R E A D E R   T O   A C C O M P A N Y

A N
I N V I T A T I O N   T O

Social Psychology

E X P R E S S I N G   A N D   C E N S O R I N G   T H E   S E L F

Dale T. Miller
Stanford University

THOMSON
™
WADSWORTH

Australia • Brazil • Canada • Mexico • Singapore • Spain
United Kingdom • United States

THOMSON

WADSWORTH

Reader to Accompany An Invitation to Social Psychology
Expressing and Censoring the Self
Dale T. Miller

Executive Editor: *Michele Sordi*
Assistant Editor: *Dan Moneypenny*
Senior Editorial Assistant: *Jessica Kim*
Technology Project Manager: *Erik Fortier*
Marketing Manager: *Raghu Reddy*
Marketing Communications Manager: *Kelley McAllister*
Project Manager, Editorial Production: *Mary Noel*
Creative Director: *Rob Hugel*

Art Director: *Vernon Boes*
Print Buyer: *Doreen Suruki*
Permissions Editor: *Joohee Lee*
Production Service: *Kalpalathika Rajan, Integra Software Services Pvt. Ltd.*
Text Designer: *Cheryl Carrington*
Copy Editor: *Sherin-de-Deepak*
Cover Designer: *Bill Stanton*
Compositor: *Integra Software Services Pvt. Ltd.*
Printer: *Webcom*

Printed in Canada
1 2 3 4 5 6 7 09 08 07 06 05

Thomson Higher Education
10 Davis Drive
Belmont, CA 94002-3098
USA

Library of Congress Control Number: 2005929903

ISBN 0-534-59206-6

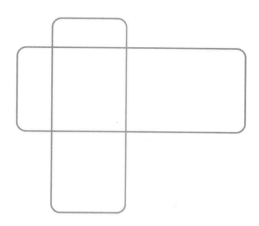

About the Author

Dale T. Miller is Professor of Psychology and Morgridge Professor of Organizational Behavior at Stanford University. Born in Canada, he received his B.A. from the University of Victoria and his Ph.D. from the University of Waterloo. Before joining the faculty at Stanford University in 2002, Miller held faculty positions at the University of Western Ontario, Simon Fraser University, University of British Columbia, and Princeton University. He has published articles in many different areas of social psychology, but his recent research has focused on the impact of social norms on social life. He is coeditor with Deborah Prentice of *Cultural Divides: The Social Psychology of Intergroup Contact* and with Michael Ross of *The Justice Motive in Everyday Life*. He has been a fellow at both the Center for Advanced Study in the Behavioral Sciences (Stanford) and the Institute for Advanced Study (Princeton). Miller has taught introductory social psychology for over thirty years.

Table of Contents

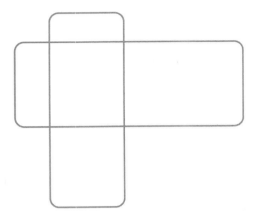

Preface

This book of readings is designed to accompany *An Invitation to Social Psychology: Expressing and Censoring the Self.* The readings, all original research reports, are reprinted in their entirety, nothing has been changed. To do justice to a research study it is necessary to read it in the original. Textbook descriptions inevitably leave unanswered many of the questions that the interested reader most wants answered, such as: "Why did the researcher decide to test this particular hypothesis?" "How exactly was the study or studies designed and executed?" "What precisely were the findings and their relation to the guiding hypothesis?" and "What does the researcher think the broader implications of his or her findings are?"

As valuable as it is to present a complete and full rendering of a particular study or set of studies, original journal reports do even more. They also show the reader how social psychology is actually done; in fact, they show the reader how science is done. Social psychology texts routinely and appropriately define social psychology as a scientific enterprise but to fully appreciate the meaning of this claim it is necessary to read original research reports. There simply is no substitute.

I thought long and hard about what articles to include in this reader. I began by deciding that I would include a total of eighteen articles, three for each of the six substantive chapters in the text. To be included I decided an article had to meet three criteria: (1) it had to be cited and at least described briefly in *An Invitation to Social Psychology*; (2) it had to address a social psychological topic of general importance, one that would be of interest to anyone interested in social psychology, not only those who had read my text; and (3) it had to be written in an accessible style such that even those with little training in social psychology could be expected to understand it reasonably well.

Finally, in deciding on the mix of articles to include I sought balance on three dimensions. First, I wanted the group of articles to convey the richness and diversity of social psychological research methods. Accordingly, I selected studies that varied along a number of dimensions including the complexity of their designs and procedures, the nature of their participants, and the particulars of their research setting. Second, I wanted the collection to span a wide range of social psychological topics. Social psychologists study many different topics and I wanted the collection to reflect that breadth. Third, I wanted the collection to achieve a balance of classic and contemporary articles. Social psychology has had a rich history and the best of it is not confined to any one time period. By spanning more than fifty years, the collection also provides a perspective on how research methods and language have evolved during that time. Readers will note that contemporary articles report more studies and ones of greater statistical and methodological sophistication than earlier ones. Readers will also note that contemporary articles avoid the inappropriate and sexist language that sometimes appears in the classic articles.

Am I pleased with the final selections? Very, and I hope you will be as well.

Acknowledgments

I am grateful to Michele Sordi for her generous and wise editorial guidance throughout this project. The expert assistance of Mary Noel and Kalpalathika Rajan during the production process is also gratefully acknowledged. For their valuable comments on the selection and organization of the readings, I also wish to thank Melissa Atkins, Marshall University; David Dunning, Cornell University; Scott Eidelman, University of Maine; Sarah Estow, Harvey Mudd College; Jennifer S. Feenstra, Northwestern College; David Livert, Penn State – Berks-Leigh Valley; and Kathryn Oleson, Reed College.

To the Student

Diverse in topic, method, design, participants and context, the articles in this reader virtually all have the same general structure. Familiarizing yourself with that structure will make your reading experience both easier and more rewarding. Journal articles all begin with an *introduction* in which the researcher states and explains the rationale for the hypothesis to be tested. The introduction is followed by the *methods* section where the researcher describes how the hypothesis was tested and who the research participants were. Following the methods section is the *results* section where the researcher describes participants' responses and characterizes their statistical significance. The final section is the *discussion* section where the researcher interprets the results and discusses their implications. If there are multiple studies in the article, this structure is repeated for each separate study. There it is.

Now some advice. You will not find reading journal articles as easy as reading textbook summaries of research. You will have to read the articles carefully and likely more than once to fully understand them. I know I do. You no doubt will find the results sections of the articles particularly heavy going. Unless you have an extensive statistical background, many of the statistical analyses reported will be difficult if not impossible to understand. Don't be alarmed by this. Convention requires that social psychologists present the statistics that they performed to test the significance of their findings. It is not sufficient to report the results of one's analyses; one must present the analyses themselves. The good news is that I have chosen articles where the researchers all do a good job of summarizing the results in narrative form so you should be able to get the gist of the findings even if you cannot follow the statistics that were used. Studying the tables and graphs will also help fill out the picture of the findings. The questions that follow the readings will also help focus your thoughts as you read them. So, yes, reading the articles will prove challenging but I expect it will prove rewarding in equal measure.

Enjoy.

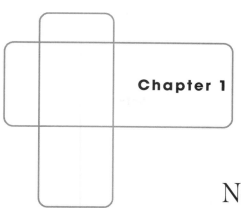

Chapter 1

Norms and Normative Behavior: Field Studies of Social Interdependence

John M. Darley and Bibb Latané

Altruism presents a problem for psychology. Altruistic behavior may please us as people, but it embarrasses traditional theories of psychology that are founded on the assumption that man is moved only by considerations of reinforcement. The hedonistic tone of traditional reinforcement theory is at variance with the simple observed fact that people do help others in circumstances in which there seem to be no gains and even considerable risk to themselves for doing so.

Reinforcement theory's traditional resolution of this dilemma is to postulate that individuals do, in fact, get rewards for altruistic acts. One line of argument is that the sight of a person in distress arouses sympathetic or empathic feelings in an observer: "Primitive passive sympathy," MacDougall said. The observer, in helping the victim, helps himself. He is motivated not to relieve the victim's suffering but to alleviate his own sympathetic distress. Whether this primitive passive sympathy is instinctive or is the result of complicated classical or instrumental conditioning, its arousal motivates a person to helping action and its termination rewards those actions.

A second resolution that preserves a reinforcement explanation of altruism postulates "norms" which the individual must learn to follow. A basic norm,

---

From *Altruism and Helping Behavior*, edited by J. Macaulay and L. Berkowitz, pp. 83–101. © 1970 Academic Press.

according to this view, is to help other individuals in distress. If a properly socialized individual within a culture violates the helping norm, he subjects himself to negative consequences which punish him for his failure to help. As with the primitive passive sympathy explanation the onlooker acts altruistically because of the negative consequences of doing otherwise. Unlike the previous explanation, the negative consequences are anticipated in the future rather than in the immediate present, and no empathic distress must be aroused in the observer. Instead, he helps because the specific case he witnesses is covered by the general normative rule.

Several theories suggest various processes by which norms are enforced. For Freudians, rules originally enforced externally, largely by the parents, become internalized in the process of development to form the superego. Norm violation leads to guilt. Other theorists locate these rules, and their enforcing mechanisms, in the other members of the society in which the individual lives. They assert that norms are enforced by the threat of the disapproval of other onlookers and also, perhaps, by more concrete negative consequences that may stem from this disapproval.

It seems to us that many discussions of altruism have confused two basic questions, and that understanding can be more profitably advanced if these questions are separated. The first question asks: "What is the underlying force in mankind toward altruism?" or "What motivates altruistic behavior?" The second question is much more specific: "What determines, in a particular situation, whether or not one person helps another in distress?" The first question is a general one, of enormous social interest and importance, and of a semi-philosophic nature. It probably will never be completely answered by reference to data. The second question is more specific, more mundane, and more amenable to research analysis.

There is no reason to expect that principles used in answering the first question should also be important or even be relevant to answering the second. It is possible, for example, that norms provide a general predisposition to help other people, but that whether or not someone will help in a particular situation is dependent on other factors.

A number of theories do make heavy use of the concept of norms to account for variations in helping from one situation to another, however. Some suggest that different norms are engaged in different situations. The "social responsibility norm" will operate at the sight of a dependent other; the "mind your own business" norm will operate when another is less dependent. The "equal outcomes" norm will operate when there is a disparity in wealth among those present in a given situation: the "do as well for yourself as you can" norm will operate when there is a smaller disparity of wealth. In other situations, other norms, such as "reciprocity," "*noblesse oblige*," and "to the victor belong the spoils" may be activated. Although, as we shall emphasize below, this diversity of norms seriously weakens their explanatory usefulness, it does allow the "explanation" of almost any kind of behavior.

A second way in which the concept of norms has been used to explain variations in helping from situation to situation is through the notion of norm "salience." A number of experimenters have shown that if one person does something, another person seeing him may be more likely also to do that thing. According to one common explanation for such effects, the model, by his behavior, increases the salience of the relevant norm for the observer, who is consequently more likely to obey this norm.

There may be considerable validity in such norm-centered accounts of behavior. We certainly hope so, since in other contexts we have used normative accounts to explain a variety of data. However, for the sake of argument, and in a mood of sporting perversity, we would like to take a rather radical position here—namely, that norms are, in general, rather unimportant determinants of behavior in specific helping situations, and that they should rarely be invoked unless all other alternative explanations fail. In the remainder of this paper, we will elaborate on some difficulties with the concept of norms, and present some data which illustrate these difficulties.

The main difficulty with norms is that they seem, at least in simple statement, contradictory. In our society, we are told to "do unto others as you would have them do unto you." We usually interpret this to mean that we should help others. Yet we are also taught "don't take candy from a stranger" or, more generally, that it is demeaning to accept help from others. It's good to help others: it's bad to be helped. This normative ambivalence toward helping and being helped is well illustrated by Adam Lindsay Gordon in his forgotten classic, *Ye Wearie Wayfarer*. Gordon exhorts us:

> Question not but live and labour
> Till yon goal be won,
> Helping every feeble neighbor,
> Seeking help from none.

> Life is mostly froth and bubble
> Two things stand like stone
> Kindness in another's trouble
> Courage in your own.

Although norms tell us we should not ask for help, we should also be able to look out for ourselves. As Mr. Deeds discovered to his chagrin, the man who attempts to help others at too great expense to himself may be looked on with suspicion and disapproval. As an example of this, a poor man recently found a sack of money that had fallen from a Brink's truck. He returned the money to Brinks (who were much startled, as they had not yet discovered the loss). Although publicized as a hero, he received scores of threatening and vilifying calls and letters castigating him for being a fool and exhorting him to look out for himself in the future.

A final way in which norms of helping conflict with other norms is that we are told to respect the privacy of others. If you intrude into another's distress, even with the best of intentions, you may find yourself resented and reviled. "Mind your own business," you may be told, "don't stick your nose in somebody else's mess." The Bible, as always, has the more elegant way of expressing this point: "He that passeth by, and meddleth with strife belonging not to him, is like one that taketh a dog by the ears" (Proverbs, 26:17).

Norms, then, seem to contradict one another. The injunction to help other people is qualified by strictures not to accept help, to look out for yourself, and not to meddle in other people's business. In any specific situation it is hard to see how norms will provide much guidance to an undecided bystander.

A second problem with norms is that they are usually stated in only the most vague and general way. There are probably good reasons why this is so. To specify norms in sufficient detail to allow them to be useful guides in specific situations would require an elaborately qualified, lengthily stated, integrated set of rules covering a wide variety of situations, many of which will arise only infrequently. It is difficult to imagine an embattled bystander watching an act, wondering what to do, and leafing through his mental rule book to exclaim "Aha! That reminds me! Section 34.62b fits this case!"

A third difficulty with normative accounts of variations in helping in specific situations is that there is little evidence that people actually think about norms when choosing a course of action. In a series of studies in which we have staged realistic emergencies and then observed people's reactions to them (Latané & Darley, [Chapter 7]), we have found that subjects typically intervene, if they intervene at all, in a matter of seconds. They seem to be guided by their first reactions, and not by a complicated choice among a variety of norms. In postexperimental interviews, we were unable to elicit any indication that subjects made explicit mental reference to norms before they decided whether or not to act. Subjects talked about their interpretations of the facts of the situations, but they did not report that they had thought about norms. This accords with our examination of our own mental processes in the minor emergencies and help-giving situations with which we have been faced. We do not often think about the golden rule when we are confronted by a beggar.

Our final reason for rejecting norm-centered explanations is that they do not seem to fit the facts adequately. For instance, a norm-centered account should argue that the presence of other people would make individuals more likely to behave in a prosocial fashion. Other people should increase the salience of norms and enforce them through the threat of negative sanctions. In our experiments on emergencies, however, the presence of other people consistently dampens altruistic ardor. Individuals seem much more likely to intervene helpfully when they are alone than when they think other people are present.

Norms, then, are contradictory and vague. People do not report thinking about them when deciding what to do. And their behavior does not always correspond to simple predictions derived from normative considerations. Having put forward these arguments, let us now try to shore them up with some data. We would like here to review several studies on helping behavior in nonemergency situations. These studies are modest ones; they were designed to explore rather different issues than the general question of the relevance of norms. It seems clearest and most sporting to present them on their own terms rather than selecting the data that best fit the point that we are trying to make. What follows, then, is rather a smorgasbord of studies in which, occasionally, immediate relevance to the central question of this paper may be sacrificed for clarity of presentation.

Parametric Studies of Compliance with a Simple Request

A major difficulty with laboratory studies of helping is that they are hard to relate to real life situations. On the one hand, subjects are under unusual pressures in the laboratory—they have been pulled out of their daily routine and are shorn of many of their usual defenses. They cannot easily leave the situation, and they may find it hard simply to ignore a request. They are known by name to the experimenter and sometimes to other subjects, and they may be anxious to gain favorable evaluations from them. These lowered defenses and heightened pressures may make the laboratory subject much more vulnerable to a request for help than the man on the street.

A second dissimilarity between laboratory helping situations and life is that in order to make a request for help believable in its laboratory context, and in order to increase the measurement utility of the response, subjects may be faced with rather unusual demands. "How many hours are you willing to spend in sensory deprivation?" "Will you help stack these papers?" "How shall we allocate these points?" Although laboratory experiments constitute an invaluable technique for testing theoretical derivations, they may not tell us much about the determinants of helping in everyday situations.

Over the past 3 years, 93 students in introductory social psychology courses at Columbia University have gone out on the streets of New York and made a variety of simple requests of some 4400 passers-by. They asked for different kinds of help, and they asked for it in different ways. The varying responses to their requests provide some information about the prevalence of altruistic compliance and the parameters influencing it.

Subjects

Students, for the most part relatively cleancut, well-dressed male (76%) undergraduates, descended on Manhattan Island in the springs of 1966–1968. Students avoided the Columbia area, but spread out over the East and West sides and the Village. Sixty-one percent of the people they asked were male, 47% were alone, 70% were moving at the time of request. Thirty percent of the requests were made in indoor locations such as subway stations and railway terminals, and 70% were made outdoors. Sixty percent of the requests were made in fairly crowded surroundings, with five or more other people within about 30 feet.

Students participated in the study as part of a class assignment. For the most part, they seemed interested in the study and found the task rather easy. The few who felt too embarrassed to "beg on the streets" were allowed to take other projects. A number of checks supported the accuracy and veracity of the students' reports of their results; the number of fabricated cases was almost certainly less than 5% of the total. Students were asked to be as unselective as possible in choosing whom to "hit"; several devices were used to prevent systematic sampling of subjects and to assign subjects randomly to experimental conditions. Although there probably was still a tendency to avoid the most seedy or most threatening prospective donees, the sample is probably not too unrepresentative of New Yorkers who show themselves in public places.

Type of Request

As Table 1 shows, the type of request made a major difference in the likelihood of receiving help. Students were very successful in getting the time, directions, or change for a quarter. They were considerably less successful in getting a dime or the name of the passerby. Less than 40% of those asked for it gave their names, and then usually only their first names. Subjects usually seemed surprised when asked for their names, and the students reported that those who gave them often seemed to do it out of sheer reflex.

TABLE 1		
Frequency of Response to Different Requests		
"Excuse me, I wonder if you could . . .	Number asked	Percentage helping[a]
a. tell me what time it is?"	92	85$_a$
b. tell me how to get to Times Square?"	90	84$_a$
c. give me change of a quarter?"	90	73$_a$
d. tell me what your name is?"	277	39$_b$
e. give me a dime?"	284	34$_b$

[a] Conditions which do not share the same subscript are significantly different by $\chi^2 (p < .05)$.

Manner of Request

A bold request for a dime worked in about one-third of the cases; requests including more information were markedly more successful, as Table 2 shows. If the subject gave his name before asking for a dime, he had about a 50–50 chance of getting help, and if he claimed that he needed to make a telephone call or had lost his wallet, he was helped two-thirds of the time.

Information preceding the request had as striking an effect when students asked for names. Students who asked simply, "Could you tell me what your name is?" were answered 30% of the time. When they said, "Excuse me, my name is _____. Could you tell me what your name is?" 59% of the 64 asked gave their names ($p < .01$ by χ^2).

Sex of Subject and of Requester

Sex had no effect on giving minor assistance. Sex affected the request for a dime: female requesters were helped by 58% of the subjects; males were helped by only 46% ($p < .02$). Sex of the subject had no effect on the request for a dime. Sex also had a large effect on the request for a name, but a different pattern of results emerged. Females were more likely to receive an answer, but only if the subject was male. Sixty-eight percent of male subjects gave their name to a female; other sex pairings achieved response rates of 37–39% ($p < .01$).

Number of Requesters

If a person, for the same cost, can help two people rather than just one, will he be more likely to help? To answer this question, male and female students

TABLE 2		
Frequency of Response as a Function of Manner of Request		
Manner of request	Number asked	Percentage helping[a]
a. "Excuse me, I wonder if you could give me a dime?"	284	34$_a$
b. "Excuse me, I wonder if you could give me a dime? I've spent all my money."	108	38$_{ab}$
c. "Excuse me, I wonder if you could tell me what time it is?" . . ." and could you give me a dime?"	146	43$_{ab}$
d. "Excuse me, my name is _____. I wonder if you could give me a dime?"	150	49$_b$
e. "Excuse me, I wonder if you could give me a dime? I need to make a telephone call."	111	64$_c$
f. "Excuse me, I wonder if you could give me a dime? My wallet has been stolen."	108	72$_c$

[a] Conditions which do not share the same subscript are significantly different by $\chi^2 (p < .05)$.

asked 1440 passers-by for 20 cents for the subway. They asked either alone or in pairs. The pairs were composed either of one male and one female, or of two males or two females. The form of request was standard in all cases: "Excuse me, could you help me (us)? I (we) have to get downtown and need 20 cents for the subway?" Table 3 presents the results.

The results were straightforward. Females were almost twice as likely to receive help as males when alone and three times as likely when in same sex pairs. The presence of a second female increased the response to a female ($p < .01$); the presence of another male slightly decreased the response to a male (n.s.). These results seem to suggest that subjects responded mainly to the person making the request, and that the presence of another person had little influence upon helping. Results from the mixed-sex pairs, however, change this picture. A female accompanied by a male was slightly less successful than a single female (n.s.), but a male accompanied by a female was much more successful than a single male ($p < .01$). It appears as if subjects do respond to the second member of a pair. They do not respond to the sum of the needs of the two persons. If there are two people asking, the response seems to be averaged.

	Alone		Same sex pair		Mixed sex pair	
TABLE 3						
Frequency of Helping as a Function of Sex and Number of Requesters for a Dime						
Sex of requester	Number asked	Percentage helping[a]	Number asked	Percentage helping[a]	Number asked	Percentage helping[a]
Female	319	57[b]	240	72[a]	323	53[b]
Male	442	30[c]	360	25[c]	317	50[b]

[a] Conditions which do not share the same subscript are significantly different by $\chi^2(p < .05)$.

Discussion

These results can easily be explained in terms of norms. People gave the correct time, change of a quarter, or directions because there is a norm to "help thy neighbor." They were less likely to give money because there is norm to "look out for yourself." They often did not give their names because there is a norm against invading privacy. If the requester gave his name before asking for a name or a dime, he was more successful because there is a norm of reciprocity. Females were more successful than males in getting money because there is a norm to help the weak. Males were more likely to give their names to females because there is a norm to be gallant. Couples were . . . but stop. We are citing one new norm to explain each successive comparison. To continue in this fashion would be nothing more than giving *ad hoc* explanations for results that we could not have predicted in advance. Further, the explanations are not really very clear. We are not convinced that normative explanations really help our understanding of the results.

The Effect of Social Class and Familiarity of Environment on Helping

An individual was identified sitting far enough removed from other people to be functionally isolated from them. A young man approached him on crutches, with his left knee bent and heavily taped. Suddenly the young man fell to the ground, clutching his knee in great pain. A rater stationed some distance away unobtrusively observed the incident and noted the reactions of the bystander to it.

Sixty such incidents were staged in each of two public locations, an underground subway station and La Guardia Airport. The results were startlingly different. In the subway, 83% of the people helped; in the airport, only 41% did ($p < .01$). This result obviously can be explained by socioeconomic differences. Middle and upper class citizens, who are much more likely to be present at airports, may be less inclined to help others. They may put a higher value on the privacy of others and thus be less likely to intrude even when the others are in distress. Lower classes, who are more frequently found in subways, have no such inhibitions. Differences in norms between social classes can obviously account for this difference in helping—or can they?

Roger Granet, who ran the studies as a class project at New York University, had a rather different hypothesis in mind. His expectation was that familiarity with the environment was the determining factor. Persons who were familiar with the physical location in which the emergency took place would be more likely to help the victim. The major reason for greater helpfulness in subways is that subway users grow familiar with the subway setting in a way that few people ever do with airports. To determine if familiarity influenced functioning in emergency situations, after each bystander had responded to the staged incident and the rater had judged the adequacy of his response, another experimenter appeared to interview the bystander about his familiarity with subways or airports. Subjects were asked about how often they used the facility and their knowledge of its entrances, exits, telephone booths, etc. The questionnaire was short, and the person administering it, though goodnatured, was large. There were only two refusals to answer. One other variable was also coded: the socioeconomic class of the bystander as judged on a five point scale from the external cues of dress and bearing. Various correlations between the class and familiarity scales gave us some confidence that they were valid. As we would expect, the socioeconomic class of bystanders in the airport was higher than that of bystanders in the subway. People were, on the average, considerably less familiar with the airport environments. More subtle results also conform to our general expectations: the higher the socioeconomic class of the respondent, the more likely he was to be familiar with the airport and the less likely he was to be familiar with the subway station.

The results on helping are quite clear. In both the airport and the subway, there was a significant correlation ($r = .29, p < .05; r = .31, p < .05$, respectively) between familiarity and responding to the emergency. In neither case was there a significant correlation between social class and helping behavior. As one would expect from this pattern of results, the relationship between familiarity and emergency functioning was not much affected by partialling out the effect of socioeconomic class. The overall pattern of the results is clear: increased familiarity with a setting is associated with an increase in the helping behavior. Socioeconomic class is not.

Granet's interpretations of these results seem to us to be the appropriate ones: a person who is more familiar with the environment is more aware of the way in which the environment works. He is not overloaded with stimuli, and his fears of embarrassment or, in the subway, actual physical harm, have moderated. He may have a greater stake in keeping that environment safe. Thus he is more likely to help. But the norms supporting helping behavior are equally relevant, regardless of environmental familiarity. Again norms do not account for the behavior of the subjects.

Down in the Subway

The next study took place in the subways of New York City, and was done by Harvey Allen as a Ph.D. dissertation at New York University. A subject was riding in a subway, and a second person stood or sat near him. A bewildered looking individual approached and asked whether the subway is going uptown or downtown. The other bystander gave the wrong answer—if the subway was going uptown, he replied "downtown," and vice versa. The dilemma for the subject was clear; should he give the right information, correcting the other bystander, or not?

The situation was, of course, prearranged. Both the question asker and the misinformer were experimenters. The dependent measure of the study was whether the bystander corrected the misinformer. In the first study, Allen varied the direction in which the original request for information was aimed. In the first condition, the request was aimed at the subject; in a second condition, the question was aimed at both bystanders; and in the third condition, the misinformer-to-be was directly addressed. These variations had major effects. When the misinformer cut in to answer the question asked of the naive subject, subjects almost always corrected him and did so immediately, impatiently, and indignantly. When the original question was addressed generally toward the two-person group, subjects corrected considerably less frequently. Finally, when the question was directed at the misinformer, subjects corrected least frequently of all. Even though norms governing response should be fairly constant, situational variables can have a strong effect on the frequency of help (Table 4).

Allen's second study demonstrates that people behave in accordance with their estimates of the cost to themselves for doing so. Again, someone asked for directions and was misinformed, putting pressure on the naive subject to correct him. (In this experiment, the question was always aimed at both the confederate and the naive bystander since that gave nearest to a

TABLE 4		
Direction of the Asker's Question and Number of Corrections Made[a]		
Direction of question	Number asked	Percentage helping
Misinformer	30	27
Group	30	47
Bystander	30	93

[a] $\chi^2 = 31.44, p < .01.$

50–50 split of responding in the previous study.) Unlike the previous study, the misinformer-to-be created a character for himself before the question asking incident occurred. He sat with his legs stretched in front of him in the subway car. Another individual (yet another confederate) walked past him and stumbled over his feet. The misinformer-to-be responded in one of three ways: by doing nothing, by looking up from his magazine on muscle-building and shouting threats of physical harm at the helpless stumbler, or by making embarrassing comments about him. Thus, in the last two conditions the misinformer-to-be established that he was quickly ready to resort to physical violence or noisy vituperation when crossed. When he subsequently misinformed the direction seeker, he presented an acute dilemma for the real subject. For him to offer the correct information required contradicting the misinformer, who might react badly to this correction.

In the third condition the misinformer-to-be made no response to the tripping incident, thus not establishing himself as belligerent. In a fourth condition, in which Allen wished to make it clear to the subject that there was a very low probability of confrontation with the misinformer, the misinformer gave a tentative answer to the request for directions (e.g., "Uptown, but I'm not sure"), making it apparent that he was not confident about his answer.

The effects of variations in potential nastiness of the misinformer are quite clear, and much as you would expect them to be. The subject was most reluctant to correct the physically threatening person and least reluctant to correct the tentatively answering person. The other two conditions fell in between in the expected positions. Clearly, subjects calculated the cost of help and modified their behavior accordingly (Table 5).

TABLE 5		
Degree of Threat and Number of Corrections[a]		
Degree of threat	Number asked	Percentage helping
Physical threat	50	16
Embarrassment	50	28
Control	50	52
Reduced embarrassment	50	82

[a] $\chi^2 = 51.56, p < .001$.

One further result is of note: if the subject had not corrected the misinformer after 30 seconds, the misinformer walked away out of ear shot, thus eliminating, for the subject, the problem of correcting the misinformer in order to help the question asker. Among subjects who had failed to correct by the time the misinformer had left, correction was still less likely among those subjects for whom the misinformer had established a threatening or an embarrassing character for himself.

In both these studies, differences between conditions showed up even though norms for helping should have been equally strong. Allen's third study tried to vary norms directly by varying the character of the direction asker, who was later to be misinformed. In one condition he was dressed as an obvious tourist, carrying a travel bag with stickers from the Midwest, and dressed in a semiwestern hat. This should arouse norms about helping strangers to the situation. In a second condition, the future direction asker established himself as a helping person. A female confederate (by this time you must have the feeling that roughly half of the population of New York served as confederates—Allen had the same feeling when he paid them), heavily laden with packages, spectacularly dropped them. The future direction asker helped her to pick them up, hopefully engaging norms of reciprocity as well as modelling a help-giving act. The third condition was a control condition; no particular character was established for the direction asker.

Although the effects were in the direction one might anticipate, no significant differences were found. In a situation in which it seems plausible to assume that norms of helping strangers and norms connected with reciprocity of helping actions were aroused, no significant differences were produced in helping behavior (Table 6).

TABLE 6		
Character of Question Asker and Number of Corrections		
Character of question asker	Number asking	Percentage helping
Tourist	50	62
Helpful	50	68
Control	50	48

[a] $\chi^2 = 4.38$, n.s.

Frisbee Study

We are all familiar with the frisbee, or pluto platter, that appears on college campuses in the spring. It is a circular, almost pie plate-shaped disk which, when propelled by an expert, can be made to fly or float through the air in complex and graceful arcs. The amount of time college students take off from more scholarly activities to devote to the study of frisbees suggests that the activity is pleasurable and even fascinating. In a study conducted in a senior social psychology seminar at New York University, Sheri Turtletaub and Harriet Ortman cleverly capitalized on this fascination to study the promotion of interaction among groups of strangers. They were concerned with factors promoting interaction among previously nonorganized groups in public places. Most specifically, their task was to turn the Grand Central Station waiting room into a frenzy of flying frisbees.

A girl sat on a bench in the waiting room at Grand Central. Soon another girl sat on a bench facing her. They recognized each other and began a conversation. One girl had been shopping, and announced that she had just bought a frisbee. The other girl asked to see it, and the first girl threw it to her. They then began to toss it back and forth. Apparently by accident, the frisbee was thrown to a third person and the reaction of this third person (an experimental confederate), was the independent variable of the study. That person either enthusiastically joined in throwing the frisbee or accused the two girls of being childish and dangerous, and kicked the frisbee back across the gap.

Whichever of these two variations occurred, the two girls continued throwing the frisbee back and forth and soon sent it to one of the 3–10 bystanders seated on the benches. They continued this until all the bystanders on the two facing benches had been probed. A bystander was counted as participating in the activity if he returned the frisbee at least twice. The percentage of bystanders present who joined in the frisbee fest was the dependent measure of the study. In all, 170 people took part in the study.

When the experimental confederate joined in the play, the other spectators were extremely likely to do so also. Over four cases, 86% of the 34 available people responded, often coming from other areas of the waiting room to participate. Indeed, in this condition the problem was not to start interaction but to terminate it so that the experimenters could leave for the next waiting room and run further incidents.

On the other hand, if the confederate refused to play, and instead negatively sanctioned the girls' activity, in four cases no other bystander of the 24 ever joined in the action. Instead, people sitting nearby would frequently get up and move to other seats to avoid being thrown a frisbee, muttering their disapproval while doing so.

The finding seems to require a normative analysis. When certain norms are made salient, they inhibit action. It also seems to fit a modelling explanation. If the third confederate participates, others do also; if she does not participate, others do not. However, the girls went on to run another condition that seemed to eliminate a simple modelling explanation. In this control condition, the confederate did not join in the action but allowed the frisbee to bounce off her accidentally and be retrieved by one of the two original girls. In this condition, a high percentage of bystander participation was observed: of 25 subjects, 74% in four cases, not significantly different from the positive participation condition. A person who was a model for nonaction failed to inhibit participation by the bystanders.

At this point we concluded that what the confederate did was less important than what the confederate said. The one treatment that significantly inhibited interaction was the one in which the confederate loudly denounced the frisbee throwers. This seemed to require a norm-centered interpretation of the results since it was to various norms that the confederate appealed. The experimenters carefully ran other conditions to tease apart exactly what norms were operative in the situation. In these further conditions, the confederate carefully confined her negative comments to an appeal to one norm. In one situation, she cited the danger to others that was caused by throwing the frisbee, in another she accused the participants of indulging in childish behavior.

These two kinds of sanctions were not significantly different from one another in the amount of action they inhibited. The overall percentage of action was about 27% of 79 subjects in 16 cases. At this point, one would be prone to conclude that both of these norms are about equally effective in inhibiting interactions since making either of them salient inhibits participation roughly equally.

However, the girls did one more manipulation, the results of which call a norm-centered account into question. The manipulation crosscut the negative sanction manipulation and consisted simply of whether or not the sanctioning person stayed to watch the frisbee players after she gave the sanctions or immediately left the waiting room. When the sanctioning individual stayed, the usual result occurred—play was greatly inhibited (11% in 33 subjects in eight cases, as reported above). But when the sanctioning person left, the percentage of participation of bystanders rose to near its original rate (60% of 46 subjects in eight cases, not significantly different from the 80% average of the other positive conditions). It was not simply the sanctioning speech given by the confederate that inhibited play, but the sanctioning speech plus her continued presence.

It might be argued that the continued presence of the sanctioning individual made the norm that she had evoked more "salient" and thus more inhibitory. This, we think, stretches the meaning of the word "salience." Even when the denouncer left, she had previously shrieked out a denunciation of the frisbee throwers. Clearly, the norms she cited were salient to bystanders in that they were forcefully reminded of the existence of these norms. However, they still participated. One explanation of the result is that the bystander simply considered the costs of participating. When the spoilsport confederate stayed around, it was clearly possible that she might yell at other bystanders who participated, call the police, or otherwise punish or embarrass the participants. We see no necessity to talk about norms to account for these data.

Discussion

These four studies, as designed, obviously have little in common with each other. They do, however, illustrate the points we feel are important about the relationship of norms to behavior. The data on responses to simple requests indicate that any serious attempt to deal with the variations in response rates in normative terms must involve the postulation of a proliferation of norms— about as many norms as Dr. MacDougall had instincts. In cases where the norms governing help can be assumed to be constant, such as the collapse of a man on crutches, environmental variables cause strong changes in the rates of helping. Finally, in the last two studies where normative and cost explanations are roughly pitted against each other, cost explanations prevail. All in all, norm-centered explanations of helping seem difficult to apply.

We have argued that a person's helping behavior is too complexly determined by situational factors to be accounted for by norms. Yet one question remains: why do some people explain their own helping behavior in normative terms? Surely this argues for the necessity for, and validity of, norm-centered accounts of helping behavior.

But perhaps not. We are familiar with other cases in which a person explains his behavior in ways that have little to do with the causes of it. The obsessive has a perfectly good account of his reasons for washing his hands— they are dirty. Or the awakened subject complies with the posthypnotic suggestion of the hypnotist and begins dancing at the sound of music, but has an explanation for why he did so if he is pressed for one. "Just practicing for a dance I'm going to," he reports.

Even when we do not infer unconscious motives from the discrepancy, we are familiar with cases in which a person's actions are not really accounted for by his explanations of them. The college student who wants permission to turn in a late paper is aware of a socially acceptable set of excuses which he is likely to offer instead of the real reasons for his tardiness. Or, nearer home, the deductive, logically sequenced steps of the normal journal article, if our cock-tail confessions are correct, may grossly misrepresent the intuitive, post hoc way a good deal of research gets done in psychology.

Looking at helping actions from this perspective, it is possible to see how a good deal of childhood training involves teaching children to give normative explanations of behaviors that are, in fact, somewhat more complexly deter-mined. The child sees the parent giving money to a Salvation Army Santa Claus and asks why. "We should share our nice things with less fortunate others," the father tells him. Thus, the child learns two things: the specific norm, and that it is appropriate to give a "should," or norm-centered account for helping behav-ior. Later, when the child gives away some valued family possession to an artful beggar, the parents' anguished explanation of why they took it back teaches the child that although norms "are very thoughtful of you, dear," their relation to behavior should not be too close.

These considerations seem to lead to a picture of norms as explanatory fictions used to explain actions after the fact, but having no behavior-guiding force of their own. But, although this is a possible conclusion to our argument, it is not a necessary one.

Some events occur and are responded to without a great deal of rational thought. This is true of emergencies; it is probably also true of the Milgrim (1965) and Brock and Buss (1962) experiments, in which subjects found themselves administering electric shocks to people. It is also true in real life situations, such as confronting a beggar, in which we have our refusal speech begun before he is half through his appeal. Only later, thinking back over the incident, does it come clear to us that ethical norms are relevant to our actions and that, under pressure of time and circumstance, we behaved in a fashion not entirely in keeping with these norms. Then we may cope with this realization in ways that have implications for our future behavior. As the research of Berscheid and Walster (1966) shows, if an opportunity to compensate the victim appropriately appears, we may take it. On the other hand, as Lerner's studies demonstrate, we may also justify our behavior toward the victim by derogating him or otherwise convincing ourselves that "he deserved what he got."

In this fashion, although normative considerations may not be important in predicting responses to sudden appeals for help, after his response the person may reflect on the discrepancies between norms and his behavior. This reflection may cause him to desire to compensate or make restitution, either toward the specific previous victim of his failure to act or to all people in distress. A person in this frame of mind might actually seek out opportunities to help and even be a wandering "good Samaritan." Less happily, the tensions between actions and norms may lead a person to rationalize the rightness of his actions by arguing that a person who needs help always deserves the difficulties in which he finds himself, which will make him even less likely to help people in distress in the future.

References

Berscheid, E., & Walster, E. When does a harm-doer compensate a victim? *Journal of Personality and Social Psychology,* 1966, **6**, 435–441.

Brock, T. C., & Becker, L. A. "Debriefing" and susceptibility to subsequent experimental manipulations. *Journal of Experimental Social Psychology,* 1966, **2**, 314–323.

Brock, T. C., & Buss, A. H. Dissonance, aggression, and evaluation of pain. *Journal of Abnormal & Social Psychology,* 1962, **65**, 197–202.

Milgram, S. Some conditions of obedience and disobedience to authority, *Human Relations,* 1965, **18**, 57–75.

Questions for Review and Discussion

1. What do you think accounted for the different response rates to the requests made of participants in the "Simple Request" Study?

2. What situational factors determined whether individuals in the "Down in the Subway" study corrected the experimental confederate who misled another confederate about the direction of the train?

3. Do you accept the authors' argument than norms are "explanatory fictions"?

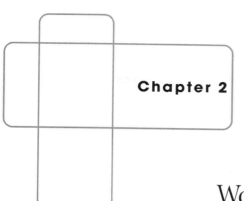

Chapter 2

Would You Drink After a Stranger? The Influence of Self-Presentational Motives on Willingness to Take a Health Risk

Kathleen A. Martin and Mark R. Leary

S elf-presentation refers to the processes by which people monitor and control how they are perceived by others (Leary, 1995; Schlenker, 1980). The impressions that people make have implications for how others perceive, evaluate, and treat them. Hence, people often are motivated to behave in ways that will create certain impressions of themselves in other people's eyes (Leary & Kowalski, 1990).

Self-presentational motives play a role in a variety of potentially danger-ous health-related behaviors, including behaviors that lead to risk of HIV infection; accidental death and injury; and alcohol, tobacco, and drug use (Leary, Tchividjian, & Kraxberger, 1994; Martin, Leary, & Rejeski, in press). The desire to be perceived as a risk-taker, brave, or one of the crowd (or conversely, concerns about being viewed as overly cautious or neurotic) may lead people to take chances with their health to create the desired image (Denscombe, 1993; Finney, 1978). For example, in a study of gay men, more

From *Personality and Social Psychology Bulletin*, Vol. 25, No. 9 (September 1999), pp. 1092–1100. © 1999 by the Society for the Personality and Social Psychology, Inc. Reprinted by permission of Sage Publications, Inc.

than one third of respondents indicated that they had failed to practice safe sex because they were concerned about making a negative impression on their partners (Catania et al., 1991). Their underlying self-presentational concern was that insisting on using a condom would lead them to be perceived as a "wimp" or as someone who is not willing to take a risk (Gold, Skinner, Grant, & Plummer, 1991).

Self-presentational concerns also can lead people to take risks that cause accidental injury and death (Leary et al., 1994). For instance, injuries often occur in recreational activities such as in-line skating and ice hockey because people fail to wear protective gear. Many people are reluctant to wear equipment such as helmets, mouth guards, and knee pads because they want to be seen as intimidating and fearless or because they are concerned about appearing excessively cautious (Cullen, Widmeyer, Dorsch, & Bishop, 1997; Williams-Avery & MacKinnon, 1996). In a similar vein, self-presentational motives can motivate risk-taking behaviors that lead to traffic injuries and fatalities. Reckless and high speed driving are major causes of vehicle crashes and are often prompted by a desire to impress others (Hingson & Howland, 1993).

Wishing to impress others and to create the impression of being adventuresome, "cool," or sociable often plays a strong role in the decision to use alcohol, tobacco, and illicit drugs. In one study, for example, the strongest intentions to smoke cigarettes were expressed by adolescents who believed that smoking was cool and who wanted others to see them as cool (Norman & Tedeschi, 1989). Likewise, a primary motive for drinking alcohol is to achieve peer acceptance and social approval (Farber, Khavari, & Douglass, 1980). Thus, whether negotiating safe sex with a new partner, contemplating a challenge to play "chicken" on the highway, or deciding to experiment with drugs at a party, people sometimes face situations in which their self-presentational goals motivate them to behave in ways that increase their chance of illness, injury, and even death.

The association between self-presentation concerns and health-risk behavior has been demonstrated in several studies examining a variety of behaviors (for reviews, see Leary et al., 1994; Martin et al., in press). Yet virtually all of the evidence for this relationship is based on correlational data, and we are unaware of any published studies that have used an experimental design to examine the effects of self-presentation on health-risk behavior. However, in one unpublished experiment (Parks & Leary, 1995), the manipulation of self-presentational concerns enhanced risk-taking behavior among men. Participants were told that they would be working with dangerous chemicals and were given the opportunity to don protective safety gear (such as goggles, gloves, and masks). Men who believed that other participants viewed them as excessively cautious elected to wear less safety gear than men who thought they were perceived as average in cautiousness. Apparently, concerns with being viewed as overly cautious prompted men to demonstrate their boldness, even at risk to their safety.

The present experiment extended these findings by examining the effects of self-presentational motives on another health-related behavior—participants' willingness to drink from a stranger's water bottle. Although this action may seem innocuous, numerous diseases can be transmitted when people share drinking containers. For example, aseptic and viral meningitis are potentially fatal infections of the cerebrospinal fluid that are transmitted across mucous membranes (Nelson, Sealy, & Schneider, 1993), and the sharing of water containers has been identified as a risk factor for transmitting these diseases (Moeller, 1997). Other illnesses such as mono-nucleosis and influenza also may be transmitted when individuals share a beverage from the same container. Furthermore, other, more serious health risk behaviors are conceptually similar to the act of sharing a drink. For example, like sharing beverage containers, sharing needles for intravenous drug use increases the risk of transmitting diseases from one person to another. However, most such behaviors cannot be examined safely and ethically in an experimental setting. Sharing a drink was chosen as the target behavior in this study because it is a potentially risky behavior that can be examined in a controlled experimental setting.

In real-world situations, self-presentational concerns become particularly salient as a result of two distinct processes, and our experimental manipulations were designed to reflect these two factors. First, people often are motivated to impression-manage when they believe that others have undesired impressions of them. Much self-presentational behavior represents people's efforts to refute others' existing impressions of them (Leary, 1995). As noted, participants in the Parks and Leary (1995) study took risks with their personal safety when they thought other people viewed them as excessively cautious. Thus, we manipulated self-presentational concern by leading some participants to believe that another person already perceived them as overly cautious and neurotic.

Second, people become motivated to impression-manage when other people directly challenge their social image by explicitly derogating them or calling their desired image into question. In situations that are relevant to health risk and accidental injury, others may taunt the individual by questioning his or her bravery, boldness, or physical skill. In response, the individual may behave in a risky fashion (driving too fast, jumping off the bridge, not using a condom, etc.) to refute the disparaging self-presentational implications of the challenge. In the present study, we manipulated this variable by introducing such a challenge in regard to drinking from a stranger's water bottle.

The primary prediction was that participants who were motivated to impression-manage—either because of a preexisting image concern or a self-presentationally relevant verbal challenge—would be more likely to drink from a stranger's bottle than those who were not motivated to impression manage. Our rationale was that people's concerns about being perceived as overly cautious would lead them to take chances with their health as a strategy for creating a desired public image. In addition, it was predicted that participants who were both concerned about their image and who were challenged to drink would be most likely to drink and those who were neither concerned nor challenged would be least likely to drink. However, we were unable to predict whether this pattern would emerge as two additive main effects or as an interaction in which the verbal challenge was particularly effective in producing risky behavior among participants who were already concerned about appearing overly cautious.

Method

Participants and Design

Participants consisted of 23 male and 26 female (M age $=$ 19.02 years, $SD =$ .83) introductory psychology students, who participated in the experiment for course credit. The confederate was a 21-year-old male college sophomore. Prior to the experiment, none of the participants had ever met the confederate. For every experimental session, the confederate was dressed in the same attire: jeans, a t-shirt, and a baseball cap. For half of the sessions, the first author served as the experimenter, and for the remaining sessions, a female undergraduate research assistant served as the experimenter. The first author and the research assistant tested the same number of male and female participants in each of the four conditions.

A completely randomized 2×2 factorial design was used in which social image–concern (low/high) was crossed with challenge to drink (challenged/not challenged). Participants were randomly assigned to one of four conditions with the restriction that equal proportions of male and female participants be assigned to each condition.

Procedure

The participant arrived at the lab before the confederate. To ensure that he or she did not bring water or any other beverage into the lab, the individual was asked to place all belongings in a separate room. The participant was then seated at a large table. It was explained that participants were being run in pairs and that the experimenter was waiting for a second participant (actually, the confederate) to arrive. While awaiting the confederate, the participant read and signed a consent form and the experimenter confirmed that he or she did not have any food allergies.

A few minutes later, the confederate arrived at the lab carrying a backpack and apologized for being late. The experimenter pretended not to see the backpack until the confederate was seated. Then, noticing it, she said, "I'm supposed to have you lock your stuff up next door, but we're already running late so could you please tuck your backpack out of the way, underneath the table." The confederate was asked to read and sign the consent form and was asked whether he had any food allergies.

Next, the experimenter presented the cover story for the experiment. She explained that she was examining the relationship between personality types, taste perception, and person perception. Specifically, she was studying how people with different personalities respond to bad tastes in terms of their ratings of those tastes and their facial responses to the tastes and how information about an individual's personality can influence how others perceive that person's facial responses. In the experiment, one participant would serve as the taster and the other participant would rate the taster's facial responses to the taste of three liquids. The participant was then asked to draw a slip of paper to determine whether he or she would be assigned the role of tasting the liquids or rating facial expressions. The drawing was rigged so that the participant was always chosen as the taster. The participant was asked to sit facing a video camera that ostensibly was to be used to record his or her facial expressions. (This detail was included to enhance the believability of the cover story.)

Next, the experimenter explained that personality profiles had been generated for all introductory psychology students as a result of their questionnaire responses from an earlier mass-testing session. The experimenter said that because she was interested in how personality influences the taster's responses, she would present only the taster's (i.e., the participant's) personality profile. (She added, however, that the confederate could see his personality profile at the end of the experiment.) The experimenter gave the participant a bogus personality profile and asked him or her to read the profile carefully and to be sure to understand it because questions would be asked about the profile later in the experiment.

Two bogus personality profiles were created for the study to manipulate social image concern. In the high image–concern condition, the profile indicated that participants were average on the dimensions of agreeableness, sociability, and self-awareness and atypically high on the dimensions of cautiousness, neuroticism, and obsessiveness. A statement at the bottom of the form gave the following interpretation: "Atypically high scores on the dimensions of cautiousness, neuroticism, and obsessiveness are consistent with the personality profile of individuals who avoid risky situations and decisions and who tend to worry unnecessarily over small concerns." In the low image–concern condition, the profile indicated that participants were average on all of the six previously listed dimensions. An interpretation statement read, "Average scores on all dimensions are consistent with the personality profile of individuals who are well adjusted and neither excessive nor deficient on the relevant attributes."

When the participant finished reading his or her profile, it was given to the confederate, who received the same instructions to read and understand the profile in preparation for subsequent questions. While the confederate read the profile, the experimenter attached two bogus electrodes over the radial artery of the participant's dominant hand and asked the participant to keep the hand very still. The experimenter explained that she was using the electrodes to collect heart rate data throughout the experiment. In reality, the participant was wired to the machinery to prevent him or her from leaving the laboratory to get a drink of water following the taste test.

Next, the experimenter placed the taste test items—three small paper cups each containing 15 ml of liquid—in front of the participant. The cups contained: (a) a highly concentrated, unsweetened, peach-flavored soft drink; (b) a very salty mixture of soy sauce and table salt; and (c) a mixture of lemon juice and yellow mustard. Prior to conducting the experiment, a panel of four tasters decided unanimously that the combined after-taste of the three liquids was unpleasant but tolerable (i.e., not so bad that participants would have no choice but to accept the drink of water from the confederate).

The participant was instructed to sample the three liquids (in the order of peach soft drink, soy sauce, lemon-mustard) by drinking the full amount in each cup and holding it in his or her mouth for 5 seconds before swallowing. The participant was instructed to verbally rate each liquid on five taste dimensions (sweet, salty, etc.) using a 5-point scale. The confederate recorded these ratings and, ostensibly, provided ratings of the participant's facial expressions.

Once all three liquids had been sampled, the experimenter removed the paper cups and said to the participant, "Well the worst is over for you, but I apologize—I'm supposed to have some bottled water for you to drink but my assistant won't be here with it for another 15 minutes and for experimental reasons I can only give you bottled water. So I'm sorry but I don't have a drink for you right now. I hope you can just sit tight until the end of the experiment." The experimenter then turned her back to the participant and pretended to prepare questionnaires. The confederate reached into his backpack underneath the table and placed a 500 ml bottle of water in front of the subject. The clear plastic bottle contained 350 ml of water so that it appeared that the confederate had already drank from it. In reality, a clean bottle was used for each participant.

In the no-challenge condition the confederate said, "That stuff must have tasted pretty nasty. Do you want a drink of my water?" In the challenge condition he made the same statement and then added ". . . if you're not worried about drinking out of the same bottle as me." The experimenter noted whether the participant accepted the drink and the amount of water consumed was measured after the participant left the lab.[1]

The experimenter turned off the video camera and announced that the experiment was over. She unhooked the participant from the heart rate recording equipment and said that she had a final questionnaire that she wanted both the participant and the confederate to complete in privacy. She gave a copy of the postexperimental questionnaire to the participant and directed the confederate to another laboratory where he ostensibly was to fill out his copy.

The postexperimental questionnaire contained four items that were included as a manipulation check. First, participants were asked to recall how they were rated on each dimension of the bogus personality profile. Second, their level of self-presentational concern was assessed. Responding on a scale ranging from 1 (*not at all*) to 12 (*extremely*), participants were asked how concerned they were that (a) the experimenter and (b) their partner (i.e., the confederate) would think negatively of them after reading the personality profile. Third, they rated the taste in their mouths following the taste test phase of the experiment on a scale ranging from 1 (*not at all bad*) to 12 (*extremely bad*). Fourth, they were asked to explain, in their own words, the purpose of the experiment.

In addition, self-presentational motives were assessed for each personality profile dimension by asking, "How much do you want others to see you as [agreeable, neurotic, etc.]?" Participants responded to these items using a scale ranging from 1 (*not at all*) to 12 (*extremely*). After completing the postexperimental questionnaire, the participant was debriefed and thanked for participating.

Results

Initially, all analyses were conducted using gender as an independent variable. Because there was no effect for gender on any of the dependent measures (all $ps > .05$), the data were subsequently collapsed and reanalyzed.

Manipulation Check

One female participant was excluded from the final sample because of suspicion regarding the confederate's role in the experiment. None of the remaining participants expressed suspicion regarding the true purpose of the study. When asked to describe the experiment's purpose, all 48 subjects provided explanations commensurate with the cover story.

The adequacy of the social image–concern manipulation was examined two ways. First, t tests were used to compare participants' recall of their scores on the personality profile. Consistent with the manipulation, participants in the high image–concern condition indicated that they were rated significantly higher on the dimensions of cautiousness, neuroticism, and obsessionality than participants in the low image–concern condition ($p < .0001$ for each dimension). Also consistent with the manipulation, no difference was obtained between the low and high image–concern conditions on the recall of ratings for agreeableness, awareness, and sociability ($p > .05$ on each dimension).

Second, the social image–concern manipulation was checked by conducting a 2 (image concern) × 2 (challenge) ANOVA with self-presentational concerns (about what the confederate thought of the participant) as the dependent measure. Consistent with the manipulation, participants in the high image–concern condition were more concerned about what the confederate thought of them ($M = 4.25$, $SD = 3.40$) than were participants in the low image–concern condition ($M = 2.83$, $SD = 1.80$), $F(1, 44) = 3.10$, $p = .08$ (one-tailed). No other effects were significant. In addition, although the important audience in this experiment was the confederate, we suspected that the social image–concern manipulation also might have influenced participants' self-presentational concerns about what the experimenter thought of them. Indeed, consistent with the manipulation, a 2 (image concern) × 2 (challenge) ANOVA revealed that participants in the high image–concern condition were more concerned about what the experimenter thought of them ($M = 3.75$, $SD = 3.07$) than were participants in the low image–concern condition ($M = 2.08$, $SD = 1.25$), $F(1, 44) = 5.87$, $p < .05$ (one-tailed). Neither the effect for challenge nor the Image Concern × Challenge interaction was significant.

To ensure that any differences in drinking behavior among participants were not due to individual differences in the perceived taste of the liquids, a 2 (image concern) × 2 (challenge) × 2 (drank/did not drink) ANOVA was conducted. Participants' responses to the question "Was there a bad taste in your mouth after you tasted the three liquids?" were used as the dependent measure. Although the mean rating confirmed that the liquids tasted *moderately bad* to *very bad* ($M = 8.90$, $SD = 2.76$ on a 12-point scale), no main effects or interactions were significant (all $ps > .05$). Thus, not only was there no difference in the taste ratings for participants in the different experimental conditions but there also was no difference in the taste ratings for those who drank versus those who did not drink.

Finally, no effects were obtained on the items asking participants the degree to which they wanted others to perceive them as agreeable, sociable, self-aware, cautious, neurotic, or obsessive (all $ps > .05$). Thus, the conditions did not differ in terms of participants' general self-presentational goals. Generally, participants wanted others to see them as very agreeable ($M = 8.77$, $SD = 1.73$ on a 12-point scale) and sociable ($M = 8.02$, $SD = 1.84$), moderately self-aware ($M = 7.33$, $SD = 2.10$) and cautious ($M = 6.27$, $SD = 1.81$), and not at all neurotic to slightly neurotic ($M = 3.63$, $SD = 2.03$) and obsessive ($M = 3.89$, $SD = 2.13$).

Drinking Behavior

To examine the effects of self-presentational motives on the degree of risk-taking behavior, a 2 (image concern) × 2 (challenge) ANCOVA was conducted using the amount of water consumed (in milliliters) as the dependent measure. The postexperimental taste rating (i.e., responses to the question "How bad was the taste in your mouth after you sampled the liquids?") was used as a covariate to control for the effects of perceived taste on drinking behavior.

Table 1 shows the average amount of water consumed in each condition. Although the standard deviation is large in the condition where participants were both concerned and challenged, none of the individual values in this condition could be considered outliers (i.e., values more than 3 standard deviations from the mean). Hence, all values were included in the analysis. In addition, Levene's test of equality of variance was not significant, $F(3, 44) = 2.62$, $p > .05$.

As hypothesized, the ANCOVA revealed a significant main effect for both image concern and challenge. Subjects who were in the high image-concern condition drank significantly more water than did participants who were less concerned, $F(1, 43) = 4.05$, $p < .05$. Also consistent with the hypothesis, participants who were challenged to drink consumed more water than did those who were not issued the challenge, $F(1, 43) = 5.89$, $p < .05$. The Image Concern × Challenge interaction was not significant.

A priori comparisons of the amount of water consumed (adjusted for the covariate) indicated that, as predicted, participants in the low image–concern/not challenged condition drank less water than did participants in the high image–concern/not challenged condition, $F(1, 21) = 5.45$, $p < .05$, the

TABLE 1					
Descriptive Statistics for the Amount of Water Consumed (ml) and the Number of Participants Who Drank in Each Condition					

	Social Image–Concern					
	Low			High		
	M	SD	n	M	SD	n
Challenged	39.17	27.29	10	59.17	60.33	9
Unchallenged	19.17	23.53	6	44.17	25.57	10

Note. $N = 48$ (12 participants in each condition). n = Number of participants who took a drink. Adjusted marginal mean for the challenged condition, averaged across both the high and low conditions, is 53.67; for the unchallenged conditions, is 27.17; for the low condition, averaged across both challenged and unchallenged conditions, is 30.07; and for the high condition, averaged across both challenged and unchallenged conditions, is 50.77.

high image–concern/challenged condition, $F(1, 21) = 7.18$, $p < .05$, and the low image–concern/challenged condition, $F(1, 21) = 4.37$, $p < .05$. However, contrary to expectation, there was no difference in the amount of water consumed by participants in the high image–concern/challenged condition and those in the high image–concern/not challenged and the low image–concern/challenged conditions (all $ps > .05$).

Table 1 also shows the number of participants in each condition who accepted the drink from the confederate. Using logistic regression analyses, models were tested to determine the effects of social image–concern, challenge, and the Image Concern × Challenge interaction on whether participants took a drink. Due to a relatively small sample size, none of the models were statistically significant (all $ps > .05$).

The above analyses included all 48 participants—those who accepted the drink as well as those who did not. To further examine whether self-presentational concerns influenced the degree of risk-taking behavior, the analyses were repeated using only those participants who took a drink from the bottle. This approach was used to examine whether, among participants who elected to drink, the amount of water consumed was affected by the experimental manipulation.

Table 2 shows the average amount of water consumed in each condition by participants who accepted the drink. Although there were no outliers in any of the groups, the sample variances were not equal, $F(3, 31) = 3.81$, $p < .05$. Subsequently, the data were transformed using a logarithmic transformation. This strategy produced four groups with similar variances, $F(3, 31) = 2.23$, $p > .05$.

	Social Image–Concern					
	Low			High		
	M	SD	n	M	SD	n
Challenged	47.00	22.39	10	78.89	57.05	9
Unchallenged	39.33	18.35	6	53.60	16.70	10

TABLE 2

Descriptive Statistics for the Amount of Water Consumed (ml) in Each Condition by Participants Who Accepted the Drink

Note. $N = 35$. Adjusted marginal mean for the challenged condition, averaged across both the high and low conditions, is 66.55; for the unchallenged condition, averaged across both high and low conditions, is 41.78; for the low condition, averaged across both challenged and unchallenged conditions, is 44.05; and for the high condition, averaged across both challenged and unchallenged conditions, is 64.29.

A 2 (image concern) × 2 (challenge) ANCOVA was then conducted using taste ratings as a covariate and the transformed variable (representing the amount of water consumed) as the dependent measure. As expected, significant main effects emerged for both image concern and challenge. Participants who accepted the drink and who were in the high image–concern condition consumed significantly more water than did participants who accepted the drink but were in the low image–concern condition, $F(1, 30) = 4.55$, $p < .05$. Also, those participants who accepted the drink after being challenged consumed more water than did those who accepted the drink but were not issued the challenge, $F(1, 30) = 4.68$, $p < .05$. The Image Concern × Challenge interaction was not significant.

A priori comparisons of the amount of water consumed (adjusted for the covariate) showed that contrary to the hypothesis, individuals in the low image–concern/not challenged condition drank just as much water as did those in the high image–concern/not challenged, the low image–concern challenged, and the high image–concern/challenged conditions (all $ps > .05$). Also contrary to expectation, there was no difference in the amount of water consumed by participants in the high image–concern/challenged condition and those in the high image–concern/not challenged and the low image–concern/challenged conditions (all $ps > .05$).

Discussion

The results of the present study support the hypothesis that self-presentational concerns can motivate behaviors that jeopardize one's good health. Individuals who were motivated to impression-manage—either because they believed that another person considered them to be excessively cautious or because they were given an explicit challenge—were more likely to engage in what most people regard as an unsavory (Haidt, McCauley, & Rozin, 1994), if not unhealthy, behavior. Specifically, participants who were concerned about their existing social image drank more water than those who were less concerned, and participants who were challenged to take a drink consumed more water than those who were not challenged.[2] Moreover, participants who were least concerned with the confederate's impression of them (i.e., in the low image–concern and unchallenged condition) drank less water than did participants in the other three conditions. These results clearly show that both preexisting social image concerns and self-presentational challenges can motivate health risk behavior.

At least two alternative explanations for the results deserve consideration. First, the confederate's challenge to drink the water ("If you're not worried about drinking out of the same bottle as me") may have led participants to be concerned not about the confederate's impression of them but rather about hurting his feelings if they refused the drink. We cannot discount this interpretation entirely. However, there are fairly strong social conventions against the sharing of food and food implements with a stranger (Rozin & Fallon, 1987). Had participants desired to do so, they should have perceived that they could have politely declined the confederate's offer, perhaps even accompanying their refusal with the claim that the aftertaste of the liquids was not really that bad. Nonetheless, even if concerns about hurting the confederate's feelings were involved, these too may also have been fueled by self-presentational considerations; participants would not have wanted to be seen as the kind of person who hurts others. If participants accepted the drink because they were concerned with the confederate's feelings, this behavior would reflect a willingness to take a health risk simply to avoid hurting someone—much like a person who does not insist on using a condom for fear of hurting his or her sexual partner's feelings.

To address the plausibility of this explanation, 23 undergraduate psychology students were given an abbreviated, written description of the experiment's procedure.[3] They were asked to imagine that they were participants in the experiment and to indicate whether they would drink from the stranger's bottle and why. Among those who said that they would accept the drink, 70% indicated that their decision was based on concerns about looking overly cautious or squeamish, and 69% said that concerns about being polite and not offending the stranger would also influence their decision. Although these findings bolster our claim that participants drank so as not to appear excessively cautious, it appears that other interpersonal motives also may have played a role.

We suspect, however, that these other interpersonal motives were consistent across the experimental conditions and cannot fully account for the observed effects. Analysis of the drinking frequency data provides some support for this position. That is, the experimental manipulations had a significant effect on the amount of water drank but they did not influence the number of participants who drank. Different patterns of findings may have emerged for these two variables because participants in all conditions were similarly motivated to create the appearance of accepting the drink, but they were not equally motivated to engage in the risk-taking behavior of drinking out of a stranger's bottle. Those who were least concerned about self-presentation took only a perfunctory sip from the bottle (perhaps to appease the confederate), whereas those who were concerned about looking overly cautious took a large gulp.

A second alternative explanation for the observed pattern of results is that the confederate's challenge may have conveyed to participants that he had considered the health risks involved in sharing his bottle and concluded that the risk was minimal. Although this interpretation cannot be dismissed outright, we believe that the phrasing of the statement was unlikely to be interpreted as reassurance.

The results of this study support the usefulness of a self-presentational perspective for understanding health risk behavior. A self-presentational approach may help to explain at least two specific features of health risk behavior. First, a self-presentational perspective adds to two other explanations that are commonly offered to account for the fact that adolescents are particularly inclined to engage in unhealthy and dangerous behaviors (National Safety Council [NSC], 1993). The first explanation suggests that adolescents have a pervasive sense of invulnerability that leads them to underestimate risk (Arnett, 1992). The second is that adolescents are less likely than adults to fully consider and foresee the long-term consequences of their actions (Trad, 1993). A self-presentation perspective adds to these explanations the possibility that images of boldness, fearlessness, and recklessness are more valued among young people than among adults. Risky behavior that might impress the friends of an 18-year-old would likely lead people to perceive a 40-year-old as unnecessarily reckless.

Second, a self-presentational approach also helps to explain why men are far more likely to be injured in accidents of all kinds than women (NSC, 1993). Images of boldness are more important to men than to women (Williams & Best, 1982), leading them to take more unnecessary risks to convey such images to other people (Dolcini et al., 1989). Consistent with this, Parks and Leary (1995) found that men's health risk behavior was affected by self-presentational concerns regarding images of boldness but that women's health risk behavior was not. The present study found no gender differences in health risk behavior, but this may have been due to the relatively low level of perceived risk associated with drinking from a stranger's bottle. Given that women are more safety conscious than men (Crowe, 1995), different results may have emerged if a more dangerous behavior had been examined. This possibility warrants further investigation.

We are not suggesting that all, or even most, unhealthy behaviors are motivated by self-presentational concerns. Health researchers have identified many other cognitive and motivational processes that lead people to jeopardize their health (e.g., the use of faulty decision-making processes or a dispositional proclivity for sensation-seeking [for a review, see Igra & Irwin, 1996]). Yet, the data support earlier speculations that people sometimes engage in unhealthy and unsafe behaviors because they believe that doing so helps to convey desired impressions of themselves to others (Leary et al., 1994; Martin et al., in press). Whether self-presentational concerns influence the effects of other health-jeopardizing cognitive and motivational processes is an issue worthy of additional study.

Research also is needed to determine the types of health risk behaviors that are affected by self-presentational concerns. Like other social factors that influence health behavior, impression management probably plays a greater role in the early or experimental stages of a health risk behavior (e.g., smoking or alcohol use) than it does later on. Once a behavior becomes habitual or enters an addiction stage, the influence of self-presentational concerns likely diminishes as personal and pharmacological factors become more predictive of its continuance (Perry & Staufacker, 1996). Thus, we suspect that the effects of self-presentational factors are moderated by the type of health risk behavior.

In addition, previous research suggests that a variety of personality attributes also moderate the effects of self-presentational factors on health behavior. People who are particularly attuned to other people's judgments of them (e.g., high in public self-consciousness), concerned with behaving in accordance with situational norms (e.g., high self-monitors), or worried about social disapproval (e.g., high approval motivation) may be particularly susceptible to self-presentational pressures (Leary, 1995). On the other hand, people who are neurotic or hypochondriacal may be so worried about their health and safety that they avoid health risks even at great cost to their social image. Such people may unwillingly project the image of a person who is afraid to behave in ways that involve only minimal risks (such as riding on a roller coaster or in an airplane).

In summary, the present study demonstrated that an experimental manipulation of self-presentational concerns was sufficient to prompt people to engage in a behavior that could be detrimental to their health. These findings may be particularly useful for understanding and preventing health risk behavior among adolescents—a group that appears especially prone to engage in danger-ous activities because of concerns with what other people think (cf. Hingson & Howland, 1993). Of importance, the manipulations used in our experimental situation paled in comparison to self-presentational pressures that people, parti-cularly adolescents and young adults, regularly face in everyday life. In our experiment, the audience was a lone stranger (rather than a group of friends), and the self-presentational challenge to accept the drink simply raised the possi-bility that the participant would worry about the implications of performing the behavior (rather than explicitly derogating his or her fearlessness). Given that effects were obtained with these relatively weak manipulations, one can only imagine the potency of self-presentational pressures in inducing people to behave dangerously in everyday life.

Notes

1. Some participants asked the experimenter for permission to drink the confederate's water. Chi-square analysis indicated that there was no differ-ence in the frequency of these requests across conditions ($p > .30$). When asked, the experimenter's response was always, "It's okay [to have a drink] so long as it's bottled water."
2. As pointed out by an anonymous reviewer, participants in the challenge condition received more than just a provocation to drink. They also received confirmation that the confederate had indeed drank from the bottle. In con-trast, the unchallenged participants may have only suspected that the confed-erate had previously drank from the bottle. Intuitively, one would expect that confirmation of the confederate's use of the bottle would make participants less likely to accept the drink. The finding that challenged participants actu-ally drank more than unchallenged participants suggests that the provocation to drink had a strong enough self-presentational effect on drinking behavior to override the effects of information about the confederate's use of the bottle.
3. The experiment was described as a study of the relationship between per-sonality and taste preferences. Participants were asked to imagine that they were partnered with another male study participant (a stranger) who would rate their facial responses as they tasted three disgusting-tasting liquids (described as unsweetened Kool-Aid, very, very salty soy sauce, and a mix-ture of mustard and lemon juice). Participants were told that after sampling

the liquids, they would have a very bad taste in their mouths. The experimenter would apologize for not having any water for the participant to drink and she would ask the participant to wait until the end of the experiment to get a drink. The partner would then take a bottle of water from his backpack and offer the participant a drink. The bottle would be three-quarters full and it would be obvious that he had already drank from it.

References

Arnett, J. (1992). Reckless behavior in adolescence: A developmental perspective. *Developmental Review, 12,* 339–373.

Catania, J. A., Coates, T. J., Stall, R., Bye, L., Kegeles, S. M., Capell, F., Henne, J., McKusick, L., Morin, S., Turner, H., & Pollack, L. (1991). Changes in condom use among homosexual men in San Francisco. *Health Psychology, 10,* 190–199.

Crowe, J. W. (1995). Safety values and safe practices among college students. *Journal of Safety Research, 26,* 187–195.

Cullen, J. D., Widmeyer, W. N., Dorsch, K. D., & Bishop, P. J. (1997). Equipment protective capabilities and perceptions of invincibility in ice hockey. *Journal of Sport and Exercise Psychology, 19,* S44.

Denscombe, M. (1993). Personal health and the social psychology of risk taking. *Health Education Research, 8,* 505–517.

Dolcini, M. M., Cohn, L. D., Adler, N. E., Millstein, S. G., Irwin, C. E., Kegeles, S. M., & Stone, S. L. (1989). Adolescent egocentrism and feelings of invulnerability: Are they related? *Journal of Early Adolescence, 9,* 409–418.

Farber, P. D., Khavari, K. A., & Douglass, F. M. (1980). A factor analytic study of reasons for drinking: Empirical validation of positive and negative reinforcement dimensions. *Journal of Consulting and Clinical Psychology, 48,* 780–781.

Finney, P. D. (1978). Personality traits attributed to risky and conservative decision-makers: Culture values more than risk. *Journal of Psychology, 99,* 187–197.

Gold, R. S., Skinner, M. J., Grant, P. J., & Plummer, D. C. (1991). Situational factors and thought processes associated with unprotected intercourse in gay men. *Psychology and Health, 5,* 259–278.

Haidt, J., McCauley, C., & Rozin, P. (1994). Individual differences in sensitivity to disgust: A scale sampling seven domains of disgust elicitors. *Personality and Individual Differences, 5,* 701–713.

Hingson, R., & Howland, J. (1993). Promoting safety in adolescents. In S. G. Millstein, A. C. Petersen, & E. O. Nightingale (Eds.), *Promoting the health of adolescents* (pp. 305–327). New York: Oxford University Press.

Igra, V., & Irwin, C. E. (1996). Theories of adolescent risk-taking behavior. In R. J. DiClemente, W. B. Hansen, & L. E. Ponton (Eds.), *Handbook of adolescent health risk behavior* (pp. 35–51). New York: Plenum.

Leary, M. R. (1995). *Self-presentation: Impression management and interpersonal behavior.* Madison, WI: Brown & Benchmark.

Leary, M. R., & Kowalski, R. M. (1990). Impression management: A literature review and two-component model. *Psychological Bulletin, 107,* 34–47.

Leary, M. R., Tchividjian, L. R., & Kraxberger, B. E. (1994). Self-presentation can be hazardous to your health: Impression management and health risk. *Health Psychology, 13,* 461–470.

Martin, K. A., Leary, M. R., & Rejeski, W. J. (in press). Self-presentational concerns in older adults: Implications for health and well-being. *Basic and Applied Social Psychology.*

Moeller, J. L. (1997). Aseptic meningitis: A seasonal concern. *Physician and Sportsmedicine, 25,* 35–42.

National Safety Council (NSC). (1993). *Accident facts.* Itasca, IL: Author.

Nelson, S., Sealy, D. P., & Schneider, E. F. (1993). The aseptic meningitis syndrome. *American Family Physician, 48,* 809–815.

Norman, N. M., & Tedeschi, J. T. (1989). Self-presentation, reasoned action, and adolescents' decisions to smoke cigarettes. *Journal of Applied Social Psychology, 19,* 543–558.

Parks, M. J., & Leary, M. R. (1995, March). *Self-presentational motives, risk-taking, and accidental injury.* Paper presented at the meeting of the Southeastern Psychological Association, Savannah, GA.

Perry, G. L., & Staufacker, M. J. (1996). Tobacco use. In R. J. DiClemente, W. B. Hansen, & L. E. Ponton (Eds.), *Handbook of adolescent health risk behavior* (pp. 53–81). New York: Plenum.

Rozin, P., & Fallon, A. E. (1987). A perspective on disgust. *Psychological Review, 94,* 23–41.

Schlenker, B. R. (1980). *Impression management: The self-concept, social identity, and interpersonal relations.* Monterey, CA: Brooks/Cole.

Trad, P. V. (1993). The ability of adolescents to predict future outcome: I. Assessing predictive abilities. *Adolescence, 28,* 533–555.

Williams, J. E., & Best, D. L. (1982). *Measuring sex stereotypes: A thirty nation study.* Beverly Hills, CA: Sage.

Williams-Avery, R. M., & MacKinnon, D. P. (1996). Injuries and use of protective equipment among college in-line skaters. *Accident Analysis and Prevention, 28,* 779–784.

Questions for Review and Discussion

1. What is self-presentation and how might self-presentation concerns be related to risk taking?

2. How did Martin and Leary manipulate self-presentation concerns in their study?

3. What factors in addition to self-presentational concerns can lead people to engage in health-endangering behaviors?

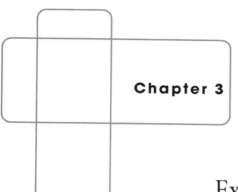

Chapter 3

Excuse Me—What Did You Just Say?!: Women's Public and Private Responses to Sexist Remarks

Janet K. Swim and Lauri L. Hyers

A s the focus of psychological research on prejudice has widened to include the target's perspective, we can no longer view those on the receiving end of prejudice and discrimination simply as passive victims (Lalonde & Cameron, 1994). Theoretical examinations have described targets as strategic negotiators of threatening situations (Goffman, 1963), as partners in a dynamic interaction (Deaux & Major, 1987), and as stress managers who actively cope through externally and internally focused responses (Fitzgerald, Swan, & Fischer, 1995).

These approaches emphasize that targets employ a variety of cognitive as well as behavioral coping strategies to withstand the injustices that they face (Crocker & Major, 1989; Feagin, 1991; Fitzgerald et al., 1995; Hyers & Swim, 1998; Lalonde & Cameron, 1994; Wright, Taylor, & Moghaddam, 1990). Understanding how targets respond to prejudice is important in order to provide a fuller picture of the way that targets negotiate social interactions in an era when encounters with prejudice are still common (Swim, Cohen, & Hyers, 1998). In the present research, we wished to examine the often underestimated role of

Reprinted from *Journal of Experimental Social Psychology*, Vol. 35, pp. 68–88, © 1999, with permission from Elsevier.

targets as active rather than passive recipients of prejudice, without neglecting to account for their more personal, private reactions.

Study 1

Public responses   In this paper, we focus on how women confront encounters with sexism. Confronting styles may vary from target group to target group because the nature of prejudice, its history, and expression are idiosyncratic to different stigmatized groups (Fiske & Stevens, 1993; Young-Bruehl, 1996). It is important to study the particular aspects of women's confronting styles for a number of reasons. Encountering sexism is commonplace for women and making decisions about whether and how to respond is a part of their every-day lives (Swim et al., 1998). Personal benefits of responding include altering or reducing this form of daily hassle and the self-satisfaction of acting on one's beliefs rather than being overpowered by a prejudiced individual (Crosby, 1993). Confronting can also aid in improving the condition of women in general by altering specific perpetrator's beliefs, altering bystanders' percep-tions of events, or altering social norms as to what is considered appropriate behavior (Blanchard, Crandall, Brigham, & Vaugh, 1994; Lalonde & Cameron, 1994). Yet, women may not respond because of social influence pressures to not respond, social pressures against identifying oneself as a feminist, fears of retaliation, or fears of being perceived as impolite or overly aggressive. These latter concerns might be especially heightened for women because confronting could be seen as inconsistent with the female gender role (Jack, 1991; Swim, Ferguson, & Hyers, 1999).

There has been very little, if any, high-impact, nonretrospective empirical work on response styles women make to encounters with prejudice. There-fore, in our first study, we placed women in a group discussion where they heard a male confederate make several sexist remarks, which allowed us to observe women's immediate responses to a specific encounter, rather than relying on long-term, retrospective recall. The sexist remarks made by our male confederate openly endorsed traditional gender roles (viewing women: as sex objects and as responsible for domestic chores). The expression of prej-udice directed toward women as a group, rather than directed at a specific woman, is pervasive and typical of women's everyday experiences with sexism (Fitzgerald et al., 1988; Swim et al., 1998). We also included a condition where women heard parallel nonsexist comments in order to obtain baseline infor-mation about women's public and private responses to the nonsexist compo-nent of these remarks.

Predicting public responding   Understanding public responding includes knowledge about factors that might influence one's decision to respond. Responding to events involves labeling an event as prejudicial, being motivated to respond to the event, and then deciding to act on that motivation. There are a number of factors that can influence labeling an event as prejudiced (e.g., Crosby, 1984; Feldman Barrett & Swim, 1998; Ruggierio & Taylor, 1997) and greater certainty that an incident is prejudicial can influence the likelihood and style of responding (e.g., Wright et al., 1990). However, labeling an event as prejudicial may not be sufficient to result in confronting. The motivation to respond is likely a function of how offensive the prejudicial incident is perceived to be (Kowalski, 1996). The decision to act on one's motivation likely involves assessing possible costs and benefits of publicly responding (Kowalski, 1996).

Endorsement of gender-related beliefs should be related to perceptions of events, motivation to respond, and decisions to respond. More specifically, identification with women as a group, such as holding gender central to the self-concept, feeling a sense of common fate with other women, and being concerned about the well-being of women in general (Branscombe, Owen, & Kobrynowicz, 1993), may increase the likelihood that a woman will label and incident as sexist (Johnston, Swim, & Stangor, 1998) and take action in response to the incident (Sauders, 1992, as cited by Fitzgerald et al., 1995). Women who have traditional attitudes about gender roles and hold modern sexist attitudes, such as believing that sexism is no longer a problem in society, may also be less likely to label an event as sexist or to publicly respond to an incident (Brooks & Perot, 1991; Jensen & Gutek, 1982; Mazer & Percival, 1989; Swim & Cohen, 1996). Finally, an active commitment to fighting sexism may be required before a woman feels the responsibility or courage to confront sexism (Crosby, 1993).

A factor that has been overlooked when considering whether people confront offensive behavior is the effect of social influence. Observations of others' behaviors after an offensive incident might influence one's interpretation of the extent to which an event is sexist and offensive. Also, group norms and diffusion of responsibility are likely to influence one's perceptions of the appropriateness of responding, motivation to respond, and assessment of the costs and benefits of responding. In the present study, the effect of social influence was examined by testing the impact of gender composition on women's public verbal responses to sexist remarks. Informational and normative social influence processes should be more powerful when bystanders are more similar to the target than when they are less similar (Abrams, Wetherell, Cochrane, Hogg, & Turner, 1990). Thus, if bystanders do not respond (as in the present study), then women's responses would be suppressed more when the nonresponding bystanders are women rather than men. Research on helping in emergencies suggests similar outcomes (Latané & Darley, 1970). The presence of bystanders creates diffusion of responsibility and lack of responding. People may feel that women are more responsible than men for confronting sexism directed at women, perhaps because women should be most qualified to decide whether the remarks need to be confronted or because they have more to gain by curbing sexism directed at women. Thus, women may believe that fellow bystanders share more responsibility for responding when the bystanders are women than when they are men.

In contrast, expectations about women's versus men's reactions to confrontations suggests that public confrontation may be *more* likely to occur when other women are present. A woman may anticipate social support from women and hostility from men if she publicly responds because of an expectation that other women would be more likely than men to share her perceptions. Thus, the cost of responding would be smaller and the likelihood of publicly responding would be greater when a women is with other women than when she is the only woman in a group.

Private responses   Choosing not to respond does not mean a lack of private responses (Kowalski, 1996). The types of private responses to prejudice described by previous researchers primarily represent different ways of coping with prejudice (e.g., denial of prejudice or making intragroup rather than intergroup comparisons, Fitzgerald et al., 1995; Tajfel & Turner, 1979). However, private responses can also be characterized by immediate thoughts and feelings about the offensiveness of the incident and whether to confront. In the present study we examine the content of women's private evaluations of the sexist remarks they encounter and the person making the remark and their thoughts about how they would like to respond to these remarks.

Self-esteem   A final purpose of the first study was to examine how encountering and confronting prejudice might affect state self-esteem. Self-blame is a common response to sexual harassment (Fitzgerald & Ormerod, 1993) and it can be associated with negative feelings about the self. Similarly, women may internalize the disempowering messages of sexist remarks (Crocker, Voelkl, Testa, & Major, 1991; Dion, 1975; Dion & Earn, 1975). However, there are ways to buffer oneself from the negative impact of prejudice (Feldman Barrett & Swim, 1998). Women who hold gender-related attitudes that would predispose them to identifying the remarks as sexist may be more likely to make self-protective attributions (Crocker & Major, 1989; Crocker et al., 1991; Landrine & Klonoff, 1997). Further, if a woman confronts a sexist person, the confronting may be self-affirming and self-esteem enhancing.

In sum, in Study 1 we examined public and private responses women make when encountering sexism directed at women. We were particularly interested in assessing the frequency and style of women's public and private responses that communicated displeasure about the sexist remark. Although we predicted that women would be more likely to publicly respond to sexist than parallel nonsexist responses, we predicted that a substantial number of women would not publicly respond to the sexist condition in contrast to the substantial number of women who would report unfavorable private thoughts and feelings about the sexist comment and person. We also predicted that those who were more gender identified, had more feminist-related beliefs, and reported being actively committed to fighting sexism would be more likely to publicly confront sexist comments. We did not make directional predictions about the effect of gender composition due to the social influence and diffusion of responsibility explanation yielding one prediction and the social support explanation providing an opposite prediction. Further, we predicted more confrontations when our female participants were the solo member of their gender in the group than when their gender was in the majority. Finally, we predicted that public confrontations, gender identification, nonsexist beliefs, and having an activist orientation would buffer women against the possible negative effects of sexist comments on self-esteem.

Method

Participants   Participants were 108 women recruited by phone from a group of students who completed a departmental prescreening questionnaire in their Introductory Psychology class. We excluded 9 participants who expressed suspicion during debriefing that the confederates were not naïve participants. In addition, thought and feeling listings and data about verbal confrontations were not available from 4 participants in the sexist condition due to technical difficulties with the video camera.

Design   The design was a 2 (gender composition: solo vs. nonsolo woman) $\times$ 2 (type of remark: sexist vs. nonsexist) between-subjects factorial. Participants were randomly assigned to conditions. In addition, the impact of several gender-related measures on the dependent measures was assessed.

Gender-related beliefs   As part of a departmental prescreening of Introductory Psychology classes, students completed several scales relevant to the present study. These included Spence, Helmreich, and Stapp's (1973) shortened version of the Attitudes Toward Women Scale and Swim, Aikin, Hall, and Hunter's (1995) Modern Sexism Scale. The Attitudes Toward Women Scale measures participants' attitudes about gender roles and gender equality (Cronbach's $\alpha = .83$). The Modern Sexism Scale measures beliefs that discrimination against women is not a problem, women complain too much about sexism, and women have gotten too much special treatment (Cronbach's $\alpha = .80$), and can be considered a measure of sensitivity to sexism (Swim & Cohen, 1996). Responses to items on these scales were on 0 (strongly agree) to 6 (strongly disagree) scales. Higher scale scores indicate more unfavorable attitudes toward women's issues on both scales.

Participants also completed the activism portion of O'Neil, Egan, Owen, and Murry's (1993) Gender Role Journey Scale and Branscombe et al.'s (1993) Gender Identity Scale. The activism subscale of the Gender Role Journey Scale included items such as "I have taken some actions in my personal life to reduce sexism" and "I am responsible for changing restrictive gender roles." Higher scores indicate greater activism (Cronbach's $\alpha = .91$). We used four subscales from the Gender Identity Scale. Higher scores on these subscales indicate that respondents (1) hold biases in favor of their own gender group (Cronbach's $\alpha = .86$), (2) have a strong emotional attachment to their own gender group (Cronbach's $\alpha = .80$), (3) feel they are a typical member of their own gender group (Cronbach's $\alpha = .84$), and (4) feel they share a common fate with members of their own gender group (Cronbach's $\alpha = .82$).

Procedure   Participants were recruited to be in a study ostensibly concerning group decision making. The experimenter escorted one participant and the three confederates to a group discussion room where they were asked to sit in preassigned seats. In the solo female participant condition, there were three male confederates. In the nonsolo female participant condition, there were two female confederates and one male confederate. The experimenter explained that the group was to select 12 individuals, from a list of 15 women and 15 men with different occupational titles, who would be best suited for survival on a deserted island. The experimenter asked group members to take turns in a clockwise order indicating their suggestion and a reason for their suggestion and asked one of the confederates to record the group's selections. This procedure allowed the participant to take part in the group discussion while the confederates said scripted comments. The script included comments about other confederates' remarks. However, the confederates were instructed to keep extraneous conversation to a minimum and always to agree with the participant's selections.

The male confederate sitting to the participant's right made either three sexist or three parallel nonsexist statements at different points during the group discussion. First, in response to another confederate's selection of an athlete/trainer, the confederate to the right of the participant said "Yeah, we definitely need to keep the (women/people in shape)." Second, during his own turn, he said "Let me see, maybe a chef? No, one of the (women/others) can cook." Third, during his final turn, he selected a female musician and said "I think we need more (women on the island to keep the men satisfied/entertainers to keep everyone happy). "The confederate made these comments to the group as a whole and did not look directly at the participant when he said them. The other two confederates were instructed not to respond to the sexist remarks or to any comments the participant might make about the remarks. After the selection of the 12 individuals was completed, one of the confederates informed the experimenter that the group had finished the task. The experimenter then led the participant and ostensibly the confederates to private rooms to complete a questionnaire.

When the participant completed the questionnaire, the experimenter led her to another room where she was informed that the group had been videotaped during the group task. In accord with Ickes, Robertson, Tooke, and Teng's (1986) naturalistic social cognition procedure, the participant was asked to view the videotape of her group task in order to help her recall the thoughts and feelings she had during the session. She was instructed to stop the tape whenever she remembered having a thought or feeling during the session and was asked to write down the thought or feeling and the time it occurred from a clock appearing on a videotape display. After she finished viewing the videotape, she was asked to rate her thoughts and feelings on several dimensions, as described below. She was then given the final debriefing and thanked for her participation in the study.

Questionnaire   Participants rated their impressions of each of the confederates.[1] Using 7-point scales, they rated the extent to which each person was cooperative, friendly, prejudiced, flexible, involved, active, responsible, expressive, comfortable, and supportive. Of particular interest were ratings of the confederates' level of prejudice. This rating was used as a single item scale with higher numbers indicating more prejudice. Based on factor analyses, three scales were formed from the remaining attributes, with higher scores representing greater perceived cooperativeness (cooperative, flexible, friendly, supportive; Cronbach's $\alpha = .84$), participation (involved, active, expressive, and comforting; Cronbach's $\alpha = .75$), and responsibility (measured by one item, "responsibility"). After these ratings, participants rated the extent to which they would like to work with the person in the future, they would like the person as a friend, and they perceived that the person had attitudes similar to their own.

Participants' feelings about themselves during the task were assessed with a modified version of Heatherton and Polivy's (1991) state self-esteem scale. We modified the scale so that it referred to participants' feelings during the group task rather than during the completion of the scale itself. The questions asked how they felt about their performance (e.g., I felt confident about my abilities), how they felt socially, (e.g., I felt concerned about the impression I was making), and how they felt about their appearance (e.g., I was pleased with my appearance). Responses to these items were recoded such that higher numbers indicated higher state self-esteem on the performance (Cronbach's $\alpha = .84$), social (Cronbach's $\alpha = .88$), and appearance (Cronbach's $\alpha = .93$) subscales.

Coding of thought and feeling listings   Participants wrote an average of 12 thoughts and feelings. After writing their recalled thoughts and feelings, participants were asked to number them and rate each thought and feeling as to whether it was (a) a thought or a feeling, (b) related to the group task, (c) negative or positive on a scale from 1 to 7, and (d) written about themselves personally, each of the confederates, or something or someone else.[2] We selected and then aggregated the ratings of those thoughts and feelings that participants had identified as being directed at the confederate sitting to their right (the confederate saying either the sexist or the nonsexist remark). There were no notable predictors of the thoughts and feelings directed at others or the participants themselves.

After the study was completed, two female coders independently rated the thoughts and feelings. Coders rated whether each thought or feeling mentioned one of the three sexist or parallel nonsexist remarks or the person saying the remarks ($\kappa = .88$). The thoughts and feelings in this subset were rated as to whether they included any mention of ways to confront the sexist comment or person ($\kappa = .55$). Private confrontations were defined as comments participants would have liked to have made or actions they would have liked to have done during the group task that would express their disagreement or displeasure with the remark.

Coding of the videotapes   Transcribers were instructed to list all comments made by the participant immediately after each sexist remark until the next scripted comment was made. Then, two female coders independently noted any confrontations, defined as verbal expressions of displeasure or disagreement with the sexist remark. The correlation between the number of confrontational responses each coder noted during each session was 0.98.

After reconciling discrepancies as to whether the response was confronta-tional, the responses were coded to capture their specific style of delivery, details not accounted for in most broad conceptual classifications (e.g., Lalonde & Cameron, 1994; Tajfel & Turner, 1979; Wright et al., 1990). Because coders could select more than one style for each response, interrater agreement was assessed separately for each style. The response styles and corresponding reliabilities were direct confrontation (e.g., saying that the person or remark was sexist or telling the perpetrator to change his behavior; $\kappa = .77$), humor or sarcasm ($\kappa = .73$), questioning of the confederate ($\kappa = .78$), giving a task-related response that contradicted the confederates remark ($\kappa = .86$), surprised exclamations ($\kappa = .77$), grumbling noise ($\kappa = .66$), and resigned acceptance ($\kappa = .88$). Coders reconciled any discrepancies through discussion. The 10% of responses that indicated resigned acceptance (e.g., "Whatever") were excluded from analy-ses of confrontational responses because they did not clearly indicate disagree-ment. It could be argued that several of the other behaviors (such as surprised exclamations or grumbling) represent immediate emotional reactions to the event rather than confrontational reactions. However, these remarks can be con-sidered confrontational because they were verbal indicators of disagreement or displeasure and were controllable.

Results

Manipulation check A 2 (gender composition) $\times$ 2 (type of remark) ANOVA was performed on the questionnaire ratings. This analysis revealed a main effect for type of remark on all but one rating. When the confederate made sexist remarks, he was perceived as more prejudiced, less responsible, and less cooperative than when he made nonsexist remarks (see Table 1). Participants also indicated a lesser preference to work with the confederate making the sexist remarks in a future group, indicated a lesser preference to have him as a friend, and perceived that his attitudes were more dissimilar from their own attitudes compared to when he made nonsexist remarks. The only rating of this confederate that was not affected by the type of remark was his level of participation in the group. There were also no main effects or inter-actions with gender composition.

Public responses Of the 44 women in the sexist condition, 4 confronted all three sexist remarks, 5 confronted two of the remarks, 11 confronted one remark, and 24 made no confrontations. Thus, 45% ($n = 20$) gave at least one verbal confrontational response in the sexist condition. In contrast, 7 of the 51 women in the nonsexist condition expressed disagreement or

			TABLE 1	
	Perceptions of Confederate Who Made the Sexist or Nonsexist Remark			
Rating	Sexist remark (M)	Nonsexist remark (M)	$F(1, 95)$	p
Prejudiced	5.06 (2.06)	1.86 (1.41)	83.57	<.001
Responsible	5.12 (1.68)	6.22 (1.01)	15.52	<.001
Cooperative	5.28 (1.28)	6.12 (.84)	14.86	<.001
Participation	5.21 (1.08)	5.31 (1.31)	.21	.70
Work with in the future	3.50 (1.98)	5.04 (1.48)	18.17	<.001
Be their friend	3.37 (1.78)	4.53 (1.41)	12.10	.001
Perceive similarity	2.67 (1.78)	4.26 (1.44)	24.52	<.001

Note. Numbers in parentheses indicate standard deviations. Higher means represent perceiving the confederate as more prejudiced, responsible, cooperative, participatory, having more favorable reactions to working with the person in the future, having more favorable reactions to being their friends, and perceiving more similarity between themselves and this person. There were 48 women in the sexist condition and 51 women in the nonsexist condition.

displeasure with the parallel nonsexist remarks. Because the parallel nonsexist remarks merely expressed a preference for certain occupations and were not designed to be offensive and few responded in the nonsexist condition, the confrontation-like responses in the nonsexist condition are used only for basic comparison purposes and will not analyzed further.

The most frequent style of confrontation made in the sexist condition was questioning the confederate ($n = 11, 25\%$). These questions included asking the confederate to repeat himself and asking the confederate rhetorical questions (e.g., "What did you say?!"). The second most frequent style of response was a task-related response ($n = 9, 20\%$) (e.g., by selecting an occupation or providing an explanation that contradicted the suggestion made by the sexist person). Next, the following three styles of responses were equally likely to occur ($n = 7, 16\%$, for each): direct comments (e.g., "You can't pick someone for that reason. Pick another person"), humor or sarcasm (e.g., making an anti-male, sexist comment), or surprised exclamations (e.g., "Oh my God. I can't believe you said that!"). The least frequent confrontational response was grumbling ($n = 1, 2\%$).

Predicting public responses[3]
Gender composition of the group. We used log-linear regressions to test whether gender composition of the group predicted publicly confronting the

sexist remarks at least once during the entire task as well as at least once to each of the three sexist remarks. We were interested in responses to each remark because each remark might be perceived differently at different points during the group task. For instance, there is a possible cumulative impact of hearing several remarks and observing others not responding to the remarks, as our confederates were instructed to behave.

While not significantly different, women were 14% more likely to confront at least once when they were the only member of their gender in the group ($n = 12, 52\%$) than when there were other women present ($n = 8, 38\%; \chi^2(1) = .88, p = .35$). Examining the number of women who gave at least one style of response after each remark revealed that gender composition had a statistically significant impact for the first remark ($\chi^2(1) = 4.24, p = .04$), but not for the later remarks. Participants were more likely to confront after the first remark when they were the solo woman present ($n = 8, 35\%$) than if there were other women present ($n = 2, 9\%$). There was no statistically significant effect of gender composition on responding to the second remark ($n = 7, 31\%$ versus $n = 5$, 22%, solo woman versus nonsolo woman, respectively), nor to the third remark ($n = 6, 27\%$ versus $n = 5, 20\%$, solo woman versus nonsolo woman).

Gender-related beliefs.   For those in the sexist remark condition, log-linear regressions were conducted to test whether any of the gender-related beliefs predicted publicly confronting the sexist remarks at least once during the study or to each remark. Separate log-linear regressions were computed for each gender-related belief. Women who reported actively confronting sexism in their lives were more likely to confront after the second ($r = .17, \chi^2(1) = 3.77, p = .05$) and third remarks ($r = .25, \chi^2(1) = 5.75, p = .02$). None of the other gender-related beliefs predicted confronting.

Private responses.   Participants' ratings of the thoughts and feelings directed at the person sitting to their right were analyzed with 2 (group composition) × 2 (type of remark) ANOVAs. A higher percentage of the thoughts and feelings were about the confederate sitting to their right when he made the sexist remarks ($M = 35.73, SD = 21$) than when he made the parallel nonsexist remarks ($M = 14.56, SD = 14.38$), $F(1, 94) = 34.84, p \leqslant .001$. With regard to the thoughts and feelings listed about the person sitting to their right, participants were more likely to list fewer thoughts, more feelings, fewer task-related thoughts and feelings, and more non-task-related thoughts and feelings in the sexist than the nonsexist remark condition (see Table 2). Further, the valence of these thoughts and feelings was more negative in the sexist ($M = 2.22, SD = 1.28$) than the nonsexist condition ($M = 4.02, SD = 1.74$), $F(1, 72) = 26.44, p < .001$. There were no main effects or interactions involving gender composition.

TABLE 2				
Quality of Thoughts and Feelings Directed to the Confederate Who Made Either the Sexist or Nonsexist Remarks				
Rating	Mean sexist remark	Mean nonsexist remark	$F(1, 72)$	p
Thought	58.99 (40.03)	82.16 (34.77)	7.81	.01
Feeling	41.01 (40.03)	17.84 (34.77)	7.81	.01
Related to task	48.98 (40.79)	79.28 (35.30)	11.63	.001
Not related to task	51.02 (40.79)	20.72 (35.30)	11.63	.001

Note.   Numbers in parentheses indicate standard deviations. Higher means indicate a higher average proportion of thoughts and feelings that the participants rated as having each characteristic. There were 43 women in the sexist condition and 31 in the nonsexist condition. The means excluded people who did not identify any of their own thoughts and feelings as being directed toward the confederate who made the sexist or nonsexist remark.

We were particularly interested in whether women's thought and feeling listings included ways to confront the sexist remarks. In the sexist condition, 43% ($n = 19$) of the participants mentioned at least one confrontational response. Of the 44 women in this condition, 1 reported four confrontational comments, 1 listed three confrontational comments, 5 listed two confrontational comments, 12 listed one confrontational comment, and 25 listed none. The confrontational comments included responses they made during the study, responses they would like to have made (e.g., arguing with him, name calling, scolding, leaving, and questioning the confederate), and responses they were not likely to have seriously considered (e.g., hitting or killing him). The two most common responses listed were arguing and taking some type of violent action like hitting the confederate. In contrast, only 3 of the 51 women in the nonsexist condition reported ways to confront the parallel nonsexist comment or person saying the comment. The confrontational responses they listed were simply thoughts about not wanting to openly disagree or argue with the confederates. Listing at least one confrontation in the thought and feeling listings was not related to whether participants made similar public responses during the study ($\chi^2(1) = 1.62, p = .20$).

Self-esteem   We predicted that hearing the sexist remark might affect how participants felt about themselves during the task in terms of their state self-esteem and this might be moderated by whether they confronted. Two (type of remark) $\times$ 2 (group composition) ANOVAs revealed that the type of remark and gender composition of the group did not affect performance, appearance, or social state self-esteem. Contrary to predictions that confronting would be self-affirming, a 2 (confronted at least once vs. never) × 2 (group composition) ANOVA for those in the sexist condition revealed no significant effects on state self-esteem.

We also predicted that gender-related beliefs would moderate the effect of hearing sexist remarks on self-esteem. Moderated regression analyses supported this prediction. First, a gender-related belief measure (kept as a continuous measure) and the type of remark made (dummy coded) were entered together in the regression equations. Second, we entered the interaction between the individual difference measure and the type of remark. We ran separate regressions for each of the gender-related beliefs and for each of the types of state self-esteem. These regressions revealed an interaction between level of activism and type of sexist remark for performance ($b = .16$, $t(86) = 2.62$, $p < .01$), appearance ($b = .32$, $t(86) = 2.63$, $p = .01$), and social ($b = .28$, $t(86) = 2.49$, $p = .01$) state self-esteem. When a sexist remark was made, less activist women reported that they had lower performance, ($r = .48$, $p < .01$), appearance, ($r = .45$, $p < .01$), and social ($r = .46$, $p < .01$) state self-esteem during the group session. When a non-sexist remark was made, level of activism was not related to performance, ($r = .01$, $p = .93$), appearance, ($r = -.07$, $p = .64$), and social ($r = .02$, $p = .91$) state self-esteem. Similar results predicting social state self-esteem were found for the Attitudes Toward Women Scale and the emotional attachment to one's own gender group subscale of the Gender Identity scale (interaction $b = -.43$, $t = -2.75$, $p = .01$; interaction $b = -.23$, $t = 2.16$, $p = .03$, respectively). When a sexist remark was made, those with more traditional gender-role attitudes and less emotional attachment to their gender group had lower social state self-esteem ($r = -.36$, $p = .02$, $r = .38$, $p = .02$, respectively), whereas when a nonsexist remark was made, these attitudes did not predict their social state self-esteem ($r = .18$, $p = .22$; $r = .05$, $p = .69$, respectively).

Discussion

Study 1 results revealed that only 16% of the women confronted the sexist person with direct verbal comments such as indicating that his remarks were inappropriate or that he should retract them. However, when including additional confronting styles, 45% of participants openly expressed their displeasure. In comparison to the near lack of confronting in the nonsexist condition, this reveals that women did not behave as passive victims to this encounter with sexism.

An examination of the private thoughts and feelings among the remaining 55% who did not publicly confront reveals that their lack of confrontation was not indicative of acceptance of the remark. First, many women privately mentioned confronting and these thoughts were unrelated to having actually confronted. Second, perceptions of the sexist confederate indicated that most participants did not think favorably about the confederate making the sexist remarks and thought that he was prejudiced. More specifically, three-quarters of those who did not publicly respond indicated that they saw him as prejudiced in their private ratings. Similarly, 91% of the women who did not confront publicly nonetheless had private negative thoughts and feelings about the confederate (i.e., the average rating of their thoughts and feelings were below the midpoint of the favorability scale).

As hypothesized, activism predicted public confrontation. This relationship was found for publicly confronting the second and third remark. This pattern suggests that after a certain amount of time had elapsed and after observing others not publicly responding one's sense of personal responsibility became a motivator. None of the other gender-related beliefs predicted confronting, suggesting that a particularly committed stance toward fighting sexism is more predictive of confronting than either being gender identified or having certain feminist beliefs. The importance of an activist orientation in women's reactions to sexism was also revealed through the impact of the sexist remarks on women's state self-esteem. In the sexist condition, women who had an activist orientation reported higher performance, appearance, and social state self-esteem than women who did not have an activist orientation. This effect is not likely a function of activist women confronting more than nonactivist women because, contrary to predictions, confrontation was not related to self-esteem.

The effect of gender composition on public confronting indicates that social influence processes affected women's choice of whether to respond more than social support. Women were more likely to confront the first remark when they were the solo female than when their gender was in the majority and, while not statistically significant, this trend existed after the other two remarks. The lack of effect of gender composition on private ratings and thoughts and feelings about the confederate and his sexist remarks suggest that social influence did not influence perceptions. Thus, the effect of group composition was not likely a result of informational influence. Instead, ingroup identification likely caused women to feel that other women's lack of response provided a better role model than the other men's lack of response. Further, they likely felt less personal responsibility for confronting when other women were present than when other men were present.

Study 2

There were two purposes for conducting Study 2. First, we tested whether women would be overconfident about the likelihood that they would respond to sexist comments. As has been long documented, people are often unaware of the impact of situations on their behaviors (Milgram, 1974). Further, people are often overconfident of their ability to predict their own and others' behaviors due, in part, to their tendency to underestimate the impact of situational forces on behavior (Ross & Nisbett, 1991). This overconfidence has important implications for assumptions about and sensitivity to women who do not respond. Demonstrating the assumptions people might make, one woman noted in her thought–feeling listings "The other two women didn't appear to find anything wrong with these comments. The two girls, I realized, have a lot to learn if they [don't] defend themselves and their gender." We predicted that women would be more likely to indicate that they would take the direct action of publicly confronting sexist remarks than women actually did in Study 1.

A second purpose of Study 2 was to test possible reasons for women's selection of responses in Study 1. After one is motivated to respond, the decision of whether and how to confront is likely a function of the anticipated costs and benefits of confronting (Kowalski, 1996). Thus, in Study 2, we examined whether the perceived costs associated with different styles of confronting might explain the responses participants selected. While there are many different costs associated with identifying events as sexist (e.g., Crosby, 1984; Feldman Barrett & Swim, 1998; Ruggiero & Taylor, 1997), we focus on two immediate costs which are particularly associated with publicly confronting sexist remarks in a group setting. Complaining can be seen as impolite because it is a violation of the social standard that says "If you don't have anything nice to say, don't say anything at all" (Crosby, 1993). This may be particularly true for women for whom assertive responding can be perceived as inconsistent with their gender role. Thus, women who confront will be viewed as impolite. Another perceived cost may be possible retaliation, ranging from mild social rejection to overt aggression. For instance, one woman noted in her thought–feeling listing, "Should I yell at a room full of guys and give them a women's lib lecture? They would laugh at me." Thus, we predicted that the most frequently selected styles of responses women made in Study 1 would most likely be those that were perceived to be the least costly (i.e., the most polite and the least risky).

Method

Participants   As part of a mass screening packet distributed in Introductory Psychology classes, 113 women responded to the scenario and activism measures described below.

Design   The study was a 2 (group composition: solo vs. nonsolo woman) × 3 (first, second, or third sexist remark) mixed factorial with repeated measures on the second factor and random assignment to one of the two group composition conditions.[4]

Scenarios and dependent measures   The scenarios described the situation that participants experienced in the sexist remark condition in Study 1. Study 2 participants were instructed to imagine that they were participating in the deserted island group task along with three men (solo condition) or along with a mixed-sex group (two women and a man, the nonsolo condition). The gender composition manipulation was accomplished by providing a diagram of the seating arrangement indicating the names of the other group members and the place where the participant was to imagine sitting. The next page of the scenario described the scripted dialogue from Study 1 and specifically noted the male confederate's remark that they needed an athlete/trainer to keep the women in shape on the island. Participants were first asked to rate how offensive (0, not very offensive; 6, very offensive) and sexist (0, not very sexist; 6, very sexist) they perceived this first remark to be. Next they were asked to indicate whether they definitely would not, probably would not, probably would, or definitely would give different styles of responses to the remark. The response styles represented the confrontational responses participants actually made during Study 1. (See Table 3 for the list of responses.) Violent responses (hitting and punching) were also included because they were frequently mentioned in the thought and feeling listings of Study 1.[5] After rating the likelihood that they would give each response, the second remark made by the sexist confederate was described and the same questions were asked. Then the third remark was described and the same questions were asked. Participants perceived the sexist remarks as offensive ($M = 3.72$, $SD = 1.84$) and sexist ($M = 4.40$, $SD = 1.69$).[6] Following the response ratings after the third remark, participants rated, from 0 (not at all) to 6 (very), the extent to which each response directly communicated disagreement or disapproval of the remark made, represented a polite or socially acceptable response, and represented a risky response in terms of how the sexist person or others would react to that response.

   In order to obtain a conservative estimate of people's anticipated responses to each remark, the results were based only on the percentage of individuals

TABLE 3		
Comparison Between Actual and Anticipated Public Responses		
Response	Percentage who actually gave the response (Study 1) ($N = 44$)	Percentage who anticipated definitely giving a response (Study 2) ($N = 109$)
No response		
1. Ignore the comment[a]	55	1
2. Wait to see what others do	55	4
Confrontational responses		
3. Question the response	25	47
4. Task-related response	20	22
5. Comment on inappropriateness	16	48
6. Sarcasm or humor	16	37
7. Surprise exclamation	16	40
8. Grumbling	2	10
9. Hit or punch	0	8
Gave at least one confrontational response	45	81

[a] Whether the lack of responses was a result of ignoring the comment and waiting to see what others do was not differentiated in Study 1.

who reported that they would definitely give each response (as opposed to those that probably would, probably would not, or definitely would not give each response). We calculated the percentage who would definitely give any of the confrontational responses at least once after each remark, the percentage who would definitely give any of the confrontational responses at least once across all three remarks, and the percentage who would definitely give each of the seven confrontational responses at least once across all three remarks. Lack of responding was calculated by the percentage of women who indicated that they would definitely not respond to all three remarks. Hence, the percentage of participants not responding was based upon the percentage of individuals who would ignore all three remarks or wait to see what others would do for all three remarks. These calculations were done to make the results from Study 2 comparable to the results from Study 1.

	TABLE 4		
	Mean Ratings of How Direct, Risky, and Polite Each Response Was Perceived to Be		
Response	Direct (M)	Risky (M)	Polite (M)
No response			
1. Ignore the comment[1]	.81[a] (1.43)	.77[a] (1.49)	4.31[ab] (2.00)
2. Wait to see what others do	.73[a] (1.14)	.61[a] (1.10)	4.15[b] (1.81)
Confrontational responses			
3. Question the response	4.27[c] (1.29)	3.61[c] (1.45)	4.17[b] (1.38)
4. Task-related response	4.19[c] (1.48)	3.41[c] (1.59)	4.67[a] (1.43)
5. Comment on inappropriateness	5.67[d] (.85)	4.53[d] (1.54)	3.74[b] (1.96)
6. Sarcasm or humor	2.89[b] (1.48)	3.20[c] (1.45)	3.13[c] (1.54)
7. Surprised exclamation	3.51[b] (1.38)	3.32[c] (1.42)	3.45[c] (1.37)
8. Grumbling	2.12[b] (1.40)	2.65[b] (1.38)	2.47[d] (1.43)
9. Hit or punch	4.28[c] (2.34)	5.60[d] (1.23)	.28[e] (.84)

Note. Numbers in parentheses indicate standard deviations. Higher numbers indicate that the response was rated as more direct, risky, and polite. Means with different superscripts *within a column* are significantly different from each other at $p < .01$, with Newman–Kuels posthoc tests. *N* ranges from 109 to 113.

Results and Discussion

Confidence in likelihood of publicly confronting   Study 2 illustrated that women were optimistic about the likelihood that they would take the direct approach of responding publicly to the sexist remarks. The total percentage of individuals predicting that they would definitely give at least one confrontational response far exceeded the number who gave at least one confrontational response during Study 1 (see Table 3). With the exception of task-related responses, the percentage of participants in Study 2 who anticipated definitely engaging in each of the confrontational behaviors at least once was greater than the percentage who actually displayed such responses in Study 1. Further, in direct opposition to the results of Study 1, very few women in Study 2 anticipated that they would not respond at all. Not responding was rated as the least direct response option (see Table 4). Thus, women anticipated being more direct than they likely would have been in a real situation.

The cost of responding   The difference in preferred style of confronting between Study 1 and Study 2 is likely a function of avoiding possible costs associated with confronting. Not responding, which was the least frequent public response women anticipated in Study 2, but the most frequent public response actually given in Study 1, was perceived to be the least risky as well as the least direct.

We wanted to examine whether the particular style of public confrontational responses women in Study 1 actually made and the women in Study 2 anticipated making were related to the possible costs of responding. We also tested whether their confidence that they would be direct would be associated with the confrontation style they used or would anticipate using. We correlated the mean ratings of how risky, polite, and direct each confrontational response was perceived to be, first with the percentage of women who actually gave each confrontational response at least once in Study 1 and second with the percentage who anticipated definitely giving each confrontational response at least once in Study 2. The less risky, more polite, and the more direct a response was perceived to be the more women actually gave the response ($r(6) = -.30$, .88, .36, respectively) and the more women anticipated giving the response ($r(6) = -.11$, .64, .46, respectively). However, the only significant correlation was between how polite the response was perceived to be and the percentage of women in Study 1 who actually gave the response ($p = .01$).[7]

General Discussion

These studies illustrate that women are not responding to sexist remarks in the manner that they would like to respond. Most women in our studies found the sexist remarks objectionable, perceived the person saying the remark as prejudiced, and would like to have publicly responded. However, the constraints of the situation impeded their responding. The effects of social constraints are illustrated by the response styles women chose and by the effect of social influence processes. First, women preferred the least risky choice of not responding. Second, when women did respond, they preferred more polite responses. Third, women were less likely to publicly confront when other women were present than when they were a solo member their gender in the group. The effect of group composition was likely a result of diffusion of responsibility or female bystanders providing a stronger normative standard about how women should respond than male bystanders.

Women who are most likely to respond are those with an activist orientation. While not endorsing traditional roles or modern sexist beliefs would be indicative of a feminist orientation, a more well developed feminist identity is associated with taking an active stance to fight sexism (Bargard & Hyde, 1991). Given that the other gender-related beliefs did not predict public responding in Study 1, the results indicate that it takes a person who is particularly committed to ending sexism to overcome the social influence processes constraining behavior.[8]

It is likely that the process leading to public responding is similar for targets of prejudice other than women (e.g., African Americans) as well as for bystanders who are not the targets (e.g., men overhearing sexist comments about women). Specifically, this process would consist of labeling an event as prejudicial, being motivated to respond to the event, and then deciding to act on the motivation. Further, an activist orientation and social influence processes are likely to affect outcomes of each of the steps in this process. Similarly, group differences may emerge due to different tendencies to label events as prejudice, motivations to respond to prejudice, and assessments of costs and benefits. For instance, compared to women, men may be less likely to label events as sexist (Russo-Devosa & Swim, 1997), feel less compelled to confront sexism, and be less afraid of appearing impolite.

Future research should explore the ramifications of confronting. People's anticipation of the costs and benefits about responding may not be correct. The discrepancy between public and private responses suggests that if a woman dissents from the social pressure not to confront, it is likely that the dissent will receive support from other women because many women would privately agree with the dissenter. The dissenter may therefore not be perceived as impolite and the response might not be as risky as assumed. Further, the benefits of confronting could be examined in future research. Confronting may serve a social role by altering other people's perceptions. Past research has shown that awareness that others do not tolerate prejudice can decrease a bystander's prejudice and tolerance of comments (Blanchard et al., 1994; Citron, Chein, & Harding, 1950). While not all the verbal confrontations in the present study are likely to have been strategically planned to influence others' perceptions, they still may have that impact. Other perhaps unintended effects of confronting include being a role model for others to express their displeasure with sexist remarks, altering social standards for what is acceptable behavior, and educating perpetrators of sexist remarks. Finally, while it may seem that confronting could make women feel efficacious and therefore heighten their self-esteem, the results from Study 1 indicated that confronting was unrelated to state self-esteem. Instead of having this personal effect, confronting may help protect the state self-esteem of women who may be uncertain as to whether the remarks were sexist by perhaps increasing the likelihood that they would label such remarks as prejudicial.

In sum, the fact that 45% of women did respond in some confrontational manner to the remarks reveals that women are not necessarily passive recipients of prejudicial encounters. This is particularly likely to be true for women personally committed to fighting sexism. However, the present study also illustrated women's struggle between their desire to challenge sexism and the social pressures that work against direct responding. Merely labeling a remark as prejudicial and wanting to respond is not likely to be sufficient to predict responding. For instance, thinking about confronting did not predict actually public confronting. Further, concerns about the costs associated with confronting support the idea that it takes courage to complain in public about sexist behaviors. The low frequency of direct comments about the remarks and the fact that 55% did not make public confrontations in contrast to the negativity of their private opinions and the desires of many to confront indicate that observers will not be privy to women's personal opinions about sexism and their views of those who make sexist remarks. This can lead to pluralistic ignorance and normative pressures not to respond, sexist people not learning that they are behaving offensively and are disliked because of this, and, in general, the perpetuation of sexist comments in the culture. We hope that recognition of pluralistic ignorance helps alleviate this ignorance and that recognition of the social barriers women face as targets of prejudice will yield more sympathetic responses to the struggles that they and others face when deciding whether to take active stances against sexism in their everyday lives.

Notes

1. Participants also completed four questions designed to assess their perceptions of social support in the group. Participants reported feeling less support from the group when a sexist remark was made. This is likely a function of perceptions of the sexist confederate rather than all members of the group because type of remark did not affect other ratings of the bystanders. Group composition did not affect the social support ratings.
2. Each participant also rated the extent to which the thought took a direct-perspective (a perception of herself, other people, the task, or the room) or a meta-perspective (a perception of other people's perception of her, other people, the task, or the room). There was some confusion for participants as to what a meta-perspective was and few participants selected this option, so we did not examine this variable.

3. We wanted to know whether perceptions of the sexist remarks would mediate the relationship between activism and confronting. However, we did not have a measure of perceptions of the sexist remark because we did not want to reveal the purpose of the study by asking the question. As a proxy for participants' perceptions of the sexist remark, we used participants' ratings of how prejudiced the sexist individual was perceived to be. The results indicate that these perceptions did not mediate the results. A possible reason this variable did not mediate the relationship is that being more likely to perceive the person as sexist, in contrast to perceiving the remark as sexist, may decrease confronting because confronting might be perceived as less effective and more risky with a more sexist person. Consistent with this explanation, log-linear regressions revealed that perceiving that the confederate was more prejudiced lead to being less likely to confront after the first remark ($r = -.23, \chi^2(1) = 4.37, p = .04$).

4. Because we anticipated that women would not be sensitive to situational cues, we anticipated that they may not be sensitive to the impact of group composition on responding. However, in contrast to their overconfidence in estimating their likelihood of responding, women accurately anticipated that they would be more likely to say they would publicly confront the sexist person in the solo status condition than the nonsolo status condition. This effect occurred for all three sexist remarks. Women in Study 2 may have assumed that they would not have needed to make as many responses because other women would be helping them. Thus, this finding could be indicative of diffusion of responsibility or expectations of social support.

5. Three additional responses were included on the form (resigned acceptance, glaring, and laughing) as other options participants might choose. These responses were not included as confrontational responses in Study 1, so they are not used in the analyses presented below.

6. We examined the impact of gender-related beliefs on perceptions of the comments and anticipated responses. Being gender identified (emotional attachment to one's gender and perceiving a common fate with other women), holding less sexist beliefs (Modern Sexism and Attitudes Toward Women), and being an activist predicted perceiving the remarks as sexist and offensive. However, being an activist predicted women being more likely to confront. Perceptions of how sexist and offensive the remarks were perceived to be mediated the effect activism, but not group composition, on the likelihood of confronting. Finally, because the questionnaire was included in a mass screening packet for all students, 45 male participants also completed all questions in the survey. Men and women found the remarks to be equally sexist but men found them to be less offensive. Men were less likely than women to anticipate that they would

definitely confront the sexist comment (50% vs. 81%). This effect remained significant after covarying out perceptions of the offensiveness of the remarks. In contrast to the women, they were less likely to anticipate confronting when the other three group members were men (33%) than when the other three group members were composed of two women and one man (62%). Even though the group composition variable resulted in the condition being all men versus an equal number of women and men, this is consistent with a diffusion of responsibility explanation, with people taking on less responsibility when other people of their gender are available to confront the sexist person. It should be noted that it is not necessary to make comparisons with men in order to understand that women did not respond as much as they wanted to and that individual differences, perceived costs, and social influence processes affected women's responding in the present study.

7. We also conducted repeated measures analyses to have a more statistically powerful test of the effect of costs on public responding. The dependent variable in these analyses was the likelihood that participants either gave a particular style of response in Study 1 or anticipated giving a particular style of response in Study 2. We excluded hitting or punching from the analyses because there was no variance on this variable for Study 1 because no participant gave this responses. We used planned contrasts with weights derived from Study 2 participants' perceptions of how direct, polite, and risky the responses were. The results revealed significant linear trends for all the variables such that the more direct, polite, and risky behaviors were perceived to be more likely to be done and anticipated. The effect for riskiness was therefore in the opposite direction to that found with the correlations. Further, higher order effects qualified all analyses with the exception of the analyses for actual responding with contrasts based upon how polite the behavior was perceived to be. Thus, like the analyses using correlations, these analyses revealed that politeness was the most parsimonious predictor of the participants' choice of response style.

8. The fact that gender-related beliefs predicted perceptions of the sexist remark but only activism predicted publicly responding (see footnote 5) is consistent with the argument that labeling an event as prejudicial is not sufficient for understanding public responses to prejudice. It is possible that the greater conceptual similarity between the activism measure and confronting accounts for its greater predictive power. However, the temporal pattern of findings from Study 1 suggest that the scales' ability to identify people more strongly committed to fighting sexism is also a viable explanation for its greater predictive power. That is, the pattern of findings suggests that participants' assessment of the situation as one in which others were not taking the responsibility to respond influenced the greater predictive power of activism as the study progressed.

References

Abrams, D., Wetherell, M., Cochrane, S., Hogg, M. A., & Turner, J. C. (1990). Knowing what to think by knowing who you are: Self-categorization and the nature of norm formation, conformity and group polarization. *British Journal of Social Psychology*, **29**, 97–119.

Bargard, A., & Hyde, J. S. (1991). Women's studies: A study of feminist identity development in women. *Psychology of Women Quarterly*, **15**, 181–201.

Blanchard, F. A., Crandall, C. S., Brigham, J. C., & Vaugh, L. A. (1994). Condemning and Condoning racism: A social context approach to interracial settings. *Journal of Applied Psychology*, **79**, 993–997.

Branscombe, N. R., Owen, S., & Kobrynowicz, D. (1993). *Measuring identification with one's gender group in women and men.* Paper presented at the American Psychological Association, Toronto, Canada.

Brooks, L., & Perot, A. R. (1991). Reporting sexual harassment: Exploring a predictive model. *Psychology of Women Quarterly*, **15**, 31–47.

Citron, A. F., Chein, I., & Harding, J. (1950). Anti-minority remarks: A problem for action research. *Journal of Abnormal Social Psychology*, **45**, 99–126.

Crocker, J., & Major, B. (1989). Social stigma and self-esteem: The self-protective properties of stigma. *Psychological Review*, **96**, 608–630.

Crocker, J., Voelkl, K., Testa, M., & Major, B. (1991). Social stigma: The affective consequences of attributional ambiguity. *Journal of Personality and Social Psychology*, **60**, 218–228.

Crosby, F. (1984). The denial of personal discrimination. *American Behavioral Scientist*, **27**, 371–386.

Crosby, F. J. (1993). Why complain? *Journal of Social Issues*, **49**, 169–184.

Deaux, K., & Major, B. (1987). Putting gender into context: An interactive model of gender-related behavior. *Psychological Review*, **94**, 369–389.

Dion, K. L. (1975). Women's reactions to discrimination from members of the same or opposite sex. *Journal of Research in Personality*, **9**, 294–306.

Dion, K. L., & Earn, B. M. (1975). The phenomenology of being a target of prejudice. *Journal of Personality and Social Psychology*, **32**, 944–950.

Feagin, J. R. (1991). The continuing significance of race: Antiblack discrimination in public places. *American Sociological Review*, **56**, 101–116.

Feldman Barrett, L., & Swim, J. K. (1998). Appraisals of prejudice and discrimination. In J. K. Swim, & C. Stangor (Eds.), *Prejudice: The target's perspective.* San Diego: Academic Press.

Fiske, S. T., & Stevens, L. E. (1993). What's so special about sex? Gender stereotyping and discrimination. In S. Oskamp & M. Costanzo (Eds.), *Gender issues in contemporary society: Applied social psychology annual* (Vol. 9, pp. 173–196). Newbury Park, CA: Sage.

Fitzgerald, L. F., & Ormerod, A. J. (1993). Breaking silence: The sexual harassment of women in academia and the workplace. In F. Denmark, & M. Paludi (Eds.), *The psychology of women: Handbook of issues and theories* (pp. 553–581). Westport, CT: Greenwood.

Fitzgerald, L. F., Shullman, S. L., Bailey, N., Richards, M., Swecker, J., Gold, Y., Ormerod, A. J., & Weitzman, L. (1988). The incidence and dimensions of sexual harassment in academia and the workplace. *Journal of Vocational Behavior, 32,* 152–175.

Fitzgerald, L. F., Swan, S., & Fischer, K. (1995). Why didn't she just report him? The psychological and legal implications of women's responses to sexual harassment. *Journal of Social Issues, 51,* 117–138.

Goffman, E. (1963). *Stigma: Notes on the management of spoiled identity.* Englewood Cliffs, NJ: Prentice Hall.

Heatherton, T. F., & Polivy, J. (1991). Development and validation of a scale for measuring state self-esteem. *Journal of Personality and Social Psychology, 60,* 895–910.

Hyers, L. L., & Swim, J. K. (1998). A comparison of the experiences of dominant and minority group members during and intergroup encounter. *Group processes and intergroup relations.*

Ickes, W., Robertson, E., Tooke, W., & Teng, G. (1986). Naturalistic social cognition: Methodology, assessment, and validation. *Journal of Personality and Social Psychology, 51,* 66–82.

Jack, D. C. (1991). *Silencing the self: Women and depression.* Cambridge, MA: Harvard Univ. Press.

Jensen, I., & Gutek, B. A. (1982). Attributions and assignment of responsibility for sexual harassment. *Journal of Social Issues, 38,* 121–136.

Johnston, K., Swim, J. K., & Stangor, C. (1998, in preparation). *The effects of enhancing gender identity on the perception of personal gender discrimination.*

Kowalski, R. M. (1996). Complaints and complaining: Functions, antecedents, and consequences. *Psychological Bulletin, 119,* 176–196.

Lalonde, R. N., & Cameron, J. E. (1994). Behavioral responses to discrimination: A focus on action. In M. P. Zanna & J. M. Olson (Eds.). *The psychology of prejudice: The Ontario symposium* (Vol. 7, pp. 257–288). Hillsdale, NJ: Erlbaum.

Landrine, H., & Klonoff, E. A. (1997). *Discrimination against women: Prevalence, consequences, remedies.* Thousand Oaks, CA: Sage.

Latané, B., & Darley, J. M. (1970). *The unresponsive bystander: Why doesn't he help?* New York: Appleton–Century–Crofts.

Mazer, D. B., & Percival, E. F. (1989). Ideology or Experience? The relationships among perceptions, attitudes, and experiences of sexual harassment in university students. *Sex Roles, 20,* 135–147.

Milgram, S. (1974). *Obedience to authority: An experimental view.* New York: Harper & Row.

O'Neil, J. M., Egan, J., Owen, S., & Murry, V. M. (1993). The gender role journey measure: Scale development and psychometric evaluation. *Sex Roles, 38,* 167–185.

Ross, L., & Nisbett, R. E. (1991). *The person and the situation: Perspectives of Social Psychology.* New York: McGraw-Hill.

Ruggiero, K. M., & Taylor, D. M. (1997). Why minority group members perceive or do not perceive the discrimination that confronts them: The role of self-esteem and perceived control. *Journal of Personality and Social Psychology, 72*, 373–389.

Russo-Devosa, Y., & Swim, J. K. (1997). *The role of Modern Sexism in perceptions of sexist attitudes and everyday sexist behaviors.* Poster presented at the annual meeting of the Midwestern Psychological Association.

Sauders, B. E. (1992). *Sexual harassment of women in the workplace: Results from the national women's study.* Presentation to the 8th Annual NC/SC Labor Law Seminar, Nashville, NC.

Spence, J. T., Helmreich, R., & Stapp, J. (1973). A short version of the Attitudes toward Women Scale (WAS). *Bulletin of the Psychonomic Society, 2*, 219–220.

Swim, J. K., Aikin, K. J., Hall, W. S., & Hunter, (1995). Sexism and racism: Old-fashioned and modern prejudices. *Journal of Personality and Social Psychology, 68*, 199–214.

Swim, J. K., & Cohen, L. L. (1996). Overt, covert, and subtle sexism: A comparison between the Attitudes Toward Women and Modern Sexism scales. *Psychology of Women Quarterly.*

Swim, J. K., Cohen, L. L., & Hyers, L. L. (1998). Experiencing everyday prejudice and discrimination. In J. K. Swim, & C. Stangor (Eds.), *Prejudice: The target's perspective.* San Diego: Academic Press.

Swim, J. K., Ferguson, M. J., & Hyers, L. L. (1999). Avoiding stigma by association: subtle prejudice against lesbians in the form of social distancing. *Basic and Applied Social Psychology.*

Tajfel, H., & Turner, J. C. (1979). An integrative theory of intergroup conflict. In W. G. Austin, & S. Worchel (Eds.), *The social psychology of intergroup relations* (pp. 33–47). Monterey, CA: Brooks/Cole.

Wright, S. C., Taylor, D. M., & Moghaddam, F. M. (1990). Responding to membership in a disadvantaged group: From acceptance to collective protest. *Journal of Personality and Social Psychology, 58*, 994–1003.

Young-Bruehl, E. (1996). *The anatomy of prejudices.* Cambridge, MA: Harvard Univ. Press.

Questions for Review and Discussion

1. What did Swim and Hyers find (Study 1) to be the most common style of confrontation taken by women when confronted with sexist remarks?

2. Why did Swim and Hyers predict that women alone would be more likely to confront the source of sexist remarks than women in the presence of other women?

3. What costs did those women confronted by a sexist remark weigh most when determining whether or not to confront the source of the remark?

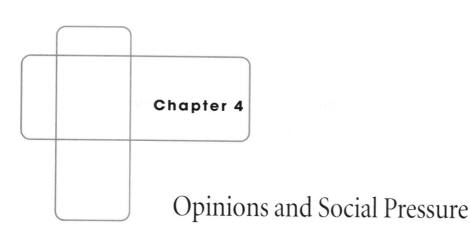

Chapter 4

Opinions and Social Pressure

Solomon E. Asch

Exactly what is the effect of the opinions of others on our own? In other words, how strong is the urge toward social conformity? The question is approached by means of some unusual experiments

That social influences shape every person's practices, judgments and beliefs is a truism to which anyone will readily assent. A child masters his "native" dialect down to the finest nuances; a member of a tribe of cannibals accepts cannibalism as altogether fitting and proper. All the social sciences take their departure from the observation of the profound effects that groups exert on their members. For psychologists, group pressure upon the minds of individuals raises a host of questions they would like to investigate in detail.

How, and to what extent, do social forces constrain people's opinions and attitudes? This question is especially pertinent in our day. The same epoch that has witnessed the unprecedented technical extension of communication has also brought into existence the deliberate manipulation of opinion and the "engineering of consent." There are many good reasons why, as citizens and as scientists, we should be concerned with studying the ways in which human beings form their opinions and the role that social conditions play.

Studies of these questions began with the interest in hypnosis aroused by the French physician Jean Martin Charcot (a teacher of Sigmund Freud) toward the end of the 19th century. Charcot believed that only hysterical patients could be fully hypnotized, but this view was soon challenged by two other physicians, Hyppolyte Bernheim and A. A. Liébault, who demonstrated

From *Scientific American*, Vol. 193, No. 5 (November 1955), pp. 31–35. © 1955 Scientific American, Inc. Reprinted with permission. © 1955 by Scientific American, Inc. All rights reserved.

that they could put most people under the hypnotic spell. Bernheim proposed that hypnosis was but an extreme form of a normal psychological process which became known as "suggestibility." It was shown that monotonous reiteration of instructions could induce in normal persons in the waking state involuntary bodily changes such as swaying or rigidity of the arms, and sensations such as warmth and odor.

It was not long before social thinkers seized upon these discoveries as a basis for explaining numerous social phenomena, from the spread of opinion to the formation of crowds and the following of leaders. The sociologist Gabriel Tarde summed it all up in the aphorism: "Social man is a somnambulist."

When the new discipline of social psychology was born at the beginning of this century, its first experiments were essentially adaptations of the suggestion demonstration. The technique generally followed a simple plan. The subjects, usually college students, were asked to give their opinions or preferences concerning various matters; some time later they were again asked to state their choices, but now they were also informed of the opinions held by authorities or large groups of their peers on the same matters. (Often the alleged consensus was fictitious.) Most of these studies had substantially the same result: confronted with opinions contrary to their own, many subjects apparently shifted their judgments in the direction of the views of the majorities or the experts. The late psychologist Edward L. Thorndike reported that he had succeeded in modifying the esthetic preferences of adults by this procedure. Other psychologists reported that people's evaluations of the merit of a literary passage could be raised or lowered by ascribing the passage to different authors. Apparently the sheer weight of numbers or authority sufficed to change opinions, even when no arguments for the opinions themselves were provided.

Now the very ease of success in these experiments arouses suspicion. Did the subjects actually change their opinions, or were the experimental victories scored only on paper? On grounds of common sense, one must question whether opinions are generally as watery as these studies indicate. There is some reason to wonder whether it was not the investigators who, in their enthusiasm for a theory, were suggestible, and whether the ostensibly gullible subjects were not providing answers which they thought good subjects were expected to give.

The investigations were guided by certain underlying assumptions, which today are common currency and account for much that is thought and said about the operations of propaganda and public opinion. The assumptions are that people submit uncritically and painlessly to external manipulation by suggestion or prestige, and that any given idea or value can be "sold" or "unsold" without reference to its merits. We should be skeptical, however, of the supposition that the power of social pressure necessarily implies uncritical submission to it:

independence and the capacity to rise above group passion are also open to human beings. Further, one may question on psychological grounds whether it is possible as a rule to change a person's judgment of a situation or an object without first changing his knowledge or assumptions about it.

In what follows I shall describe some experiments in an investigation of the effects of group pressure which was carried out recently with the help of a number of my associates. The tests not only demonstrate the operations of group pressure upon individuals but also illustrate a new kind of attack on the problem and some of the more subtle questions that it raises.

A group of seven to nine young men, all college students, are assembled in a classroom for a "psychological experiment" in visual judgment. The experimenter informs them that they will be comparing the lengths of lines. He shows two large white cards. On one is a single vertical black line—the standard whose length is to be matched. On the other card are three vertical lines of various lengths. The subjects are to choose the one that is of the same length as the line on the other card. One of the three actually is of the same length; the other two are substantially different, the difference ranging from three quarters of an inch to an inch and three quarters.

The experiment opens uneventfully. The subjects announce their answers in the order in which they have been seated in the room, and on the first round every person chooses the same matching line. Then a second set of cards is exposed; again the group is unanimous. The members appear ready to endure politely another boring experiment. On the third trial there is an unexpected disturbance. One person near the end of the group disagrees with all the others in his selection of the matching line. He looks surprised, indeed incredulous, about the disagreement. On the following trial he disagrees again, while the others remain unanimous in their choice. The dissenter becomes more and more worried and hesitant as the disagreement continues in succeeding trials; he may pause before announcing his answer and speak in a low voice, or he may smile in an embarrassed way.

What the dissenter does not know is that all the other members of the group were instructed by the experimenter beforehand to give incorrect answers in unanimity at certain points. The single individual who is not a party to this prearrangement is the focal subject of our experiment. He is placed in a position in which, while he is actually giving the correct answers, he finds himself unexpectedly in a minority of one, opposed by a unanimous and arbitrary majority with respect to a clear and simple fact. Upon him we have brought to bear two opposed forces: the evidence of his senses and the unanimous opinion of a group of his peers. Also, he must declare his judgments in public, before a majority which has also stated its position publicly.

The instructed majority occasionally reports correctly in order to reduce the possibility that the naive subject will suspect collusion against him. (In only a few cases did the subject actually show suspicion; when this happened, the experiment was stopped and the results were not counted.) There are 18 trials in each series, and on 12 of these the majority responds erroneously.

How do people respond to group pressure in this situation? I shall report first the statistical results of a series in which a total of 123 subjects from three institutions of higher learning (not including my own, Swarthmore College) were placed in the minority situation described above.

Two alternatives were open to the subject: he could act independently, repudiating the majority, or he could go along with the majority, repudiating the evidence of his senses. Of the 123 put to the test, a considerable percentage yielded to the majority. Whereas in ordinary circumstances individuals matching the lines will make mistakes less than 1 per cent of the time, under group pressure the minority subjects swung to acceptance of the misleading majority's wrong judgments in 36.8 per cent of the selections.

Of course individuals differed in response. At one extreme, about one quarter of the subjects were completely independent and never agreed with the erroneous judgments of the majority. At the other extreme, some individuals went with the majority nearly all the time. The performances of individuals in this experiment tend to be highly consistent. Those who strike out on the path of independence do not, as a rule, succumb to the majority even over an extended series of trials, while those who choose the path of compliance are unable to free themselves as the ordeal is prolonged.

The reasons for the startling individual differences have not yet been investigated in detail. At this point we can only report some tentative generalizations from talks with the subjects, each of whom was interviewed at the end of the experiment. Among the independent individuals were many who held fast because of staunch confidence in their own judgment. The most significant fact about them was not absence of responsiveness to the majority but a capacity to recover from doubt and to reestablish their equilibrium. Others who acted independently came to believe that the majority was correct in its answers, but they continued their dissent on the simple ground that it was their obligation to call the play as they saw it.

Among the extremely yielding persons we found a group who quickly reached the conclusion: "I am wrong, they are right." Others yielded in order "not to spoil your results." Many of the individuals who went along suspected that the majority were "sheep" following the first responder, or that the majority were victims of an optical illusion; nevertheless, these suspicions failed to free them at the moment of decision. More disquieting were the reactions of subjects who construed their difference from the majority as a sign of some general deficiency in themselves, which at all costs they must hide. On this basis they desperately tried to merge with the majority, not realizing the longer-range consequences to themselves. All the yielding subjects underestimated the frequency with which they conformed.

Which aspect of the influence of a majority is more important—the size of the majority or its unanimity? The experiment was modified to examine this question. In one series the size of the opposition was varied from [1] to 15 persons. The results showed a clear trend. When a subject was confronted with only a single individual who contradicted his answers, he was swayed little: he continued to answer independently and correctly in nearly all trials. When the opposition was increased to two, the pressure became substantial: minority subjects now accepted the wrong answer 13.6 per cent of the time. Under the pressure of a majority of three, the subjects' errors jumped to 31.8 per cent. But further increases in the size of the majority apparently did not increase the weight of the pressure substantially. Clearly the size of the opposition is important only up to a point.

Disturbance of the majority's unanimity had a striking effect. In this experiment the subject was given the support of a truthful partner–either another individual who did not know of the prearranged agreement among the rest of the group, or a person who was instructed to give correct answers throughout.

The presence of a supporting partner depleted the majority of much of its power. Its pressure on the dissenting individual was reduced to one fourth: that is, subjects answered incorrectly only one fourth as often as under the pressure of a unanimous majority. The weakest persons did not yield as readily. Most interesting were the reactions to the partner. Generally the feeling toward him was one of warmth and closeness; he was credited with inspiring confidence. However, the subjects repudiated the suggestion that the partner decided them to be independent.

Was the partner's effect a consequence of his dissent, or was it related to his accuracy? We now introduced into the experimental group a person who was instructed to dissent from the majority but also to disagree with the subject. In some experiments the majority was always to choose the worst of the comparison lines and the instructed dissenter to pick the line that was closer to the length of the standard one; in others the majority was consistently intermediate and the dissenter most in error. In this manner we were able to study the relative influence of "compromising" and "extremist" dissenters.

Again the results are clear. When a moderate dissenter is present, the effect of the majority on the subject decreases by approximately one third, and extremes of yielding disappear. Moreover, most of the errors the subjects do make are moderate, rather than flagrant. In short, the dissenter largely controls the choice of errors. To this extent the subjects broke away from the majority even while bending to it.

On the other hand, when the dissenter always chose the line that was more flagrantly different from the standard, the results were of quite a different kind. The extremist dissenter produced a remarkable freeing of the subjects; their errors dropped to only 9 per cent. Furthermore, all the errors were of the moderate variety. We were able to conclude that dissent *per se* increased independence and moderated the errors that occurred, and that the direction of dissent exerted consistent effects.

In all the foregoing experiments each subject was observed only in a single setting. We now turned to studying the effects upon a given individual of a change in the situation to which he was exposed. The first experiment examined the consequences of losing or gaining a partner. The instructed partner began by answering correctly on the first six trials. With his support the subject usually resisted pressure from the majority: 18 of 27 subjects were completely independent. But after six trials the partner joined the majority. As soon as he did so, there was an abrupt rise in the subjects' errors. Their submission to the majority was just about as frequent as when the minority subject was opposed by a unanimous majority throughout.

It was surprising to find that the experience of having had a partner and of having braved the majority opposition with him had failed to strengthen the individuals' independence. Questioning at the conclusion of the experiment suggested that we had overlooked an important circumstance; namely, the strong specific effect of "desertion" by the partner to the other side. We therefore changed the conditions so that the partner would simply leave the group at the proper point. (To allay suspicion it was announced in advance that he had an appointment with the dean.) In this form of the experiment, the partner's effect outlasted his presence. The errors increased after his departure, but less markedly than after a partner switched to the majority.

In a variant of this procedure the trials began with the majority unanimously giving correct answers. Then they gradually broke away until on the sixth trial the naive subject was alone and the group unanimously against him. As long as the subject had anyone on his side, he was almost invariably independent, but as soon as he found himself alone, the tendency to conform to the majority rose abruptly.

As might be expected, an individual's resistance to group pressure in these experiments depends to a considerable degree on how wrong the majority is. We varied the discrepancy between the standard line and the other lines systematically, with the hope of reaching a point where the error of the majority would be so glaring that every subject would repudiate it and choose independently. In this we regretfully did not succeed. Even when the difference between the lines was seven inches, there were still some who yielded to the error of the majority.

The study provides clear answers to a few relatively simple questions, and it raises many others that await investigation. We would like to know the degree of consistency of persons in situations which differ in content and structure. If consistency of independence or conformity in behavior is shown to be a fact, how is it functionally related to qualities of character and personality? In what ways is independence related to sociological or cultural conditions? Are leaders more independent than other people, or are they adept at following their followers? These and many other questions may perhaps be answerable by investigations of the type described here.

Life in society requires consensus as an indispensable condition. But consensus, to be productive, requires that each individual contribute independently out of his experience and insight. When consensus comes under the dominance of conformity, the social process is polluted and the individual at the same time surrenders the powers on which his functioning as a feeling and thinking being depends. That we have found the tendency to conformity in our society so strong that reasonably intelligent and well-meaning young people are willing to call white black is a matter of concern. It raises questions about our ways of education and about the values that guide our conduct.

Yet anyone inclined to draw too pessimistic conclusions from this report would do well to remind himself that the capacities for independence are not to be underestimated. He may also draw some consolation from a further observation: those who participated in this challenging experiment agreed nearly without exception that independence was preferable to conformity.

Questions for Review and Discussion

1. Which aspect of the influence of the majority did Asch find was more important—the size of the majority or its unanimity?
2. Do you think that the effect of group pressure would be stronger or weaker if the judgment had concerned the beauty of an object rather than its size?
3. Why do you think that the presence of another participant who disagreed with the majority reduced a participant's tendency to conform even when the other dissenter disagreed with the participant?

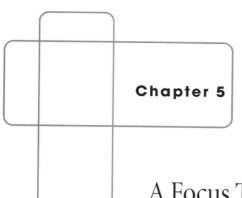

Chapter 5

A Focus Theory of Normative Conduct: Recycling the Concept of Norms to Reduce Littering in Public Places

Robert B. Cialdini, Raymond R. Reno, and Carl A. Kallgren

Although social norms have a long history within social psychology, support for the concept as a useful explanatory and predictive device is currently quite mixed. Some researchers have used and championed the concept as important to a proper understanding of human social behavior (e.g., Berkowitz, 1972; Fishbein & Ajzen, 1975; McKirnan, 1980; Pepitone, 1976; Sherif, 1936; Staub, 1972; Triandis, 1977). Others have seen little of value in it, arguing that the concept is vague and overly general, often contradictory, and ill-suited to empirical testing (e.g., Darley & Latané, 1970; Krebs, 1970; Krebs & Miller, 1985; Marini, 1984). In addition, a parallel controversy has developed within academic sociology where ethnomethodological and constructionist critics have faulted the dominant normative paradigm of that discipline (Garfinkel, 1967; Mehan & Wood, 1975).

The effect of these criticisms has been positive in pointing out problems that must be solved before one can have confidence in the utility of normative explanations. One such problem is definitional. Both in common parlance and academic usage, *norm* has more than one meaning (Shaffer, 1983). When

From *Journal of Personality and Social Psychology*, Vol. 58, pp. 1015–1026. Copyright © 1990 by the American Psychological Association. Reproduced with permission.

considering normative influence on behavior, it is crucial to discriminate between the *is* (descriptive) and the *ought* (injunctive) meaning of social norms, because each refers to a separate source of human motivation (Deutsch & Gerard, 1955). The descriptive norm describes what is typical or *normal*. It is what most people do, and it motivates by providing evidence as to what will likely be effective and adaptive action: "If everyone is doing it, it must be a sensible thing to do." Cialdini (1988) has argued that such a presumption offers an information-processing advantage and a decisional shortcut when one is choosing how to behave in a given situation. By simply registering what most others are doing there and by imitating their actions, one can usually choose efficiently and well. Researchers have repeatedly found that the perception of what most others are doing influences subjects to behave similarly, even when the behaviors are as morally neutral as choosing a consumer product (Venkatesan, 1966) or looking up at the sky (Milgram, Bickman, & Berkowitz, 1969). The injunctive meaning of norms refers to rules or beliefs as to what constitutes morally approved and disapproved conduct. In contrast to descriptive norms, which specify what is done, injunctive norms specify what ought to be done. That is, rather than simply informing one's actions, these norms enjoin it through the promise of social sanctions. Because what is approved is often what is typically done, it is easy to confuse these two meanings of norms. However, they are conceptually and motivationally distinct, and it is important for a proper understanding of normative influence to keep them separate, especially in situations where both are acting simultaneously.

A second source of confusion surrounding the concept of social norms is that, although they are said to characterize and guide behavior within a society, they should not be seen as uniformly in force at all times and in all situations. That is, norms should motivate behavior primarily when they are activated (i.e., made salient or otherwise focused on); thus, persons who are dispositionally or temporarily focused on normative considerations are most likely to act in norm-consistent ways (Berkowitz, 1972; Berkowitz & Daniels, 1964; Gruder, Romer, & Korth, 1978; Miller & Grush, 1986; Rutkowski, Gruder, & Romer, 1983; Schwartz & Fleishman, 1978). Of course, salience procedures should be effective for both descriptive and injunctive norms. In fact, in situations with clear-cut descriptive and injunctive norms, focusing individuals on *is* versus *ought* information should lead to behavior change that is consistent only with the now more salient type of norm.

One purpose of this research was to test this assertion as it applies to individuals' decisions to litter in public places. The choice of littering behavior for this study occurred for several reasons: (a) it provides a clearly observable action that is governed by a widely held injunctive norm (Bickman, 1972; Heberlein,

1971; Keep America Beautiful, Inc., 1968) and (b) it constitutes a growing social problem of considerable aesthetic, financial, and health-related costs to the culture. In California alone, for example, litter has increased by 24% over a recent span of 15 years, requiring $100 million annually in cleanup costs (California Waste Management Board, 1988) and posing health threats to humans and wildlife through water pollution, fire hazards, rodent and insect infestations, highway accidents, and thousands of injuries suffered from discarded cans and broken bottles (Geller, Winett, & Everett, 1982). Thus, a better understanding of the normative factors moderating deliberate littering would be of both conceptual and practical value.

A common finding in the literature on littering is that the act is significantly more likely in a littered setting than in a clean setting (e.g., Finnie, 1973; Geller, Witmer, & Tuso, 1977; Heberlein, 1971; Krauss, Freedman, & Whitcup, 1978; Reiter & Samuel, 1980). Although this finding is congruent with the normative view that, in most settings, individuals tend to act in accordance with the clear behavioral norm there (Krauss et al., 1978), it is also consistent with other motivational accounts. For example, it might be argued that the tendency to litter more in a littered environment is due to simple imitation. Or, it might be argued that individuals are more likely to litter into a littered environment because they perceive that their litter will do less damage to the state of the environment than if it were clean.

Study 1

In our first experiment, subjects were given the opportunity to litter into either a previously clean or a fully littered environment after witnessing a confederate who either littered into the environment or walked through it. By varying the state of the environment (clean vs. littered), we sought to manipulate the perceived descriptive norm for littering in the situation. By manipulating whether the confederate dropped litter into the environment, we sought to affect the extent to which subjects were drawn to focus attention on the state of the environment and, consequently, on the relevant descriptive norm there.

We had two main predictions: First, we expected that subjects would be more likely to litter into an already littered environment than into a clean one. This expectation is consistent with the findings of prior research on littering (e.g., Krauss et al., 1978; Reiter & Samuel, 1980) and with the view that, in most settings, individuals are at least marginally aware of the existing norms and tend to act in accordance with them. Second, and more important, we expected the effect of the descriptive norm for littering in the situation (as indicated by the state of the environment) to be significantly enhanced when subjects' attention was drawn to the environment by a littering other. This expectation was predicated on considerable prior evidence (see Fiske & Taylor, 1984, for a review) indicating that substantial psychological impact can result from salience procedures involving simple shifts in the visual prominence of stimulus information, including normative information (Feldman, Higgins, Karlovac, & Ruble, 1976; Ferguson & Wells, 1980; Manis, Dovalina, Avis, & Cardoze, 1980; Ruble & Feldman, 1976; Trope & Ginnosar, 1986). Specifically, then, we predicted an interaction such that subjects who saw the confederate litter into a fully littered environment would litter more than those who saw no such littering; whereas subjects who saw the confederate litter into a clean environment would litter less than those who saw no such littering.

Should we obtain this interaction, we would have good support for our focus model of normative conduct. It should be noted that the second component of this predicted interaction adds important conceptual weight to our test in that it is contrary to what would be anticipated by rival accounts. It is opposite to what would be expected if subjects were motivated simply by a greater reluctance to litter into a clean versus littered environment because of the greater relative damage to the respective environments that such littering would cause; by that account, subjects should be more likely to litter after observing littering in a clean environment because the environment will have already been damaged. Similarly, the second component of our predicted interaction pits the norm focus/salience interpretation against a straightforward imitation formulation, in which an unpunished litterer would be expected to increase the littering tendencies of observers in either type of environment. By postulating that a littering other will concentrate attention on evidence of what the majority of people have done, thereby highlighting normative considerations, only the (descriptive) norm focus/salience account predicts that observed littering will reduce subsequent littering in a clean environment.

Method

Subjects and procedure
Norm salience.   Subjects were 139 visitors to a university-affiliated hospital who were returning to their cars in an adjacent, multilevel parking garage during the daylight hours of 5 days within a period of 8 consecutive days. Approximately 5 s after emerging from an elevator, subjects encountered an experimental confederate of college age walking toward them. In half of the instances, the confederate appeared to be reading a large, 21.6 × 35.6 cm (8½ × 14 in.) handbill, which he or

she dropped into the environment approximately 4.5 m (5 yd) before passing the subjects (high norm salience). A second confederate judged whether a subject had noticed the littering incident and, consequently, had deflected his or her attention at least momentarily to the parking garage floor. The great majority (93%) were judged to have done so, and only they were examined as to their subsequent littering behavior. In the other half of the instances, the confederate merely walked past the subject without carrying a handbill, so as to provide an equivalent degree of social contact (low norm salience).

Existing descriptive norm. For some of the subjects, the floor of the parking structure had been heavily littered by the experimenters with an assortment of handbills, candy wrappers, cigarette butts, and paper cups (existing prolittering norm). For the remaining subjects, the area had been cleaned of all litter (existing antilittering norm). The state of the environment (littered or clean) was alternated in 2-hr blocks, with the initial state determined randomly at the start of each day. On arriving at their cars, subjects encountered a large handbill that was tucked under the driver's side windshield wiper so as to partially obscure vision from the driver's seat. The handbill, identical to that dropped by the confederate, carried a stenciled message that read, "THIS IS AUTOMOTIVE SAFETY WEEK. PLEASE DRIVE CAREFULLY." A similar handbill had been placed on all other cars in the area as well.

Measure of littering. From a hidden vantage point, an experimenter noted the driver's sex, estimated age, and whether the driver littered the handbill. Littering was defined as depositing the handbill in the environment outside of the vehicle. Because there were no trash receptacles in the area, all subjects who failed to litter did so by taking and retaining the handbill inside their vehicles before driving away.

Analyses Analyses in this and subsequent studies were conducted using the SPSS-X loglinear program, wherein tests for effects within dichotomous data are examined through the nesting of hierarchical models. This technique allows the testing of individual parameters by comparing the differences in the likelihood ratio chi-square of a pair of nested models. The differenced likelihood ratio is reported as a chi-square.

Results and Discussion

Gender and age differences in littering have sometimes been found in past research (see Geller et al., 1982, for a review). Therefore, before proceeding to tests of

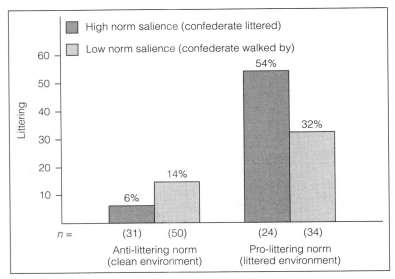

Figure 1 ■ Percentages of subjects littering as a function of norm salience, and the direction of the descriptive norm regarding littering: Study 1.

our theoretical hypotheses, we explored the data for gender or age differences. None were found; consequently, neither variable was included in subsequent analyses.

Figure 1 depicts the amount of littering that occurred in each of the four experimental conditions. Loglinear analysis of those data produced a set of results that conforms to that predicted by our norm focus model. First, as expected, there was a main effect for the existing descriptive norm, in that subjects littered more in a littered environment than in a clean environment (41% vs. 11%), $\chi^2(1, N = 139) = 17.06$, $p < .001$. Second, this effect occurred to a much greater extent under conditions of high norm salience, when subjects' attention was drawn to the existing descriptive norm for the environment. That is, the size of the existing descriptive-norm effect when the confederate littered (6% vs. 54%), $\chi^2(1, N = 55) = 16.52$, $p < .001$, was significantly greater than when the confederate did not litter (14% vs. 32%), $\chi^2(1, N = 84) = 3.99$, $p < .05$; the resultant interaction was tested as a planned comparison that proved highly reliable, $\chi^2(1, N = 139) = 20.87$, $p < .001$. The significant interaction provides confirmation of our hypothesis that procedures designed to shift attention within a setting to just one type of operative norm—in this case, the descriptive norm—will generate behavior change that is consistent only with that type of norm. Apparently, this is so even when the behavior in question is governed by an injunctive norm—in this case, the antilittering norm—that is strongly and widely held in the society (Bickman, 1972; Heberlein, 1971; Keep America Beautiful, Inc., 1968).

The pattern of results also supported the directional predictions made from our model. That is, under conditions of high (descriptive) norm salience, subjects littered more in a littered environment (54% vs. 32%) but less in a clean one (6% vs. 14%), although neither simple effect was statistically significant, χ^2s $= 2.76$ and 1.18, respectively.

It is this latter finding, showing the least littering among subjects in the high norm salience/clean environment condition, that seems the most provocative of our study and, therefore, worthy of pursuit. After all, from an applied standpoint, we should be principally interested in strategies for litter abatement. Moreover, the fact that the least littering occurred among subjects who observed prior littering into a clean environment is of considerable conceptual interest, as it supports norm focus predictions over those that spring from a straightforward imitation or environmental damage account. Good reason exists, however, for caution in drawing strong conceptual conclusions from this finding. Although part of a theoretically predicted, significant interaction, the drop in littering due to high norm salience in the clean environment was far from significant by itself. Of course, this lack of significance might well have occurred because of a floor effect, owing to the low level of littering (14%) in the low norm salience/clean environment condition; nonetheless, in the interest of enhanced statistical confidence, a replication seemed warranted.

Study 2

In planning to replicate and extend our initial study, we recognized a pair of testable implications that flowed from our earlier analysis. First, consistent with the outcomes of Study 1, a subject who witnessed evidence of littering in an otherwise clean environment should litter less as a result; however, the evidence would not have to take the form, as it did in Study 1, of observed littering action. That is, the consequence of such action—a single piece of litter lying in an otherwise clean environment—should have the same effect, because of its conspicuousness, by drawing attention to an environment whose descriptive norm (except for one aberrant litterer) was clearly antilitter. Second, as the amount of litter increases progressively in a setting, so should the likelihood that a subject will litter into it because, by definition, that litter will change the descriptive norm for the setting. The upshot of this pair of implications of our normative analysis is a nonintuitive prediction: The likelihood that an individual will litter into an environment bearing various pieces of perceptible, extant litter will be described by a check-mark-shaped function. Little littering should occur in a clean environment; still less should occur with a sole piece of litter in an otherwise clean environment, but progressively greater littering should occur as litter accumulates and the descriptive norm for the situation changes from antilitter to prolitter.

Method

Subjects and procedure   Subjects were 358 visitors to an amusement park in a large southwestern city during the evening hours of a pair of weekends in early summer. Immediately before turning a particular corner on a park walkway, subjects encountered a college-age experimental confederate passing out handbills that read "DON'T MISS TONIGHT's SHOW," which referred to an entertainment program sponsored by the park on weekend nights. The confederate was instructed to give a handbill, at 1-min intervals, to the first passing adult walking alone or to one adult (the physically closest) in the first passing group. On turning the walkway corner, subjects, who were no longer visible to the confederate, faced a path of approximately 55 m (60 yd) from which no exit was possible except at its ends.

State of the environment.   All litter had been removed from the path except for varying numbers of handbills of the sort that subjects had just been given by a confederate. Depending on the experimental condition, the path contained 0, 1, 2, 4, 8, or 16 handbills that were visible from the path entrance.

Measurement of littering.   Because no litter receptacles were available on the path, a subject who deposited a handbill into the environment at any point along the path's length was considered a litterer. Subjects' littering behavior was covertly observed by a hidden, second experimental confederate, who also timed subjects' latency to litter (failure to litter was given a score of 100s) and who removed any newly littered handbills from the path. On exiting the path, subjects turned a corner to find a pair of previously unseen litter receptacles; virtually all subjects who had not littered to that point dropped their handbills into one of the receptacles.

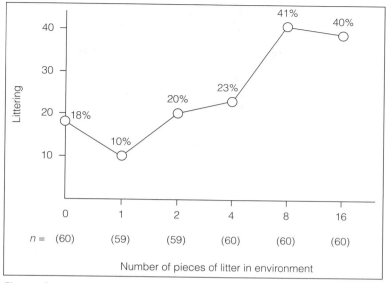

Figure 2 ■ Percentages of subjects littering as a function of the number of pieces of litter in the environment: Study 2.

Results and Discussion

As in Study 1, we first examined the littering data for age and gender differences. No significant effects were obtained because of subject age. However, we did find a significant tendency for men to litter more frequently than women (31% vs. 19%), $\chi^2(1, N = 358) = 7.41, p < .01$.

Figure 2 depicts the percentage of litterers in each of the experimental conditions of Study 2. The data pattern closely reflects the predicted checkmark shape of our normative analysis. The checkmark function hypothesis was tested in a two-step process. First, we constructed a planned comparison using trend weights that modeled the checkmark shape $(-2, -4, -1, 1, 2, 4)$. It proved significant, $\chi^2(1, N = 358) = 21.80, p < .01$. A second planned comparison was then performed to test whether a difference in littering occurred between the zero littering condition and the one-piece-of-environmental-litter condition. No significant difference was found, $\chi^2(1, N = 229) = 1.64, p < .20$. Comparable analyses were conducted on the latency to litter data shown in Figure 3. As with frequency to litter, the first contrast proved significant, $F(1, 352) = 20.65$, $p < .01$, whereas the second did not $(F < 1)$. There was no significant interaction between any of these contrasts and gender.

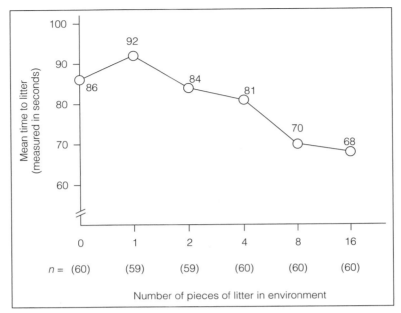

Figure 3 ■ Mean latency to litter as a function of the number of pieces of litter in the environment: Study 2.

Study 3

Even though the general form of the findings of Study 2 confirmed our predictions, one crucial feature of the results offered only ambiguous support. The hypothesized decline in littering from the clean environment condition to the one-piece-of-litter condition of the study, although present (18% vs. 10%), was not conventionally significant, allowing the possibility that it may have been the overall linearity of the checkmark pattern, rather than its elbow-like bend, that accounted for the significance of our general planned comparison. This ambiguity is especially frustrating because, as in Study 1, it appears that a floor effect in the data may have prevented a clear demonstration of reduced littering under the circumstances predicted by our formulation. It is difficult to generate significantly less littering than that of a clean environment when the clean environment generates so little littering itself.

Consequently, we decided to conduct a conceptual replication of the theoretically relevant conditions of Study 2 that was designed to overcome the floor-effect problem. One way to deal with a floor effect of the sort that faced us is to increase the statistical power associated with our significance tests by increasing the number of subjects run in each condition. Thus, we used an experimental setting that would allow us to record the littering decisions of large numbers of subjects in a relatively short period of time. Additionally, in an attempt to sharpen the impact of our single-piece-of-litter manipulation, we chose a more conspicuous single piece of litter than we had used in Study 2.

Specifically, subjects were college dormitory residents who found a public service flier in their mailboxes. The environment in front of the mailboxes had been arranged so that it contained (a) no litter, (b) one piece of highly conspicuous litter (a hollowed-out, end piece of watermelon rind), or (c) a large array of various types of litter, including the watermelon rind. The dependent variable was subjects' tendencies to litter with the fliers. On the basis of our normative analysis and the pattern of results of Studies 1 and 2, we made a pair of predictions. First, we anticipated that subjects would litter more into a fully littered environment than into a clean one. Second, we expected that they would litter least into an otherwise clean environment that contained a single, attention-focusing piece of litter.

Method

Subjects   Subjects were 484 residents of a densely populated, high-rise women's dormitory on the campus of a large state university.

Procedure   The residents' mailboxes were located in rows at one corner of the dormitory's main lobby. The mailbox area was cut off visually from most of the lobby by a translucent partition. Once past the partition, subjects encountered an open area that fronted the mailboxes. During a 10 a.m. to 4 p.m. schoolday period, residents who opened their mailboxes to find a public service flier placed there as part of the experiment were counted as subjects, provided that no one else was simultaneously in the area getting her mail.

Depending on the experimental condition, subjects passing through the open area in front of their mailboxes encountered an environment that contained no litter or a single piece of litter (a hollowed-out, heel section of watermelon rind), or a large number of pieces of litter of various kinds (e.g., discarded fliers, cigarette butts, paper cups, candy wrappers, and soft drink cans), including the watermelon rind. A subject was considered to have littered if she deposited the flier anywhere in the environment (all waste containers had been removed) before exiting the lobby onto an elevator or through a set of doors leading to the campus. Of those subjects who littered, the great majority were observed by an unobtrusively placed experimenter to do so in the area in front of the mailboxes.

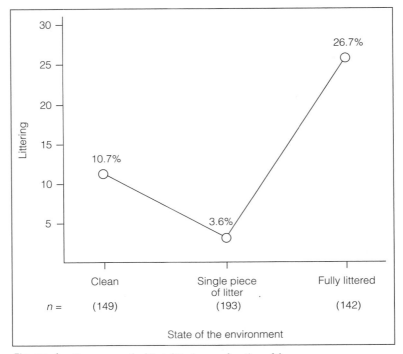

Figure 4 ■ Percentages of subjects littering as a function of the amount of litter in the environment: Study 3.

Results and Discussion

The percentages of littering in the three experimental conditions are presented in Figure 4. Their pattern accords well with predictions based on our normative perspective; indeed, the expected quadratic trend was highly significant, $\chi^2(1, N = 484) = 23.12, p < .001$. Moreover, planned contrast tests of our two experimental predictions were supportive at conventional levels of significance. First, subjects were more likely to litter into a fully littered environment than into an unlittered one (26.7% vs. 10.7%), $\chi^2(1, N = 291) = 12.62$, $p < .001$. Second, subjects were less likely to litter into an environment when it contained a single, salient piece of litter than when it was unlittered (3.6% vs. 10.7%), $\chi^2(1, N = 335) = 6.79, p < .01$.

Theoretical implications   To this point, we have reported data from three experiments in three different natural settings that seem to converge sufficiently to allow the generation of statements about the conceptual and pragmatic value of those data. On the conceptual side, it appears that norms can be influential in directing human action; however, in keeping with the spirit of prior criticism of normative explanations, it is necessary for norm theorists to be specific about both the type of norm (injunctive or descriptive) thought to be acting in a situation and about the conditions under which it is likely to act. Distinguishing between injunctive and descriptive norms is crucial, because both types can exist simultaneously in a setting and can have either congruent or contradictory implications for behavior. For example, in Study 1 we showed that through procedures designed to highlight differing descriptive norms, we could enhance or undermine compliance with the societywide injunctive norm against littering. Such a finding should not be interpreted to mean that descriptive norms are, in this instance or in general, more powerful than injunctive norms. Rather, it is the differential focusing of attention on one or the other sort of norm that is the key. Indeed, even within the same type of norm, it seems to be the case from our findings that focus of attention is an important component. In all three experiments, exposing subjects to a single piece of litter in an otherwise clean environment—a procedure designed to draw subjects' attention to what most people had done in the setting (i.e., the descriptive norm)—reduced littering there.

Practical applications   Because littering is a social problem, it is appropriate to consider the potential practical applications of our data as well. The finding of greatest applied value appears to be that subjects in three different settings littered least after encountering a single piece of litter in an otherwise unlittered place. At first glance, such a result might seem to suggest that individuals seeking to retard the accumulation of litter in a particular environment might affix a single, prominent piece of litter there. On closer consideration, however, it becomes clear that such an approach would be inferior to beginning with a totally clean environment. Examination of Figures 2 and 3, showing the average likelihood and latency of littering among subjects in our amusement park study, illustrates the point. Subjects who encountered a perfectly clean environment tended not to litter there, resulting in long delays before anyone despoiled it with a handbill. Once a single handbill appeared in the setting, subjects were even less likely to litter, generating even longer latencies before the second piece of litter appeared. At that point, with two pieces of litter visible in the environment, the descriptive norm began to change, and subjects' reluctance to litter into the setting began to deteriorate steadily, leading to shorter and shorter littering latencies with increasing accumulations of litter. Anyone wishing to preserve the state of a specific environment, then, should begin with a clean setting so as to delay for the greatest time the appearance of two pieces of litter there, because those two pieces of litter are likely to begin a slippery-slope effect that leads to a fully littered environment and to a fully realized perception that "everybody litters here." This logic further suggests that environments will best be able to retard littering if they are subjected to frequent and thorough litter pickups that return them to the optimal litter-free condition.

In considering the practical implications of our data, we recognized a weakness in our decision to focus subjects' attention on the descriptive rather than injunctive norm for littering: Procedures that focus subjects on the descriptive norm will only reduce littering when the environment is wholly or virtually unspoiled. Indeed, as was suggested in the data of Study 1, a descriptive norm focus when the environment is substantially littered will tend to increase littering there—hardly a desirable outcome for any but theory-testing purposes. A descriptive norm-focusing procedure, then, should only have socially beneficial effects in environments that do not need much help. The circumstances are different, however, when the injunctive norm is made salient and when, consequently, individuals are focused on what people typically approve and disapprove rather than on what they typically do in a situation. By making the injunctive norm against littering more prominent, we should expect reduced littering even in a heavily littered environment.

A test of this hypothesis seemed instrumental to a pair of potentially valuable goals. First, on the practical level, it might establish norm focus procedures that could be used for litter abatement in a variety of environments. Second, on the conceptual level, it would generate evidence for or against our contention that focusing attention on either *is* or *ought* information will lead to behavior change that is consistent only with the now more salient type of norm; to this point in the research program, we had examined only half of that contention by concentrating just on descriptive norms.

Study 4

Recall that in Study 1, we argued that a confederate's act of dropping a flier into the environment would draw subjects' attention to that environment and to clear evidence (that we had manipulated) concerning whether people typically littered there. In this way, we sought to manipulate focus of attention to the existing descriptive norm regarding littering in the setting. Presumably, if instead the environment were to give clear evidence of what is societally approved or disapproved there, the same attention-focusing device would function as an injunctive norm activator, because societally based approval or disapproval is the distinguishing characteristic of injunctive norms (Birnbaum & Sagarin, 1976; Marini, 1984; Sherif & Sherif, 1969).

The question of what clear approval/disapproval cue could be placed effectively in a natural environment to test our formulation was answered serendipitously while conducting Study 1. That study was run in a parking garage whose walls rose only halfway from the floor to the roof at each level. On one especially windy day, the litter we had distributed all around the garage floor in the fully littered environment condition was blown against an inside wall, as if someone had swept it there in a neat line. When a confederate dropped a handbill into that environment, virtually no subjects littered, whereas, on previous days the majority of subjects in that experimental condition had littered. In the course of puzzling over the discrepancy, we realized that the littering tendency of windy-day subjects may have declined when attention was called to the considerable litter in the environment because that litter gave the (mistaken) impression of having been swept—a clear disapproval cue.

Armed with this potential insight, we decided to conduct a partial replication and extension of Study 1, in which subjects saw a confederate who either did or did not drop a handbill into an environment that contained a large amount of either swept or unswept litter. In the case of unswept litter, we expected to replicate the data pattern of Study 1 for the comparable experimental cells; that is, we anticipated that by dropping a handbill, the confederate would focus subjects' attention on the environment and its evidence that people typically litter there, which should cause littering to increase. By dropping a handbill into a setting where prior litter had been swept (into piles), we anticipated that the confederate would once again focus subjects' attention on the environment. But in this instance, subjects would encounter a mixed message, composed of a descriptive norm cue (abundant litter) that would incline them toward littering and an injunctive norm cue (swept litter) that would incline them against it. Accordingly, we predicted that the difference in littering found in the unswept conditions would be reversed or at least reduced. Statistically, then, we expected an interaction between our two independent variables of whether a confederate dropped a handbill into the environment (high or low norm salience) and whether the environment contained swept or unswept litter (presence or absence of an injunctive norm cue). Furthermore, we expected a specific form for that interaction, such that any difference in littering found between the swept and unswept litter conditions under low-norm salience procedures would be significantly enhanced under high-norm salience procedures. That is, it was our belief that, under the low salience conditions, the normative forces present would be registered only minimally by subjects, resulting in only a minimal swept/unswept difference. However, under high salience conditions with normative issues now focal, the effect would be magnified.

Method

Subjects and procedure

Norm salience.   Subjects were 127 visitors to a university-affiliated hospital during the late afternoon and early evening hours of 6 days within a 13-day period. They underwent the same norm salience procedures as subjects in Study 1. That is, after emerging from a parking garage elevator, they encountered a college-age confederate who either dropped a distinctively colored handbill onto the floor in subjects' view or simply walked past without carrying a handbill.

Presence of an injunctive norm cue.   For some subjects, the floor of the parking structure had been heavily littered by the experimenters, with the litter distributed across the environment in a fashion identical to that of Study 1. For the remaining subjects, all of this ambient litter had been swept into three large piles situated approximately 9 m (10 yd) apart in a line. In the high-norm salience/swept litter condition, the confederate dropped a handbill onto the floor approximately 1.5 m (5 ft) after passing the piles of litter. It was decided to have the confederate drop the handbill immediately in front, but in full view, of the litter piles to avoid an imitation explanation for our predicted effect. That is, if subjects had seen the confederate drop a handbill into one of the piles, then the predicted reduction in subjects' subsequent littering could be interpreted as simple modeling of a decision not to litter. The swept or unswept litter conditions were run in alternating 2-hr blocks, with the first run of the day determined randomly.

Measure of littering.   Littering was assessed as it was in Study 1.

Results and Discussion

The influence of age and gender on littering rates was examined in an initial analysis; no significant effects occurred. Thus, these variables were not included in further analyses.

The percentage of subjects who littered in each of the experimental conditions of our design is displayed in Figure 5. Those percentages occurred in a pattern consistent with the form of the interaction that we were led to anticipate from our norm focus formulation. Using loglinear analyses, we tested that interaction with a planned comparison that contrasted the difference between the two low-norm salience cells (29% vs. 33%), $\chi^2(1, N = 68) = 0.18$, ns, against the difference between the two high-norm salience cells (18% vs. 45%), $\chi^2(1, N = 59) = 5.19$, $p < .02$. That interaction test proved significant, $\chi^2(1, N = 127) = 4.91, p < .03$.

Looking at the interaction pattern in another way, we can see that it is composed of two opposing trends—neither significant by itself, but significantly

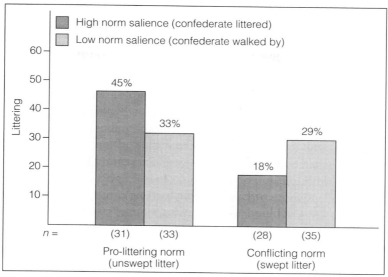

Figure 5 ▪ Percentages of subjects littering as a function of norm salience, and the configuration of litter in the environment: Study 4.

different in contrast to one another—both instigated by the same attention-focusing procedure. That is, when a dropped handbill drew attention to an unswept environment that, by its fully littered nature, gave evidence of a clear descriptive norm favoring littering there, littering tendencies rose (33% vs. 45%). However, when the same device drew attention to an environment that included a clearly conflicting injunctive norm cue as well, littering tendencies were reversed (29% vs. 18%). This pattern of effects accords well with each of the goals we set for Study 4. First, it supports our theoretical assertion that both descriptive and injunctive norm can elicit behavior change, with the prominence of one or the other type of norm accounting for the direction of the change. Second, it offers grounds for hope that certain kinds of undesirable action (littering, drinking and driving, tax cheating, highway speeding, etc.) can be restrained by the use of procedures that temporarily focus individuals on injunctive norms in the settings where the action is most likely to take place.

Study 5

To this point in our research program, we have examined the validity of our norm focus formulation by using an attention-focusing procedure designed to make subjects mindful of a specific descriptive norm (Studies 1–3) or of conflicting descriptive and injunctive norms (Study 4) governing littering in a situation. The first three studies found resultant behavior changes wholly in line with the descriptive norm. The fourth study, which added evidence of a contradicting injunctive norm to the perception of the existing descriptive norm, broke the dominance of the descriptive norm over subjects' behavior; it actually produced a (nonsignificant) reduction of littering in an environment where a clear, prolittering descriptive norm existed. It seemed to us that the logical next step in this progression was to conduct one additional study that removed any prolittering descriptive norm focus and that concentrated subjects exclusively on the injunctive, antilittering norm. It was our expectation that such an uncontaminated, injunctive norm focus would then lead to a significant reduction in littering.

We saw another reason for conducting an additional experiment. In Studies 1 through 4, our norm-focusing manipulation involved the dropping of a noticeable piece of litter into an environment (either by a seen or an unseen individual) so as to draw subjects' attention to the normative information present in that environment. There were several advantages of using that particular attention-focusing device, including the ability to make certain nonintuitive predictions that would not have flowed from rival theoretical accounts. We also recognized, however, that there would be certain drawbacks to using the same procedure yet again. First, the generality of our conceptual argument could be seen as untested beyond the range of our specific norm salience manipulation. More important, though, using littering to highlight the norms related to littering could create interpretational ambiguities. That is, the littering act itself is not neutral. It carries social meanings (depending on the situation in which it occurs) that are likely to generate various kinds of perceptions of the littering agent. It is possible that one or another of these perceptions could have acted to incline subjects to follow or reject the litter's lead. For instance, although it is unlikely that someone who littered into a fully littered environment, as occurred in Study 4, would be seen positively by subjects, someone who littered into an environment of neatly swept litter might be seen in an especially negative light; it is possible that this more negative view may have accounted for the reduction in littering among such subjects in Study 4. Similarly, it is conceivable that subjects in Studies 1 through 3 may have had an unpleasant reaction to any litterer who would litter into a previously clean setting and, hence, may have failed to litter so as to distance themselves from such an unsavory person.

To avoid interpretations of this sort, which are based on subjects' perceptions of a litterer, it was necessary to design a focus shift manipulation that would draw subjects' attention to the injunctive norm against littering but would do so without the action of a littering agent. To this end, in Study 5 we relied on the device of cognitive priming, wherein one concept can be activated in an individual by focusing that individual's attention on a related concept (see Higgins & Bargh, 1987, for a review). Most, although not all (cf. Ratcliff & McKoon, 1988), explanations of priming effects incorporate the notion of spreading activation, which posits that similar concepts are linked together in memory within a network of nodes and that activation of one concept results in the spreading of the activation along the network to other related concepts (Anderson, 1976, 1983; Collins & Loftus, 1975; McClelland & Rumelhart, 1981). A key determinant of whether the presentation of one concept will cause activation of another is their semantic or conceptual proximity.

If, as research by Harvey and Enzle (1981) indicates, norms are concepts stored in a network format, then focusing subjects on a particular norm should activate other norms that are perceived to be semantically close to it. Moreover, the greater the semantic proximity, the stronger should be the resultant activation. To test this possibility, we first had a large number of norms rated as to their similarity to the antilittering norm. Next, on the basis of those ratings, we selected three norms that, although alike in rated normativeness, differed in their perceived similarity (conceptual proximity) to the antilittering norm. Finally, we included reference to one or another of the norms on handbills that we placed on car windshields in a local library parking lot. We expected that the handbills containing a message reminding subjects of the most distant norm from the antilittering norm (voting) would be littered relatively often but that as the handbill messages referred to norms rated closer (energy conservation) and closer (recycling) to the antilittering norm, fewer and fewer subjects would litter them. We also expected that handbills containing no normative message would be littered most of all, whereas handbills containing the target, antilittering message would be littered least.

Method

Preliminary ratings study   A list of 35 norms that had been generated by the researchers and their colleagues (e.g., "Driving at a safe speed," "Recycling," "Paying taxes," and "Not littering") were shown to 95 undergraduate psychology students during a class session at a large state university. The students were asked to indicate the extent to which they found each item on the list to be normative or nonnormative on 9-point scales, anchored by the labels *extremely normative* (1) and *not at all normative* (9); the scale midpoint was labeled *somewhat normative* (5). A definition of norms was provided at the top of the list that read "Norms are shared beliefs within a culture as to what constitutes socially appropriate conduct."

A second list was shown to a different class of 87 undergraduate psychology students at the same university during a meeting of their class. In addition to the definition of norms at the top of the list, this list contained comparisons of each of the selected norms with the norm against littering. Subjects were asked to "indicate how closely related you believe each of the pairs of norms are" on 9-point scales anchored by the labels *identical* (1) and *unrelated* (9); the scale midpoint was labeled *somewhat close* (5). Examples of the comparison items are "The norm against littering and the norm for recycling" and "The norm against littering and the norm for returning library books on time."

Selection of the experimental norms.   Means for both types of ratings were computed. The norm for not littering was rated as 4.25 on the 9-point normativeness scale. We then limited our choices for the additional experimental norms to those that had means for both male and female subjects within one scale point of 4.25 on rated normativeness. From this pool and on the basis of the similarity scale ratings, we selected three norms to be close to, moderately close to, and far from the norm against littering. Those three norms and their rated distances from the norm against littering were, respectively, the norm for recycling (3.57), the norm for turning off lights when last to leave a room (5.74), and the norm for voting (7.12).

Generating the normative messages.   For each of the four experimental norms, a message was constructed that was suitable for presentation on a handbill. For the antilittering norm (identical to the target norm), it read, "April is Keep Arizona Beautiful Month. Please Do Not Litter." For the recycling norm (close to the target norm), it read, "April is Preserve Arizona's Natural Resources Month. Please Recycle." For the turning off lights norm (moderately close to the target norm), it read, "April is Conserve Arizona's Energy Month. Please Turn Off Unnecessary Lights." For the voting norm (far from the target norm), it read, "April is Arizona's Voter Awareness Month. Please Remember That Your Vote Counts." Finally, a control message was constructed that carried no injunctive norm; it read, "April is Arizona's Fine Art's Month. Please Visit Your Local Art Museum."

Subjects and procedure   Participants were 133 female patrons and 126 male patrons of a municipal public library branch who parked their cars in the library lot. After leaving the library and returning to their cars, subjects found on the driver's side of the windshield a handbill that had been placed there by an experimenter. The handbill carried one of the five experimental messages designed to focus subjects differentially on the norm against littering. Drivers' decisions to litter the handbill were recorded by an unobtrusively placed

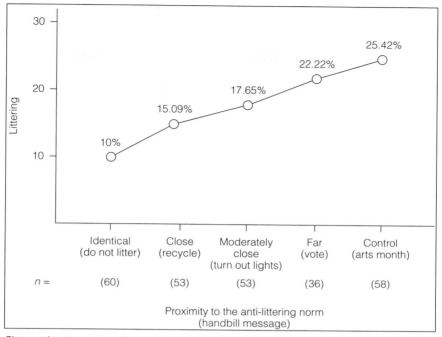

Figure 6 ▪ Percentages of subjects littering a handbill message as a function of its proximity to the injunctive norm against littering: Study 5.

observer. Typically, subjects who littered did so immediately after reading the handbill message and virtually always within 5 s of having done so. Consequently, we felt confident that the priminglike effects we anticipated were well within the range of priming-effect durations found by other investigators (see Higgins & Bargh, 1987, for a review). No efforts were made to change the moderate amount of naturally occurring litter on the library grounds and parking lot, which consisted of a variety of cigarette butts and an occasional paper cup or soft drink can.

Results and Discussion

In tests for gender effects within the data, only the main effect was significant, $\chi^2(1, N = 259) = 3.92$, $p < .05$, indicating that men littered more frequently than women (22% vs. 14%). To examine our hypothesis that as the conceptual distance between the antilittering norm and the handbill messages increased, littering rates would increase commensurately, we conducted a trend analysis. Only the predicted, linear trend (displayed in Figure 6) proved significant,

$\chi^2(1, N = 259) = 5.48$, $p < .02$. Within the five experimental message means, only one comparison was significant, that between the target, antilittering norm (10%) and the no-norm control message (25%), $\chi^2(1, N = 118) = 4.87, p < .03$.

As in Study 4, focusing subjects differentially on the injunctive norm against littering, this time through the processes of priming and spreading activation, led to littering rates corresponding to the predicted degree of injunctive norm focus. Thus, as expected, subjects in Study 5 (a) littered least after encountering a message focusing them directly on the antilittering norm, (b) littered progressively more frequently as the encountered (equally normative) messages directed focus progressively away from the antilittering norm, and (c) littered most when the encountered message was not normative.

General Discussion

We began this article by reporting the mixed support for the utility of social norms in accounting for much of human behavior; the claim that the concept, as traditionally conceived, possesses great explanatory power currently has strong proponents and equally strong opponents. From the perspective of the research we have presented, it would appear that both camps are right. Norms clearly do have a considerable impact on behavior, but the force and form of that impact can only be usefully understood through conceptual refinements that have not been traditionally or rigorously applied. That is, to predict properly the likelihood of norm-consistent action requires, first, that one specify the type of norm—descriptive or injunctive—said to be operating. Second, one must take into account the various conditions that would incline individuals to focus attention on or away from the norm.

We have argued that our experimental manipulations worked to focus subjects on descriptive norms in Studies 1 through 3, on descriptive and injunctive norms in Study 4, and on injunctive norms in Study 5. Although the patterns of results in those studies are consistent with that argument, there is certainly room for alternative views. For example, it could be contended that, for subjects in Studies 1 through 3, seeing litter in another wise clean environment did not simply engage the descriptive norm against littering but engaged the injunctive norm as well. That is, a single piece of litter may have reminded subjects of societal objections to littering, and thus it may have been the activation of the injunctive norm that produced reduced littering in those studies. Alternative accounts of this sort for specific segments of our data, although not parsimonious in explaining the overall pattern of results, remain conceivable nonetheless.

That is so in part because our work was conducted in naturally occurring field settings where it was not possible to assess the precision and effectiveness of our norm-focus manipulations through the methods typically available to laboratory investigators. Detailed checks on the strength, specificity, and functional impact of a subject's attentional focus could not have been practicably administered in our research situations. The consequent absence of such measures allows questions to arise as to whether our experimental manipulations worked as planned. Without the corroboration of these measures, one may have less confidence that the type of norm we intended to be functional actually mediated our findings. Fortunately, the effectiveness of injunctive social norms, about which there has been doubt in the scientific community (Darley & Latané, 1970; Garfinkel, 1967; Krebs, 1970; Krebs & Miller, 1985; Marini, 1984), has the clearest support in our data. That is, although it does seem possible to explain our data patterns without recourse to the well-established concept of descriptive norms, it does not seem plausible to do so without recourse to the more disputed and interesting concept of injunctive social norms, especially in Studies 4 and 5. Nonetheless, future research should be done in ways that allow direct assessments of the mediating processes presumed to be active in the present work.

Throughout this research program, we have exposed subjects to acute situational conditions designed to focus them on or away from particular norms. We recognize, however, that enduring cultural and dispositional conditions may also influence one's normative focus. This distinction among cultural, situational, and dispositional factors strikes us as important in the realm of norms. In thinking about the concept, we have been led to speculate that norms function at the cultural/societal level, the situational level, and the individual level. Although they may not have developed such a tripartite conceptualization, norm theorists have recognized normative influences at each of these levels. At the first (cultural/societal) level, the influence of global norms on behavior within a culture or social group has often been noted (Birnbaum & Sagarin, 1976; Paicheler, 1976; Pepitone, 1976; Triandis, 1977; Triandis, Marin, Lisansky, & Betancourt, 1984). Indeed, many definitions of norms refer exclusively to this level. For example, Ross (1973) considered norms to be "cultural rules that guide behavior within a society" (p. 105). At the second level, others have recognized that cultural norms may not apply equally to all situations (Peterson, 1982). Consequently, definitions of norms often include an explicit situational component. For example, Popenoe (1983) defined social norms as expectations "of how people are supposed to act, think, or feel in specific situations" (p. 598). Finally, other social scientists have evidence that norms exist at the individual level as well. Most notable in this regard is the groundbreaking work of Schwartz (1973, 1977) on the concept of personal norms.

Our view is that what is normative (i.e., most often done or approved or both) in a society, in a setting, and within a person will, in each case, have demonstrable impact on action, but that the impact will be differential depending on whether the actor is focused on norms of the culture, the situation, or the self. Research is planned to test the implications of this conception.

References

Anderson, J. R. (1976). *Language, memory, and thought.* Hillsdale, NJ: Erlbaum.

Anderson, J. R. (1983). *The architecture of congnition.* Cambridge, MA: Harvard University Press.

Berkowitz, L. (1972). Social norms, feelings, and other factors affecting helping and altruism. In L. Berkowitz (Ed.), *Advances in experimental social psychology* (Vol. 6, pp. 63–108). San Diego, CA: Academic Press.

Berkowitz, L, & Daniels, L. R. (1964). Affecting the salience of the social responsibility norm. *Journal of Abnormal and Social Psychology, 68,* 275–281.

Bickman, L. (1972). Environmental attitudes and actions. *Journal of Social Psychology, 87,* 323–324.

Birnbaum, A., & Sagarin, E. (1976). *Norms and humar behavior.* New York: Praeger.

California Waste Management Board. (1988). *The California litter problem.* Sacramento, CA: Author.

Cialdini, R. B. (1988). *Influence: Science and practice* (2nd ed.). Glenview, IL: Scott, Foresman.

Collins, A. M., & Loftus, E. F. (1975). A spreading-activation theory of semantic processing. *Psychological Review, 82,* 407–428.

Darley, J. M., & Latané, B. (1970). Norms and normative behavior: Field studies of social interdependence. In J. Macaulay & L. Berkowitz (Eds.), *Altruism and helping behavior* (pp. 83–102). San Diego, CA: Academic Press.

Deutsch, M., & Gerard, H. B. (1955). A study of normative and informational social influence upon individual judgment. *Journal of Abnormal and Social Psychology. 51,* 629–636.

Feldman, N. S., Higgins, E. T., Karlovac, M., & Ruble, D. N. (1976). Use of consensus information in causal attributions as a function of temporal presentation and availability of direct information. *Journal of Personality and Social Psychology, 34,* 694–698.

Ferguson, T. J., & Wells, G. L. (1980). Priming of mediators in causal attribution. *Journal of Personality and Social Psychology, 38,* 461–470.

Finnie, W. C. (1973). Field experiments in litter control. *Environment and Behavior, 5,* 123–144.

Fishbein, M., & Ajzen, I. (1975). *Belief, attitude, intention, and behavior.* Reading, MA: Addison-Wesley.

Fiske, S. T., & Taylor, S. E. (1984). *Social cognition.* Reading, MA: Addison-Wesley.

Garfinkel, H. (1967). *Studies in ethnomethodology.* Englewood Cliffs, NJ: Prentice-Hall.

Geller, E.S., Winett, S., & Everett, P. B. (1982). *Preserving the environment.* New York: Pergamon Press.

Geller, E. S., Witmer, J. F., & Tuso, M. A. (1977). Environmental interventions for litter control. *Journal of Applied Psychology, 62,* 344–351.

Gruder, C. L., Romer, D., & Korth, B. (1978). Dependency and fault as determinants of helping. *Journal of Experimental Social Psychology, 14,* 227–235.

Harvey, M. D., & Enzle, M. E. (1981). A congnitive model of social norms for understanding the transgression-helping effect. *Journal of Personality and Social Psychology, 41,* 866–875.

Heberlein, T. A. (1971). Moral norms, threatened sanctions, and littering behavior. *Dissertation Abstracts International, 32,* 5906A. (University Microfilms No. 72–2639).

Higgins, E. T., & Bargh, J. E. (1987). Social cognition and social perception. *Annual Review of Psychology, 38,* 369–425.

Keep America Beautiful, Inc. (1968). *Who litters and why.* New York: Public Opinion Surveys.

Krauss, R. M., Freedman, J. L., & Whitcup, M. (1978). Field and laboratory studies of littering. *Journal of Experimental Social Psychology, 14,* 109–122.

Krebs, D. L. (1970). Altruism: An examination of the concept and a review of the literature. *Psychological Bulletin, 73,* 258–302.

Krebs, D. L., & Miller, D. T. (1985). Altruism and aggression. In G. Lindzey & E. Aronson (Eds.), *The handbook of social psychology* (3rd ed.). New York: Random House.

Manis, M., Dovalina, I., Avis, N. E., & Cardoze, S. (1980). Base rates can affect individual prediction. *Journal of Personality and Social Psychology, 38,* 231–248.

Marini, M. M. (1984). Age and sequencing norms in the transition to adulthood. *Social Forces, 63,* 229–244.

McClelland, J. L., & Rumelhart, D. E. (1981). An interactive activation model of context effects in letter perception. *Psychological Review, 8,* 375–407.

McKiran, D. J. (1980). The conceptualization of deviance: A conceptualization and initial test of a model of social norms. *European Journal of Social Psychology, 10,* 79–93.

Mehan, H., & Wood, H. (1975). *Reality of ethnomethodology.* New York: Wiley.

Milgram, S., Bickman, L., & Berkowitz, O. (1969). Note on the drawing power of crowds of different size. *Journal of Personality and Social Psychology, 13,* 79–82.

Miller, L. E., & Grush, J. E. (1986). Individual differences in attitudinal versus normative determination of behavior. *Journal of Experimental Social Psychology, 22,* 190–202.

Paicheler, G. (1976). Norms and attitude change: Polarization and styles of behavior. *European Journal of Social Psychology, 6,* 405–427.

Pepitone, A. (1976). Toward a normative and comparative biocultural social psychology. *Journal of Personality and Social Psychology, 34,* 641–653.

Peterson, L. (1982). An alternative perspective to norm-based explanations of modeling and children's generosity. *Merrill Palmer Quarterly, 28,* 283–290.

Popenoe, D. (1983). *Sociology* (5th ed.). Englewood Cliffs, NJ: Prentice-Hall.

Ratcliff, R., & McKoon, G. (1988). A retrieval theory of priming in memory. *Psychological Review, 95,* 385–408.

Reiter, S. M., & Samuel, W. (1980). Littering as a function of prior litter and the presence or absence of prohibitive signs. *Journal of Applied Social Psychology, 10,* 45–55.

Ross, H. L. (1973). *Perspectives on social order.* New York: McGraw-Hill.

Ruble, D. N., & Feldman, N. S. (1976). Order of consensus, distinctiveness, and consistency information and causal attributions. *Journal of Personality and Social Psychology, 34,* 930–937.

Rutkowski, G. K., Gruder, C. L., & Romer, D. (1983). Group cohesiveness, social norms, and bystander intervention. *Journal of Personality and Social Psychology, 44,* 545–552.

Shaffer, L. S. (1983). Toward Pepitone's vision of a normative social psychology: What is a social norm? *Journal of Mind and Behavior, 4,* 275–294.

Schwartz, S. H. (1973). Normative explanations of helping behavior: A critique, proposal, and empirical test. *Journal of Experimental Social Psychology, 9,* 349–364.

Schwartz, S. H. (1977). Normative influences on altruism. In L. Berkowitz (Ed.), *Advances in experimental social psychology* (Vol. 10, pp. 221–279). San Diego, CA: Academic Press.

Schwartz, S. H., & Fleishman, J. A. (1978). Personal norms and the mediation of legitimacy effects on helping. *Social Psychology, 41,* 306–315.

Sherif, M., (1936). *The psychology of social norms.* New York: Harper.

Sherif, M., & Sherif, C. W. (1969). *Social Psychology.* New York: Harper & Row.

Staub, E. (1972). Instigation to goodness: The role of social norms and interpersonal influence. *Journal of Social Issues, 28,* 131–150.

Triandis, H. C. (1977). *Interpersonal behavior.* Monterey, CA: Brooks/Cole.

Triandis, H. C., Marín, G., Lisansky, J., & Betancourt, H. (1984). *Simpatia as a cultural script of Hispanics. Journal of Personality and Social Psychology, 47,* 1363–1375.

Trope, Y., & Ginnosar, Z. (1986). On the use of statistical and nonstatistical knowledge. In D. Bar Tal & A. Kruglanski (Eds.), *The social psychology of knowledge.* New York: Cambridge Press.

Venkatesan, M. (1966). Experimental study of consumer behavior, conformity, and independence. *Journal of Marketing Research, 3,* 384–387.

Questions for Review and Discussion

1. In Study 1 what factor(s) increased or decreased participants' littering when they observed a confederate littering?
2. Why did Cialdini et al. predict that participants in Study 3 would be less likely to litter in an environment when it contained a single, conspicuous piece of literature than when it was unlittered?
3. What is the difference between an injunctive and descriptive norm and how did the Cialdini et al create each type of norm in Studies 4 and 5?

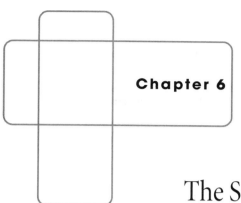

Chapter 6

The Silence of the Library: Environment, Situational Norm, and Social Behavior

Henk Aarts and Ap Dijksterhuis

Because humans are social animals, human behavior is strongly influenced by behavior of other humans. This influence is often very direct. When we interact with others, these others provide direct input for our own thinking and doing. However, direct influence may not reflect the essence of the success of humans as social animals. After all, animals that are decidedly less social, such as cats, are directly influenced by behavior of other cats. Instead, being a successful social animal is largely dependent on more indirect forms of social influence. When we are standing behind a bookshelf in a library, there is often no direct influence of others. Still, our behavior is affected by others (albeit indirectly): We keep the level of noise down as much as possible. In such cases, our behavior is guided by social norms. It is controlled by the activation of behavior that we believe other people expect from us (Cialdini & Trost, 1998). Such social norms are pervasive and form an essential mechanism by which human social behavior is directed (Birenbaum & Sagarin, 1976; Dewey, 1922; Pepitone, 1976; Sherif, 1936).

Most research on social norms has hitherto concentrated mainly on why and how norms are learned and whether norms predict behavior, whereas the question of how social norms become active in directing everyday behavior has received only little theoretical analysis and empirical attention. The present

From *Journal of Personality and Social Psychology*, Vol. 84, No. 1, pp. 18–28. © 2003 by the American Psychological Association. Reproduced with permission.

study attempts to push this important issue forward by focusing on *situational norms*. Situational norms represent generally accepted beliefs about how to behave in particular situations and are learned by associating normative behavior to these situations. Behaving silently when visiting a library or church are examples of such well-established norms. Thus, situational norms refer to knowledge or mental representations of appropriate behavior that guide behavior in a certain situation or environment.

The present research examines the processes underlying the role of situational norms in guiding social behavior. More specifically, stimulated by recent work on automaticity in social behavior (Aarts & Dijksterhuis, 2000; Bargh & Chartrand, 1999; Dijksterhuis & Bargh, 2001), we will test whether, and under which circumstances, environments are capable of activating (mental representations of) normative behavior automatically. In other words, is it possible that normative behavior is elicited by environments, without a consciously expressed fiat or mandate?

Social Influence: The Development and Enactment of Situational Norms

How do we learn to behave in a socially expected way in a given environment? Research on social influence suggests that there are two ways by which we learn situational norms (Cialdini & Trost, 1998; Deutsch & Gerard, 1955; Kelley, 1952). First, people learn how to behave in ways they believe other people approve of, and avoid those behaviors they think others disapprove of. This *normative social influence* is based on the fundamental need to be accepted by others. Such beliefs about what others think we should or should not do are also known as subjective norms (Fishbein & Ajzen, 1975) or injunctive norms (Cialdini, Kallgren, & Reno, 1991).

Sometimes people consult the behavior of those around them to find out what to do. That is, people can also learn situational norms through *informational social influence*. They see others' behavior as a source of information to help them define social reality and maximize the effectiveness of their social behavior. These beliefs about what the majority of people do in specified environments are also referred to as descriptive norms (Cialdini et al., 1991). Apart from influence through observing behavior of others, descriptive norms can also be verbally communicated (Latané, 1996; Miller & Prentice, 1996).

Several researchers have incorporated the concept of social norms in behavior models to optimize the prediction and explanation of human action (Fishbein & Ajzen, 1975; Schwartz & Tessler, 1972; Triandis, 1980; Zuckerman & Reis, 1978). There is an abundance of findings demonstrating that self-reported measures of social norms (and especially subjective norms) correlate with, and independently predict, a variety of behaviors over and above attitudes, especially when the behavior occurs in social settings (for reviews, see Ajzen, 1991; Armitage & Conner, 2001; Eagly & Chaiken, 1993).

Of importance, although the observed correlations between measured constructs provide valuable information about proximal determinants of behavior, the research designs and measurement procedures commonly used in these studies (i.e., correlational data obtained by self-reports in a questionnaire setting) do not allow one to draw firm conclusions about the processes under-lying these relations. For instance, when confronted by questionnaires probing the relevant constructs, people are fully aware of, and capable of retrieving, the reasons that underlie their behavioral acts. This deliberate or reflective mode of responding necessarily leads to an emphasis on conscious processes as deter-mining normative behavior. Indeed, the influence of explicitly expressed social norms on behavior is often found to be mediated by behavioral intentions, thereby suggesting that normative behavior occurs intentionally and con-sciously. But is this always the case?

Environment, Norm, and Behavior

In a series of experiments relevant to this question, Cialdini, Reno, and Kallgren (1990; see also Reno, Cialdini, & Kallgren, 1993) studied under which envi-ronmental conditions students will act on the situational norm of behaving orderly in public spaces. They stuffed handbills into students' mailboxes located in a mailroom and observed what students would do with them. When the floor was already covered with many handbills, students dropped handbills on the floor themselves. Conversely, under conditions of a spotless mailroom, students behaved more orderly and dropped fewer handbills on the floor. Of interest, the condition under which students littered least was a condition in which the mailroom was spotless except for one very salient exception: An almost finished piece of watermelon. Thus, people behaved in an orderly way when the situation in the environment vividly reminded them of the norm that everybody behaved orderly except for "the pig that spoiled the place." Once the norm is activated, virtually all students behave in line with it by putting the handbills in their bag.

One could assume that people were aware of the norm to engage in normative behavior in the "watermelon condition." It represents the violation of a norm and it is likely that such effects of norm violation on behavior are mediated by conscious awareness of the norm. However, the difference between the conditions in which nobody littered (the spotless mailroom) and the one in which many people littered is more ambiguous. Were people in these conditions aware of the norm? Perhaps, perhaps not. In any event, we would like to argue that awareness of a norm is not necessary for evoking normative behavior.

Automaticity in Normative Behavior

Instead, we would like to argue that situational norms can guide social behavior automatically. As argued earlier, situational norms are knowledge-based beliefs about how to behave in particular situations that are shaped by social influence. Insights into human development suggest that these norms evolve in a stepwise manner (Craig, 1996; Hetherington & Baltes, 1988). First, in the course of socialization, individuals learn and practice common ways of conduct that are characteristic for the society. This way, people develop mental representations of how to execute generally accepted or normative behaviors (e.g., being quiet by lowering one's voice or behaving orderly by cleaning up a table or room). These hierarchically ordered behavior representations or "action concepts" (according to the terminology suggested by Hommel, 1998) form part of our behavioral repertoire, and can be readily accessed to guide and adjust behavior when required (see also Jeannerod, 1997; Powers, 1973). Later, the social environment (e.g., parents, grandparents, friends, teachers, and the media) recurrently communicates and enforces beliefs about which normative behaviors should be exhibited in which situation. This way, situational norms become socially shared and well-established (Cialdini & Trost, 1998). It is also, and at the same time, likely that normative behaviors become mentally associated with the specific situation to which they apply (Harvey & Enzle, 1981). Consequently, the situation can activate mental representations of normative behaviors automatically. And once activated, these representations provide the knowledge necessary for guiding one's own situationally appropriate behavior. The idea that situational norms are behavioral guides that we apply effortlessly and automatically in producing behavior is noncontroversial (Barker & Wright, 1955; Schank & Abelson, 1977).

Our reasoning about the activation of normative behavior bears similarity to recent findings of behavioral effects on the perception of social stimuli. This research shows that the presence of stereotyped groups (e.g., elderly) not only leads to activation of semantically associated behavioral traits (e.g., slow), but also to subsequent behavior in line with these traits (Bargh, Chen & Burrows,

1996; Chen & Bargh, 1997; Dijksterhuis & van Knippenberg, 1998; Macrae et al., 1998; for a review, see Dijksterhuis & Bargh, 2001). The theoretical basis for predicting these effects is the overlap between perceptual and behavioral representations for the same type of behavior. Behavioral traits (e.g., moving slow) thus provide the knowledge and the mechanisms for producing the behavior oneself. Accordingly, the mere activation or perception of behavioral traits (either primed by stereotypical information or members of a social group) is capable of tuning behavior one is already engaging, and thus causes one to adjust on going behaviors without a consciously expressed intent to do so. We believe that, like traits about groups, our knowledge about situational norms can affect our behavior along the same lines.

But do physical environments always activate normative behavior? That is, do we keep the level of noise down automatically on the mere activation of the symbolic representation of a library? The behavioral effects discussed above occur because of direct activation of behavioral traits. This direct activation is possible as people develop strong and chronic associations between social targets and traits (Devine, 1989; Hamilton & Sherman, 1994; Stangor & Lange, 1994). These associations streamline the social perception process, and help us to understand other people's behavior in order to respond with an appropriate action of one's own (Macrae & Bodenhausen, 2000). In other words, social stimuli have direct behavioral implications.

In the case of physical (or built) environments, however, a different picture may emerge. Contrary to social stimuli, physical environments do not comprise behavioral implications per se, that is, they do neither display nor call for normative behavior directly. Therefore, there is no necessity to access behavior representations on the mere perception of physical environments to select a proper social response. For example, imagine a person passing (and seeing) the library on his or her way to the cafeteria. Under such circumstances, there would be little point in reducing the volume of one's voice because this normative behavior is not relevant to the person's current goal. Whether library primes (representations of) normative behaviors is likely to depend on whether the environment is of immediate behavioral relevance (Barker, 1968; Leff, 1978). That is, as situational norms refer to socially expected ways of behaving when being in an environment, these norms are readily accessed to direct ongoing actions when visiting the environment (Bargh, 1990). Accordingly, normative behavior is more likely to be materialized when being behaviorally involved in, or having a *goal* to visit the environment. Central to our process-oriented approach toward normative behavior, then, is the idea that well-established situational norms are put into operation automatically on the goal to visit environments.

The Present Research

We report three experiments that were designed to investigate the processes underlying the role of situational norms in guiding behavior. The following questions are addressed. First, is the mere activation of a symbolic representation of an environment (e.g., a picture of a library) sufficient to activate mental representations of normative behavior or does it require the goal to visit the library (Experiment 1)? Second, does automatic activation of these behavior representations elicit overt behavior (Experiment 2)? Third, are these effects dependent on the associative strength between environment and normative behavior (Experiment 3). In the first two experiments we focused on the norm of behaving silently in libraries, and in the third experiment we used the social norm of behaving mannerly in exclusive restaurants.

Before presenting these experiments, we first present two pilot studies demonstrating that the specific behaviors examined in our experiments are indeed normative. To the extent that they are normative, the behaviors should uniquely correlate with subjective norms or descriptive norms toward the behaviors. Accordingly, we conducted two survey studies in which several potential determinants of the behavior under investigation were measured and scrutinized for interrelations.

Pilot Studies 1 and 2

Method

Two different samples of undergraduates participated in a survey study. They were first exposed to a picture of a library ($n = 66$) or exclusive restaurant ($n = 62$), and then asked to respond to several questions related to the environment displayed on the picture. In line with previous research on the role of social norms in attitude–behavior models (e.g., Schaalma, Kok, & Peters, 1993; Sheeran & Orbell, 1999, see also Fishbein & Ajzen, 1975), the following constructs were measured: *Self-reported frequency of past visits* to libraries (or exclusive restaurants) was assessed by asking participants to indicate how often they had visited the respective environment in the last 2 weeks. Participants responded on a 10-point scale, varying from *never* (1) to *very often* (10). *Attitude* toward being silent in libraries (or being well-mannered in exclusive restaurants) was measured by one bipolar 10-point item ranging from *very bad* (1) to *very good* (10). *Subjective norm* was operationalized as the extent to which one believes important others think that one should perform the given behavior in the respective environment. *Descriptive norm* was assessed by asking participants to what extent they believe the majority of other people are silent in libraries (or behave well-mannered in exclusive restaurants). *Mere belief* was operationalized as the extent to which one believes that libraries (or exclusive restaurants) are silent (or well-mannered) places. These three items were accompanied by a 10-point scale, varying from *not at all* (1) to *absolutely* (10). As a measure of *behavior*, participants indicated to what extent they are silent when visiting libraries (or well-mannered when visiting exclusive restaurants) on a 10-point scale, varying from *never* (1) to *always* (10).

Results and Discussion

Table 1 presents means and intercorrelations of the measured constructs for the act of behaving silently in libraries and behaving well-mannered in exclusive restaurants separately. As the means show, our respondents are regular visitors of the library but less frequent visitors of an exclusive restaurant. In addition, attitudes, beliefs, subjective norms, descriptive norms, and experiences are quite in favor of displaying the two actions in the environments, and considering the low variance, there is much consensus about this. By and large, then, our students exhibit the behaviors when visiting the environments. Of more importance, however, both the subjective norm and descriptive norm correlated significantly with the behavioral measures.

To test which constructs were most predictive of behavior, two separate stepwise multiple regression analyses were performed, in which behavior was predicted by the measured constructs. First, for the act of being silent in libraries, the analyses showed that the behavior was significantly predicted by subjective norms, β-subjective norm $= 0.373$, $t(60) = 3.21$, $p < .01$, whereas the contribution of the other variables was nonsignificant, β-past frequency $= 0.165$, $t(60) = 1.43$, *ns*; β-attitude $= 0.031$, $t(60) = 0.26$, *ns*; β-mere belief $= 0.065$, $t(60) = 1.34$, *ns*; β-descriptive norm $= 0.155$, $t(60) = 0.50$, *ns*. In other words, only subjective norms shared unique variance with the behavioral measure. A similar pattern of results emerged for the act of behaving well-mannered in exclusive restaurants: Behavior was significantly predicted by subjective norms, β-subjective norm $= 0.456$, $t(56) = 3.96$, $p < .001$, whereas the contribution of the other variables was nonsignificant, β-past frequency $= -0.062$, $t(56) = -0.53$, *ns*; β-attitude $= 0.111$, $t(56) = 0.86$, *ns*; β-mere belief $= -0.033$, $t(56) = -0.57$, *ns*; β-descriptive norm $= 0.096$, $t(56) = -0.27$, *ns*.

In short, our regression analysis approach suggests that our sample population (i.e., undergraduates) conceive of their act of behaving silently in libraries

TABLE 1							
Means, Standard Deviations, and Intercorrelations of Past Frequency of Visits, Attitude, Subjective Norm, Descriptive Norm, Mere Belief, and Behavior in Pilot Studies							
Measure	*M*	*SD*	2	3	4	5	6
Behavior: Behaving silent in libraries ($n = 66$)							
1. Past frequency of visits	6.30	1.70	.027	−.015	.103	.003	.202
2. Attitude	8.81	1.40		.157	.302*	.053	.141
3. Mere belief	8.70	1.12			.434***	.431***	.214
4. Subjective norm	9.02	0.90				.291*	.373**
5. Descriptive norm	8.06	1.30					.257*
6. Behavior	7.72	1.35					
Behavior: Well-mannered in exclusive restaurants ($n = 62$)							
1. Past frequency of visits	2.63	0.96	.015	−.012	.190	.032	.027
2. Attitude	8.26	1.04		.163	.459***	.384**	.297*
3. Mere belief	7.95	1.53			.286*	.300*	.107
4. Subjective norm	8.68	1.04				.730***	.456***
5. Descriptive norm	8.08	1.51					.377**
6. Behavior	7.76	1.53					

*$p < .05$ **$p < .01$ ***$p < .001$.

and well-mannered in exclusive restaurants as being largely normative. That is, when asked to indicate whether one performs the two behaviors, participants tend to base their responses on situational norms.

Experiment 1

In the first experiment, we tested the hypothesis pertaining to our key assumption that situational norms can be conceived of as mental associations between an environment and normative behavior, and hence, that the goal to go to a library automatically enhances the accessibility of the normative behavior. Participants were exposed to a picture of one of two environments (a library or railway station). After being exposed to the picture, a lexical decision task was assessed to tap the accessibility of action concepts representing the norm of being silent. Following previous work of this kind, it was assumed that the time taken to recognize the behavioral concepts in this task would reflect relative accessibility of representations of normative behavior (Aarts & Dijksterhuis, 2000; Macrae, Bodenhausen, & Milne, 1995; Neely, 1991). Thus, response latencies on these concepts served as a measure for the activation of the situational norm. If the accessibility of appropriate behavior representations is conditional on the presence of a behavioral goal, as we hypothesize, priming of library would decrease the speed of responding to behavioral concepts referring to the situational norm only when being instigated with the goal to go to the library. However, if the mere exposure to library suffices to affect the responses, priming of library should enhance the accessibility, irrespective of goal activation.

Method

Participants and design   Fifty undergraduates participated in the experiment, receiving 6 Dutch Guilders (approximately $2.50) in return. They were randomly assigned to either a goal-control prime, no-goal-library prime, or goal-library prime condition.

Experimental task and procedure   On arrival at the laboratory, participants were told that they would take part in research conducted by different research teams, and that they had to perform tasks on a computer. The computer program provided the instructions. Participants worked in separate cubicles and were provided with two consecutive tasks.

The first task was announced as the "Picture Task." Participants learned that they were going to be briefly exposed to a picture of a certain environment for 30 s. As a cover story, all participants were told that they had to examine the picture and to answer some questions about it later. Furthermore, two thirds of the participants also learned they had to visit the environment after the experiment. Some participants were exposed to a picture of a library, showing the interior design of it (hence, this condition is referred to as the *goal-library prime* condition). The other participants were shown a picture of a railway station, showing an empty platform. Because the latter group of participants was not primed with an environment typically associated with the norm of behaving silently, this condition can be treated as a *goal-control prime* condition. Apart from the goal-control prime and goal-library prime condition we added a no-goal condition: One third of the participants were also exposed to the library picture. However, instead of anticipating a visit to the environment, these participants were merely asked to carefully scrutinize the picture. Because these participants were not instigated with the goal to visit the library, this condition is referred to as the *no-goal-library prime* condition. None of the pictures displayed people in the environment. Furthermore, the names of the respective environments were not mentioned.

Next, participants were confronted with the lexical decision task in which they had to respond to 24 words. Twelve of the words were existing words and 12 were nonsense words. For every word appearing on the screen, they were asked to decide as fast and as accurately as possible whether the word was a meaningful word or not. Participants pressed keys on the computer's keyboard marked *yes* or *no*. All words appeared at the same location on the screen, preceded by a fixation point, for 500 ms. Response latencies were measured in milliseconds from the onset of the words to the time participants pressed a key. The time interval between word trials was 2 s. The words were presented in random order, and were preceded by 4 practice trials. Among the existing words, 4 target words represented the normative behavior (i.e., being silent) of interest: *silent, quiet, still, whisper*. The other 8 existing words were neither relevant for the concept of being silent nor related to the two environments (*large, small, middle, begin, weak, strong, proceed, little*). The length of the words was controlled for. That is, the mean length of the silence and control words was equal ($M = 6.0$ letters).[1]

After the task, participants were thoroughly debriefed. The debriefing indicated that participants were unaware of the hypotheses under investigation. Moreover, they did not perceive any connection between the different tasks. Not surprisingly, some participants spontaneously asked when they were supposed to visit the environment on the picture, revealing that we succeeded in the instigation of actual behavioral goals. Of course, we told all participants that these instructions were only given to test our hypotheses.

Results and Discussion

The average response latency on the 4 silence words and 8 control words were subjected to a 3 (prime: goal-control vs. no-goal-library vs. goal-library) between-participants × 2 (type of word: silence vs. control) within-participants analysis of variance (ANOVA). Incorrect ("no") responses across these words were excluded from the analyses (3% out of all responses). The analysis yielded a significant Prime × Type of Word interaction, $F(2, 47) = 3.52$, $p < .04$. No other effects were reliable ($Fs < 1$). Simple effect analysis showed that response latencies differed between prime conditions for silence words, $F(2, 47) = 4.38$, $p < .02$, but not for control words ($F < 1$). Planned comparison further

	TABLE 2		
	Response Latencies (in Milliseconds) as a Function of Goal Prime and Type of Word in Experiment 1		
Type of words	Goal-control prime	No-goal-library prime	Goal-library
Silence words	578 (39)	568 (79)	524 (35)
Control words	562 (49)	566 (76)	553 (66)

Note. Standard deviations are shown in parentheses.

revealed that participants' responses to silence words were faster in the goal-library condition than in the goal-control condition, $F(1, 47) = 7.60, p < .01$, and in the no-goal-library condition, $F(1, 47) = 5.18, p < .03$. There was no significant difference between the control and no-goal-library conditions ($F < 1$). Means are presented in Table 2.

The results of Experiment 1 support our predictions. The activation of a library enhanced the speed of responding to concepts related to normative behavior displayed in that environment. However, these effects only emerged when participants had the goal to visit that environment. The speed of responding to concepts related to normative behavior was equivalent across the control and no-goal-library conditions. These results indicate that the goal of doing things in a library heightens the accessibility of the behavior representation of the social norm of being silent.

Experiment 2

So far, the results of Experiment 1 showed that the instigation of the goal to visit a certain physical environment facilitates access to behavior representations that are associated with the situational norm pertaining to the environment. In Experiment 2, our aim was to investigate whether the priming effects indeed lead to changes in overt behavior.[2]

To assess changes in behavior, we measured the sound pressure level (i.e., intensity) of participants' voices while speaking. On the basis of the results of the previous experiment, we expected priming of library to decrease the intensity of participants' voice, but this decrease will be most pronounced for participants that are instigated with the goal to go to the library.

Experiment 2 served two further purposes. First, we included mediator variables to rule out alternative accounts for the observed behavioral priming effects. For instance, going to the library may affect participants' mood or modify their level of arousal. Effects of priming on behavior (i.e., voice intensity) may be attributable to variances in these variables. Hence, for the present purpose, two potential variables seemed relevant to test for mediator effects: mood and arousal.

Furthermore, earlier we argued that situational norms are socially shared beliefs that are the result of socialization and associative learning. Generally accepted behaviors that are characteristic of a society are well-learned and subsequently linked to specific situations. Although it is likely that the establishment of situational norms (and mental associations between situations and normative behavior) does not require much direct practice or regular experience, it may be questioned whether this logic also pertains to the automatic activation of the normative behavior itself. That is, do situational norms automatically become active in guiding behavior on the goal to visit an environment without regular experiences with the environment and associated normative action? To explore this important question, we assessed participants' frequency of past behavior to test whether regular direct experiences with the library enhance the effects of environmental priming on behavior.

Method

Participants and design   Sixty-nine undergraduates participated in the experiment, receiving 6 Dutch Guilders in return. They were randomly assigned to one of the conditions described in Experiment 1.

Experimental task and procedure   On arrival at the lab, participants were told that they would take part in research conducted by different research teams, and that they had to perform tasks on a computer. The computer program provided the instructions. Participants worked in cubicles and were tested individually. They were provided with four consecutive tasks: a priming task, a word pronunciation task, the Affect–Arousal Scale, and a measure of past direct experiences with the library.

First, participants were exposed to the picture task used in Experiment 1. Next, participants were confronted with the word pronunciation task assessing the sound pressure level of their voice in dB(A). For this task they were instructed to read aloud 10 words that were presented on the computer screen. This information was allegedly helpful for the purpose of designing new communication systems. No explanation or instructions were given regarding the way participants should pronounce the words. Each word remained on the screen for 2 s. The time interval between words was 3 s. To reduce noise in the sound pressure level score, 10 short words were chosen that only comprise "soft" phonemes (see Fletcher, 1953), that is, they did not contain letters like *t* or *s*. Participants were provided with a microphone attached to a headset. To keep the distance fixed, the microphone was placed 10 cm away from the mouth of the participants. Data of each spoken word was filed by the computer, and subsequently converted into dB(A) using audio software (GIPOS; Gigi & Vogten, 1998). The microphone-recording system was calibrated to a 70 dB audio source (white noise) reference tone (see Baken, 1987, for a more elaborate discussion on the measurement of voice intensity). The dependent variable was the mean dB(A) across the 10 words, representing a measure of voice intensity.

Immediately after the word pronunciation task, a modified version of the Affect–Arousal Scale (Salovey & Birnbaum, 1989) was administered. The questionnaire contained six items differentiating feelings of mood and arousal on 10-point scales. The mood items were *bad–good, sad–happy,* and *displeased–pleased.* The arousal items were *calm–excited, tired–energetic,* and *sedate–aroused.*[3] Participants responded to each item in terms of how they felt at that moment.

Furthermore, as part of a larger questionnaire on activities in daily life, participants were asked to indicate how often they had visited the library in the past month. To attenuate possible influences of the previous tasks on the frequency estimates of past direct experiences, participants were explicitly instructed to be as accurate as possible in their recall (Aarts & Dijksterhuis, 1999). The frequency estimates served as a measure of past behavior.

At the end of the experiment, participants were debriefed. As usual, debriefing revealed that participants were not aware of a possible effect of the priming task on later performance.

Results and Discussion

Effects on behavior: Voice intensity scores   Voice intensity has been found to differ between males and females (e.g., Coleman, Mabis, & Hinson, 1977; Huber, Stathopoulos, Curione, Ash, & Johnson, 1999). Hence, to control for gender differences, the voice intensity scores [dB(A)] were subjected to a 3 (prime: goal-control vs. no-goal-library vs. goal-library) × 2 (gender: male vs. female) between-participants ANOVA. The main effect of gender was highly significant, $F(1, 63) = 25.96$, $p < .001$. Males produced a louder voice ($M = 85.21$) than females ($M = 81.99$). However, the analysis further showed that the effect of prime was significant, $F(2, 63) = 3.46$, $p < .04$. The Prime × Gender interaction was not significant ($F < 1$). Planned comparison revealed that participants' voices in the goal-library condition ($M = 83.16$) were reliably less loud than participants' voices in the goal-control condition ($M = 84.48$), $F(1, 63) = 4.98$, $p < .03$, and in the no-goal-library condition ($M = 84.62$), $F(1, 63) = 5.83$, $p < .02$. There was no significant difference between the control and no-goal-library conditions ($F < 1$).

Controlling for mood and arousal effects   With the assessment of the mood and arousal scales, we wanted to rule out potential mediators. We first conducted a multivariate analysis of variance using priming condition and gender as the independent variable and the average of the three mood items ($\alpha = 0.81$) and the average of the three arousal items ($\alpha = 0.50$) as the dependent variable. Next, we performed 3 (prime: goal-control vs. no-goal-library vs. goal-library) $\times$ 2 (gender: male vs. female) between-participants analyses of covariance (ANCOVAs), with the mood and arousal measures as covariates.

ANOVAs revealed no significant main effect of priming on the two dependent variables ($Fs < 1$), indicating that mood and arousal were not affected by the prime conditions. ANCOVAs yielded the same pattern of significant results for gender, prime, and the interaction effect after controlling for mood—$F(1, 62) = 25.70$, $p < .001$; $F(2, 62) = 3.72$, $p < .04$; and $F(2, 62) < 1$, respectively—and after controlling for arousal—$F(1, 62) = 27.35$, $p < .001$; $F(2, 62) = 3.37$, $p < .05$; and $F(2, 62) < 1$, respectively. Taken together, then, these analyses indicate that the observed pattern of results is neither attributable to changes in mood nor to variations in arousal.

The role of past behavior.   The mean frequency of past visits to the library was 3.17 ($SD = 2.28$), and all participants had at least visited the library once in the last month. To test whether the library prime effects on vocal performance are conditional on the number of direct experiences with the library and associated normative behavior, we subjected the behavioral measure (voice intensity) to a moderated hierarchical multiple regression analysis (Baron & Kenny, 1986), in which the behavior is predicted by gender (coded as male = 1, female = 2), prime (coded as goal-control prime = 1, no-goal-library prime = 2, goal-library prime = 3), past behavior, and the Prime $\times$ Past Behavior interaction term. To reduce multicollinearity bias, all variables were standardized before the cross-product was computed (Dunlap & Kemery, 1987). This analysis showed that the prediction of behavior by gender and prime was significant, β-gender = -0.518, $t(64) = -4.93$, $p < .01$; β-prime = -0.238, $t(64) = -2.27$, $p < .03$ (these effects are similar to the ones resulting from the original ANOVAs). However, including the main effect of past behavior and the interaction term did not significantly add to the prediction of behavior, β-past behavior = 0.075,

$t(64) = 0.72$, *ns*; β-interaction $= -0.056$, $t(64) = -0.60$, *ns*. The nonsignificant interaction effect indicates that the library prime effects on vocal behavior are unconditional on the number of direct experiences.

In sum, the results of Experiment 2 showed that the priming of representations of behaviors by physical environments extends to overt behavior. Participants' voice intensity decreased when they were exposed to a picture of a library, indicating that they behaved in line with the primed behavior of being silent. However, this effect was qualified by the presence of the goal to go to the library: The library only affected the intensity of the voice under conditions of processing the environment in behavioral term. Controlling for differences in mood and arousal did not modify the pattern of results. Furthermore, the priming effects did not interact with frequency of past behavior, suggesting that normative behavior can be automatically activated without regular direct experiences with the situational norm.

Experiment 3

The reasons behind conducting Experiment 3 were three-fold. First, we tried to replicate the priming effects on normative behavior in a different domain, namely behavior associated with the situational norm of behaving well-mannered in exclusive restaurants. Second, we attempted to provide more direct support for the mediating role of the mental representations producing the priming effects. According to the present conceptualization of situational norms, effects of environmental priming on over behavior should depend on the strength of the association between environment and normative behavior. Assuming that differences in associative strength exist, it follows that the stronger the association, the stronger the automatic effects of an environment on behavior will be (for a similar logic, see, e.g., Dijksterhuis, Aarts, Bargh, & van Knippenberg, 2000; Fazio, Jackson, Dunton, & Williams, 1995). Third, in Experiment 2 we found no evidence for the idea that frequency of direct experiences with the environment (and the associated normative behavior) moderates the priming effects. It should be noted, however, that our research sample consisted of participants that had all direct experiences with the environment. Thus, the sensitivity of the measure might have been insufficient to detect reliable moderating effects of direct experiences. Therefore, we again assessed the frequency of direct experiences with an exclusive restaurant (which is probably not visited by all participants on a regular basis; see also the pilot studies) to explore moderating role of practice in behavioral priming effects.

In Experiment 3, associative strength was first measured by means of a response latency paradigm in which participants were briefly exposed to a picture of an environment (e.g., an exclusive restaurant) and subsequently indicated as fast as possible whether a presented action concept (e.g., well-mannered) described the way one should behave in that environment. The speed of responding thus represents an indirect measure of the ease of activating the normative behavior by the environment. Next, effects of environmental prime on behavior were observed during eating. We anticipated that priming of an exclusive restaurant leads to well-mannered behavior. However, the size of this effect should be dependent on the associative strength between environment and socially expected behavior. People who strongly associate an exclusive restaurant with behaving mannerly will show stronger behavioral effects than those with relatively weak associations. In the control condition, however, associative strength should have no effect, as the behavioral norm of behaving well-mannered is not activated.

Method

Participants and design   Forty-two undergraduates participated in the experiment, receiving 12 Dutch Guilders (approximately $6) in return. They were randomly assigned to either the goal-control prime or goal-restaurant prime condition.

Experimental task and procedure   The experiment was conducted in the lab and consisted of two parts. First, the associative strength between environment and normative behavior was measured. One month later the effects of environmental priming were tested on behavior.

Associative strength.   After participants entered the lab, they were told that they would take part in several studies. Participants were seated in cubicles containing a computer. First, we measured how strongly the action concept of "behaving mannerly" was associated with an exclusive restaurant. This was done with an association task. Participants were told that pictures would be briefly (400 ms) presented on the screen, designating a variety of environments. Furthermore, they learned that after each picture, an action concept would be presented on the screen, and that their task was to indicate as fast as possible whether the given action describes the appropriate way of behaving in the environment on the picture. Some pictures were succeeded with action concepts that are socially not expected to be displayed in the environment (e.g., park–litter), and some pictures were followed by action concepts that are socially expected to be exhibited in the environment (e.g., exclusive restaurant–well-mannered).

It should be noted that we did not ask participants to indicate what one can do, but how one should behave in the respective environments, that is, the situational norm. In total, 80 pictures (20 different environments) appeared on the screen, and 4 comprised a picture of the same exclusive restaurant (identical to the one used in the experimental prime condition later on). The 4 words succeeding this picture were related to the norm of mannerly behavior (*well-mannered, decent, orderly, tidy*).

An association trial consisted of the following sequence of events: (a) presentation of a (12 cm $\times$ 8 cm) gray rectangle for 500 ms, (b) presentation of a picture (color photograph of the same size) for 400 ms, (c) presentation of a gray rectangle for 100 ms, and (d) presentation of the action concept in the middle of the rectangle. The action concept remained on the screen until the participant responded. Everything appeared at the same location on the screen. Responses were collected from the computer keyboard—participants pressed a key marked *yes* or *no*. Response latencies were measured in milliseconds from the onset of the action concepts to the time participants pressed a button. The time interval between trials was 2 s. The trials were presented in random order, and preceded by four practice trials. The mean reaction time on the four "restaurant" trials is indicative for the associative strength. All participants responded with *yes* to the four trials, indicating that they shared the norm of behaving mannerly in the environment (see also the earlier presented pilot study).

Environmental priming manipulations.   After 1 month, all participants were contacted again with the request to participate in several tests that were designed by different research teams. We were able to recruit 42 persons who also participated in the first part. Thus, we could relate their associative strength between the exclusive restaurant and behaving mannerly with the data obtained later. Participants worked in a cubicle on computers and were tested individually. After participants were seated in the cubicle, they were exposed to the picture task. All participants first received the goal to visit the environment on the picture. Next, they were exposed to either the prime control (railway station) condition or the exclusive restaurant prime condition.

Assessing behavioral effects.   Immediately after the picture task, participants were confronted with the "execution of mundane action task." Participants were told that a team of researchers was pilot-testing a set of mundane tasks for upcoming research, which lasted for about 3 min. Hence, participants were requested to perform short tasks, and to answer some questions afterwards. They were seated at a table that was cleaned before each session. For one of the tasks, participants were required to eat a round-shaped biscuit that usually

gives crumbs when one bites into it. A hidden video camera recorded participants while they ate. The video allowed a clear view of participants' hand
movements at the table while consuming the biscuit. The dependent measure
we assessed was the extent to which participants kept their table clean and tidy.
Accordingly, two raters blind to experimental conditions and hypotheses rated
the videotapes on frequency of cleaning the table during the consumption
of the biscuit. Concretely, they counted the number of times participants
removed crumbs from the table during the task. The correlation between the
two raters was .94, and by averaging their ratings for each participant, we
obtained a measure representing well-mannered behavior.

Furthermore, participants were asked to indicate how often they had visited
an exclusive restaurant in the last month. This frequency estimate served as a
measure of past behavior. Finally, participants were thoroughly debriefed. The
debriefing indicated that participants did not perceive any connection between
the tasks. Thus, as in the previous experiments they were not aware of any influence of the priming task on their later performance. However, 2 participants
did not complete the biscuit task. Hence, these participants were excluded from
further analyses.

Results and Discussion

Effects on behavior   The measure of mannerly behavior was subjected to a 2
(prime: control vs. restaurant) between-participants ANOVA. In line with our
prediction, the effect of prime was significant, $F(1, 38) = 5.85, p < .03$. Participants removed the crumbs substantially more often in the restaurant condition
($M = 1.79$) than in the control condition ($M = 0.60$), thereby replicating the
behavioral priming effect of Experiment 2.

The mediating role of environment–behavior associative strength   According to
our hypothesis, the priming effects should be dependent on associative strength:
After activation of an exclusive restaurant, people who strongly associate that
restaurant with behaving mannerly will show stronger behavior effects than those
who weakly associate that restaurant with behaving mannerly. Thus, the prime is
supposed to moderate the relation between associative strength and actual performance. To test this effect, we subjected the behavioral measure to a moderated
hierarchical multiple regression analysis, in which the behavior is predicted by
prime (coded as goal-control prime = 1, goal-restaurant prime = 2), associative
strength, and the Prime × Associative Strength interaction term. To reduce
multicollinearity bias, all variables were standardized before the cross-product
was computed. This analysis showed that the prediction of behavior by prime,

β-prime = 0.366, $t(36) = 2.67$, $p < .02$, and associative strength, β-associative strength = -0.417, $t(36) = -3.05$, $p < .01$, was significantly improved by including the interaction term, β-interaction = -0.372, $t(36) = -2.99$, $p < .01$.

The nature of the interaction effect is revealed when computing Pearson correlations between the associative strength measure and behavior under restaurant priming condition and under control condition. First, there was no relation between associative strength and behavior in the control prime condition ($r = -.10$, ns), which of course is due to the fact that the behavioral norm of behaving well-mannered was not activated. Of more importance, the predicted relation between the associative strength measure and normative behavior in the restaurant prime condition was highly significant ($r = -.65$, $p < .01$): As the speed of responding to appropriate behavior increases (i.e., when accessibility is higher), so does the frequency of displaying normative actions. In other words, the effect of the goal to visit an exclusive restaurant on behaving well-mannered is mediated by the ease of accessing representations of normative behavior.

The role of past behavior   The mean frequency of past visits to an exclusive restaurant was 1.43 ($SD = 1.15$). Ten participants (25%) had not visited an exclusive restaurant in past month. As in Experiment 2, we again sought to test whether the effects of restaurant activation on behavioral effects are conditional on the frequency of past behavior. Accordingly, the behavioral measure (behaving well-mannered) was subjected to a moderated hierarchical multiple regression analysis, in which the behavior is predicted by the prime conditions (coded as control prime = 1, restaurant prime = 2), past behavior measure, and the Prime × Past Behavior interaction term. As in the previous analyses, all variables were standardized before the cross-product was computed. The regression analysis showed that the prediction of behavior by prime was significant, β-prime = 0.361, $t(36) = 2.37$, $p < .03$. However, the main effect of past behavior and the interaction term did not share significant variances with behavior, β-past behavior = -0.081, $t(36) = -0.53$, ns; β-interaction = -0.140, $t(36) = -0.92$, ns. These results indicate that the restaurant prime affected actual performance regardless of the number of direct experiences with the environment and associated normative behavior in the past.

General Discussion

The present research adopted a process-oriented approach to investigate how situational norms guide social behavior. It was posited that situational norms can be seen as associations between environment and normative behavior in memory that are shaped by social influence. Because of these associations, it is possible to automatically elicit the (mental representations of) behavior by activating the goal to visit the environment. Three experiments provided support for these ideas.

In the first two experiments, we established that library only enhanced the accessibility of mental representations of being silent and made participants talk less loud when they had a goal to visit the library. These findings indicate that mere exposure to library does not guide normative behavior directly. The present results thus differ from findings obtained in inquiries on behavioral priming effects of social stimuli. This research establishes that mere perception of social targets suffices to activate representations of behavior traits and corresponding behavior, demonstrating the strong and direct behavioral implications of social stimuli (Dijksterhuis & Bargh, 2001). Physical (or built) environments, however, seem to impinge on social behavior in a different way. In appreciating a functional view on human behavior, we believe that people do not access representations of the norm of being silent automatically on the mere perception of a library. It takes an additional step to prime the normative behavior and, as the present results show, this happens when having the goal to visit the environment.

Another way to interpret the effects of goals is to posit that instructions to visit the environment simply prime more nodes in memory, and thus renders representations of normative behavior more accessible. However, it should be noted that our data indicate that mere perception of environments (i.e., when participants only scrutinized the interior features within the same amount of time) does not suffice to facilitate normative behavior directly (compared with controls). This effect resembles recent findings on the role of processing goals in trait activation on the perception of social targets (Macrae, Bodenhausen, Milne, Thorn, & Castelli, 1997). Macrae et al. (1997) did not find the typical trait activation effect after mere exposure to a picture of a woman or when participants processed the picture in socially meaningless terms (if they had to indicate whether there was a dot on the picture). A picture of a woman only activated these traits if participants had the goal to process the picture in socially relevant terms (e.g., "Is the object on the picture a living thing?"). In line with this research, we believe that the goal to visit the library renders the environment of immediate behavioral relevance, and as a result, facilitates access to representations of normative behavior (cf. Bargh, 1990). That is, the goal to visit an environment activates (albeit implicitly) thoughts about how one should behave in a socially accepted way, thus triggering the normative behavior associated with the environment automatically. In fact, given our experimental procedures, the conditional role of goals in normative behavior activation effect can be classified as an instance of unintended goal-dependent automaticity (Bargh, 1989)—unintended in the sense that it occurs as a result of the intentional instigation of another goal (e.g., visiting the library).

Furthermore, we obtained evidence for the idea that the environmental priming effects on behavior are conditional on the associative strength between the representations of the environment and normative behavior. In Experiment 3, participants indicated as fast as possible whether specific action concepts (well-mannered) represent the normative way of behaving in a certain environment briefly presented on a picture (an exclusive restaurant). Results showed that the priming effects of an exclusive restaurant on well-mannered behavior were more pronounced for participants with strong associations than for those who possessed weak associations. This pattern of data concurs with other research showing that accessibility of concepts after priming depends on the associative strength between the concept and prime (Higgins, 1996). These results thus provide crucial information, as they show that the respective normative behavior was more accessible for some than for others, and moreover, that the priming effects of physical environment were mediated by these variances in mental accessibility.

Situational Norms Versus Personal Habits

The present conceptualization on the role of situational norms in directing behavior bears similarity with recent treatments about habitual social behavior (Aarts & Dijksterhuis, 2000; Bargh & Gollwitzer, 1994; Ouellette & Wood, 1998). In both cases, goals automatically prime behavior according to an "if-then" rule. However, situational norms and habits differ in how these automatic effects originate. Habits are conceived of as idiosyncratically learned goal–mean links in memory that gain strength by extensive direct practice. These links emanate from a selection process in which an action is regularly selected and performed that is perceived to be most effective in obtaining a goal (e.g., taking the bicycle instead of a bus to go to the university). Thus, Aarts and Dijksterhuis (2000) found that cycling was automatically activated by the goal to travel to the university, but only for those persons that regularly use the bicycle for this trip.

Situational norms are socially shared beliefs representing links between specific situations and normative behaviors. These norms are also known as customs or social conventions that are the product of socialization and cultural construal (e.g., Camic, 1986; Durkheim, 1893/1964), and do not require much direct practice to become well-established (Sperber, 1990). Direct practice may be essential to learn how to execute the behavioral part (e.g., lower one's voice to be quiet) of situational norms, but not to associate normative behavior to a given situation. Such associations can easily be established by indirect experiences (Lieberman, 2000). Situational norms thus are able to automatically become active in a situation without much direct experience with that situation (cf. Cohen, 1997). Indeed, the present data show that past behavior did not enhance the priming effects. Of course, socialization may cause people to differ in how well situational norms establish (Cialdini & Trost, 1998). For example, some people grow up in an environment in which the importance of well-mannered behavior in exclusive establishments is more stressed, and therefore develop stronger links between that situation and behavior. Hence, differences in associative strength are likely to occur because of differences in culture and social background.

Situational Norms and Control Over Social Behavior Revisited

The most important theoretical significance of the present research lies in demonstrating that situational norms are able to guide social behavior directly, an observation that diverges from findings in correlational survey studies on attitude–behavior models. As the present studies show, however, not all situational norms guide social behavior directly. Only situational norms that are well-established, in the sense of strong associations between environment and normative behavior, are automatically put in operation on the goal to visit the environment. For those who weakly (or not at all) associate the environment with normative behavior, the behavior representation is not spontaneously facilitated, and hence, does not become accessible in guiding overt behavior. Presumably, these people have to be consciously reminded (or prompted) to the situational norm to enact the normative behavior (e.g., Cialdini et al., 1990; see also Zimbardo & Leippe, 1991). For example, it may have been the case that participants in the Cialdini et al. studies (1991) did not have such strong links between public spaces and behaving orderly after all, and thus the additional piece of watermelon made them more aware of the normative behavior. In other words, under conditions of weak situational norms, individuals are more prone to intentional control, as they have to rely on conscious intents to assimilate their ongoing behavior to the norm pertaining to the situation at hand. However, because this general perspective to automatic and intentional control of normative behavior as a function of associative strength is not directly tested in the current experiments, it still awaits further empirical scrutiny.

Situational norms are rules and standards that are understood by members of a group or society, and that guide behavior without the force of laws. Although some norms may be rather local and transient, this "lawless" force makes the concept of norms of particular interest to social psychology. Recently, Cialdini and Trost (1998) stated that "There has been some debate about the usefulness of norms as an explanatory concept, . . . and in fact, the variety of conceptualizations may have contributed to the confusion concerning the actual role of social norms in directing our behavior" (p. 152). One may argue that the present analysis may further confuse the matter by conceptualizing situational norms as associations between environment and normative behavior. However, our findings that were predicted from this conceptualization may be quite instructive. That is, the idea that normative behavior is directly evoked by environments when (a) goals are active that render environments behaviorally relevant, and (b) behavior representations become accessible as a result of socially shaped associations between environment and normative behavior suggests that automatic normative behavior follows similar principles that are postulated in contemporary social cognition research to account for the emergence of other automatic social behavior. In so doing, we feel that we have become closer to capture the mechanism that tells us how, when, and where normative behavior may be expected.

Notes

1. In the lexical decision task, Dutch words were used. Here, we report the English translations of the original words.
2. Obviously, activation of a behavior representation is not yet the same as actual behavioral change. Recent neurophysiological evidence however demonstrates that activation of a behavior representation (e.g., a gesture) leads to the same activation in the anterior cingulate cortex as actually performing this same behavior (Decety, Jeannerod, Germain, & Pastene, 1991; Jeannerod, 1997; Paus, Petrides, Evans, & Meyer, 1993; see also Dijksterhuis & Bargh, 2001). That is, performing an action and merely activating the representation of this action results in activation of the same so-called "motor programs." These motor programs are ultimately responsible for actual behavior. According to these findings, activation of a behavior representation should—all else being equal—lead to corresponding changes in overt behavior. Hence, on the basis of the findings of Experiment 1 in which we obtained evidence for activated behavior representations, we can expect actual behavioral changes to occur in Experiment 2.
3. These items are from "Influence of Mood on Health-Relevant Cognitions," by P. Salovey and D. Birnbaum, 1989, *Journal of Personality and Social Psychology, 57*, pp. 539–551. Copyright 1989 by the American Psychological Association. Reprinted with permission of the author.

References

Aarts, H., & Dijksterhuis, A. (1999). How often did I do it: Experienced ease of retrieval and frequency estimates of past behavior. *Acta Psychologica, 103*, 77–89.

Aarts, H., & Dijksterhuis, A. (2000). Habits as knowledge structures: Automaticity in goal-directed behavior. *Journal of Personality and Social Psychology, 78*, 53–63.

Ajzen, I. (1991). The theory of planned behavior. *Organizational Behavior and Human Decision Processes, 50*, 179–211.

Armitage, C. J., & Conner, M. (2001). Efficacy of the theory of planned behavior: A meta-analytical review. *British Journal of Social Psychology, 40*, 471–499.

Baken, R. J. (1987). *Clinical measurement of speech and voice.* London: Taylor & Francis.

Bargh, J. A. (1989). Conditional automaticity: Varieties of automatic influence in social perception and cognition. In J. S. Uleman & J. A. Bargh (Eds.), *Unintended thought* (pp. 3–51). New York: Guilford Press.

Bargh, J. A. (1990). Auto-motives: Preconscious determinants of social interaction. In R. M. Sorrentino & E. T. Higgins (Eds.), *Handbook of motivation and cognition* (pp. 93–130). New York: Guilford Press.

Bargh, J. A., & Chartrand, T. L. (1999). The unbearable automaticity of being. *American Psychologist, 54*, 462–476.

Bargh, J. A., Chen, M., & Burrows, L. (1996). The automaticity of social behavior: Direct effects of trait concept and stereotype activation on action. *Journal of Personality and Social Psychology, 71*, 230–244.

Bargh, J. A., & Gollwitzer, P. M. (1994). Environmental control of goal-directed action: Automatic and strategic contingencies between situations and behavior. In W. D. Spaulding (Ed.), *Nebraska symposium on motivation* (Vol. 41, pp. 71–124). Lincoln: University of Nebraska Press.

Barker, R. G. (1968). *Ecological psychology: Concepts and methods for studying the environment of human behavior.* Stanford, CA: Stanford University Press.

Barker, R. G., & Wright, H. F. (1955). *Midwest and its children: The psychological ecology of an American town.* New York: Row, Peterson.

Baron, R. M., & Kenny, D. A. (1986). The moderator-mediator variable distinction in social psychological research: Conceptual, strategic, and statistic considerations. *Journal of Personality and Social Psychology, 51*, 1173–1182.

Birenbaum, A., & Sagarin, E. (1976). *Norms and human behavior.* New York: Praeger Publishers.

Camic, C. (1986). The matter of habit. *American Journal of Sociology, 91*, 1039–1087.

Chen, M., & Bargh, J. A. (1997). Nonconscious behavioral confirmation processes: The self-fulfilling nature of automatically-activated stereotypes. *Journal of Experimental Social Psychology, 33*, 541–560.

Cialdini, R. B., Kallgren, C. A., & Reno, R. R. (1991). A focus theory of normative conduct: A theoretical refinement and revaluation of the role of norms in human behavior. In M. P. Zanna (Ed.), *Advances in experimental social psychology* (Vol. 24, pp. 201–234). San Diego, CA: Academic Press.

Cialdini, R. B., Reno, R. R., & Kallgren, C. A. (1990). A focus theory of normative conduct: Recycling the concept of norms to reduce littering in public places. *Journal of Personality and Social Psychology, 58*, 1015–1026.

Cialdini, R. B., & Trost, M. R. (1998). Social influence: Social norms, conformity, and compliance. In D. T. Gilbert, S. T. Fiske, & G. Lindzey (Eds.), *The handbook of social psychology* (Vol. 2, pp. 151–192). Boston: McGraw-Hill.

Cohen, D. (1997). Ifs and thens in cultural psychology. In R. S. Wyer Jr. (Ed.), *Advances in social cognition* (Vol. 10, pp. 121–131). Mahwah, NJ: Erlbaum.

Coleman, R. F., Mabis, J. H., & Hinson, J. K. (1977). Fundamental frequency-sound pressure level profiles of adult male and female voices. *Journal of Speech, Language and Hearing Research, 20*, 197–204.

Craig, G. J. (1996). *Human development.* Upper Saddle River, NJ: Prentice-Hall.

Decety, J., Jeannerod, M., Germain, M., & Pastene, J. (1991). Vegetative response during imagined movement is proportional to mental effort. *Behavioural Brain Research, 42*, 1–5.

Deutsch, M., & Gerard, H. G. (1955). A study of normative and informational social influence upon individual judgment. *Journal of Abnormal and Social Psychology, 51*, 629–636.

Devine, P. G. (1989). Stereotypes and prejudice: Their automatic and controlled components. *Journal of Personality and Social Psychology, 56*, 5–18.

Dewey, J. (1922). *Human nature and conduct: An introduction to social psychology.* New York: Holt.

Dijksterhuis, A., Aarts, H., Bargh, J. A., & van Knippenberg, A. (2000). Past contact, stereotype strength, and automatic behavior. *Journal of Experimental Social Psychology, 36*, 531–544.

Dijksterhuis, A., & Bargh, J. A. (2001). The perception-behavior expressway: The automatic effects of social perception on social behavior. In M. P. Zanna (Ed.), *Advances in experimental social psychology* (Vol. 33, pp. 1–40). San Diego, CA: Academic Press.

Dijksterhuis, A., & van Knippenberg, A. (1998). The relation between perception and behavior or how to win a game of Trivial Pursuit. *Journal of Personality and Social Psychology, 74*, 865–877.

Dunlap, W. P., & Kemery, E. R. (1987). Failures to detect moderating effects: Is multicollinearity the problem? *Psychological Bulletin, 102*, 418–420.

Durkheim, E. (1964). *The division of labor in society* (G. Simpson, Trans.). Original work published 1893.

Eagly, A. H., & Chaiken, S. (1993). *The psychology of attitudes.* Fort Worth, TX: Harcourt Brace Jovanovich.

Fazio, R. H., Jackson, J. R., Dunton, B. C., & Williams, C. J. (1995). Variability in automatic activation as an unobtrusive measure of racial attitudes: A bona fide pipeline? *Journal of Personality and Social Psychology, 69*, 1013–1027.

Fishbein, M., & Ajzen. I. (1975). *Belief, attitude, intention and behavior: An introduction to theory and research.* Reading, MA: Addison Wesley.

Fletcher, H. (1953). *Speech and hearing in communication.* New York: van Nostrand.

Gigi, E. F., & Vogten, L. L. M. (1998). GIPOS. *IPO Annual Progress Report, 32*, 105–110.

Hamilton, D. L., & Sherman, J. W. (1994). Stereotypes. In R. S. Wyer Jr. & T. K. Srull (Eds.), *Handbook of social cognition* (Vol. 2, pp. 1–68). Hilldale NJ: Erlbaum.

Harvey, M. D., & Enzle, M. E. (1981). A cognitive model of social norms for understanding the transgression-helping effect. *Journal of Personality and Social Psychology, 41*, 866–875.

Hetherington, E. M., & Baltes, P. B. (1988). Child psychology and lifespan development. In E. M. Hetherington, R. Lerner, & M. Perlmutter (Eds.), *Child development in life-span perspective* (pp. 1–20). Hillsdale, NJ: Erlbaum.

Higgins, E. T. (1996). Knowledge activation: Accessibility, applicability, and salience. In E. T. Higgins & A. W. Kruglanski (Eds.), *Social psychology; Handbook of basic principles* (pp. 133–168). New York: Guilford Press.

Hommel, B. (1998). Perceiving one's own action—and what it leads to. In J. S. Jordan (Ed.), *Systems theories and a priori aspects of perception* (pp. 143–179) Amsterdam: Elsevier Science.

Huber, J. E., Stathopoulus, E. T., Curione, G. M., Ash, T. A., & Johnson, K. (1999). Formants of children, women, and men: The effects of vocal intensity variation. *Journal of Acoustical Society of America, 106*, 1532–1542.

Jeannerod, M. (1997). *The cognitive neuroscience of action*. Malden, MA: Blackwell Publishers.

Kelley, H. H. (1952). Two functions of reference groups. In G. E. Swanson, T. M. Newcomb, & E. L. Hartley (Eds.), *Readings in social psychology* (pp. 410–414). New York: Holt.

Latané, B. (1996). Dynamic social impact: The creation of culture by communication. *Journal of Communication, 46*, 13–25.

Leff, H. L. (1978). *Experience, environment, and human potential*. New York: Oxford University Press.

Lieberman, D. A. (2000). *Learning: Behavior and cognition*. Belmont, CA: Wadsworth.

Macrae, C. N., & Bodenhausen (2000). Social cognition: Thinking categorically about others. *Annual Review of Psychology, 51*, 93–120.

Macrae, C. N., Bodenhausen, G. V., & Milne, A. B. (1995). The dissection of selection in person perception: Inhibitory processes in social stereotyping. *Journal of Personality and Social Psychology, 69*, 397–407.

Macrae, C. N., Bodenhausen, G. V., Milne, A. B., Thorn, T. M. J., Castelli, L., Schloerscheidt, A. M., & Greco, S. (1998). On activating exemplars. *Journal of Experimental Social Psychology, 34*, 330–354.

Macrae, C. N., Bodenhausen, G. V., Milne, A. B., Thorn, T. M. J., & Castelli, L. (1997). On the activation of social stereotypes: The moderating role of processing objectives. *Journal of Experimental Social Psychology, 33*, 471–489.

Miller, D. T., & Prentice, D. A. (1996). The construction of social norms and standards. In E. T. Higgins & A. W. Kruglanski (Eds.), *Social psychology; Handbook of basic principles* (pp. 799–829). New York: Guilford Press.

Neely, J. (1991). Semantic priming effects in visual word recognition: A selective review of current findings and theories. In D. Besner & G. Humpreys (Eds.), *Basic processes in reading: Visual word recognition* (pp. 264–336). Hillsdale, NJ: Erlbaum.

Ouellette, J., & Wood, W. (1998). Habit and intention in everyday life. The multiple processes by which past behavior predicts future behavior. *Psychological Bulletin, 124,* 54–74.

Paus, T., Petrides, M., Evans, A. C., & Meyer, E. (1993). Role of human anterior cingulate cortex in the control of oculomotor, manual and speech response: A positron emission tomography study. *Journal of Neurophysiology, 70,* 453–469.

Powers, W. T. (1973). *Behavior: The control of perception.* Chicago: Aldine.

Pepitone, A. (1976). Toward a normative and comparative biocultural social psychology. *Journal of Personality and Social Psychology, 34,* 641–653.

Reno, R. R., Cialdini, R. B., & Kallgren, C. A. (1993). The transituational influence of social norms. *Journal of Personality and Social Psychology, 64,* 104–112.

Salovey, P., & Birnbaum, D. (1989). Influence of mood on health-relevant cognitions. *Journal of Personality and Social Psychology, 57,* 539–551.

Schaalma, H. P., Kok, G. J., & Peters, L. (1993). Determinants of consistent condom use by adolescents: The impact of experience with sexual intercourse. *Health Education Research, 8,* 255–269.

Schank, R. C., & Abelson, R. P. (1977). *Scripts, plans, goals, and understanding.* Hillsdale, NJ: Erlbaum.

Schwartz, S. H., & Tessler, R. C. (1972). A test of a model for reducing attitude-behavior discrepancies. *Journal of Personality and Social Psychology, 24,* 225–236.

Sheeran, P., & Orbell, S. (1999). Augmenting the theory of planned behavior: Roles for anticipated regret and descriptive norms. *Journal of Applied Social Psychology, 29,* 2107–2142.

Sherif, M. (1936). *The psychology of social norms.* New York: Harper.

Sperber, D. (1990). The epidemiology of beliefs. In C. Fraser & G. Gaskell (Eds.), *The social psychological study of widespread beliefs* (pp. 25–44). New York: Clarendon Press/Oxford University Press.

Stangor, C., & Lange, J. E. (1994). Mental representations of social groups: Advances in understanding stereotypes and stereotyping. In M. P. Zanna (Ed.), *Advances in experimental social psychology* (Vol. 26, pp. 357–416). San Diego, CA: Academic Press.

Triandis, H. C. (1980). Values, attitudes, and interpersonal behavior. In H. E. Howe Jr. & M. Page (Eds.), *Nebraska Symposium on Motivation* (Vol. 27, pp. 195–259). Lincoln: University of Nebraska Press.

Zimbardo P. G., & Leippe, M. R. (1991). *The psychology of attitude change and social influence.* New York, NY: McGraw-Hill.

Zuckerman, M., & Reis, H. T. (1978). Comparisons of three models for predicting altruistic behavior. *Journal of Personality and Social Psychology, 46,* 498–528.

Questions for Review and Discussion

1. How do Aarts and Dijksterhuis propose that an environment can automatically direct normative behavior?
2. How do Aarts and Dijksterhuis define situational norms and how do they create them in Studies 1 and 2?
3. Who did Aarts and Dijksterhuis predict would be most likely to behave in a well-mannered way after being briefly exposed to a picture of a restaurant?

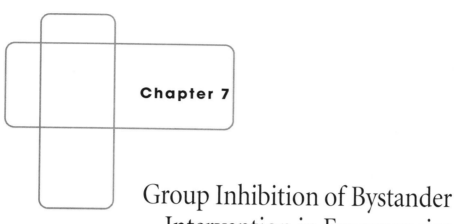

Chapter 7

Group Inhibition of Bystander Intervention in Emergencies

Bibb Latané and John M. Darley

Emergencies, fortunately, are uncommon events. Although the average person may read about them in newspapers or watch fictionalized versions on television, he probably will encounter fewer than half a dozen in his lifetime. Unfortunately, when he does encounter one, he will have had little direct personal experience in dealing with it. And he must deal with it under conditions of urgency, uncertainty, stress, and fear. About all the individual has to guide him is the secondhand wisdom of the late movie, which is often as useful as "Be brave" or as applicable as "Quick, get lots of hot water and towels!"

Under the circumstances, it may seem surprising that anybody ever intervenes in an emergency in which he is not directly involved. Yet there is a strongly held cultural norm that individuals should act to relieve the distress of others. As the Old Parson puts it, "In this life of froth and bubble, two things stand like stone—kindness in another's trouble, courage in your own." Given the conflict between the norm to act and an individual's fears and uncertainties about getting involved, what factors will determine whether a bystander to an emergency will intervene?

We have found (Darley & Latané, 1968) that the mere perception that other people are also witnessing the event will markedly decrease the likelihood that an individual will intervene in an emergency. Individuals heard

From *Journal of Personality and Social Psychology*, Vol. 10, No. 3, pp. 215–221. © 1968 by the American Psychological Association. Reproduced with permission.

a person undergoing a severe epileptic-like fit in another room. In one experimental condition, the subject thought that he was the only person who heard the emergency; in another condition, he thought four other persons were also aware of the seizure. Subjects alone with the victim were much more likely to intervene on his behalf, and, on the average, reacted in less than one-third the time required by subjects who thought there were other bystanders present.

"Diffusion of responsibility" seems the most likely explanation for this result. If an individual is alone when he notices an emergency, he is solely responsible for coping with it. If he believes others are also present, he may feel that his own responsibility for taking action is lessened, making him less likely to help.

To demonstrate that responsibility diffusion rather than any of a variety of social influence processes caused this result, the experiment was designed so that the onlookers to the seizure were isolated one from another and could not discuss how to deal with the emergency effectively. They knew the others could not see what they did, nor could they see whether somebody else had already started to help. Although this state of affairs is characteristic of many actual emergencies (such as the Kitty Genovese murder in which 38 people witnessed a killing from their individual apartments without acting), in many other emergencies several bystanders are in contact with and can influence each other. In these situations, processes other than responsibility diffusion will also operate.

Given the opportunity to interact, a group can talk over the situation and divide up the helping action in an efficient way. Also, since responding to emergencies is a socially prescribed norm, individuals might be expected to adhere to it more when in the presence of other people. These reasons suggest that interacting groups should be better at coping with emergencies than single individuals. We suspect, however, that the opposite is true. Even when allowed to communicate, groups may still be worse than individuals.

Most emergencies are, or at least begin as, ambiguous events. A quarrel in the street may erupt into violence, but it may be simply a family argument. A man staggering about may be suffering a coronary or an onset of diabetes; he may be simply drunk. Smoke pouring from a building may signal a fire; on the other hand, it may be simply steam or air-conditioning vapor. Before a bystander is likely to take action in such ambiguous situations, he must first define the event as an emergency and decide that intervention is the proper course of action.

In the course of making these decisions, it is likely that an individual bystander will be considerably influenced by the decisions he perceives other bystanders to be taking. If everyone else in a group of onlookers seems to regard an event as nonserious and the proper course of action as nonintervention, this consensus may strongly affect the perceptions of any single individual and inhibit his potential intervention.

The definitions that other people hold may be discovered by discussing the situation with them, but they may also be inferred from their facial expressions or their behavior. A whistling man with his hands in his pockets obviously does not believe he is in the midst of a crisis. A bystander who does not respond to smoke obviously does not attribute it to fire. An individual, seeing the inaction of others, will judge the situation as less serious than he would if he were alone.

In the present experiment, this line of thought will be tested by presenting an emergency situation to individuals either alone or in the presence of two passive others, confederates of the experimenter who have been instructed to notice the emergency but remain indifferent to it. It is our expectation that this passive behavior will signal the individual that the other bystanders do not consider the situation to be dangerous. We predict that an individual faced with the passive reactions of other people will be influenced by them, and will thus be less likely to take action than if he were alone.

This, however, is a prediction about individuals; it says nothing about the original question of the behavior of freely interacting groups. Most groups do not have preinstructed confederates among their members, and the kind of social influence process described above would, by itself, only lead to a convergence of attitudes within a group. Even if each member of the group is entirely guided by the reactions of others, then the group should still respond with a likelihood equal to the average of the individuals.

An additional factor is involved, however. Each member of a group may watch the others, but he is also aware that the others are watching him. They are an audience to his own reactions. Among American males it is considered desirable to appear poised and collected in times of stress. Being exposed to public view may constrain an individual's actions as he attempts to avoid possible ridicule and embarrassment.

The constraints involved with being in public might in themselves tend to inhibit action by individuals in a group, but in conjunction with the social influence process described above, they may be expected to have even more powerful effects. If each member of a group is, at the same time, trying to appear calm and also looking around at the other members to gauge their reactions, all members may be led (or misled) by each other to define the situation as less critical than they would if alone. Until someone acts, each person only sees other nonresponding bystanders, and, as with the passive confederates, is likely to be influenced not to act himself.

This leads to a second prediction. Compared to the performance of individuals, if we expose groups of naive subjects to an emergency, the constraints on behavior in public coupled with the social influence process will lessen the likelihood that the members of the group will act to cope with the emergency.

It has often been recognized (Brown, 1954, 1965) that a crowd can cause contagion of panic, leading each person in the crowd to overreact to an emergency to the detriment of everyone's welfare. What is implied here is that a crowd can also force inaction on its members. It can suggest, implicitly but strongly, by its passive behavior, that an event is not to be reacted to as an emergency, and it can make any individual uncomfortably aware of what a fool he will look for behaving as if it is.

Method

The subject, seated in a small waiting room, faced an ambiguous but potentially dangerous situation as a stream of smoke began to puff into the room through a wall vent. His response to this situation was observed through a one-way glass. The length of time the subject remained in the room before leaving to report the smoke was the main dependent variable of the study.

Recruitment of subjects.   Male Columbia students living in campus residences were invited to an interview to discuss "some of the problems involved in life at an urban university." The subject sample included graduate and professional students as well as undergraduates. Individuals were contacted by telephone and most willingly volunteered and actually showed up for the interview. At this point, they were directed either by signs or by the secretary to a "waiting room" where a sign asked them to fill out a preliminary questionnaire.

Experimental manipulation.   Some subjects filled out the questionnaire and were exposed to the potentially critical situation while alone. Others were part of three-person groups consisting of one subject and two confederates acting the part of naive subjects. The confederates attempted to avoid conversation as much as possible. Once the smoke had been introduced, they stared at it briefly, made no comment, but simply shrugged their shoulders, returned to the questionnaires and continued to fill them out, occasionally waving away the smoke to do so. If addressed, they attempted to be as uncommunicative as possible and to show apparent indifference to the smoke. "I dunno," they said, and no subject persisted in talking.

In a final condition, three naive subjects were tested together. In general, these subjects did not know each other, although in two groups, subjects reported a nodding acquaintanceship with another subject. Since subjects arrived at slightly different times and since they each had individual questionnaires to work on, they did not introduce themselves to each other, or attempt anything but the most rudimentary conversation.

Critical situation. As soon as the subjects had completed two pages of their questionnaires, the experimenter began to introduce the smoke through a small vent in the wall. The "smoke" was finely divided titanium dioxide produced in a stoppered bottle and delivered under slight air pressure through the vent.[1] It formed a moderately fine-textured but clearly visible stream of whitish smoke. For the entire experimental period, the smoke continued to jet into the room in irregular puffs. By the end of the experimental period, vision was obscured by the amount of smoke present.

All behavior and conversation was observed and coded from behind a one-way window (largely disguised on the subject's side by a large sign giving preliminary instructions). If the subject left the experimental room and reported the smoke, he was told that the situation "would be taken care of." If the subject had not reported the presence of smoke by 6 minutes from the time he first noticed it, the experiment was terminated.

Results

Alone condition. The typical subject, when tested alone, behaved very reasonably. Usually, shortly after the smoke appeared, he would glance up from his questionnaire, notice the smoke, show a slight but distinct startle reaction, and then undergo a brief period of indecision, perhaps returning briefly to his questionnaire before again staring at the smoke. Soon, most subjects would get up from their chairs, walk over to the vent, and investigate it closely, sniffing the smoke, waving their hands in it, feeling its temperature, etc. The usual alone subject would hesitate again, but finally walk out of the room, look around outside, and, finding somebody there, calmly report the presence of the smoke. No subject showed any sign of panic; most simply said, "There's something strange going on in there, there seems to be some sort of smoke coming through the wall. . . ."

The median subject in the alone condition had reported the smoke within 2 minutes of first noticing it. Three-quarters of the 24 people who were run in this condition reported the smoke before the experimental period was terminated.

Two passive confederates condition. The behavior of subjects run with two passive confederates was dramatically different; of 10 people run in this condition, only 1 reported the smoke. The other 9 stayed in the waiting room as it filled up with smoke, doggedly working on their questionnaire and waving the fumes away from their faces. They coughed, rubbed their eyes, and opened the window—but they did not report the smoke. The difference between the response rate of 75% in the alone condition and 10% in the two passive confederates condition is highly significant ($p < .002$ by Fisher's exact test, two-tailed).

Three naive bystanders.   Because there are three subjects present and available to report the smoke in the three naive bystander condition as compared to only one subject at a time in the alone condition, a simple comparison between the two conditions is not appropriate. On the one hand, we cannot compare speeds in the alone condition with the average speed of the three subjects in a group, since, once one subject in a group had reported the smoke, the pressures on the other two disappeared. They legitimately could (and did) feel that the emergency had been handled, and any action on their part would be redundant and potentially confusing. Therefore the speed of the *first* subject in a group to report the smoke was used as the dependent variable. However, since there were three times as many people available to respond in this condition as in the alone condition, we would expect an increased likelihood that *at least* one person would report the smoke even if the subjects had no influence whatsoever on each other. Therefore we mathematically created "groups" of three scores from the alone condition to serve as a base line.[2]

In contrast to the complexity of this procedure, the results were quite simple. Subjects in the three naive bystander condition were markedly inhibited from reporting the smoke. Since 75% of the alone subjects reported the smoke, we would expect over 98% of the three-person groups to contain at least one reporter. In fact, in only 38% of the eight groups in this condition did even 1 subject report ($p < .01$). Of the 24 people run in these eight groups, only 1 person reported the smoke within the first 4 minutes before the room got noticeably unpleasant. Only 3 people reported the smoke within the entire experimental period.

Cumulative distribution of report times.   Figure 1 presents the cumulative frequency distributions of report times for all three conditions. The figure shows the proportion of subjects in each condition who had reported the smoke by any point in the time following the introduction of the smoke. For example, 55% of the subjects in the alone condition had reported the smoke within 2 minutes, but the smoke had been reported in only 12% of the three-person groups by that time. After 4 minutes, 75% of the subjects in the alone condition had reported the smoke; no additional subjects in the group condition had done so. The curve

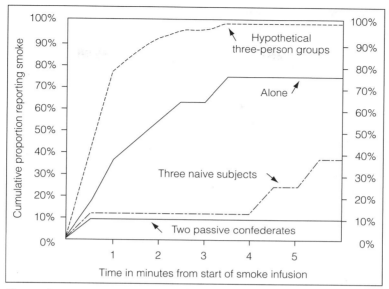

Figure 1 ▪ Cumulative proportion of subjects reporting the smoke over time.

in Figure 1 labeled "Hypothetical Three-Person Groups" is based upon the mathematical combination of scores obtained from subjects in the alone condition. It is the expected report times for groups in the three-person condition if the members of the groups had no influence upon each other.

It can be seen in Figure 1 that for every point in time following the introduction of the smoke, a considerably higher proportion of subjects in the alone condition had reported the smoke than had subjects in either the two passive confederates condition or in the three naive subjects condition. The curve for the latter condition, although considerably below the alone curve, is even more substantially inhibited with respect to its proper comparison, the curve of hypothetical three-person sets. Social inhibition of response was so great that the time elapsing before the smoke was reported was greater when there were more people available to report it (alone versus group $p < .05$ by Mann-Whitney U test).

Superficially, it appears that there is a somewhat higher likelihood of response from groups of three naive subjects than from subjects in the passive confederates condition. Again this comparison is not justified; there are three people free to act in one condition instead of just one. If we mathematically combine scores for subjects in the two passive confederates condition in a similar manner to that described above for the alone condition, we would obtain an expected likelihood of response of .27 as the hypothetical base line. This is not significantly different from the .37 obtained in the actual three-subject groups.

Noticing the smoke.   In observing the subject's reaction to the introduction of smoke, careful note was taken of the exact moment when he first saw the smoke (all report latencies were computed from this time). This was a relatively easy observation to make, for the subjects invariably showed a distinct, if slight, startle reaction. Unexpectedly, the presence of other persons delayed, slightly but very significantly, noticing the smoke. Sixty-three percent of subjects in the alone condition and only 26% of subjects in the combined together conditions noticed the smoke within the first 5 seconds after its introduction ($p < .01$ by chi-square). The median latency of noticing the smoke was under 5 seconds in the alone condition; the median time at which the first (or only) subject in each of the combined together conditions noticed the smoke was 20 seconds (this difference does not account for group-induced inhibition of reporting since the report latencies were computed from the time the smoke was first noticed).

This interesting finding can probably be explained in terms of the constraints which people feel in public places (Goffman, 1963). Unlike solitary subjects, who often glanced idly about the room while filling out their questionnaires, subjects in groups usually kept their eyes closely on their work, probably to avoid appearing rudely inquisitive.

Postexperimental interview.   After 6 minutes, whether or not the subjects had reported the smoke, the interviewer stuck his head in the waiting room and asked the subject to come with him to the interview. After seating the subject in his office, the interviewer made some general apologies about keeping the subject waiting for so long, hoped the subject hadn't become too bored and asked if he "had experienced any difficulty while filling out the questionnaire." By this point most subjects mentioned the smoke. The interviewer expressed mild surprise and asked the subject to tell him what had happened. Thus each subject gave an account of what had gone through his mind during the smoke infusion.

Subjects who had reported the smoke were relatively consistent in later describing their reactions to it. They thought the smoke looked somewhat "strange," they were not sure exactly what it was or whether it was dangerous, but they felt it was unusual enough to justify some examination. "I wasn't sure whether it was a fire but it looked like something was wrong." "I thought it might be steam, but it seemed like a good idea to check it out."

Subjects who had not reported the smoke also were unsure about exactly what it was, but they uniformly said that they had rejected the idea that it was a fire. Instead, they hit upon an astonishing variety of alternative explanations, all sharing the common characteristic of interpreting the smoke as a nondangerous event. Many thought the smoke was either steam or air-conditioning vapors, several thought it was smog, purposely introduced to simulate an urban environment, and two (from different groups) actually suggested that the smoke was a "truth gas" filtered into the room to induce them to answer the questionnaire accurately. (Surprisingly, they were not disturbed by this conviction.) Predictably, some decided that "it must be some sort of experiment" and stoically endured the discomfort of the room rather than overreact.

Despite the obvious and powerful report-inhibiting effect of other bystanders, subjects almost invariably claimed that they had paid little or no attention to the reactions of the other people in the room. Although the presence of other people actually had a strong and pervasive effect on the subjects' reactions, they were either unaware of this or unwilling to admit it.

Discussion

Before an individual can decide to intervene in an emergency, he must, implicitly or explicitly, take several preliminary steps. If he is to intervene, he must first *notice* the event, he must then *interpret* it as an emergency, and he must decide that it is his personal *responsibility* to act. At each of these preliminary steps, the bystander to an emergency can remove himself from the decision process and thus fail to help. He can fail to notice the event, he can fail to interpret it as an emergency, or he can fail to assume the responsibility to take action.

In the present experiment we are primarily interested in the second step of this decision process, interpreting an ambiguous event. When faced with such an event, we suggest, the individual bystander is likely to look at the reactions of people around him and be powerfully influenced by them. It was predicted that the sight of other, nonresponsive bystanders would lead the individual to interpret the emergency as not serious, and consequently lead him not to act. Further, it was predicted that the dynamics of the interaction process would lead each of a group of naive onlookers to be misled by the apparent inaction of the others into adopting a nonemergency interpretation of the event and a passive role.

The results of this study clearly support our predictions. Individuals exposed to a room filling with smoke in the presence of passive others themselves remained passive, and groups of three naive subjects were less likely to report the smoke than solitary bystanders. Our predictions were confirmed—but this does not necessarily mean that our explanation for these results is the correct one. As a matter of fact, several alternatives are available.

Two of these alternative explanations stem from the fact that the smoke represented a possible danger to the subject himself as well as to others in the building. Subjects' behavior might have reflected their fear of fire, with subjects in groups feeling less threatened by the fire than single subjects and thus being less concerned to act. It has been demonstrated in studies with humans (Schachter, 1959) and with rats (Latané, 1968; Latané & Glass, 1968) that togetherness reduces fear, even in situations where it does not reduce danger. In addition, subjects may have felt that the presence of others increased their ability to cope with fire. For both of these reasons, subjects in groups may have been less afraid of fire and thus less likely to report the smoke than solitary subjects.

A similar explanation might emphasize not fearfulness, but the desire to hide fear. To the extent that bravery or stoicism in the face of danger or discomfort is a socially desirable trait (as it appears to be for American male undergraduates), one might expect individuals to attempt to appear more brave or more stoic when others are watching than when they are alone. It is possible that subjects in the group condition saw themselves as engaged in a game of "Chicken," and thus did not react.

Although both of these explanations are plausible, we do not think that they provide an accurate account of subjects' thinking. In the postexperimental interviews, subjects claimed, *not* that they were unworried by the fire or that they were unwilling to endure the danger; but rather that they decided that there was no fire at all and the smoke was caused by something else. They failed to act because they thought there was no reason to act. Their "apathetic" behavior was reasonable—given their interpretation of the circumstances.

The fact that smoke signals potential danger to the subject himself weakens another alternative explanation, "diffusion of responsibility." Regardless of social influence processes, an individual may feel less personal responsibility for helping if he shares the responsibility with others (Darley & Latané, 1968). But this diffusion explanation does not fit the present situation. It is hard to see how an individual's responsibility for saving himself is diffused by the presence of other people. The diffusion explanation does not account for the pattern of interpretations reported by the subjects or for their variety of nonemergency explanations.

On the other hand, the social influence processes which we believe account for the results of our present study obviously do not explain our previous experiment in which subjects could not see or be seen by each other. Taken together, these two studies suggest that the presence of bystanders may affect an individual in several ways; including both "social influence" and "diffusion of responsibility."

Both studies, however, find, for two quite different kinds of emergencies and under two quite different conditions of social contact, that individuals are less likely to engage in socially responsible action if they think other bystanders are present. This presents us with the paradoxical conclusion that a victim may be more likely to get help, or an emergency may be more likely to be reported, the fewer people there are available to take action. It also may help us begin to understand a number of frightening incidents where crowds have listened to but not answered a call for help. Newspapers have tagged these incidents with the label "apathy." We have become indifferent, they say, callous to the fate of suffering others. The results of our studies lead to a different conclusion. The failure to intervene may be better understood by knowing the relationship among bystanders rather than that between a bystander and the victim.

Notes

1. Smoke was produced by passing moisturized air, under pressure, through a container of titanium tetrachloride, which, in reaction with the water vapor, creates a suspension of [titanium] dioxide in air.

2. The formula for calculating the expected proportion of groups in which at least one person will have acted by a given time is $1 - (1 - p)^n$ where p is the proportion of single individuals who act by that time and n is the number of persons in the group.

References

Brown, R. W. Mass phenomena. In G. Lindzey (Ed.), *Handbook of social psychology.* Vol. 2. Cambridge: Addison-Wesley, 1954.

Brown, R. *Social psychology.* New York: Free Press of Glencoe, 1965.

Darley, J. M., & Latané, B. Bystander intervention in emergencies: Diffusion of responsibility. *Journal of Personality and Social Psychology,* 1968, 8, 377–383.

Goffman, E. *Behavior in public places.* New York: Free Press of Glencoe, 1963.

Latané, B. Gregariousness and fear in laboratory rats. *Journal of Experimental Social Psychology*, 1968, in press.

Latané, B., & Glass, D. C. Social and nonsocial attraction in rats. *Journal of Personality and Social Psychology*, 1968, 9, 142–146.

Schachter, S. *The psychology of affiliation*. Stanford: Stanford University Press, 1959.

Questions for Review and Discussion

1. Why did Latané and Darley predict that groups of individuals would be less likely than solitary individuals to respond to potential emergencies involving themselves?

2. How critical do you think it was to the results that the participants were actively engaged in a task (completing a survey) when the smoke started to appear?

3. What did the post-experimental interview reveal about the thought processes of those who did not report the smoke in the group condition?

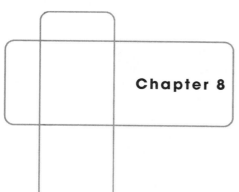

Chapter 8

Pluralistic Ignorance
and Alcohol Use on Campus:
Some Consequences
of Misperceiving the Social Norm

Deborah A. Prentice and Dale T. Miller

Few issues have fascinated social psychologists as much or for as long as the relation between private attitudes and social norms. Conventional wisdom has it that when individuals perceive their attitudes to be different from the normative attitudes of their social group, they will experience discomfort and will resolve the discrepancy, usually by changing their attitudes in the direction of the norm. This analysis rests on an assumption that has gone largely unexamined by social psychologists: that people can accurately identify the social norm. In this article, we report four studies that challenge the generality of this assumption and document the consequences of its violation.

Although social influence has been a major topic of research for the past century (see Moscovici, 1985; Turner, 1991), the question of how people identify the social norm has scarcely arisen. Laboratory investigators have typically created situations in which the norm either is formed by subjects as part of the experimental task or is given unambiguously by the experimental procedure. For example, subjects in Sherif's (1936) autokinetic experiments were in

From *Journal of Personality and Social Psychology*, Vol. 64, No. 2, pp. 243–256. Copyright © 1993 by the American Psychological Association. Reproduced with permission.

a situation in which no norm existed. As part of the judgment task, they jointly (or individually) developed perceptual norms. Subjects in Asch's (1951) conformity studies, on the other hand, were in a situation with a strong and unambiguous norm: They were asked to give a judgment after hearing numerous "other subjects" give the same (objectively incorrect) answer. Sherif's subjects were free to negotiate the norm; Asch's subjects were provided with a clear, consensual group norm. In neither of these prototypical cases was it the subject's task to identify a preexisting norm.

Field research on social influence might logically be expected to have more to say about how people identify the social norm. However, most field studies have focused primarily on the effects of norms to the exclusion of considerations about how people locate those norms. For example, in Newcomb's (1943) study of attitude change among students at Bennington College, the fact that the prevailing norms of the college were liberal was presented as an unambiguous property of the social context. Presumably, the newcomer to Bennington found enough evidence of liberal views in the outward behavior of the residents to ascertain that these views were, in fact, the norm. Similarly, Festinger, Schachter, and Back's (1950) investigation of pressures toward uniformity in the Westgate and Westgate West housing projects examined adherence to prevailing norms without providing any evidence of how those norms were established or communicated. More recent investigations have shown a similar tendency to focus on the effects, rather than on the identification, of norms (e.g., Cialdini, Kallgren, & Reno, 1991; Crandall, 1988).

Despite the dearth of direct evidence regarding how people identify existing norms, the classic influence studies do suggest two general properties of norms that determine how they are perceived and communicated. First, social norms are defined by people's public behavior. The negotiated reality of Sherif's subjects, the public judgments of Asch's confederates, the liberal views expressed by Bennington students, and the attitudes expressed by the residents of Westgate and Westgate West all were public statements that defined the social norm. To the extent that public statements accurately reflect the private attitudes and judgments of their proponents, the subjective norm that they instantiate will coincide with the actual norm of the group. To the extent that they misrepresent people's private views, the subjective norm will diverge from the actual norm.

In addition to their public nature, norms are imbued with an impression of universality: People assume that all members of a group endorse that group's social norms (Allport, 1924), and, in turn, the power of norms to affect an individual's attitudes and behavior is heavily dependent on their perceived universality. As consensus (or the appearance of consensus) breaks down, the norm loses its influence. The Asch (1951) studies provide clear evidence of the importance of universality: When just one confederate deviated from the normative response (even by giving an alternative wrong answer), conformity dropped to nearly zero.

Pluralistic Ignorance

Although the social psychological literature offers little evidence of how people identify social norms, it does provide some striking examples of systematic errors in norm estimation. Many of these examples come from research on pluralistic ignorance. *Pluralistic ignorance* is a psychological state characterized by the belief that one's private attitudes and judgments are different from those of others, even though one's public behavior is identical (Miller & McFarland, 1991). It develops most commonly under circumstances in which there is widespread misrepresentation of private views. In these cases, people's tendency to rely on the public behavior of others to identify the norm leads them astray, for the social norm that is communicated misrepresents the prevailing sentiments of the group. If participants understood this state of affairs, the situation would be self-correcting. However, they typically make the mistake of assuming that even though others are acting similarly, they are feeling differently. Their own behavior may be driven by social pressure, but they assume that other people's identical behavior is an accurate reflection of their true feelings.

Although many studies have demonstrated pluralistic ignorance, both in and out of the laboratory (see, e.g., Breed & Ktsanes, 1961; Miller & McFarland, 1987; O'Gorman, 1975; Packard & Willower, 1972; Schanck, 1932), little research has addressed the question of how victims of pluralistic ignorance respond to the perceived discrepancy between their private attitudes and the social norm. These individuals have several strategies available to them for reducing the discrepancy: They can move their private attitudes closer to the (perceived) norm, bring the norm closer to their attitudes, or reject the group altogether. Given that the last two of these options will often appear too costly or too difficult to effect, at least in the short run, the simplest way for individuals to eliminate the discrepancy is to change their private attitudes. This internalization of the norm will most often occur in situations in which private attitudes or judgments are not well established (see Kelman, 1958). One such situation is the classic case of the unresponsive bystander. In seeking to explain why bystanders fail to help a victim of an emergency, Latané and Darley (1970) suggested that pluralistic ignorance is at the root of this inaction. They argued that individual bystanders fail to act because they are unsure about the seriousness of the situation; however, these same bystanders often assume that the inaction of others reflects a high degree of confidence that the situation is not serious. In this case, pluralistic ignorance is easily resolved through internalization of the social norm: Bystanders will adopt a consensual (if erroneous) definition of the situation as a nonemergency.

In other cases of pluralistic ignorance, private attitudes and judgments are well established; here, individuals will be unable to internalize the normative position. One such case is a classroom dynamic investigated by Miller and McFarland (1987, 1991). The situation is as follows: A professor who has just presented difficult material will typically ask students if they have any questions. This request for students to acknowledge their confusion often fails to elicit a response, even though confusion is widespread. The students' inaction is driven by pluralistic ignorance: Individual students are inhibited from raising their hands out of fear of asking a stupid question, but they interpret their classmates' identical behavior as an indication that everyone else understands the material. In this situation, pluralistic ignorance will not be resolved by students deciding that they actually do understand the material. They have ample and irrefutable evidence that they do not understand it. Instead, pluralistic ignorance will likely persist, leaving students feeling deviant and alienated from each other.

The research reported in this article was designed to explore these consequences of pluralistic ignorance. In all four studies, we examined pluralistic ignorance in the context of students' attitudes toward alcohol drinking on campus. We chose this particular issue because attitudes toward drinking are currently in a period of transition at Princeton, as the university becomes more sensitive to the negative effects of alcohol use on academic and social life. Many theorists have argued that pluralistic ignorance frequently accompanies such periods of social change, with private attitudes changing more quickly than social norms (see Breed & Ktsanes, 1961; Fields & Schuman, 1976; Miller & McFarland, 1991). Thus, we expected the issue of alcohol use to provide an excellent context for our empirical studies.

Alcohol Use on Campus

Alcohol use by college undergraduates has become a major concern of university administrators and public health officials across the country (Berkowitz & Perkins, 1986; Maddox, 1970; Straus & Bacon, 1953). A recent survey revealed that whereas the use of other recreational drugs has dropped significantly over the past 2 decades, alcohol use has declined more slowly (Barringer, 1991). According to the College Health Association, alcohol is the single greatest risk to the health of university students. One powerful predictor of adolescent alcohol use, and of other forms of substance use, is peer influence (e.g., Graham, Marks, & Hansen, 1991; Kandel, 1980; Perkins, 1985; Stein, Newcomb, & Bentler, 1987). Moreover, the impact of peers appears to increase, rather than decrease, as adolescents mature (Huba & Bentler, 1980; Zucker & Noll, 1982).

The alcohol situation at Princeton is exacerbated by the central role of alcohol in many of the university's institutions and traditions. For example, at the eating clubs, the center of social life on campus, alcohol is on tap 24 hours a day, 7 days a week. Princeton reunions boast the second highest level of alcohol consumption for any event in the country after the Indianapolis 500 (Clitherow, 1991). The social norms for drinking at the university are clear: Students must be comfortable with alcohol use to partake of Princeton social life.

In the face of these strong norms promoting alcohol use, we suspected that students' private attitudes would reveal substantial misgivings about drinking. Within their first few months at college, students are exposed to vivid and irrefutable evidence of the negative consequences of excessive alcohol consumption: They nurse sick roommates, overlook inappropriate behavior and memory losses, and hear about serious injuries and even deaths that result from drinking. They may have negative experiences with alcohol themselves and may notice its effects on their academic performance. This accumulating evidence of the ill effects of alcohol is likely to affect their private attitudes but not the social norm: Indeed, believing that others are still comfortable with alcohol, students will perpetuate that norm by continuing to adopt a nonchalant demeanor that masks their growing concerns. If this analysis is, in fact, correct, we should find clear evidence of pluralistic ignorance regarding students' comfort with alcohol use on campus.

The present studies sought to document the existence of pluralistic ignorance regarding alcohol use and to investigate some of its consequences for individuals' attitudes and behavior. Study 1 was designed to demonstrate pluralistic ignorance by showing a divergence between private attitudes and the social norm as well as a belief in the university of that norm. Study 2 extended this effect by showing a similar divergence between private attitudes and perceptions of the attitudes of one's friends. Study 3 explored the extent to which individuals respond to pluralistic ignorance by internalizing the social norm over time. Study 4 examined the behavioral manifestations of alienation produced by feeling deviant from the norm. The first three studies focused on comfort with alcohol use; the fourth study examined attitudes toward the university's policy banning beer kegs on campus.

Study 1

In our first study, we tested the assumption that students' attitudes toward alcohol drinking on campus are characterized by a divergence between private attitudes and perceptions of the social norm. We also examined the extent to which social norms are imbued with an illusion of universality by asking subjects to estimate the variability, as well as the central tendency, of other students' attitudes.

Method

Subjects.   Subjects were 132 undergraduates, who voluntarily attended a mass testing session in which they participated in this and other short studies for pay. The sample included 69 women and 63 men, with approximately even distribution of women and men across the 1st- through 4th-year classes.[1]

Procedure.   Subjects responded to a brief, one-page questionnaire that was included in a large booklet. The questionnaire was preceded by a page of instructions on how to use the response scales. The first question asked the following:

1.   How comfortable do you feel with the alcohol drinking habits of students at Princeton?

Subjects indicated their own comfort by circling a number on the corresponding 11-point scale (1 = *not at all comfortable* and 11 = *very comfortable*). Then they were asked to estimate the comfort of other students:

2.   How comfortable does the average Princeton undergraduate feel with the alcohol drinking habits of students at Princeton? (Please circle the average student's response and then bracket the two values between which the attitudes of 50% of students fall.)

Again, subjects indicated the average student's comfort by circling a number on the corresponding 11-point scale and then bracketed the two numbers on the same scale within which they believed the attitudes of 50% of students fall.

Results and Discussion

We expected that students would vary in their own comfort with alcohol drinking on campus but that they would believe other students to be uniformly more comfortable than they are. Means and standard deviations for the two comfort questions are presented in Table 1. Subjects' ratings indicated a sharp divergence between their own comfort and their subjective estimates of the comfort of others. A 2 (sex) × 2 (target) analysis of variance (ANOVA) revealed a highly

	TABLE 1	
Ratings of Own and Average Student's Comfort with Alcohol Drinking in Study 1		
Measure	Self	Average student
Women		
M	4.68	7.07
SD	2.69	1.68
Men		
M	6.03	7.00
SD	2.76	1.57
Total		
M	5.33	7.04
SD	2.73	1.63

Note.   All ratings were made on 11-point scales (1 = not at all comfortable and 11 = very comfortable).

significant main effect of target, $F(1, 130) = 55.52$, $p < .0001$: Respondents were much less comfortable with the alcohol drinking habits of Princeton undergraduates than they believed the average student to be. This main effect of target was qualified by a significant Sex × Target interaction, $F(1, 130) = 9.96$, $p < .005$, indicating that the gap between ratings of own and others' comfort was substantially larger for women than for men. Nevertheless, the self-other difference was significant for both male, $F(1, 62) = 10.35$, $p < .005$, and female subjects, $F(1, 68) = 51.95$, $p < .0001$.

A closer analysis of the distributions of comfort ratings indicated that students' perceptions of the attitudes of others converged on a highly consistent norm. Although their own comfort ratings spanned the entire 11-point scale in a relatively uniform distribution, their estimates of the average student's comfort assumed an almost perfectly normal distribution, with high agreement on an average of approximately 7. A statistical comparison of the variances of the two distributions revealed a highly significant difference, $F(131, 131) = 2.99$, $p < .0001$.

In addition, subjects' estimates of the variability of others' attitudes provided strong evidence for the illusion of universality. The median estimate of the range within which the attitudes of 50% of students fell (i.e., the interquartile range) was 4, with a lower bound of 5 and an upper bound of 9. (We use medians here to facilitate comparison with the actual distribution. The means are very close to the medians in all cases.) Thus, students' subjective distributions of attitudes toward drinking on campus had a mean of approximately 7, with an interquartile range from 5 to 9. By contrast, the actual distribution of attitudes, as reflected by subjects' own comfort ratings, had a mean of 5.33, with an interquartile range from 3 to 8. These distributions demonstrate the two defining features of pluralistic ignorance: A divergence of subjective from actual norms and an illusion of universality.

Study 2

The results of Study 1 provided strong support for our expectation that students' attitudes toward campus alcohol practices would be characterized by pluralistic ignorance. However, two methodological features of the study allowed for alternative interpretations of the results. First, our question about the social norm asked students to rate the comfort of the average Princeton undergraduate with alcohol drinking on campus. Although we believed that ratings of the average student would provide a good indication of the perceived norm, it is also possible that the category "average student" lacked psychological reality for our subjects. Second, we asked the two comfort questions in a fixed order, with the question about the self always preceding the question about the average student. It is possible that subjects rated the average student as more comfortable simply because they made that rating second.

To preclude these alternative explanations for the findings of Study 1, we conducted a second study, in which we manipulated the order of the self and other questions and included an additional question that assessed the comfort of the respondent's friends with alcohol drinking on campus. Unlike ratings of the average student, ratings of friends were certain to be made with a group of real people in mind.

Method

Subjects.   Subjects were 242 undergraduates, who voluntarily attended a mass testing session in which they filled out this and other questionnaires for pay. The sample included 145 women and 97 men, with an approximately even distribution of women and men across the 1st- through 4th-year classes.

Procedure.   Subjects answered the two questions asked in Study 1 (minus the variability estimates) and a third question that asked them to rate how comfortable their friends feel with the alcohol drinking habits of students at Princeton. Half of the subjects (77 women and 44 men) rated themselves first and the average student second; the other half (68 women and 53 men) rated the average student first and themselves second.

TABLE 2			
Ratings of Own and Others' Comfort with Alcohol Drinking in Study 2			
Measure	Self	Friend	Average student
Self-question first Women			
M	5.84	6.49	6.96
SD	2.69	2.42	1.41
Men			
M	6.02	6.82	7.11
SD	2.66	2.12	1.20
Total			
M	5.91	6.61	7.01
SD	2.68	2.32	1.34
Other-question first Women			
M	5.06	6.13	7.16
SD	2.47	2.34	1.72
Men			
M	5.87	6.94	7.47
SD	2.54	2.12	1.37
Total			
M	5.41	6.49	7.30
SD	2.50	2.24	1.57

Note. All ratings were made on 11-point scales (1 = *not at all comfortable* and 11 = *very comfortable*).

Results and Discussion

Means and standard deviations for the three comfort questions are shown in Table 2. A 2 (sex) $\times$ 3 (target) $\times$ 2 (question order) ANOVA revealed a highly significant effect of target, $F(2, 476) = 54.52$, $p < .0001$. Pairwise comparisons of the three means indicated that ratings of own comfort were significantly lower than ratings of friends' comfort or of the average student's comfort (using Tukey tests, with $p < .05$). The main effect of target was qualified by a significant

Target × Order interaction, $F(2, 476) = 3.45$, $p < .05$, indicating that the differences between comfort ratings for the three targets were greater when the question about the average student came first. However, separate pairwise comparisons within each form of the questionnaire showed that ratings of own comfort were significantly lower than ratings of the other two targets for both question orders. Friends' comfort was rated as intermediate between own comfort and the average student's comfort in all cases, but the difference between ratings of friends and of the average student was significant only when the average student question came first (for all reported differences, $p < .05$).

Students' perceptions of the comfort of the average student again converged on a highly consistent norm. Ratings of the average student were significantly less variable than ratings of the self, $F(241, 241) = 3.14$, $p < .0001$, and of friends, $F(241, 241) = 2.46$, $p < .0001$. Not surprisingly, ratings of friends' comfort showed considerable variability across subjects, although still not quite as much variability as self-ratings.

These results, especially concerning perceptions of friends, raise some interesting questions about the relation between local (friend) and global (campus) norms and about the role of these norms in producing pluralistic ignorance. In the case of alcohol use on campus, both types of norms are on the side of greater comfort with alcohol than students privately feel, and thus it is difficult to disentangle them. In theory, however, local and global norms may be quite distinct and may contribute independently to producing the perceived self–other differences. Misestimation of the local norm may occur because, as in the bystander and classroom cases, students base their estimates on observations of their friends' public behavior and erroneously assume that that behavior is diagnostic of their private attitudes. Misestimation of the global norm may be driven, in part, by a similar process but may also be influenced by the collective representation of Princeton as a drinking campus and by the importance of a liberal position on alcohol to the college student identity. We return to a consideration of the mechanisms underlying pluralistic ignorance in the general discussion.

In summary, the results of Studies 1 and 2 confirmed our intuition that students' comfort with alcohol use on campus would manifest the classic characteristics of pluralistic ignorance. Although the subjects in these studies were volunteers and thus may not have been representative of the student body (a weakness we remedy in the next study), we believe that the phenomenon demonstrated here is quite general: Undergraduates believe that everybody is more comfortable with drinking than they are themselves (see also Perkins & Berkowitz, 1986). The situation of drinking on campus shares much in common with the classic examples of pluralistic ignorance cited in the introduction. In all cases, individuals assume that others' outward display of comfort and ease reflects their actual feelings, even though those individuals' own identical behavior is somewhat at odds with their internal states.

Study 3

Armed with evidence for the validity of our assumptions about the alcohol issue, we designed the next two studies to explore some of the consequences of pluralistic ignorance. Study 3 addressed the question of how individuals respond to pluralistic ignorance over time. One prediction is that when individuals perceive their attitudes to be different from the normative attitudes of their social group, they will gradually change their attitudes in the direction of the group norm, either because they are persuaded by the group's position or because they internalize the sentiments that they originally expressed inauthentically. This conformity prediction has considerable precedent in the social influence literature, which has always placed a heavy emphasis on conformity as a means of resolving self–group discrepancies (see Moscovici, 1985). However, in the case of alcohol use on campus, the presence of irrefutable evidence of the ill effects of excessive drinking might make it very difficult for students to decide that they are, in fact, comfortable with the drinking norms. If students are unable to internalize the (perceived) normative position, we should observe no reduction in pluralistic ignorance over time.

To examine the extent to which students would change their attitudes to reduce pluralistic ignorance, we surveyed a random sample of college sophomores at two time points: Initially, in September, when they had just returned from summer vacation and had had little recent exposure to college drinking norms, and then again in December, after they had spent several months as active members of the college community. We assumed that 8 to 9 weeks between interviews would be sufficient to observe internalization effects, if such effects existed. In addition, we asked two questions to assess their recent and typical levels of alcohol consumption. Although we expected no gross changes in drinking habits over the course of the semester, we were interested in the relation of drinking behavior to both private attitudes and estimates of the norm. These behavioral questions were included in both interviews.

We tested for internalization effects in two ways. Our first expectation was that students would increasingly adopt the normative position toward alcohol use on campus over the course of the semester. Thus, we predicted that their private attitudes would show a change in the direction of greater comfort over time. Our second expectation was that internalization would result in greater consistency among private attitudes, estimates of the norm, and drinking behavior. Thus, we predicted that the correlations among these variables would increase over time.

Method

Subjects.   Fifty 2nd-year undergraduates (25 women and 25 men) participated in this study. We chose 2nd-year students because we assumed that they would be familiar with student culture and, in particular, with norms for drinking but that they would still be new enough at the university to be concerned about fitting in. Subjects were selected at random from the student telephone directory and were each interviewed twice over the telephone.

Procedure.   Subjects were contacted for the first interview during the 2nd or 3rd week of the fall term. They were asked to participate in a telephone survey of students' attitudes toward the university's alcohol policies. The interviewer explained that their telephone numbers had been chosen at random from the telephone directory and that their responses would be completely anonymous. Over 90% of the students contacted agreed to participate.

The interview began with several questions about the university's alcohol policies that are irrelevant to the present investigation. The critical questions regarding their own attitudes toward drinking and their estimates of the average student's attitude were as follows:

1. Now, I'd like to know how you feel about drinking at Princeton more generally. How comfortable do you feel with the alcohol drinking habits of students here? I'd like you to use a 0-to-10 scale, where 0 means you're not at all comfortable and 10 means you're very comfortable.
2. How comfortable would you say the average Princeton undergraduate feels with the alcohol drinking habits of students here at Princeton, where 0 means not at all comfortable and 10 means very comfortable?

Subjects responded to each question by giving the interviewer a number from 0 to 10. Finally, subjects were asked about their own drinking habits. After reassuring them of their anonymity, the interviewer asked two open-ended questions:

3. How many alcoholic drinks have you had in the last week?
4. How many alcoholic drinks do you have in a typical week during the semester?

Subjects estimated their weekly alcohol intake. At the conclusion of the interview, subjects were informed that we would be calling back later in the term to find out whether people's attitudes had changed over time. The interviewer explained that "When we do [call back], we would like to talk to you

	TABLE 3			
	Ratings of Own and Others' Comfort with Alcohol Drinking in Study 3			
	September		December	
Group	Self	Average student	Self	Average student
Women				
M	6.08	7.16	5.94	7.74
SD	2.47	1.55	3.10	1.20
Men				
M	5.84	7.48	7.08	7.58
SD	3.01	1.45	2.70	1.27
Total				
M	5.96	7.32	6.51	7.66
SD	2.75	1.50	2.91	1.24

Note. All ratings were made on 11-point scales (0 = *not at all comfortable* and 10 = *very comfortable*). We added 1 point to each observation to make the scale comparable with the scale used in Studies 1 and 2.

again, so if you could let your roommates know that you're the survey person, we'd really appreciate it."

Approximately 8 weeks after the first interview, subjects were recontacted for the second interview. All 50 students again agreed to participate. They were asked the same questions as in the first survey, including the questions about their own comfort with drinking, the average student's comfort with drinking, and their recent and typical alcohol intake.

Results

Attitudes and norms.   The social psychological literature contains many compelling demonstrations of the power of social influence to move individual attitudes in the direction of the social norm. We tested the prediction that people will internalize what they perceive to be the social norm by examining changes in subjects' ratings of their own comfort and the average student's comfort with alcohol drinking over the course of the semester. Means and standard deviations for the two comfort questions are shown in Table 3. (We added 1 point to each observation to make the scales comparable with those used in Study 1.) Inspection of the means suggests that in the face of relatively stable social norms, men, but not women, did indeed bring their own attitudes into line.

	Women		Men	
TABLE 4				
Correlations Among Drinking Behavior, Own Attitudes, and Estimates of Others' Attitudes				
Measure	September	December	September	December
Own and others' attitudes	.60**	−.08	.34†	.76***
Behavior and own attitudes	.56**	.45*	.28	.59**
Behavior and others' attitudes	.13	−.16	−.11	.34†

†$p < .05$, one-tailed.   *$p < .05$, two-tailed.   **$p < .01$, two-tailed.   ***$p < .001$, two-tailed.

Inferential statistics confirmed this observation. A 2 (sex) × 2 (target) × 2 (time) ANOVA revealed a significant three-way interaction, $F(1, 48) = 3.92$, $p = .05$. Female subjects rated themselves as significantly less comfortable with alcohol drinking than the average Princeton undergraduate across both interviews; for target main effect, $F(1, 24) = 11.94$, $p < .005$; Target × Time interaction, $F < 1$. Male subjects showed a similar self–other difference in the first interview, $F(1, 24) = 8.24$, $p < .01$; by the second interview, the difference was eliminated, $F(1, 24) = 1.69$, $p > .10$; Target × Time interaction, $F(1, 24) = 3.92$, $p = .06$. Thus, men behaved in the way social influence theorists would expect: They changed their own attitudes toward drinking in the direction of the social norm. Women, on the other hand, showed no change in attitudes over time.

Correlational analyses provided further evidence of internalization among male, but not among female, subjects. If individuals respond to perceived deviance by bringing their attitudes into line with their perceptions of the norm, we would expect the correlation between attitudes and norms to increase over time. Male subjects showed just such an increase. Correlations between attitudes and norms are presented in the top line of Table 4. For men, the correlation between attitudes and norms increased from .34 in the first interview to .76 after 8 weeks. For women, the attitude–norm correlation showed a substantial decrease from .60 in the first interview to −.08 in the second interview.

Again, as in Studies 1 and 2, estimates of the comfort of the average Princeton student with alcohol were much less variable than subjects' own comfort ratings. A statistical comparison of the variances of the two distributions yielded a highly significant difference at both time points, $Fs(49, 49) = 3.36$ and 5.51 for the first and second interviews, respectively, $ps < .0001$.

Drinking behavior. We examined the relation of private attitudes and social norms to drinking behavior as well. Subjects' estimates of the number of drinks they had had in the past week and the number of drinks they had in a typical week

Group	September	December
TABLE 5		
Self-Reported Drinking Behavior		
Women		
M	3.60	1.79
SD	5.28	2.92
Interquartile range	0–5	0–3
Men		
M	5.74	6.44
SD	8.74	7.26
Interquartile range	0–9	1–9

Note. Drinking behavior was measured by averaging subjects' estimates of the number of alcoholic drinks they had in the past week and the number they had in a typical week.

correlated highly ($r = .78$ for the first interview and .93 for the second interview) and so we averaged them to form a single index of drinking behavior at each interview. Means and standard deviations for this index are shown in Table 5.[2] We expected drinking habits to be reasonably stable among our sophomore subjects, and indeed an initial ANOVA revealed a significant gender difference in drinking ($M = 2.69$ for women and 6.16 for men), $F(1, 46) = 5.17, p < .05$, but no change in drinking over time ($F < 1$) nor any Sex × Time interaction, $F(1, 46) = 1.61$, $p > .10$.[3] However, correlational analyses provided some indirect evidence of increased consistency of attitudes, norms, and behavior again among male, but not among female, subjects.

Correlations of behavior with attitudes and norms are shown in the last two lines of Table 4. For female subjects, both sets of correlations remained fairly stable over time. The attitude–behavior correlation was around .5 at both interviews, and the norm–behavior correlation was not significantly different from zero at either time point. For male subjects, both the attitude–behavior and the norm–behavior correlations increased over the course of the semester: The attitude–behavior correlation went from .28 at the first interview to .59 at the second interview, and the norm–behavior correlation went from −.11 at the first interview to .34 at the second interview.[4] Of course, we can draw no causal inferences on the basis of these results. Still, the pattern of correlations for men is quite consistent with the operation of conformity pressures to bring attitudes, norms, and behavior into line.

	TABLE 6	
Predicting Own Attitudes from Drinking Behavior and Estimates of Others' Attitudes		
Group	Adjusted R	Adjusted R^2
Women		
September	.75**	.56
December	.36†	.13
Men		
September	.44*	.20
December	.85**	.73

†$p < .05$, one-tailed.   *$p < .05$, two-tailed.   **$p < .001$, two-tailed.

One final set of analyses lent further support to this conclusion. We performed separate multiple regression analyses for men and women within interviews to test a model of individual attitudes as a joint function of drinking behavior and social norms. The results of these analyses are shown in Table 6. For women, their own comfort with drinking was predicted quite well from their drinking habits and their estimates of others' comfort with drinking at the start of the term; that prediction grew substantially worse over time. For men, the opposite was true: Their alcohol drinking habits and their estimates of others' comfort with drinking provided a relatively poor prediction of their own comfort at the start of the term, but that prediction became much better over time.[5] Again, these results for men are consistent with theorizing about conformity pressures in social groups; the results for women, on the other hand, suggest increasing alienation over the course of the semester.

Discussion

The pattern of results in this study clearly indicates internalization on the part of men and alienation on the part of women. The obvious question raised by these results is why men and women responded to pluralistic ignorance so differently. Because these gender differences were not predicted, we have no ready-made explanation for them. However, one potential explanatory factor is suggested by the finding that male subjects reported an alcohol consumption rate over double that reported by female subjects. One interpretation of this difference is that alcohol consumption is a more central or integral aspect of male social life than of female social life. If so, men might be expected to feel greater pressures to learn to be comfortable with alcohol. By contrast, women, and particularly women at historically male institutions, may be accustomed to finding themselves at odds with the social norm concerning alcohol. As a result, they may have come to view that norm as less relevant to their behavior than to the behavior of men.

Another possibility is that men are simply more inclined to react to feeling deviant from the norm with conformity, whereas women react to deviance with alienation. Although this suggestion that men conform more readily than women runs contrary to previous theorizing about gender differences in influenceability (see Eagly, 1978), there is some supporting evidence for it in the literature on gender differences in ego defenses. Considerable research suggests that in the face of ego threat, men react with externalizing defenses, such as projection and displacement, whereas women react with internalizing defenses, such as repression and reaction formation (Cramer, 1987; Levit, 1991). In the case of pluralistic ignorance, these differences in ego defenses may translate into a greater tendency of men to internalize the norm: Whereas women turn against themselves for being deviant, men take constructive steps to be less deviant.

One final point deserves consideration. Although men appear to have been able to resolve pluralistic ignorance through internalization, it is important to note that at the beginning of their 2nd year in college, both men and women were experiencing pluralistic ignorance in equal measure. Furthermore, Studies 1 and 2 provided evidence of pluralistic ignorance in a cross-section of the male population, including older as well as younger students. These findings suggest that internalization of the norm may provide only a temporary resolution of the perceived self-other discrepancy in comfort with alcohol; when social pressures are less immediate (e.g., during school breaks) or when those pressures change (e.g., as they do in students' 3rd and 4th years at Princeton), men may experience recurring concerns about students' excessive drinking habits.

Study 4

Study 3 provided evidence that, at least for women, pluralistic ignorance cannot easily be resolved through internalization. In Study 4, we explored the link between pluralistic ignorance and feelings of alienation from an institutional norm and from the institution itself. We were particularly interested in testing Noelle-Neumann's (1986) contention that people will be unwilling to express their opinions publicly when they feel that those opinions are deviant. This hypothesis, applied to a context of pluralistic ignorance, yields a provocative prediction, namely even when people's private attitudes are in line with the norm of the group, they should be hesitant to express those attitudes if they mistakenly believe they are deviant.

To test this hypothesis, we needed a case of pluralistic ignorance in which the attitude in question had clearly available means of public expression. Such an issue arose in the fall of 1991 when the university instituted a campus-wide policy banning kegs of beer. The keg ban was imposed unilaterally by the president of Princeton, who saw it largely as a symbolic act designed to demonstrate the university's concern about drinking on campus. The policy was immediately unpopular: Editorials appeared in the student newspaper and other publications, and there was even protest from alumni groups (who would no longer have kegs at reunions).

Despite the apparent consensus around a negative attitude toward the keg ban, we suspected that private sentiments were not nearly so negative. It was a time of great concern about alcohol use on campus, and many students privately expressed approval that the president of the university was willing to take action on the issue. Also, because the ban affected only kegs, students would still be free to drink bottled beer and other forms of alcohol if they wished. In short, it was a symbolic act that was unlikely to have dire consequences for social life at Princeton.

Thus, the keg ban provided the perfect issue for our investigation of the behavioral manifestations of alienation. We expected that we would find evidence of pluralistic ignorance on the keg ban issue, with people's private attitudes being much less negative than the prevailing social norm. In addition, unlike general comfort with alcohol, attitudes toward the keg ban had a clear means of public expression: We could ask students how willing they were to participate in social actions designed to protest the ban. Our hypothesis was that regardless of their actual attitude toward the keg ban, feeling deviant from the norm would inhibit students from taking any action to protest the ban and might produce more general symptoms of alienation from the university as well.

Method

Subjects.   Ninety-four undergraduates voluntarily attended a mass testing session, in which they participated in this and other short studies for pay. The sample included 52 women and 42 men, with approximately even distribution of women and men across the 1st- through 4th-year classes.

Procedure.   Subjects responded to a brief, two-page questionnaire that was included in a large booklet. The questionnaire was presented as a study of attitudes about the keg ban, about alcohol use on campus, and about life at Princeton more generally. The first question assessed their attitudes toward the keg ban:

1. How do you feel about the university's new policy banning kegs on campus? Please indicate your feelings by circling a number from 0 to 10.

Subjects circled a number on the accompanying scale, with 0 labeled *totally opposed* and 10 labeled *totally in favor*. Next, they were asked to estimate the attitudes of other students, using a comparative scale:

2. Compared to you, how does the average Princeton undergraduate feel about the university's policy banning kegs on campus?

Subjects circled a number from 1 to 5 on the accompanying scale, with the numbers labeled *much more negative, somewhat more negative, about the same, somewhat more positive*, and *much more positive*. The next two questions concerned their willingness to take social action to protest the keg ban:

3. How many signatures in protest of the ban would you be willing to go out and collect? Please circle a response from 0 signatures to 100 or more signatures.
4. How much of your time would you be willing to spend discussing ways to protest the ban? Please circle a response from no time to 10 or more hours.

Subjects circled a number from 0 to 100 (in increments of 10) to indicate how many signatures they would be willing to collect and a number from 0 to 10 (in increments of 2) to indicate how many hours they would be willing to discuss. Finally, they answered two questions that were designed to measure their connection to the university:

5. What percentage of reunions do you expect to attend after you graduate from Princeton?
6. How likely are you to donate money to Princeton after you graduate?

Subjects circled a number from 0 to 100 (in increments of 10) to indicate the percentage of reunions they expect to attend and a number from 1(*not at all likely*) to 9 (*very likely*) to indicate how likely they are to donate money to Princeton after graduation.

Results

We divided subjects into two categories on the basis of their responses to the question of how the average student feels about the keg ban compared with themselves. Forty women and 29 men indicated that the average student was either much more negative or somewhat more negative about the keg ban than they were; these subjects constituted the *others-more-negative* group. Eleven women and [eleven] men indicated that the average student felt about the same as they did; these subjects constituted the *others-the-same* group. (Two men and one woman indicated that the average student was more positive than they were; because this group was too small to analyze, the responses of

TABLE 7					
Ratings of Attitude Toward the Keg Ban. Willingness to Take Action, and Connection to the University of Comparative Attitude of the Average Student					
		Average student's attitude			
		Women		Men	
Measure		More negative	Same	More negative	Same
Keg ban attitude					
M		4.70	0.64	4.97	1.09
SD		2.55	0.92	2.61	1.30
Signatures					
M		6.05	49.09	3.14	30.00
SD		19.04	27.00	8.48	33.47
Hours					
M		0.40	2.55	0.34	1.45
SD		1.03	1.57	0.94	1.81
% reunions					
M		33.88	57.27	34.29	47.27
SD		22.37	25.73	24.10	29.70
Donations					
M		4.65	6.27	4.69	6.00
SD		2.28	2.32	2.54	2.49

these subjects were discarded). The distribution of subjects into these two categories confirmed our expectation that students' attitudes toward the keg ban, like their general comfort with alcohol, would be characterized by pluralistic ignorance: They showed a systematic tendency to believe that the average student felt more negatively about the keg ban than they did.

We predicted that subjects who believed themselves to be different from the average student would be less likely to take social action against the keg ban and would be less connected to the university compared with subjects who believed themselves to be the same as the average student, controlling for actual attitudes toward the ban. Means and standard deviations for the attitude and behavior questions are shown in Table 7. Not surprisingly, subjects' own attitudes toward the ban corresponded to their comparative ratings of others' attitudes: Subjects in the others-more-negative group expressed more favorable attitudes toward the ban than did subjects in the others-the-same group, $F(1, 90) = 48.26$, $p < .0001$. However, even controlling for this difference in private attitudes, subjects who felt that their attitude was different from the norm still were less willing to take action against the ban.[6] A 2 (sex) × 2 (comparison group) analysis of covariance, controlling for attitudes, yielded a significant effect of comparison group on willingness to collect signatures, $F(1, 90) = 18.94$, $p < .0001$, willingness to work hours, $F(1, 90) = 10.99$, $p < .005$, and percentage of reunions expected to attend, $F(1, 89) = 8.10$, $p < .01$. The effect of comparison group on likelihood of donating money was not significant, $F(1, 90) = 1.08$, $p > .10$, although the means were in the expected direction. There was also a significant gender difference in willingness to collect signatures, $F(1, 90) = 4.57$, $p < .05$, and a marginally significant gender difference in willingness to work hours, $F(1, 90) = 3.42$, $p < .07$. None of the Sex × Comparison Group interaction effects were significant.

Discussion

These results provide clear evidence that people who feel deviant from the norm of their social group are inhibited from acting. Regardless of their actual position on the keg ban, subjects who believed that others felt more negatively than they did were less likely to act on the ban and were also less connected to the university, as measured by their plans to attend reunions after graduation. These results demonstrate that mistakenly believing oneself to be deviant is associated with considerable alienation from the group. However, it is also important to note that the results of this study are correlational and do not enable us to make causal statements about the precise role of feeling deviant on the keg ban issue in producing the observed effects.

The results of this study, combined with those of Study 3, provide an interesting picture of the consequences of pluralistic ignorance regarding alcohol use for male and female students. For men, the pattern of result followed quite closely the predictions of the social influence literature: When they perceived their attitudes to be different from the normative attitudes of their group, men showed signs of alienation (Study 4) and responded to their perceived deviance by changing their attitudes in the direction of the norm (Study 3). For women, the pattern of results was more anomalous: They also showed signs of alienation when they perceived their attitudes to be deviant, but did not respond by moving toward the norm. Indeed, if anything, they appeared to grow more alienated over time (Study 3).

We believe that the most parsimonious account for these results focuses on the different relations of men and women to both the norm in question and to the group. As noted in connection with Study 3, norms related to alcohol use are likely to be much more central for men than for women. Likewise, fitting in at the university is likely to be more critical for men than for women. Even though Princeton had admitted female students for more than 2 decades, male students are still both the statistical and the psychological norm. (Many of the university's institutions and traditions were developed when it was an all-male school). Thus, whereas Princeton men are likely to feel strong conformity pressures, Princeton women may have less ability and less motivation to conform to the norms of the group. They may see some degree of deviance and alienation as inherent in their position within a historically male institution. Of course, this explanation is speculative, but it is consistent both with previous theorizing about social groups (e.g., Festinger et al., 1950) and with the present results.

General Discussion

In pursuit of an answer to the question of how people respond to perceived differences between themselves and the group, social psychologists have largely ignored the more preliminary questions of how, and with what degree of accuracy, people identify social norms. In most laboratory investigations of social influence, the task of identifying group norms is eliminated by flat of experimental design. (If the norm is measured at all, it is only done so as a manipulation check). In real-world social groups, however, the task of identifying the group norm can be highly complex and demanding, so much so that members' estimates of the norm are often seriously in error. The present studies documented significant errors in college students' estimates of social norms relating to comfort with alcohol (Studies 1, 2, and 3) and attitudes toward a new university-mandated policy to reduce alcohol abuse (Study 4). Especially interesting was the systematic nature of the errors: Students erred by overestimating their fellow students' support for the status quo. Indeed, they assumed that the average other student was more in favor of the status quo than they themselves were. In short, students were victims of pluralistic ignorance: They believed that the private attitudes of other students were much more consistent with campus norms than were their own.

Norm Misperception: Possible Interpretations

The reported discrepancy between students' own attitudes and those they attribute to their friends and peers may have many sources. The least interesting interpretation, from a psychological standpoint, is that the reported discrepancy is merely that: a reported discrepancy that does not reflect true perceptions.

By this impression management account, students may not actually think they are deviant but only portray themselves as such. Their descriptions of themselves as deviating from the status quo could simply constitute strategic attempts to present themselves as nonconformists, as people who are less supportive of their group's norm than the average group member. By presenting themselves in this way, the students might have hoped to convey the impression (if they assumed that the researcher disapproved of the group's norm) that they were more mature, more progressive, or more enlightened than their peers.

An impression management account could be applied to virtually all the studies that have reported erroneous perceptions of one's own attitudinal or behavioral deviance. The form that pluralistic ignorance takes in these studies is almost always the same: Subjects report that they are more sympathetic to the positions or concerns of some out-group than are their peers. For example, Whites portray themselves as more sympathetic to Blacks than their fellow Whites (Fields & Schuman, 1976), teachers portray themselves as more sympathetic to students than their fellow teachers (Packard & Willower, 1972), and prison guards portray themselves as more sympathetic to prisoners than their fellow guards (Kauffman, 1981).

Although it is possible that students in the present studies were motivated to portray themselves as more sympathetic to the position of the university administration than their fellow students, there are a number of reasons to doubt this self-presentational account. First, the anonymous nature of the data collection provided subjects with very little incentive to self-present. Second, the finding in Study 4 that subjects' estimates of their attitudinal deviance correlated positively with various measures of alienation, even when equating for their own attitudes, is hard to reconcile with a self-presentational interpretation. Subjects not only described themselves as being out of step with the social norm, but they also acted as though they were out of step with this norm. Even more problematic for the self-presentational account is the finding in Study 3 that male subjects moderated their perception of their deviance over time by shifting their attitudes toward their estimates of the social norm. If these subjects were attempting to present themselves as being more progressive or enlightened than their peers, it is unlikely that they would have reported their attitudes to be closer to the norm at one time than another. In short, the present findings are much more consistent with the view that the pluralistic ignorance observed in the present studies represented authentic perceptions of deviance and not just ones offered for public consumption.

Another possible interpretation of students' perceived deviance focuses on the representativeness of the public data from which they inferred others' attitudes. These data may have been skewed in the direction of the perceived norm. For example, campus publications may have tended to express more pronorm opinions than antinorm opinions. Similarly, students who strongly supported campus norms may have expressed their attitudes more vociferously than those who only weakly supported them or who disapproved of them. Korte (1972) offered the following general summary of this process:

> The side of an issue representing a cultural (or subcultural) value is more prominent, more frequently and loudly advocated by its adherents. From the point of view of the individual, this source of bias constitutes an unrepresentative sampling of the relevant population. (p. 586)

Through an accurate reading of a biased distribution of publicly expressed opinions, students may have been led to erroneous perceptions of their peers' attitudes. Interestingly, this account implies that pluralistic ignorance could arise without students misrepresenting their true opinions. It suggests that pluralistic ignorance may require a silent majority but not a dissembling one.

We cannot rule out the biased sample hypothesis, but it has difficulty accounting for the data on friends' attitudes in Study 2. There, we found that subjects revealed pluralistic ignorance not just when estimating the attitudes of the average Princeton student but also when estimating the attitudes of their friends. It seems implausible that students would use the public expressions of their vocal friends to infer the private attitudes of their silent friends. Inferences concerning the population of a campus must be estimated from a sample of that population, but inferences concerning the population of one's friends need not depend on sample-to-population generalization.

Two other possible accounts of the pluralistic ignorance observed in these studies focus on students' interpretation and encoding of their own and others' behavior. The first of these accounts, which we call the *differential interpretation hypothesis*, suggests that students display pluralistic ignorance in their reactions to alcohol issues because they (a) present themselves as being more supportive of campus norms than they are and (b) fail to recognize that others are also misrepresenting their true feelings. The first of these points is well documented: Many authorities have noted that group members often display more public support for group norms than they privately feel (Goffman, 1961; Matza, 1964; Schanck, 1932). As Goffman (1961) stated, "when the individual presents himself before others, his performance will tend to incorporate and exemplify the officially accredited values of the society, more so, in fact, than does his behavior as a whole" (p. 35).

Comfort with alcohol and opposition to alcohol restrictions may not be "officially accredited" campus values, but they may serve a similar function. Alcohol on most college campuses, and certainly on the Princeton campus, is not simply a critical feature of social life: It is also an important source of in-group-out-group polarization. Nothing is more central to the power struggle between students and the administration, faculty, and larger community than campus alcohol policy. Thus, even if students do not privately support the student position on alcohol, they may feel compelled to do so publicly out of a sense of group loyalty. Acknowledging that the other side has a point, or is not all bad, can carry a stiff social penalty.

There may be many reasons for students to exaggerate publicly their support for campus alcohol norms, but why do they not assume that their peers' public behavior is similarly inauthentic? One possibility, suggested by Miller and McFarland (1987, 1991), is that people hold a general belief that they are more fearful of appearing deviant than is the average person. Thus, students may be disposed to accept as authentic the public pronorm behaviors of their peers, despite recognizing that their own public pronorm behaviors are inauthentic.

A final explanation for the observed pluralistic ignorance points to potential differences in the way students encode their own and others' behavior. According to this differential encoding account, students may fail to recognize how pronorm their public behavior actually is, mistakenly believing that their private discomfort with alcohol practices is clear from their words and deeds. If students do suffer from an *illusion of transparency* (Miller & McFarland, 1991), they might reasonably assume that because the words and deeds of others signal more comfort than they themselves feel (and supposedly express), they must be alone in their discomfort.

Although both the differential interpretation and differential encoding hypotheses are plausible accounts of pluralistic ignorance in the present context, we have no direct evidence to support or to distinguish between them. It is quite possible that the two operate in parallel, along with other biases, to make pluralistic ignorance an overdetermined phenomenon. Future research could shed light on these accounts by determining whether students do (a) misrepresent their private attitudes in their public pronouncements or (b) generate different interpretations for what they saw as similar public behavior in themselves and others.

Before leaving our analysis of pluralistic ignorance effects, we should comment briefly on the apparent inconsistency between this phenomenon and the well-documented *false consensus effect:* people's tendency to overestimate their similarity to others (Marks & Miller, 1987; Ross, Greene, & House, 1977). The two phenomena are different but are not incompatible (see Suls, 1986). The norm misperception that arises in cases of pluralistic ignorance is most appropriately operationalized as a mean difference between the actual group norm and the perceived group norm; false consensus, on the other hand, is most appropriately operationalized as a positive correlation between ratings of the self and ratings of others. Theoretically, it is possible for there to be both a positive correlation between people's judgments of self and others and a mean difference in self-other ratings. Indeed, we found precisely this pattern of results in Study 1 (for the self-other correlation, $r = .37$, $p < .001$) and in Study 2 ($r = .27$, $p < .01$). Thus, although students anchored their estimates of the average student's level of comfort on their own (hence the positive correlation), they also perceived there to be a systematic difference between their comfort level and the comfort of others. Nisbett and Kunda (1985) provided numerous other examples in which subjects displayed both false consensus effects and systematic biases in central tendency estimates.

Norm Misperception: Social and Psychological Consequences

What are the consequences of mistakenly assuming that the views of one's peers are different from one's own? Although illusory norms may not have the force of overt social pressure behind them, they still can have powerful social and psychological consequences.

Social consequences. Pluralistic ignorance has traditionally been linked to two consequences: the social construction of emergency situations as nonemergencies and the perpetuation of unsupported social norms. Defined broadly, the pluralistic ignorance found in the present studies may have had both of these consequences. Consider emergency nonintervention first. We obviously did not focus on emergency situations directly in these studies, but it is quite possible that most of our subjects had witnessed situations involving alcohol abuse that they viewed as potentially serious. If so, we can surmise that the pluralistic ignorance dynamic described by Latané and Darley (1970) may have been replicated frequently on the Princeton campus, resulting in (a) the withholding of assistance to inebriated students about whom all members of groups were concerned and (b) increased confidence on the part of nonacting, but nonetheless concerned, bystanders that they were much less cool about the consequences of excessive drinking than were their friends and fellow bystanders.

The role of pluralistic ignorance in perpetuating unsupported or weakly supported social norms in the present context is also easy to sketch. Alcohol may have continued to play a central role in campus life not because students wanted it that way but because they thought that everyone else wanted it that way. For example, students themselves might often, or even generally, be indifferent to the availability of alcohol at a party, but they may assume that most other students have a strong preference for parties at which alcohol is present. This logic could have many consequences, the most obvious of which is that students, assuming that more people will come to parties that serve alcohol, will seek out parties with alcohol. It also suggests that students hosting parties will assume that they must provide alcohol to satisfy their guests. In short, attempts to institute alcohol-free social activities or institutions may fail to generate support because students mistakenly (and self-fulfillingly) assume they will not be widely supported.

One additional social consequence illustrated by the present findings is that individuals may actually conform to their mistaken estimates of the group norm. Previous research on substance use has shown that people's estimates of the prevalence of drug use among their peers influences their own use, whether these estimates are accurate or inaccurate (Kandel, 1980; Marks, Graham, & Hansen, 1992; Sherman, Presson, Chassin, Corty, & Olshavsky, 1983). Similarly, in Study 3, male subjects modified their private attitudes over time in the direction of the position they mistakenly assumed was held by the average student. In effect, they achieved a level of comfort that few students initially felt simply because they thought that everyone felt that way. This analysis highlights the fact that the norms of a social group may be largely independent of the norms of a social group may be largely independent of the norms of the group members (Turner & Killian, 1972). The desire to be correct and to fit in may lead people to conform, even without social pressure, to what they (mis)perceive to be the norm of the group. In these cases, pluralistic ignorance will be highly ephemeral. If people come to believe what they mistakenly attribute to everyone else, then an originally erroneous perception of the situation will become accurate at the private, as well as the public, level. Misjudgments of others will drive out correct judgments of the self.

Psychological consequences.   Our discussion suggests that the social consequences of pluralistic ignorance are significant. However, as the present research indicates, pluralistic ignorance has powerful psychological consequences as well. As documented in our studies, many of the consequences of mistakenly perceiving oneself as deviant are not much different from the consequences of accurately perceiving oneself as deviant. Discomfort, alienation, and an inclination to move in the direction of the majority appear to characterize the phenomenology of illusory deviants as well as real deviants. Indeed, because victims of pluralistic ignorance will typically be involuntary deviants, they may experience the pain of their deviance quite acutely. They may lack the comforting belief that they chose to march to the beat of a different drummer.

Whether victims of pluralistic ignorance do or do not experience their deviance more acutely than voluntary deviants, we have evidence that they manifest real symptoms. For the male subjects in Study 3, for example, the pain of perceiving themselves as deviant may have been a critical factor motivating them to conform to the (illusory) norm of their social group. Moreover, the present findings suggest that people may be much less inclined to conform to majority influence, real or imagined, than is generally assumed by social psychologists. Female subjects in Study 3 retained their (self-perceived) deviant attitudes, a response consistent with other signs of alienation found in both male and female subjects in Study 4. These results raise the possibility that conformity may not play as dominant a role in resolving self–group discrepancies as most psychological equilibrium models have posited.

Conclusions

The reported studies illustrate a number of important points about the relation between private attitudes and social norms. Taken together, they indicate that people can often err considerably in situating their attitudes in relation to those of their peers and that these errors have real consequences, both for the individual and for the group. Because little research attention has been given to questions of norm estimation, we know very little about the processes through which individuals identify and represent the norms of their social groups. The present results suggest that further attention to these questions may lead to a better understanding of the ways in which norms can perpetuate social problems, like alcohol use, and can inhibit social change.

The findings of these studies have practical implications as well. In particular, our analysis of the role of pluralistic ignorance in perpetuating dysfunctional social norms has clear implications for programs designed to effect social change. Programs aimed at the individual, such as informational campaigns or individual counseling sessions, may change private attitudes, but they are likely to leave social norms, and in many cases public behavior, untouched. Indeed, our research suggests that recent attempts by universities to raise consciousness about alcohol abuse on campus may have been effective at changing the attitudes of individual students (see also Trice & Beyer, 1977) but not at changing their perceptions of the attitudes of their peers. A more effective way to facilitate social change may be to expose pluralistic ignorance in a group setting and to encourage students to speak openly about their private attitudes within the group. Such an approach would promote social change by demonstrating that it has, in effect, already occurred at the individual level and simply needs to be acknowledged at the social level.

Notes

1. The data for Studies 1, 2, and 4 were collected at Questionnaire Day sessions, which are organized by the psychology department each semester. These sessions are advertised in the student newspaper with notices posted

around campus and are also announced in the large introductory-level psychology courses. Students come to a large lecture hall anytime during the afternoon or evening, fill out a questionnaire booklet anonymously, and receive $6 for their participation. To ensure that participants feel completely anonymous, we collect demographic information regarding only their sex and class. Although the samples are self-selected, they typically represent a cross-section of the undergraduate population in terms of these demographic characteristics.

2. Initial exploration of the distribution of scores on the drinking measure (separately for men and women at each time point) revealed several outliers: Two men and one woman in September and one man and one woman in December reported levels of drinking that were extremely high compared with the rest of their distribution. To ensure that these points did not unduly affect the results, we analyzed the data [in] three ways: (a) including these values, (b) replacing them with the closest values that were not outliers (i.e., with the value of the inner fence; see Tukey, 1977), and (c) excluding them. The patterns of results from these three sets of analyses were identical and led to the same substantive conclusions. Thus, in the text, we report the results of the analyses with all values included; the results of the two alternative analyses are provided in footnotes.

3. With replacement of outliers: in September, women ($M = 3.22$, $SD = 4.06$), men ($M = 5.13$, $SD = 7.04$); in December, women ($M = 1.61$, $SD = 2.31$), men ($M = 6.46$, $SD = 7.16$). With exclusion of outliers: in September, women ($M = 2.72$, $SD = 3.64$), men ($M = 3.53$, $SD = 4.51$); in December, women ($M = 1.39$, $SD = 1.95$), men ($M = 4.70$, $SD = 5.76$). For all analyses, the sex difference was the only significant effect.

4. With replacement of outliers: attitude-behavior correlations in September and December, respectively, for women were .57 and .44 and for men .26 and .59; norm-behavior correlations in September and December, respectively, for women were .11 and −.22 and for men −.17 and .33. With exclusion of outliers, attitude-behavior correlations in September and December, respectively, for women were .50 and .31 and for men were .00 and .53; norm–behavior correlations in September and December, respectively, for women were .06 and −.30 and for men were −.42 and .26.

5. With replacement of outliers: women in September ($R = .77$), in December ($R = .33$); men in September ($R = .45$), in December ($R = .82$). With exclusion of outliers: Women in September ($R = .73$), in December ($R = .10$); men in September ($R = .32$), in December ($R = .80$).

6. The use of analysis of covariance as a way of equating the two groups on attitudes is a reasonable but not perfect strategy; see Huitema (1980) for a full discussion of the assumptions and limitations of this statistical approach.

References

Allport, F. H. (1924). *Social psychology*. Boston: Houghton Mifflin.

Asch, S. E. (1951). Effects of group pressure upon the modification and distortion of judgments. In H. Guetzkow (Ed.), *Group leadership and men* (pp. 177–190). Pittsburg, PA: Carnegie Press.

Barringer, F. (1991, June 23). With teens and alcohol, it's just say when. *New York Times*, p. 1.

Berkowitz, A. D., & Perkins, H. W. (1986). Problem drinking among college students: A review of recent research. *Journal of American College Health, 35,* 21–28.

Breed, W., & Ktsanes, T. (1961). Pluralistic ignorance in the process of opinion formation. *Public Opinion Quarterly, 25,* 382–392.

Cialdini, R. B., Kallgren, C. A., & Reno, R. R. (1991). The focus theory of normative conduct: A theoretical refinement and reevaluation of the role of norms in human behavior. In M. P. Zanna (Ed.), *Advances in experimental social psychology* (Vol. 24, pp. 201–234). San Diego, CA: Academic Press.

Clitherow, R. (1991). What is to be done? Alcohol abuse at Princeton. *The Princeton Tory, 7* (March), 8–13.

Cramer, P. (1987). The development of defenses. *Journal of Personality, 51,* 79–94.

Crandall, C. (1988). Social contagion and binge eating. *Journal of Personality and Social Psychology, 55,* 588–598.

Eagly, A. (1978). Sex differences in influenceability. *Psychological Bulletin, 85,* 86–116.

Festinger, L., Schachter, S., & Back, K. (1950). *Social pressure in informal groups*. New York: Harper & Row.

Fields, J. M., & Schuman, H. (1976). Public beliefs and the beliefs of the public. *Public Opinion Quarterly, 40,* 427–448.

Goffman, E. (1961). *Asylums: Essays on the social situation of mental patients and other inmates*. Garden City, NJ: Anchor Books.

Graham, J. W., Marks, G., & Hansen, W. B. (1991). Social influence processes affecting adolescent substance use. *Journal of Applied Psychology, 76,* 291–298.

Huba, G. J., & Bentler, P. M. (1980). The role of peer and adult models for drug taking at different stages in adolescence. *Journal of Youth and Adolescence, 9,* 449–465.

Huitema, B. E. (1980). *The analysis of covariance and alternatives*. New York: Wiley.

Kandel, D. B. (1980). Drug and drinking behavior among youth. In A. Inkeles, N. J. Smelser, & R. Turner (Eds.), *Annual review of sociology* (Vol. 6, pp. 235–285). Palo Alto, CA: Annual Reviews.

Kauffman, K. (1981). Prison officer attitudes and perceptions of attitudes. *Journal of Research in Crime Delinquency, 18,* 272–294.

Kelman, H. (1958). Compliance, identification, and internalization: Three processes of attitude change. *Journal of Conflict Resolution, 2,* 51–60.

Korte, C. (1972). Pluralistic ignorance about student radicalism. *Sociometry, 35,* 576–587.

Latané, B., & Darley, J. (1970). *The unresponsive bystander: Why doesn't he help?* New York: Appleton-Century-Crofts.

Levit, D. B. (1991). Gender differences in ego defenses in adolescence: Sex roles as one way to understand the differences. *Journal of Personality and Social Psychology, 61,* 992–999.

Maddox, G. L. (Ed.) (1970). *The domesticated drug: Drinking among collegians.* New Haven, CT: College and University Press.

Marks, G., Graham, J. W., & Hansen, W. B. (1992). Social projection and social conformity in adolescent alcohol use: A longitudinal analysis. *Personality and Social Psychology Bulletin, 18,* 96–101.

Marks, G., & Miller, N. (1987). Ten years of research on the false-consensus effect: An empirical and theoretical review. *Psychological Bulletin, 102,* 72–90.

Matza, D. (1964). *Delinquency and drift.* New York: Wiley.

Miller, D. T., & McFarland, C. (1987). Pluralistic ignorance: When similarity is interpreted as dissimilarity. *Journal of Personality and Social Psychology, 53,* 298–305.

Miller, D. T., & McFarland, C. (1991). When social comparison goes awry: The case of pluralistic ignorance. In J. Suls & T. Wills (Eds.), *Social comparison: Contemporary theory and research* (pp. 287–313). Hillsdale, NJ: Erlbaum.

Moscovici, S. (1985). Social influence and conformity. In G. Lindzey, & E. Aronson (Eds.), *The handbook of social psychology* (3rd ed., Vol. 2, pp. 347–412). New York: Random House.

Newcomb, T. M. (1943). *Personality and social change.* New York: Holt, Rinehart & Winston.

Nisbett, R. E., & Kunda, Z. (1985). Perceptions of social distributions. *Journal of Personality and Social Psychology, 48,* 297–311.

Noelle-Neumann, E. (1986). *The spiral of silence.* Chicago: University of Chicago Press.

O'Gorman, H. J. (1975). Pluralistic ignorance and White estimates of White support for racial segregation. *Public Opinion Quarterly, 39,* 313–330.

Packard, J. S., & Willower, D. J. (1972). Pluralistic ignorance and pupil control ideology. *Journal of Education Administration, 10,* 78–87.

Perkins, H. W. (1985). Religious traditions, parents, and peers as determinants of alcohol and drug use among college students. *Review of Religious Research, 27,* 15–31.

Perkins, H. W., & Berkowitz, A. D. (1986). Perceiving the community norms of alcohol use among students: Some research implications for campus alcohol education programming. *International Journal of Addictions, 21,* 961–976.

Ross, L., Greene, D., & House, P. (1977). The "false consensus effect": An egocentric bias in social perception and attributional processes. *Journal of Experimental Social Psychology, 13,* 279–301.

Schanck, R. L. (1932). A study of community and its group institutions conceived of as behavior of individuals. *Psychological Monographs, 43*(2), 1–133.

Sherif, M. (1936). *The psychology of social norms.* New York: Harper.

Sherman, S. J., Presson, C. C., Chassin, L., Corty, E., & Olshavsky, R. (1983). The false consensus effect in estimates of smoking prevalence: Underlying mechanisms. *Personality and Social Psychology Bulletin, 9,* 197–207.

Stein, J. A., Newcomb, M. D., & Bentler, P. M. (1987). An 8-year study of multiple influences on drug use and drug use consequences. *Journal of Personality and Social Psychology, 53,* 1094–1105.

Straus, R., & Bacon, J. M. (1953). *Drinking in college.* New Haven, CT: Yale University Press.

Suls, J. (1986). Notes on the occasion of social comparison theory's thirtieth birthday. *Personality and Social Psychology Bulletin, 12,* 289–296.

Trice, H. M., & Beyer, J. M. (1977). A sociological property of drugs: Acceptance of users of alcohol and other drugs among university undergraduates. *Journal of Studies on Alcohol, 33,* 58–74.

Tukey, J. (1977). *Exploratory data analysis.* Reading, MA: Addison-Wesley.

Turner, J. (1991). *Social influence.* Pacific Grove, CA: Brooks/Cole.

Turner, R., & Killian, L. (1972). *Collective behavior* (2nd ed.). Englewood Cliffs, NJ: Prentice-Hall.

Zucker, R. A., & Noll, R. B. (1982). Precursors and developmental influences on drinking and alcoholism: Etiology from a longitudinal perspective. *Alcohol consumption and related problems* (Alcohol and Health Monograph No. 1, pp. 289–327). Rockville, MD: National Institute on Alcohol Abuse and Alcoholism.

Questions for Review and Discussion

1. Define pluralistic ignorance.
2. How did Prentice and Miller interpret the finding that students thought that their peers were more comfortable with campus drinking practices than they were?
3. What was the difference in the way males and females reacted to their (mis)perception that their peers were more comfortable with drinking practices than they were?

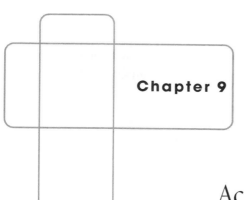

Chapter 9

Actual Versus Assumed Differences in Construal: "Naive Realism" in Intergroup Perception and Conflict

Robert J. Robinson, Dacher Keltner, Andrew Ward, and Lee Ross

We tend to resolve our perplexity arising out of the experience that other people see the world differently than we see it ourselves by declaring that these others, in consequence of some basic intellectual and moral defect, are unable to see things "as they really are" and to react to them "in a normal way." We thus imply, of course, that things are in fact as we see them, and that our ways are the normal ways. (Ichheiser, 1949, p. 39)

The recognition that human beings actively construe and even construct the phenomena they encounter, and the further recognition that the impact of any objective stimulus depends on the subjective meaning attached to it by the actor, have long been among psychology's most important intellectual contributions. As early as the 1930s, when objectivist behaviorism was dominating most of American psychology, European psychologists including Piaget and Bartlett were discussing the active role that schemas and other cognitive structures play in guiding the interpretation of information and creating individual differences in such interpretation. In the decades that followed, two of social psychology's most important intellectual leaders, Solomon Asch and Kurt Lewin, repeatedly emphasized the importance of attending to the *actor's* subjective understanding or "definition" of his or her situation. During that period, personality researchers

From *Journal of Personality and Social Psychology*, Vol. 68, No. 3, pp. 404–417. Copyright © 1995 by the American Psychological Association. Reproduced with permission.

and clinicians (most notably George Kelly, 1955) similarly stressed the importance of subjectivist considerations in understanding individual differences in behavior (Ross, 1990; Ross & Nisbett, 1991).

Since the flowering of the cognitive tradition in social and personality psychology in the 1970s, it has become clear that there really are two separate insights to be gained about subjectivism. The first and more familiar insight is simply that subjective construal matters—that in many contexts people's interpretations play an important role in determining their responses and that variability and uncertainty of construal contributes significantly to the variability and unpredictability of important classes of human behavior. The second and less familiar insight, captured in our opening quotation from Ichheiser, is that people tend to be "naive realists" (Griffin & Ross, 1991; Ross & Ward, in press-a). That is, people do not fully appreciate the subjective status of their own construals, and, as such, they do not make sufficient allowance for the uncertainties of construal when called on to make behavioral attributions and predictions about others (Griffin, Dunning, & Ross, 1990; Ross, 1990; Ross & Nisbett, 1991).

It is easy to imagine how blindness to intersubjective differences in construal might exacerbate misunderstanding, distrust, and dislike. Disputants may fail to recognize the extent to which their adversaries' judgments and decisions are predicated on different factual beliefs, ontological assumptions, or interpretations of relevant information. In other words, they may fail to recognize the extent to which their adversaries are essentially responding to a "different object of judgment" (Asch, 1940; Ichheiser, 1970), which in turn may lead them to see their adversaries as stubborn, illogical, or distorted by some combination of ideological bias and self-interest (Bar-Tal & Geva, 1986; Fisher & Ury, 1981).

In the context of social debate between relatively well-defined partisan factions, however, a subtler source of misattribution and antipathy may make its influence felt. The opposing partisans may be well aware (in fact, all members of the body politic may be well aware) that the two groups construe the world differently. They similarly may be aware that the construal differences in question tend to be congruent with the groups' differing ideological positions. However, these same partisans may attribute such construal differences to the biasing effects on others (but not, of course, on themselves) of ideology or self-interest. In other words, individuals may feel that whereas they themselves have proceeded from available evidence to reasonable interpretations and beliefs, those who hold opposing beliefs (and, to a lesser extent, even those who share their general ideological position) have done just the opposite, (i.e., that other people's construals of evidence, in contrast to their own, are the consequence rather than the cause of preexisting values and biases).

The result of such interpersonal perceptions and attributions should be not an underestimation of construal differences and ideological congruence but an overestimation. People should tend to believe that they alone struggle with the ambiguities, complexities, and even inconsistencies of objective reality, that others tend to perceive the world in simple, ideologically consistent, black or white terms, while they alone appreciate fully the subtler grays. Ironically, the intergroup consequences that follow from such an appreciation, or even exaggeration, of construal differences are apt to be as unfortunate as the consequences that follow from obliviousness to construal differences. That is, partisans involved in conflict may continue to see the other side as extreme, unreasonable, and unreachable, and to see their own side as similarly (albeit, somewhat less) extreme and biased. Partisans, accordingly, are apt to underestimate the possibility of finding common ground that could provide the basis for conciliation and constructive action; as a consequence, they could be reluctant to enter into the type of frank dialogue that could reveal such commonalities in interests or beliefs.

The two types of social perception bias we have identified may seem quite different and even contradictory (one involves obliviousness to construal differences, and the other involves anticipation or even exaggeration of such differences). However, both types of bias actually have a common theme, the one noted in our introductory quote from Ichheiser. This theme is prominent in research on "phenomenal absolutism" (Bar-Tal & Geva, 1986; Segall, Campbell, & Herskovitz, 1966) or, as we prefer to call it, *naive realism* (Griffin & Ross, 1991; Ross & Ward, in press-a), and it has long been noted in research on in-group versus out-group attitudes (Allport, 1954; Brewer, 1979; Sumner, 1906). It speaks to the individual's unshakable conviction that he or she is somehow privy to an invariant, knowable, objective reality—a reality that others will also perceive faithfully, provided that they are reasonable and rational, a reality that others are apt to misperceive only to the extent that they (in contrast to oneself) view the world through a prism of self-interest, ideological bias, or personal perversity. Theorists and researchers concerned with intergroup conflict, in turn, have noted some of the potential social consequences of this naivete, including the tendency to misattribute the other side's words and deeds, to blame the other side exclusively for shared problems (Blumenthal, Kahn, Andrews, & Head, 1972; Eldridge, 1979), to doubt their sincerity (Deutsch, 1973; Thomas & Pondy, 1977), and to overlook opportunities for identifying commonalities in goals, values, and interests (Fisher & Ury, 1981; Keltner & Robinson, 1993; Pruitt & Rubin, 1986; Schelling, 1963).

In two studies, we compared actual and perceived discrepancies in social construal. More specifically, we explored three separate questions prompted by our foregoing discussion of subjective construal and conflict. First, we examined the extent to which members of the opposing partisan groups actually did construe the various objects of their judgment differently, in accord with their differing political or ideological stances. Second, we tested the hypothesis that the group members—and perhaps nonpartisan neutrals as well—will tend to overestimate group extremity and ideological consistency and therefore overestimate intergroup differences. Finally, we examined the attributions or interpretations that the partisans place on whatever construal differences they perceive or assume to exist.

Our two studies concerned two different types of partisan dispute. Study 1 dealt with the general issue of abortion; Study 2 dealt with a specific incident of interracial violence. In both studies, college students holding opposing political views were asked to specify some of the factual assumptions and construals underlying those views. They were also asked to estimate the assumptions and construals of partisans on the other side and partisans on their own side as well. Both studies also addressed the attribution issue through various questionnaire items asking the antagonists to estimate the impact of objective or evidential factors versus subjective or ideological factors in determining such construals. The design of Study 2, however, added an important new feature. It included nonpartisan, or "neutral," participants as well as ideological adversaries, thus allowing us to determine whether overestimation of partisan ideological congruence and extremity arises solely from the rater's own partisanship or, as we suspect, is actually a more general feature of social perception.

Study 1: Pro-Choice and Pro-Life Views of Partisanship in the Abortion Debate

In Study 1 we sought, through two separate questionnaire administrations, to examine the actual extent to which members of opposing partisan groups differed in the way that they construed the facts underlying the issue of abortion and the extent to which the group members believed that they differed.[1] The initial questionnaire dealt with the types of individuals, circumstances, and considerations that prompt abortion decisions. The follow-up questionnaire dealt both with matters of biology and medicine (in particular, the age at which a fetus becomes viable and the age of the fetus at the point when abortions are commonly performed) and with pragmatic considerations (i.e., the consequences likely to follow from enactment of particular laws and policies restricting the practice of abortion). Also, whereas the initial questionnaire used members of partisan organizations, the follow-up questionnaire used self-descriptions as a basis for respondent selection and characterization. Both questionnaires, however, asked the pro-choice and pro-life advocates not only to specify their own construals and assumptions relevant to the abortion issue but also to estimate the views both of those on the other side in the abortion debate and of those on their own side. In the initial questionnaire, participants were also asked to assess the relative importance of various factors (some evidential, some pragmatic, and some philosophical or ideological) first in determining their own views and then in determining the views of the two opposing sides.

Method

Participants.   The initial questionnaire dealing with abortion was administered to 27 pro-choice and 25 pro-life participants recruited from relevant campus groups concerned with the issue. These participants were paid $5.[2] The second questionnaire, on the same topic, was administered to students enrolled in an introductory psychology class, 66 of whom ultimately labeled themselves as strongly pro-choice and 22 of whom labeled themselves as strongly pro-life.[3] These "partisans," who constituted roughly 30% of the class, received credit toward a class requirement in lieu of payment.

Procedure.   The first part of the initial questionnaire featured six scenarios or vignettes that assessed the participants' assumptions and beliefs about the circumstances that lead to abortion. Each scenario dealt with a particular woman's decision to undergo an abortion. Three scenarios were designed to present relatively sympathetic cases. One involved a pregnancy resulting from rape; a second involved a pregnancy in which the fetus was at risk of a genetically transmitted disease; and a third scenario involved the pregnancy of a high school teenager. The other three scenarios were designed to present relatively less sympathetic cases. One dealt with a pregnancy resulting from a casual affair; one dealt with a pregnancy that posed a threat to career aspirations; and one dealt with the pregnancy of an older mother with grown children. Participants assessed both how much sympathy they felt for the individual deciding to undergo abortion in each case and how typical they found each of the abortion cases (1 = *not at all typical,* 7 = *extremely typical*). The respondents filling out the initial questionnaire subsequently were asked to estimate the percentage of all abortions that fell into each of several categories, again some relatively sympathetic (e.g., abortion following rape or incest) and some relatively less sympathetic (e.g., abortion to terminate a pregnancy following a casual affair).

Respondents to Questionnaire 1 were then asked about the bases for their opinions and beliefs about abortion. Specifically, they were asked to indicate (on 7-point scales) the extent they had been influenced by each of several stipulated factors, including actual cases they knew or had heard about; practical consequences of laws permitting or limiting abortion; religious, moral, or ethical considerations; general philosophical beliefs; and general political orientation. When participants had completed all of these ratings pertaining to their own construals and beliefs, they were again presented with the same set of items, but this time asked about the responses that would be made to each item by "typical pro-choice" and "typical pro-life" partisans at Stanford University.[4]

The questionnaire administered to the respondents who participated in the second phase of Study 1 further explored beliefs of pro-choice and pro-life partisans enrolled in an introductory psychology class. One set of questions dealt with pragmatic considerations. Participants assessed as true or false five statements about specific consequences that might follow if the courts substantially restricted legal access to abortion through a decision overturning *Roe v. Wade.* Three of the consequences were negative (e.g., "more women would die because of illegal abortions"; "there would be more mistreated children"; and "only rich women would be able to get abortions"). Two of the stipulated consequences were positive or ameliorative (e.g., "there would be more wide-spread use of birth control"; and "most of the unwanted babies would be adopted"). For each item, participants first offered their own assessment, then estimated in turn the percentage of pro-choice and of pro-life supporters in their introductory psychology class who would respond *true or false* to each item. A second set of items dealt with factual or scientific matters, including, most notably, the percentage of early abortions (i.e., those occurring in the 10th week of pregnancy or before) and the week of pregnancy during which the fetus becomes viable. For each of these items, respondents again first offered their own numerical estimate and then guessed the estimate offered by their pro-choice and pro-life classmates.

Results

Sympathy for scenario characters choosing abortion. Participants' sympathy ratings for the three relatively sympathetic and three relatively unsympathetic scenarios in the first questionnaire administration were combined to provide composite measures, as shown in Table 1. As one might expect, pro-choice respondents expressed significantly more sympathy than pro-life respondents for the women choosing abortion. This was true for the "sympathetic" scenarios, $t(49) = 2.81$, $p < .01$, the "unsympathetic" scenarios, $t(49) = 5.62$, $p < .001$, and the six-scenario composite, $t(49) = 5.19$, $p < .001$. As predicted, however, this sympathy gap proved to be far smaller than the members of either

TABLE 1

Actual Versus Estimated Differences in Assessments of Sympathetic and Unsympathetic Abortion Scenarios and Categories (Questionnaire 1)

Item	Actual ratings					Pro-choice estimates						Pro-life estimates					
	By PCs (n = 27)		By PLs (n = 25)		Difference[1]	Of PCs[2]		Of PLs[2]		Difference[3]		Of PCs[2]		Of PLs[2]		Difference[3]	
	M	SD	M	SD		M	SD	M	SD	M	SD	M	SD	M	SD	M	SD
Sympathy for women in vignette:																	
Sympathetic scenarios	7.8	1.5	6.7	1.2	1.1**	8.1	1.3	5.9	1.9	2.2[a]	2.2	8.4	1.1	5.2**	1.8	3.2[b]	2.2
Unsympathetic scenarios	4.9	2.1	2.0	1.6	2.9*	5.6	1.9	1.2*	1.0	4.4[b]	2.5	5.9	1.7	1.6	1.3	4.3[a]	2.1
All scenarios	6.3	1.6	4.3	1.1	2.0**	6.9**	1.5	3.6*	1.2	3.3[b]	2.1	7.1	1.2	3.4**	3.4	3.7[b]	1.9
Assessed typicality of unsympathetic–sympathetic scenarios (mean difference)	0.0	3.5	0.9	4.3	−0.9	0.4	4.2	4.4**	4.1	−4.0[a]	5.6	−0.5	3.4	1.9	4.7	−2.4	4.5
Estimated percentage of abortions in unsympathetic–sympathetic categories (mean difference)	5.9	6.1	9.3	6.7	−3.4	7.3	5.7	14.7**	5.7	−7.4	6.1	4.8	5.4	12.4**	6.3	−7.6	6.2

Note. PCs = pro-choice participants; PLs = pro-life participants.

[1] Asterisks indicate *actual difference* between groups significantly different from zero: $^* p < .05$. $^{**} p < .01$.

[2] Asterisks indicate *estimated rating* significantly different from corresponding *actual rating*: $^* p < .05$. $^{**} p < .01$.

[3] Superscripts indicate *estimated difference* significantly greater than corresponding *actual difference*: [a] $p < .05$. [b] $p < .01$.

the pro-choice, $t(49) = 3.46$, $p < .01$, for the composite measure, or the pro-life group, $t(49) = 3.10$, $p < .01$, for the composite measure, had presumed it to be (see Table 1). The source of this discrepancy between presumption and reality was clear. We found that pro-life respondents actually expressed significantly more sympathy for the women electing abortion than either the pro-choice participants, $t(50) = 2.41$, $p < .05$, or the pro-life participants themselves, $t(24) = 3.62$, $p < .01$, had presumed. We similarly found that the pro-choice respondents actually expressed less sympathy for these women than the pro-life respondents, $t(49) = 1.96$, $p < .06$, or the pro-choice respondents themselves, $t(25) = 3.49$, $p < .01$ had presumed.

Perceived typicality of particular types of abortions.   Participants' estimates of typicality for the three relatively sympathetic scenarios were subtracted from their estimates for the three relatively unsympathetic scenarios. The resulting difference scores thus provided an index assessing participants' tendency to perceive unsympathetic abortion scenarios rather than sympathetic ones as typical; a higher score, accordingly, reflected a tendency to perceive the distribution of unsympathetic versus sympathetic abortion decisions in a manner ideologically congruent with the pro-life position rather than the pro-choice position. Respondents' percentage estimates for the frequency of cases in unsympathetic versus sympathetic abortion categories were treated similarly, again yielding difference scores for which more positive values were more reflective of biases congruent with the pro-life as opposed to the pro-choice stance (see Table 1).

Analyses of these composite measures revealed only a modest tendency for pro-life respondents to see unsympathetic abortion scenarios and categories as relatively more typical, and sympathetic scenarios and categories as relatively less typical, than did pro-choice respondents (see Table 1). This difference proved to be marginally statistically significant for the "category" measure, $t(50) = 1.94$, $p < .06$, but not for the "scenario" measure $(t < 1)$. Once again, however, these differences proved to be smaller than the partisans themselves had assumed. In the case of the pro-choice raters, the relevant discrepancy between actual and perceived partisan differences reached the conventional significance level for the scenario measure, $t(49) = 2.37$, $p < .05$, and fell just short of that level for the category measure, $t(48) = 1.99$, $p < .06$. In the case of the pro-life raters, the discrepancies in question, although in the predicted direction, did not reach conventional significance levels for either measure.[5]

Further examination revealed that it was the ideological consistency of the pro-life faction that was most likely to be overestimated, again by pro-choice and pro-life partisans alike. For the scenario measure, the degree of overestimation regarding pro-life participants was significant for pro-choice estimators, $t(50) = 3.04$, $p < .01$, but not for pro-life estimators, $t(24) = 1.03$, *n s*; for the category measure, the degree of overestimation regarding pro-life respondents was significant both for pro-choice estimators, $t(48) = 3.07$, $p < .01$, and for the pro-life estimators themselves, $t(24) = 4.43$, $p < .001$.

Perception of medical and scientific facts. Participants responding to the follow-up questionnaire in Study 1 were asked their beliefs about two factual or scientific matters of obvious concern to partisans in the abortion debate: (a) the percentage of abortions performed before or during the 10th week of pregnancy (i.e., the relative commonness of early, and therefore ethically less troubling, abortions) and (b) the week of pregnancy during which the fetus becomes viable.

The participants' responses to these items revealed modest differences between the factual assumptions of pro-choice and pro-life partisans, which was statistically significant in the case of the early abortion item, $t(82) = 2.03$, $p < .05$, but nonsignificant in the case of the week-of-viability item, $t(75) = 1.23$. As predicted, both of the "real" differences were smaller than the differences assumed by the two partisan groups. Specifically, pro-choice raters significantly overestimated pro-choice/pro-life differences on both the early abortion item, $t(61) = 2.40$, $p < .05$, and the viability item, $t(58) = 2.24$, $p < .01$.[6] For pro-life raters, the discrepancy between actual and estimated pro-choice/pro-life differences was marginally significant for the early abortion item, $t(19) = 2.08$, $p < .06$, and nonsignificant for the viability item, $t(17) = 1.15$.

Assumed consequences of limiting access to abortion. The items in the second questionnaire that dealt with anticipated harmful versus benign consequences of more restrictive abortion policies revealed several substantial differences between the views of the two partisan groups (see Table 2). Pro-choice participants were unanimous in agreeing that more deaths from illegal abortion would occur. They were close to unanimous in agreeing that more babies would be mistreated. In addition, almost half believed that abortion access would be restricted to the rich. (The mean percentage of agreement over the three items was roughly 79%.) Pro-life advocates were less convinced about each of these harmful consequences (the mean percentage of agreement was roughly 59%). Disagreements pertaining to the two items dealing with benign or mitigating consequences were even more pronounced. Whereas nearly 73% of pro-life partisans expected more widespread use of birth control, only 44% of pro-choice partisans agreed. Similarly, although 57% of pro-life partisans expected that "most unwanted babies would be adopted," the corresponding percentage for the pro-choice partisans was only 12%.

TABLE 2

Mean Actual Versus Estimated Differences in Factual Beliefs and Construal Pertinent to the Abortion Issue (Questionnaire 2)

Item	Actual ratings					Pro-choice estimates						Pro-life estimates					
	By PCs (n = 27)		By PLs (n = 25)		Difference[1]	Of PCs[2]		Of PLs[2]		Difference[3]		Of PCs[2]		Of PLs[2]		Difference[3]	
	M	SD	M	SD		M	SD	M	SD	M	SD	M	SD	M	SD	M	SD
Factual beliefs																	
% of Early abortions	65.9	24.1	53.4	24.3	12.5*	68.2	21.7	49.0	23.7	19.2[a]	21.9	68.4	23.7	46.8	19.2	21.6	19.6
Week fetus viable	21.6	7.8	18.8	10.0	2.8	22.8	8.4	15.6*	11.1	7.2[b]	9.3	22.3	9.8	16.8	9.4	5.5	9.9
Consequences of abortion restrictions:																	
Negative consequences[4]																	
More deaths from illegal abortions	100.0		81.8		18.2**[6]	85.9**		24.7**		61.2[b]		82.3**		40.8**		41.6[b]	
More mistreated babies	89.4		59.1		30.3**	70.4**		24.1**		46.3[b]		62.0**		31.3**		30.7	
Access restricted to the rich	46.1		36.4		9.7	54.4*		25.6**		28.8[b]		55.3		37.5		17.8	

T A B L E   2 (*continued*)

Mean Actual Versus Estimated Differences in Factual Beliefs and Construal Pertinent to the Abortion Issue (Questionnaire 2)

Item	Actual ratings						Pro-choice estimates							Pro-life estimates					
	By PCs (n = 27)		By PLs (n = 25)		Difference[1]		Of PCs[2]		Of PLs[2]		Difference[3]			Of PCs[2]		Of PLs[2]		Difference[3]	
	M	SD	M	SD			M	SD	M	SD	M	SD		M	SD	M	SD	M	SD
Combined[5]	78.5		59.1		19.4		70.2		24.8		45.4			66.5		36.5		30.0	
Benign consequences[4]																			
More widespread use of birth control	44.0		72.7		−28.7*		40.1		61.0**		−20.9			46.6		64.0*		−17.4	
Most unwanted babies adopted	12.1		57.1		−45.0**		27.4**		70.8**		−43.4			28.3**		63.7		−35.4	
Combined[5]	28.1		64.9		−36.8		33.8		65.9		−32.2			37.5		63.9		−26.4	

Note.   PCs = pro-choice participants; PLs = pro-life participants.

[1] Asterisks indicate *actual difference* between groups significantly different from *zero*. *p < .05.   **p < .01.

[2] Asterisks indicate *estimated rating* significantly different from corresponding *actual rating*. *p < .05.   **p < .01.

[3] Superscripts indicate *estimated difference* significantly different from corresponding *actual difference*. [a]p < .05.   [b]p < .01.

[4] Means represent actual and estimated percentages of respondents agreeing that the stated consequences of abortion restrictions will occur.

[5] These combined measures represent the average of the percentages for the individual item listed above them. Although useful for summary and illustrative purposes, discrepancies between actual and estimated differences for these combined measures cannot be compared via standard *t* tests.

[6] By Fisher's exact test.

For the three items that dealt with the anticipated negative consequences of increased abortion restrictions (i.e., "more deaths from illegal abortions," "more mistreated babies," and "abortion access restricted to the rich"), pro-choice estimators consistently overestimated partisan group differences (all $ps < .01$), believing in particular that pro-life respondents would respond in a more ideologically congruent fashion than they actually did. Pro-life raters also significantly overestimated their own group's tendency to respond in a manner consistent with ideology on two of the three items (i.e., the death and mistreatment items), but on those same two items they actually significantly underestimated pro-choice extremity (as did the pro-choice raters them-selves). Pro-life perceptions were generally accurate for both partisan groups on the third "negative" item ("abortion access restricted to the rich"). Contrary to our predictions, the gap in assumptions regarding potential benign or posi-tive consequences actually was slightly (albeit never significantly) larger than either partisan group had predicted.

Bases of beliefs.   The first questionnaire asked respondents to assess the bases both of their own abortion stance and that of typical partisans on the two sides of the issue. Specifically, they were asked to estimate (using 7-point scales) the impact exerted by six specific factors including both objective or pragmatic considerations (e.g., knowledge of actual cases or anticipated consequences of changing the laws) and ideological considerations (e.g., political orientation and religious or ethical concerns). The results of these assessments (see Table 3) are revealing. Both pro-choice and pro-life partisans cited "general philosophi-cal beliefs" as the most important determinant of their own views, with mean ratings of 5.8 and 5.6, respectively, on the relevant 7-point scale. Both claimed that they personally had been moderately influenced both by knowledge of actual cases and by the presumed consequences of laws permitting freer access to abortion. The groups differed primarily in their assessment of the impact of "genuine religious, moral, and ethical considerations" (pro-life respondents claimed to have been more influenced by these considerations than did pro-choice respondents, but not significantly so) and the impact both of "general political orientation" and the "anticipated consequences of laws restricting abortion" (pro-choice respondents claimed to have been more influenced by both types of considerations than pro-life participants claimed).

When we looked at the partisans' beliefs about the bases of each other's views, some interesting differences in perception emerged. Thus, pro-choice respondents believed that their fellow pro-choice partisans had been heavily influenced by their concerns about the potential impact of more restrictive abortion laws but that their pro-life antagonists had been largely unmoved

TABLE 3

Basis of Abortion Views: Mean Assessed Impact of Various Factors on Own Views, on Views of Own Side, and on Views of Other Side

Item	Rated influence on self					Rated influence on pro-choice				Rated influence on pro-life			
	By PCs (n = 26)		By PLs (n = 25)		Difference[1]	By PCs[2]		By PLs[2]		By PCs[2]		By PLs[2]	
	M	SD	M	SD		M	SD	M	SD	M	SD	M	SD
Knowledge of actual cases	3.5	1.8	3.4	1.7	0.1	4.4*	1.3	5.5**	0.9	3.6	1.5	4.2*	1.3
Anticipated consequences of laws restricting abortion	4.8	1.8	3.6	1.7	1.2*	5.4*	1.2	5.5	1.1	2.3**	1.3	3.7	1.7
Anticipated consequences of laws permitting abortion	4.1	1.9	4.1	2.0	0.0	4.4	1.5	4.8	1.4	4.5	2.0	4.8	1.6
General philosophical beliefs	5.8	1.1	5.6	1.1	0.2	5.7	0.9	5.5	1.4	5.7	1.3	5.8	1.1
General political orientation	3.8	2.1	2.2	1.5	1.6**	4.3	1.5	5.1*	1.0	4.6**	1.6	4.4**	1.5
Religious, moral, ethical convictions	4.6	1.8	5.5	1.8	-0.9	4.4	1.2	3.7*	1.2	6.3	0.6	6.1	0.7

Note. PCs = pro-choice respondents; PLs = pro-life respondents.

[1] Asterisks indicate actual difference between groups in ratings of influence on self significantly different from zero. *p < .05. **p < .01.

[2] Asterisks indicate rated influence on an average group member significantly different from corresponding rating for influence on self. *p < .05. **p < .01.

by such pragmatic concerns. The roughly .3-point difference in question was significantly greater than the 1.2-point difference apparent in the participants' self-reports regarding this consideration, $t(50) = 4.25$, $p < .01$, and, incidentally, greater than the 1.8-point difference expected by pro-life participants, which itself did not differ significantly from the actual difference. At the same time, both groups seemed to exaggerate pro-choice versus pro-life differences regarding the impact of religious, moral, and ethical convictions, $ts(50) = 2.00$ and 2.57, $ps < .06$ and .05, for pro-choice and pro-life perceivers, respectively. The findings most relevant to our naive realism thesis, however, are those that involved assessments about the influence of ideology or politics. Our respondents felt that they personally had been less heavily influenced by their political orientation than had either their peers or their adversaries. The data in Table 3 make it clear that our participants were willing to admit that their own views on abortion had been influenced by nonfactual, nonpragmatic concerns, but they preferred to label such influences as philosophical or even religious and ethical. Only in taking into account the views of other people, especially the other side, were they inclined to cite the potentially biasing effect of political orientation.

Study 2: Liberals and Conservatives Interpret an Incident of Racial Violence

Study 1 dealt with actual versus estimated differences in construal relevant to a broad social issue, namely, the practice of abortion. In Study 2, the emphasis shifted somewhat. We sought to examine the extent to which opposing partisans—this time, self-described liberals and conservatives—would similarly overestimate differences in their construals of the facts surrounding one specific controversial incident, an incident involving interracial violence.

Racial animosity between Blacks and Whites remains an important problem in America, one that generally leads liberals and conservatives not only to offer rather different analyses of the nation's problems and to propose rather different solutions, but also to construe specific events that they hear or read about in a rather different fashion. One such event, the so-called "Howard Beach" incident, involved the death, in November 1986, of a young Black man, Michael Griffith, who was struck by a passing car as he attempted to escape from a group of White pursuers in the Howard Beach neighborhood of New York City. The incident ultimately led to the trial and conviction of some (but not all) of the young man's pursuers. Many details of the case remain ambiguous and highly controversial and as such offered an ideal target for our study of real versus perceived construal biases. Thus, in accord with our theoretical concerns, we first contrasted liberal and conservative construals and then explored the two groups' assumptions about the other side's construals versus their own side's construals.

In Study 2 we also asked a group of self-described political neutrals to predict the construals of both liberals and conservatives. The tendency for partisan respondents in Study 1 to overestimate the ideological consistency and extremity not only of the other side but of their own side as well suggested that the phenomenon in question had less to do with the way in which partisans perceive groups than the way in which partisan groups are perceived. Accordingly, and consistent with our conceptual analysis of naive realism, we expected that political middle-of-the-roaders, or "neutrals," like the political partisans themselves, would overestimate the construal biases and ideological consistency of both partisan groups.

There was also a change in the way we identified the target of the participants' various assessments. Rather than asking them to make assessments about the "typical" member of the partisan faction at Stanford, we asked them to estimate the mean responses of those of their classmates who had checked the two most extreme points on the relevant self-description item. In other words, we relied on an accurate and precise "operational" definition of the groups whose responses were to be estimated.

Method

Item preparation.   Item selection in this study depended heavily on the contribution of a group of student raters. These raters were provided with a large number of statements about the Howard Beach case, obtained from The New York Times and other newspapers, which they were asked to classify into three categories: (a) statements that reflected poorly on the White perpetrators of the assault (who became the defendants in the ensuing trial), (b) statements that reflected poorly on the Black victim in the case, and (c) statements that were relevant to the case but did not reflect poorly or well on any party in the case. From this larger pool of items, 14 were chosen that had elicited widespread agreement from the raters. Of these, 6 were "anti-perpetrator" items (e.g., "the White pursuers [the perpetrators] deliberately chased Michael Griffith [the victim] into the path of oncoming traffic"); 6 were "anti-victim" items (e.g., "Michael Griffith had consumed cocaine on the night in question"); and 2 were neutral, or "buffer," items (e.g., "The Howard Beach incident damaged New York City's reputation").

Participants.   A political preference question was administered to Stanford undergraduates who either were enrolled in introductory psychology classes or were recruited in their dormitories. The questionnaire results allowed us to identify and recruit 23 liberals and 20 conservatives, all of whom had characterized themselves using the most extreme points (i.e., 1 or 7) or next to most extreme points (i.e., 2 or 6) on the relevant 7-point liberal–conservative rating scale. Another 16 neutral or middle-of-the-road students, all of whom had characterized themselves using the middle of the scale (i.e., 4), were also identified and recruited. Participants received either course credit or a payment of $5 for their participation.

Procedure.   All participants, political partisans and neutrals alike, were given the same one-page synopsis of the Howard Beach case (i.e., a description of the events leading up to the death of Michael Griffith, along with a summary of the jail sentences handed down) and were asked to complete a questionnaire that presented them with the 14 prepared statements about the case. Respondents were asked to indicate, using 7-point Likert-type scales, the degree to which they believed each statement to be true. They were also asked to predict how liberal and conservative undergraduates would rate the truth of the same statements (order of rating tasks was counterbalanced in the design). In all cases respondents were provided with an operational definition of liberals and conservatives; that is, they were told (accurately) that the terms *liberal* and *conservative* referred to those participants in our study who had characterized themselves using either the two most extreme or the two next-to-most extreme points on the relevant 7-point self-rating scale.

After completing all assessments pertaining to these 14 rater-generated construal items, participants read one-page summaries of the defense and prosecution closing trial statements and responded to several additional items created by us. The topics dealt with in these items included the accuracy of the defense and prosecution statements, the "harshness" of the defendants' treatment, and the treatment the defendants likely would have received had the racial situation been reversed (i.e., if the defendants had been Black and the victim White). Once again, for each of the items, respondents both provided their own ratings and estimated the mean ratings that liberal and conservative respondents would offer for that item.[7] Finally, as in Study 1, respondents were again asked to indicate the bases for their own assessments and those of the two partisan groups. However this time, instead of judging the basis of a stance on a general topic such as abortion, respondents were asked to characterize the bases for the judgments made in the Howard Beach case. Participants considered the impact of the available evidence and the impact of political ideology or beliefs, as well as the impact of their knowledge about the racial situation in New York. Furthermore, for these items dealing with influences on other people, participants were asked to report not only the influences they believed had actually determined the partisans' responses but also the influences they expected the relevant partisan groups to report.

Results

Construal measures and predictions.   Composite scores were calculated for each respondent using the 12 items deemed sensitive to potentially liberal or conservative biases in construal.[8] These scores were then transformed to percentage scores, such that 0 indicated the most extreme anti-victim bias possible and 100 indicated the most extreme anti-perpetrator bias possible. A one-way analysis of variance performed on these scores revealed a significant difference among the three groups' construals, $F(2, 56) = 6.27, p < .01$. More specifically, a focused contrast indicated a statistically significant, $t(41) = 3.14, p < .01$, but seemingly modest difference (i.e., 9 points on the relevant 100-point scale) between liberal and conservative construals (see Table 4). That is, liberal participants, as one might anticipate, interpreted the events in question in a way that reflected slightly more negatively on the White perpetrators (and less negatively on the Black victim) than did conservative respondents ($Ms = 63.2$ for liberals vs. 54.2 for conservatives). The neutrals, as one might also anticipate, offered construals that fell in between those of the two partisan groups ($M = 55.6$), although they were much closer to those of the conservatives.

The most striking result, however, and the one most relevant to our research hypothesis, was the overestimation of this difference by partisans and nonpartisans alike. The primary source of this overestimation can be seen in Table 4 and Figure 1. That is, all three groups of respondents significantly overestimated the extent to which the conservatives would interpret the Howard Beach events in ways that blamed the Black victim and exonerated the White perpetrators, $t(41) = 6.04, p < .001$, for liberals; $t(19) = 6.37, p < .001$, for conservatives; $t(33) = 5.38, p < .001$, for neutrals. In addition, although to a lesser extent, all three groups overestimated the tendency for liberal participants to show an opposite (i.e., anti-perpetrator) bias, $t(22) = 2.73, p < .05$, for liberals; $t(41) = 3.63, p < .001$, for conservatives; and $t(365) = 3.10, p < .01$, for neutrals. The result, of course, was highly significant overestimation of liberal–conservative differences in construal by all three groups of raters ($ps < .01$ in each case).[9]

The consistency of such overestimates bears further examination and emphasis. Not one of the 20 conservative participants showed the degree of pro-perpetrator bias that the liberals, the neutrals, or even the conservatives themselves expected to be average for such respondents. By the same token, only 3 of the 23 liberal respondents displayed the degree of anti-perpetrator bias predicted to be average for the group by conservatives, only 2 displayed the degree predicted to be average by the neutrals, and only 7 displayed the degree that the liberals themselves had predicted to be average for their peers.

TABLE 4

Actual Versus Estimated Liberal–Conservative Differences in Mean Judgments and Construals Concerning the Howard Beach Case

Item	Participants' construal[4]	Prosecution close[5]	Defense close[5]	Difference	Court treatment[6]	Treatment if race reversed[6]
Actual ratings						
By LIBS (n = 23)	63.2	71.8	19.0	52.9	3.2	1.5
By CONS (n = 20)	54.2	57.1	47.8	9.3	2.8	2.1
Difference[1]	8.9**	14.7*	−28.8**	43.6**	0.4	−0.6*
Estimates by LIBS[2]						
Of LIBS	68.9*	81.2**	22.3	58.9	3.6*	1.5
Of CONS	32.3**	33.1**	70.2**	−37.1**	2.0**	2.6*
Difference[3]	36.5[b]	48.1[b]	−48.0[a]	96.0[b]	1.6[b]	−1.1
Estimates by CONS[2]						
Of LIBS	72.9**	80.5	18.9	61.5	4.1**	1.4
Of CONS	36.8**	40.6**	68.2**	−27.6**	2.2*	2.9**
Difference[3]	36.0[b]	39.9[b]	−49.3[a]	89.2[b]	1.9[b]	−1.5[b]
Estimates by NEUTS[2]						
Of LIBS	74.1**	80.9	24.8	56.1	3.9	1.4
Of CONS	33.3**	35.4**	65.2*	−29.9**	2.3	2.9**
Difference[3]	40.8[b]	45.6[b]	−40.4	86.0[a]	1.6[a]	−1.4[a]

Note.   LIBS = liberals; CONS = conservatives; NEUTS = neutrals.

[1] Asterisks indicate *actual difference* significantly different from *zero.* $*p < .05.$ $**p < .01.$
[2] Asterisks indicate *estimated rating* significantly different from corresponding *actual ratings.*
  $*p < .05.$ $**p < .01.$
[3] Superscripts indicate *estimated difference* significantly greater than corresponding *actual difference.*
  $^a p < .05.$ $^b p < .01.$
[4] Higher mean scores reflect construals of events hostile to the White perpetrators and favorable to the Black victim.
[5] Means reflect participants' perceptions of accuracy (i.e., higher scores indicate greater perceived accuracy).
[6] Means are based on 5-point scale (1 = *far too harsh,* 5 = *far too lenient*).

Assessment of prosecution and defense closing statements.   The liberal and conservative respondents' assessments of the relative accuracy of prosecution and defense closing statements in the Howard Beach case showed differences consistent both with their general political stance and with their differing

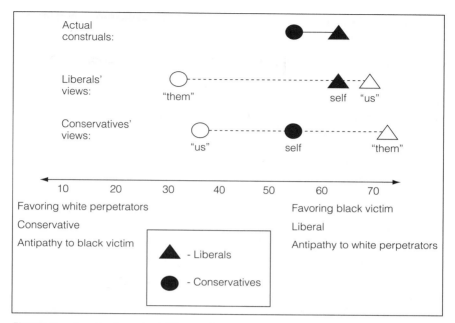

Figure 1 ■ Actual and perceived differences between politically liberal and conservative participants in their interpretations of the Howard Beach incident.

interpretations and construals of the specific events that had occurred (see Table 4). Respectively, liberals gave somewhat higher mean ratings to the prosecution closing statements than did conservatives ($Ms = 71.8$ vs. 57.1 on the 100-point scale), $t(41) = 2.24$, $p < .04$, and they gave substantially lower ratings to the defense closing statements ($Ms = 19.0$ vs. 47.8), $t(41) = 5.06$, $p < .001$. Once again, however, these actual differences of 14.7 and 28.8 points, respectively, although statistically significant, were dwarfed by the magnitude of the differences that the three groups had predicted (i.e., roughly 40 points or more in every instance). As Table 4 indicates, the relevant overestimations of liberal-conservative differences by all three groups were statistically significant for the prosecution closing (and prosecution vs. defense closing) ratings. For ratings of the defense closing, only the liberal–conservative difference predicted by neutral participants failed to differ significantly from the actual difference.

Again, it was predictions about the conservative raters that proved to be the most discrepant from the actual state of affairs. The discrepancy between actual and estimated conservative assessments, with respect to both the defense and prosecution closings, was statistically significant not only for liberal raters but also for neutral raters and for the conservatives themselves (with t tests all yielding probability values less than .01). By contrast, predictions about liberals were generally accurate. Liberals and neutrals slightly (but nonsignificantly) underestimated the ideologically consistent disapproval liberals would show in rating the defense closing, whereas conservative raters were right on target. Similarly, although all three groups overestimated the positivity of the liberal response to the prosecution closing, only the discrepancy between liberals' own estimates and their self-ratings attained a conventional level of significance (i.e., $p < .01$ for liberal raters, $p > .10$ for neutral and conservative raters).

Treatment of the defendants.   Despite their general political stance, liberals and conservatives actually differed little (see Table 4) in assessing the leniency or severity of the treatment afforded the defendants by the court ($p > .15$). On the other hand, they did differ significantly (in the direction one might expect in light of their political stances) in their ratings about the harshness of the treatment the defendants would have received if the racial status of the White perpetrators and Black victim had been reversed, $t(41) = 2.14$, $p < .04$. Most important, however, when we went from actual to perceived differences, the now-familiar pattern emerged. On both the court treatment and racial reversal items, all three groups expected greater differences between liberal and conservative assessments than those actually found, with the discrepancy between actual and perceived differences reaching the conventional statistical significance level in every case (all $ps < .02$), except liberal raters' estimation of partisan differences on the racial reversal item ($p < .10$).

Once again, the gap between expectation and reality on these measures was primarily attributable to the overestimation, by all groups, of the degree to which conservative respondents would respond in an ideologically congruent fashion. On the racial reversal question, this overestimation was statistically significant for all three groups ($ps < .02$). On the court treatment issue, the overestimation was significant for the liberals and conservatives (both p values $< .01$), although it just failed to reach the conventional significance level for the neutrals, $t(34) = 1.99$, $p < .06$. Liberals were also misperceived, but less consistently so. Although their liberal bent on the court treatment question was overestimated to a statistically significant degree by conservatives, $t(41) = 3.39$, $p < .01$, and fellow liberals, $t(22) = 2.75$, $p < .02$, it was overestimated only marginally by neutrals, $t(37) = 1.89$, $p < .07$. On the racial reversal question, there was no evidence of such overestimation vis-á-vis liberals by any of the three groups.

Perceived bases for judgments.   Participants were asked to rate the extent to which the various ratings and judgments reflecting construals of the Howard Beach case (both their own construals and those of the two partisan groups) had been influenced by three different factors: (a) the available evidence, (b) the participants' political ideology or beliefs, and (c) the participants' knowledge about the racial situation in New York. Respondents were asked not only to predict the extent to which liberals and conservatives would report having been influenced by each of these factors but also the extent to which these two groups really had been influenced.

Our analyses indicated that liberals and conservatives differed little in their claims about the influence exerted on their own assessments by either the available evidence or their political ideology. (Liberals did, however, report a significantly greater influence of their knowledge about New York's racial situation than did either of the other groups). Consistent with our account of "naive realism," however, participants across the political spectrum felt that other people, that is, both liberals and conservatives (in contrast to themselves), had been heavily influenced by ideology and relatively uninfluenced by evidence (see Table 5). Participants in all three groups further felt that liberals and conservatives alike had been influenced by ideology to an extent that was greater than those partisans had claimed (in all but one case, the relevant probability values reached the .01 level). Liberals and neutrals alike (and to some extent even the conservatives themselves) also felt that conservatives had been influenced less than they claimed by evidence ($ps < .01$ for liberal and neutral raters, $p < .01$ for conservative raters). Also, conservatives ($p < .07$), neutrals ($p < .01$), and even liberals ($p < .02$) felt the same way about the actual versus self-reported influence of evidence on liberals.

Discussion

Despite the changes in topic, groups, definitions, and the wording or emphasis of questionnaire items, the results of Study 2 closely resembled those of Study 1. Liberals and conservatives apparently interpreted the facts of the Howard Beach incident and ensuing trial somewhat differently, in accord with their ideological biases; however, as was the case with the pro-choice versus pro-life views explored in Study 1, the magnitude of these real construal differences was far exceeded by the magnitude of the differences assumed by the relevant partisans. Also, participants in Study 2 again overestimated the extremity and ideological consistency not only of the other side but of their own side as well. An asymmetry in these effects, noted somewhat parenthetically in Study 1, was once again apparent, however. Specifically, the overestimation proved to be much greater with respect to conservative views than with respect to liberal views (just as it had with respect to presumably more conservative pro-life views than presumably more liberal pro-choice views). As a result, whereas both partisan groups were about equally guilty of overestimating the gap in construals, liberals proved to be less accurate than conservatives in their perceptions of their adversaries, whereas conservatives proved to be less accurate than liberals in their perceptions of their peers.

Basis of Judgments and Construals: Mean Assessed Impact of Three Factors on Own Construal, on Own Construals of Own Side, and on Construals of Other Side

Item	Rated influence on self					Rated influence on liberals						Rated influence on conservatives					
	By LIBS (n = 23)		By CONS (n = 20)		Difference	By LIBS[1]		By CONS[1]		By NEUTS[1]		By LIBS[1]		By CONS[1]		By NEUTS[1]	
	M	SD	M	SD		M	SD	M	SD	M	SD	M	SD	M	SD	M	SD
Available evidence	4.7	1.4	5.2	1.3	−0.5	4.0*	1.4	3.9	1.3	3.4**	1.3	3.7**	1.5	4.5	1.5	3.7**	1.4
Political ideology or beliefs	4.2	1.7	3.7	1.4	0.5	5.1**	1.3	5.7**	1.1	5.5*	1.2	5.5**	1.3	5.4**	1.3	5.6**	0.9
Racial knowledge	4.6	1.6	3.4	1.8	1.2	5.1	1.1	5.5*	1.1	5.2	1.4	3.9	1.7	4.1	1.4	3.7	1.1

Note. LIBS = liberals; CONS = conservatives; NEUTS = neutrals.

[1] Asterisks indicate rated actual influence on an average group member significantly different from corresponding actual rating for influence on self. * $p < .05$.   ** $p < .01$.

Two findings of theoretical importance are also worth emphasizing. First, the neutral participants in Study 2 shared the tendency to overestimate both partisan ideological extremity and group differences in construal. This finding, along with the fact that partisan respondents in both studies tended to overestimate the extremity of the views of their own side as well as those of their ideological adversaries, indicates that partisanship on the part of the respondent making the relevant estimates was not the key to such overestimation. Rather, the data strongly suggest the key was all participants' shared (but exaggerated) notions about the impact that partisanship would exert on construals and beliefs. Second, the results of Study 2 also provided further evidence relevant to our theoretical contentions regarding naive realism. That is, although members of the two partisan groups differed little in characterizing the bases of their own assessment, they clearly believed that other people in general, and people on the other side in particular, had been much more influenced than they themselves by political ideology and somewhat less influenced by the available evidence.

General Discussion

Results of our two studies suggest that partisans involved in social-political conflicts tend to overestimate the extremity and ideological congruency of the underlying beliefs and construal of the other side, and often of their own side as well. Critically, nonpartisans or neutrals similarly tend to overestimate the polarization of partisan views. Thus, partisans and nonpartisans alike are prone to overestimate the gap between the two sides, the gap between their own personal views and those of the other side, and especially the gap between their ideological partners and those of their ideological adversaries. The evidence further suggests that the partisans in our studies believed that their own views and assumptions were generally less shaped by political ideology than by objective or rational pragmatic concerns compared with the views of their adversaries or even their fellow partisans. These findings are highly compatible with and closely akin to the polarization effects documented by Moscovici (1981; see also Judd & Kulik, 1980; Pratkanis, 1989). Our results, however, also extend those findings by demonstrating that it is erroneous and exaggerated inferences about the way partisans perceive the world, rather than partisan biases on perception, that lie at the heart of the phenomena we have reported.

Perhaps most surprising was the extent to which our respondents believed that their own side would be guilty of the same biases attributed to the other side. In both studies participants assumed that even those who shared their basic positions would not share their willingness to see relevant factual issues or pragmatic concerns in an objective rather than ideologically dictated fashion. Thus, in contrast to various discussions of stereotyping, particularly the typical in-group favoritism noted in accounts of ethnocentrism (Brewer, 1979) and out-group delegitimization (Bar-Tal, 1990), partisans in our studies tended to view not only the other side but also the members of their own side as extremist and unduly influenced by ideology and bias. In effect, partisans within ideological groups tended to view themselves as atypical vis-à-vis their group: atypical in their moderation, in their freedom from bias, and in their capacity to "see things as they are in reality" even when that reality proves to be ideologically inconvenient or "politically incorrect."

Another noteworthy, perhaps surprising, feature in our data may be the tendency for those holding the conservative position on the relevant issue to be perceived less accurately than those holding the liberal position, a tendency shared by liberals, by neutrals, and by conservatives themselves. It is conceivable that this result is an artifact arising from the distribution of political views on the predominantly liberal Stanford campus (i.e., Stanford liberals may in fact more closely resemble commonly held stereotypes than do conservatives). It is also possible that the term *liberal* (at least on the Stanford campus) may be relatively well understood and agreed on, whereas the label conservative may produce less agreement and may cover a broader range of political ideologies, (i.e., libertarian, traditionalist, authoritarian, etc.). In short, it remains to be seen whether this result reflects some more widespread and noteworthy phenomenon about the actual nature of, beliefs about, and misperceptions about the two groups (see Fields & Schuman, 1976). Obviously, broader, more representative sampling of liberal and conservative respondents (and, of course, issues) will be required before hazarding any guesses about the robustness, much less the sources, of such a phenomenon.[10]

Before discussing possible theoretical or practical implications of our findings, we note some methodological limitations arising from the nature of our respondent sample. First, the sample was small, a problem that reduced the statistical power of any comparisons that obliged us to estimate rather than stipulate the actual differences to which predicted differences could be compared. Second, it is conceivable that our undergraduate partisans generally are more moderate and less doctrinaire than those holding the relevant political positions within the larger society; it is also conceivable (although less likely) that our partisans were less well informed than citizens in general about the views of their adversaries. These concerns should, at the least, make us reluctant to generalize too readily to the broader body politic.

A subtler but more serious problem concerns the task faced by our participants. Although we went to considerable pains to emphasize that they were to estimate average responses, or percentages of partisans opting for one response or another, we cannot rule out the possibility that some of our respondents nevertheless insisted on estimating "prototypical" responses (i.e., those most "exemplary" or "distinguishing" of the group) instead of, as we had specified, responses of "average or typical group members" (Study 1) or "the mean response" of all participants checking the appropriate points on the relevant self-description scales (Study 2). We also cannot rule out the possibility that simple "nonregressiveness" in prediction, abetted by reliance on the representativeness heuristic (Tversky & Kahneman, 1974), played a role. However, we can assure the reader that not even the most extreme group members (in terms of either their self-characterizations or their involvement in activist political groups) showed the degree of ideological bias and extremity in construal assumed by our respondents. We also remind the reader that if participants insist on using extreme, prototypic, or "stereotypic" group members as the basis for their inferences even in a laboratory study where they were told not to do so, it is virtually certain that such a tendency produces even more distorted and exaggerated judgments in everyday ideological confrontations outside the laboratory.

Finally, we recognize that there are some obvious problems in using self-reports to assess the accuracy of social perceptions. In particular, it is conceivable that respondents may be unwilling or unable to report their own views accurately and that our respondents' actual perceptions, assumptions, and construals may have been more thoroughly and closely in accord with the political positions they espoused, and more in accord with the predictions made by ideological peers, adversaries, and neutrals alike, than their self-reports in this study have suggested. We add that we have no reason to assume that systematic biases in self-assessment or self-report did occur (or, more to the point, no reason to assume that it was any such biases that produced the pattern of results we obtained). Nevertheless, we do recognize the need for caution in interpreting and generalizing results that use self-assessments, especially discrepancies in self-assessments, to test the accuracy of social beliefs and predictions.

Theoretical Implications

Our analyses and findings help to illuminate the complex possibilities for misunderstanding and misattribution that arise in the context of social–political debate. It has long been recognized that opposing partisans may not simply be disagreeing about the most reasonable position to be adopted concerning the issue at hand. Rather, they may be proceeding from different factual assumptions about, or different construals of that issue; that is, in Asch's (1940, 1948) terms, disagreeing not about the "judgment of the social object" but about the (nature of) the "object of judgment." To the extent that the opposing partisans fail to recognize, or fail to make allowance for such construal differences, misattributions and misunderstandings become inevitable. Our studies of partisan perception and perceptions of partisanship, however, produced notably few examples of such blindness to differences in perception or construal. On the contrary, on measure after measure our participants overestimated such differences. This recognition, even exaggeration, of construal differences vis-à--vis ideological adversaries however, did not reflect a charitable interpretation of the corresponding differences in political positions (e.g., the view that one's adversaries were fair-minded people who had proceeded logically from different factual assumptions and interpretations to reach different but not unreasonable conclusions). Instead, our measures suggest that the opposing partisans, and neutrals as well, deemed the relevant construal differences to be the product rather than the source of ideological or political bias. Our participants, in short, assumed that they alone proceeded from facts or reasonable factual assumptions, guided by reasonable ethical and philosophical principles, but generally untainted by ideological or political bias.

Underlying this seemingly smug and self-congratulatory stance, we have argued, is a more fundamental illusion, one that has been central to social psychology's long-standing exploration of subjectivism or naive realism (Asch, 1940; Griffin & Ross, 1991; Lewin, 1948; Ross & Nisbett, 1991; Ross & Ward, in press-a). The basis for this illusion is the individual's conviction that he or she perceives reality objectively and that reality will be similarly perceived by those who share that objectivity. This conviction, in turn, may lead people to treat the viewpoints held and expressed by those who disagree with them about important social or political issues as evidence of subjective bias on the part of those opponents, bias not only in proceeding from evidence to conclusions but also in construing the evidence itself. Indeed, once people decide that others are guided by ideology (rather than the evidence and common sense), it becomes logical to assume that these others, friends and foes alike, will differ significantly from them in their construals and beliefs about a wide range of issues. They decide that these others, unlike themselves, will perceive the world in a manner that is consistent with, indeed reinforcing of, such ideological biases. They insist that they alone, unfettered by ideological blinders, will be able to see and be forced to confront the complexity of issues and problems, obliged to choose not between black and white but among subtle shades of gray. Although our findings are consistent with such theorizing, they obviously do not demand it. Indeed, we are well aware that conventional theories of stereotyping could generate predictions of exaggerated ideological extremity and consistency (although such theories would surely have to be stretched mightily to encompass construals, rather than actions and attributes, to embrace perceptions of in-groups as well as those of out-groups and to address differences in the sources of own vs. others' views). However, we do regard our findings as an encouraging development in our continuing efforts to link social misunder-standing and misattribution to more basic cognitive or motivational processes (see Griffin & Ross, 1991; Ross & Ward, in press-b).

Before turning from theoretical implications to practical ones, an obvious question remains: When are construal differences likely to be unanticipated and unrecognized (or at least underestimated) and when are such differences likely to be anticipated and even exaggerated? One answer involves the level and salience of social debate. Issues such as abortion rights and racial animosity are the topic of ongoing, outspoken, social dialogue. Even if many people once tac-itly assumed that those on the other side of such issues were proceeding from the same facts and assumptions as they themselves, years of exposure to parti-sans on the other side, especially through the news media, are likely to have disabused them. Indeed, the dynamics of informal and formal social debate are apt to heighten one's impressions and assumptions about the construal biases exhibited by the other side. That is, in social discussion people are generally less interested in revealing the complexities and sources of ambivalence in their positions—particularly if they are publicly representing one side to a dispute (Druckman, 1971)—than in defending their basic stance and persuading others. Nor, as decades of group dynamics research taught us, do partisans lightly reveal their doubts or ambivalence to their ideological peers—lest they face coolness, suspicion, criticism, or even ostracism. As a result, people are likely to hear biased samples of partisan assumptions and construals from fellow partisans and adversaries alike. In other words, the theories people hold about partisan differences in construal and the data they receive about such views from everyday experience are likely to be mutually reinforcing.

By the same token, when there is an absence of social debate, when sharply defined factions have failed to emerge and identify themselves, people are not apt to be confronted with differences in construal or even obliged to consider the possibility that such differences may exist. Indeed, in our study (and, no doubt, often in everyday social experience), people may be induced to assume and even exaggerate the extent of construal differences only when they are explicitly required to consider the question of construal similarities and differences. When not prompted to do so, the norm may be a type of "mindlessness" (Langer, 1978) in which no consideration of construal, much less differences in construal, occurs at all. That is, like young children, people characteristically may not stop to contemplate the difference between appearance and reality (Flavell, 1985) or to consider the possibility that others may not share their perspectives. Instead, people may simply respond to what seem to them to be the opportunities and demands of the environment, with little consideration of the reasons why others might be responding differently to that same environment. Indeed, when one finds that another person has responded differently to an object of social, political, or ethical judgment than one has, and no basis for assuming ideological differences presents itself, one may still conclude that the other person lacks objectivity. For in failing to recognize the inherent subjectivity of one's own construal, one is prone to presume bias on the part of the other.

Implications for Conflict Resolution

Although we did not explicitly address the topic of conflict resolution, a few observations may be in order. First, members of opposing factions who overestimate differences in their working assumptions, priorities, and sympathies are apt to be overly pessimistic about the prospect of finding common ground in their views, interests, or goals (Clark & Marshall, 1981). Members of pro-choice and pro-life factions, we believe, who took the trouble to candidly air the details of their views might find more in the way of shared interests than they anticipate (Keltner & Robinson, 1993). For instance, they might find that they agree not only about the need for programs designed to prevent unwanted pregnancies but also about the need for programs—such as on-site day care for working mothers—that would make alternatives to abortions less daunting. Yet, the discussion and negotiation necessary to become aware of such areas of potential agreement may be precluded by erroneous assumptions about the ideological orthodoxy of the other side.

Our research thus suggests the value of candid, relatively informal discussions (and of developing personal relations and settings that encourage such candor), discussions in which participants talk about their factual assumptions and the complexities of their values rather than simply defending their positions (for related research on the benefits of this type of discussion, see Druckman, Broome, & Korper, 1988; Thompson, 1991; Walcott, Hopmann, & King, 1977). Even if such discussions do not lead to consensus about policy, they could at least reduce stereotyping (by neutral observers as well as by the partisans themselves) and allow the partisans to see the other side as less of an unreasoning, unreasonable, ideologically driven monolith. In fact, such discussions would also free partisans of some illusions that they hold not only about their ideological adversaries but about their own side as well (i.e., illusions of homogeneity, moral consensus [Janis, 1972], and extremism), which would in turn make it easier for them to express their own dissenting views. Indeed, it has been proposed that both third parties (Rubin, 1980) and moderates within groups (Jacobson, 1981) can play a valuable role in facilitating the relevant dialogue, especially in encouraging partisans predisposed toward extremism to get beyond rhetoric and statements of position to underlying interests, assumptions, concerns, and especially sources of uncertainty and ambivalence (see also Fisher & Ury, 1981; Pruitt & Rubin, 1986; Susskind & Cruikshank, 1987).

Beyond any specific applied implications, our research serves simply to refocus attention on the subjective world of people who are in social conflicts. It is difficult enough to deal with the hostility and distrust that arise from real differences in viewpoints arising from real differences in objective interests and experiences. Researchers must therefore do what they can to recognize and attenuate any hostility and distrust that arises from misperceptions and misattributions. In particular, they must be vigilant for instances in which people respond less to each other's actual views than to tacit but erroneous assumptions about such views and about the character of those who hold them.

Notes

1. At the time of Study 1 (summer 1989), both the attention given to the abortion issue and the zeal of pro-choice and pro-life factions were at a high point because of the various cases pending before the United States Supreme Court.
2. In both Study 1 and Study 2, 1 or 2 respondents failed to answer the relevant questionnaire completely. As a result, degrees of freedom varied slightly for different statistical comparisons.
3. This self-labeling occurred at the end of the questionnaire on a two-part item. The first part asked respondents to circle either pro-choice or pro-life. The second part asked them to indicate how *strongly* they believed in their position, using a 7-point scale (1 = *not strongly at all*, 7 = *very strongly*, 4 = *with moderate strength*). Only the questionnaires of partisans circling the two most extreme points (i.e., 6 or 7) were used in the study.
4. This simple wording used to elicit respondents' estimates or perceptions regarding the views of the two partisan groups merits some comment. On the one hand, the wording was *conservative* with regard to our overestimation hypothesis, because the partisans whose views we actually tallied, rather than being typical, were activists who belonged to campus organizations concerned with the abortion issue (and thus were likely to hold views more extreme than the statistical mean, median, or mode of their group). On the other hand, to some respondents the word *typical* might connote *prototypical* or *most exemplary* and thus prompt them to offer not estimates of statistical averages (i.e., means, medians, or modes) but characteristics shown by the most extreme group members. It will become apparent later that the class of partisans about whom estimates were to be made was defined somewhat differently in our two studies. As will also become apparent, the pattern of findings to be discussed did not depend either on the way the target groups were characterized or on the types of estimates (means, proportions, etc.) that were being made about those groups.
5. We should note parenthetically that the statistical significance of *all* these findings, and some others to follow, would have greatly increased if a less conservative test had been used (i.e., a test determining whether the actual difference

obtained fell within a confidence interval for the participants' estimates). Instead, unless otherwise indicated, we treated each observed or actual mean difference as a sample statistic subject to estimation error (indeed, a statistic based on a relatively small sample) and as a result markedly, but we think appropriately, reduced the power of our test.

6. For this second phase of Study 1, unlike the initial phase of Study 1 (and, for that matter, unlike Study 2), we analyzed the data using tests that treated the means of the actual reports as population parameters rather than sample statistics. This less conservative approach seemed appropriate because participants in this second phase were specifically asked, beyond providing self-reports, to estimate the responses of pro-choice and pro-life supporters in the particular introductory psychology class of which they were a member. Thus, the respondents' self-reports made up the entire population of responses to which their estimates were compared.

7. For these tasks, and the other items discussed later the order of items and response measures was varied such that some participants offered all three ratings (i.e., self, liberal, and conservative) for each of the items in turn, some filled out self-ratings for all items before filling out liberal and conservative ratings, and the rest filled out liberal and conservative ratings before providing self-ratings. Analysis revealed no significant interactions (all probability values were greater than .10) between response order and response type on any of these items; accordingly, order effects receive no further consideration in our subsequent analyses and discussion.

8. The interitem reliability (Cronbach's alpha) of these 12 statements was 68.

9. It is worth noting that the 9 liberal respondents who characterized themselves as extreme (1 on our scale) displayed no greater pro-victim bias than the 14 who characterized themselves as less extreme (2 on our scale). In fact, these more extreme liberals exhibited slightly *less* provictim bias ($M = 62.6$) than did the less extreme liberals ($M = 63.5$). By the same token, although only 1 of the 20 conservative respondents chose to use the most extreme point on the 7-point preference scale, the degree of bias shown by that respondent was virtually indistinguishable from the mean level shown by the 19 respondents who characterized their conservatism with a 6 on the 7-point scale ($Ms = 52.8$ vs. 54.3, respectively). Accordingly, it seems unlikely that using samples of partisans that had included more individuals who checked 1 or 7 (instead of 2 or 6) would have yielded partisan construals that matched the respondents' extreme predictions. In other words, the overestimation phenomena in question is unlikely to represent an artifact arising either from the particular operational definition of partisanship that we adopted or from any tendency for respondents to overestimate the proportion of 1s and 7s in the partisan groups whose responses they were being asked to estimate.

10. Robinson and Keltner (1994) and Keltner and Robinson (1994) have undertaken further survey research to clarify this issue.

References

Allport, G. W. (1954). *The nature of prejudice.* Cambridge, MA: Addison-Wesley.

Asch, S. E. (1940). Studies in the principles of judgments and attitudes: II. Determination of judgments by group and by ego standards. *Journal of Social Psychology, 12,* 433–465.

Asch, S. E. (1948). The doctrine of suggestion, prestige, and imitation in social psychology. *Psychological Review, 55,* 250–276.

Bar-Tal, P. (1990). Causes and consequences of relegitimization: Models of conflict and enthnocentrism. *Journal of Social Issues, 46,* 65–81.

Bar-Tal, D., & Geva, N. (1986). A cognitive basis of international conflicts. In S. Worchel, & W. G. Austin (Eds.), *Psychology of intergroup relations* (pp. 118–133). Chicago: Nelson Hall.

Blumenthal, M. D., Kahn, R. L., Andrews, F. M., & Head, K. B. (1972). *Justifying violence.* Ann Arbor: University of Michigan Press.

Brewer, M. B. (1979). In-group bias in the minimal intergroup situation: A cognitive-motivational analysis. *Psychological Bulletin, 86,* 307–324.

Clark, H. H., & Marshall, C. R. (1981). Definite reference and mutual knowledge. In A. K. Joshi, B. Webber, & I. Sag (Eds.), *Linguistics structure and discourse setting* (pp. 10–63). Cambridge, England: Cambridge University Press.

Deutsch, M. (1973). *The resolution of conflict.* New Haven, CT: Yale University Press.

Druckman, D. (1971). On the effects of group representation. *Journal of Personality and Social Psychology, 18,* 273–274.

Druckman, D., Broome, B. J., & Korper, S. H. (1988). Value differences and conflict resolution. *Journal of Conflict Resolution, 32,* 489–510.

Eldridge, A. F. (1979). *Images of conflict.* New York: St. Martin's Press.

Fields, J. M., & Schuman, H. (1976). Public beliefs about the beliefs of the public. *Public Opinion Quarterly, 40,* 427–448.

Fisher, R., & Ury, W. (1981). *Getting to YES: Negotiating agreement without giving in.* Boston: Houghton Mifflin.

Flavell, J. H. (1985). *Cognitive development.* Englewood Cliffs, NJ: Prentice Hall.

Griffin, D. W., Dunning, D., & Ross, L. (1990). The role of construal processes in over-confident predictions about the self and others. *Journal of Personality and Social Psychology, 59,* 1128–1139.

Griffin, D. W., & Ross, L. (1991). Subjective construal, social inference, and human misunderstanding. *Advances in Experimental Social Psychology, 24,* 319–359.

Ichheiser, G. (1949). *Misunderstandings in human relations: A study in false social perception.* Chicago: University of Chicago Press.

Ichheiser, G. (1970). *Appearances and realities.* San Francisco: Jossey-Bass.

Jacobson, D. (1981). Intraparty dissensus and interparty conflict resolution. *Journal of Conflict Resolution, 25,* 471–494.

Janis, I. L. (1972). *Victims of groupthink.* Boston: Houghton Mifflin.

Judd, C. M., & Kulik, J. A. (1980). Schematic effects of social attitudes on information processing and recall. *Journal of Personality and Social Psychology, 38,* 569–578.

Kelly, G. A. (1955). *The psychology of personal constructs.* New York: Norton.

Keltner, D., & Robinson, R. J. (1993). Imagined ideological differences in conflict escalation and resolution. *International Journal of Conflict Management, 4,* 249–262.

Keltner, D., & Robinson, R. (1994). *Lone moderates in ideological disputes.* Manuscript in preparation.

Langer, E. J. (1978). Rethinking the role of thought in social interaction. In J. H. Harver, W. J. Ickes, & R. F. Kidd (Eds.), *New directions in attribution research* (Vol. 2), (pp. 35–38). Hillsdale, NJ: Erlbaum.

Lewin, K. (1948). *Resolving social conflicts.* New York: Harper.

Moscovici, S. (1981). On social representations. In J. P. Forgas (Ed.), *Social cognition: Perspectives on everyday understanding* (pp. 181–209). San Diego, CA: Academic Press.

Pratkanis, A. R. (1989). The cognitive representation of attitudes. In A. R. Pratkanis, S. J. Breckler, & A. G. Greenwald (Eds.), *Attitude structure and function* (pp. 71–98). Hillsdale, NJ: Erlbaum.

Pruitt, D. G., & Rubin, J. Z. (1986). *Social conflict: Escalation, stalemate, and settlement.* New York: Random House.

Robinson, R., & Keltner, D. (1994). *Much ado about nothing? Revisionists and traditionalists choose an introductory English syllabus.* Manuscript submitted for publication.

Ross, L. (1990). Recognizing the role of construal processes. In I. Rock (Ed.), *The legacy of Solomon Asch* (pp. 77–96). Hillsdale, NJ: Erlbaum.

Ross, L., & Nisbett, R. E. (1991). *The person and the situation.* New York: McGraw-Hill.

Ross, L., & Ward, A. (in press-a). Naive realism: Implications for misunderstanding and divergent perceptions of fairness and bias. In T. Brown, E. Reed, & E. Turiel (Eds.), *Values and knowledge,* Hillsdale, NJ: Erlbaum.

Ross, L., & Ward, A. (in press-b). Psychological barriers to dispute resolution. *Advances in Experimental Social Psychology.*

Rubin, J. Z. (1980). Experimental research on third-party intervention in conflict: Toward some generalizations. *Psychological Bulletin, 87,* 379–391.

Schelling, T. C. (1963). *The strategy of conflict.* New York: Oxford University Press.

Segall, M. H., Campbell, D. T., & Herskovitz, M. J. (1966). *The influence of culture on visual perception.* Indianapolis, IN: Bobbs-Merrill.

Sumner, W. G. (1906). *Folkways.* Lexington, MA: Ginn.

Susskind, L., & Cruikshank, J. (1987). *Breaking the impasse.* New York: Basic Books.

Thomas, K. W., & Pondy, L. R. (1977). Toward an "intent" model of conflict management among principal parties. *Human Relations, 30,* 1089–1102.

Thompson, L. L. (1991). Information exchange in negotiation. *Journal of Experimental Social Psychology, 27,* 161–179.

Tversky, A., & Kahneman, D. (1974). Judgement under uncertainty: Heuristics and biases. *Science, 185,* 1124–1131.

Walcott, C., Hopmann, P. T., & King, T. D. (1977). The role of debate in negotiation. In D. Druckman (Ed.), *Negotiations: Social-psychological perspectives* (pp. 193–211). Newbury Park, CA: Sage.

Questions for Review and Discussion

1. Define naïve realism?
2. What was the relation between the actual and perceived differences in the beliefs of the partisans in Studies 1 and 2?
3. Why do you think that the various groups of partisans in both studies overestimated the extremeness of their peers' beliefs as well as their opponents?

Chapter 10

"I'm Not as Thin as You Think I Am": The Development and Consequences of Feeling Discrepant from the Thinness Norm

Catherine A. Sanderson, John M. Darley, and Candace S. Messinger

One of the most fundamental concepts in social psychology is that individuals look to their environment to learn about what they should think (Cantril, 1941) and how they should behave (Sherif, 1936). In turn, both theory and research describe the power of social norms, namely attributes of a group that are considered both descriptive and prescriptive for its members (Miller & Prentice, 1996). For example, the theories of reasoned action/planned behavior (Fishbein & Ajzen, 1975), social impact theory (Latané & Wolf, 1981), social identity theory (Tajfel & Turner, 1986), and self-categorization theory (Turner, 1985) all describe social norms as an important predictor of attitudes and behavior. Classic research on social influence such as Asch's (1951) line judgment task, Newcomb's (1943) study of attitude change among Bennington College students, and Festinger and colleagues' (Festinger, Schachter, & Back, 1950) examination of attitudes among residents of housing projects also has shown the powerful effects of norms.

The present research contributes to prior work on the influence of social norms by examining whether individuals sometimes believe that their own attitudes and behaviors differ from those of others in their social group as well as

From *Personality and Social Psychology Bulletin*, Vol. 28, No. 2 (February 2002), pp. 172–183. © 2002 by the Society for the Personality and Social Psychology, Inc. Reprinted by permission of Sage Publications, Inc.

how this perceived discrepancy evolves over time and the consequences of perceiving such a discrepancy. To examine this issue, we chose to assess a norm that is particularly salient for women, namely the norm of thinness (Rodin, Silberstein, & Striegel-Moore, 1985). Although norms of female beauty have varied considerably over time, from the curved and plump body shape epitomized by Marilyn Monroe in the 1950s to the thin and childlike figure epitomized by Twiggy in the 1960s, the trend in recent years has been decidedly toward a norm of thinness (Goodman, 1995; Seid, 1989; Wolf, 1991). For example, the size of Miss America contestants, *Playboy* centerfolds, and magazine ad models have all become increasingly thinner in terms of both body weight and measurements over time (Garner, Garfinkel, Schwartz, & Thompson, 1980). We posit that these vivid examples of the societal norm of thinness lead women to perceive this norm as particularly strong and universally held, both in terms of behavior (e.g., weight, exercise frequency) and attitudes (e.g., desire to be thin, comfort with the thinness norm), which may not reflect their own behaviors and attitudes. This research will therefore examine whether women feel discrepant from others in their endorsement of the thinness norm, the development of this perceived discrepancy over time, and the consequences of feeling discrepant on symptoms of eating disorders.

Processes leading to inaccuracy in norm perception   Considerable research on social groups has shown that people are motivated to model the attitudes and behaviors that are characteristic of their group (Festinger, 1950), in part because an important part of individuals' self-concept derives from their social identity (i.e., their group memberships) (Tajfel & Turner, 1986; Turner, 1982, 1985). However, this process of norm construction involves at least three potentially difficult issues that may engage in particular types of behavior as a method of self-presentation that are in line with social norms but not necessarily with their own attitudes (Jones & Pittman, 1982; Schlenker, 1986; Tetlock & Manstead, 1985). For example, Zanna and colleagues (von Baeyer, Sherk, & Zanna, 1981; Zanna & Pack, 1975) have shown that women who believe they are interacting with a man who holds traditional attitudes toward women behave in particularly feminine ways, such as wearing more makeup and jewelry. Second, in determining norms about attitudes and beliefs, individuals must rely on others' public statements, which may or may not accurately reflect their private beliefs. In fact, individuals may at times voice an attitude publicly that misrepresents their true belief and thereby lead to erroneous attitude norms (Miller & McFarland, 1987; Prentice & Miller, 1993). Prentice and Miller (1993), for example, found that students were less comfortable with alcohol use at Princeton than they believed other students were, presumably because students may have publicly exaggerated their support for campus alcohol norms out of group loyalty (e.g., against the administration and faculty). Finally, because people tend to infer that the norms of the group's most active and typical members correspond to those of people in the group in general (Miller & McFarland, 1987; Miller & Prentice, 1994), they may infer social norms that do not accurately represent those of the broader group. For example, Schanck (1932) found that within a small Methodist community, a vocal minority led to the perception of strong community norms against gambling, drinking, and smoking, even though most residents were both supporting and engaging in such activities. In sum, although individuals look to others in their social group to learn the normative attitudes and behavior of group members, several factors may lead them to misperceive group norms.

Given individuals' tendency to look to the attitudes and behavior of others to get a sense of the norms of a given community (Bandura & Walters, 1963; Festinger, 1954), their accuracy in assessing such norms should generally increase as they spend more time in, and hence gain more familiarity with, a particular environment. However, public expressions are often characterized by a conservative lag, in that individuals continue to express support for those values they believe are held by others in their social group even after they have privately changed their views (see Miller & Prentice, 1994, 1996). For example, research by O'Gorman and colleagues demonstrated that individuals changed their private views about the civil rights movement long before they were willing to express these views publicly (Breed & Ktsanes, 1961; Fields & Schuman, 1976; O'Gorman, 1975; O'Gorman & Garry, 1976). Individuals may therefore continue to express those views they believe are held by their peers, even when such views do not represent their true opinions, which can then lead to greater norm misperception over time.

Consequences of feeling discrepant from the norm Given the importance of social groups in defining individuals' own self-concepts (Hogg & Abrams, 1988; Tajfel & Turner, 1986; Turner, 1982), people are motivated to have their attitudes and behaviors correspond with those of their valued social groups. In fact, the more important a social group is to a person, and the more representative or typical a given attitude or behavior is of that group, the more pressure individuals feel to learn and conform to such norms (Festinger et al., 1950). Moreover, the consequences of deviation can be quite negative, such as a reduction in popularity, feelings of alienation, and even rejection from the group (Prentice & Miller, 1993; Schachter, 1951), which again serves to increase individuals' conformity to such norms as a strategy for resolving perceived self-other differences (Moscovici, 1985). Thus, if one believes their own attitudes and behaviors are discrepant from those of the norm, they have three options: They can attempt to move their attitudes and behavior closer to the norm, they can attempt to move the norms of the group closer to their own, or they can reject the group entirely (Festinger et al., 1950). Given that the latter two options are quite difficult (practically and/or psychologically) for individuals, the easiest way for individuals to resolve their perceived discrepancy from group norms is to change their private attitudes and public behavior so that they become more like those of the perceived norm.

In turn, individuals' perceptions of the norms in their valued social groups do influence their own attitudes and behaviors. For example, Prentice and Miller (1993) found that students' erroneous perceptions of the campus drinking norm led to more positive attitudes toward drinking, at least for male students. Similarly, research has shown that people's estimates of the frequency of such use among their peers influences their own use, regardless of the accuracy of these estimates (Baer & Carney, 1993; Baer, Stacy, & Larimer, 1991; Marks, Graham, & Hansen, 1992; Sherman, Presson, Chassin, Corty, & Olshavsky, 1983) and that individuals' perceptions of the frequency of condom use by their peers is associated with their own rates of condom use (White, Terry, & Hogg, 1994; Winslow, Franzini, & Hwang, 1992). Thus, although the perceived norms of a social group may be largely independent of the actual norms of group members (Turner & Killian, 1972), over time the mere perception of norm discrepancy can lead individuals to change their attitudes and behavior toward those of the perceived norm.

Eating Disorders on College Campuses

Considerable research indicates that college women are at high risk for developing eating disorders, which have substantial and often lifetime physical and psychological consequences (Drewnowski, Hopkins, & Kessler, 1988; Schotte & Stunkard, 1987). The mean age at which such symptoms occur is between 15 and 20 years (Johnson, Stuckey, Lewis, & Schwartz, 1982), and the vast majority of people with eating disorders are women (Gandour, 1984). Estimates of disordered eating in college women range from 12% for vomiting (Halmi, Falk, & Schwartz, 1981) to 90% for binge eating (Hawkins & Clement, 1980). Although relatively few undergraduate women meet the DSM-IV criteria for an eating disorder, research indicates that many do show some symptoms of disordered eating. For example, one study of undergraduate women found that 54% reported using one or more dieting behaviors at least daily (e.g., counting calories, eating low-calorie foods, skipping meals) and 19% reported engaging in even more extreme measures of weight control at least monthly (e.g., taking laxatives, taking appetite control pills, vomiting) (Mintz & Betz, 1988). Thus, eating disorders represent a serious problem for many women and hence have received considerable attention in both the scientific community (Gandour, 1984; Schlesier-Stropp, 1984; Striegel-Moore, Silberstein, & Rodin, 1986) and the popular press (Boskind-Lodahl & Sirlin, 1977).

Processes leading to feeling discrepant from the thinness norm in college
Although we described previously how the norm for thinness in women is a general one in society, the college environment in particular may emphasize this norm. One of the most normative and involving tasks during late adolescence is that of social dating—in particular the forming of close, intimate relationships with others (Cantor, Acker, & Cook-Flannagan, 1992; Erikson, 1950; Sanderson & Cantor, 1995). In turn, considerable research demonstrates both that people are attracted to those who are physically attractive (Berscheid & Walster, 1974; Hatfield & Sprecher, 1986) and that at least for women, attractiveness is highly associated with thinness (Polivy, Garner, & Garfinkel, 1986; Silverstein, Perdue, Peterson, & Kelly, 1986; Stewart, Tutton, & Steele, 1973). For example, both men and women rate thin women as more feminine than normal-weight or overweight women (Guy, Rankin, & Norvell, 1980), and women who eat less are seen as more feminine (Pliner & Chaiken, 1990). Given the strong focus on social dating during the college years and the desire to be attractive to potential dating partners, women may be particularly focused on conforming to the thinness norm during this life period.

Although one could posit that the very public nature of eating and exercise in college may lead women to easily assess such norms, we posit that several processes instead lead women to feel discrepant from other women in terms of their endorsement of the thinness norm. First, although eating is a relatively public behavior given the nature of campus dining halls, the societal pressures toward thinness in women may lead at least some women to engage in public behavior that is in line with the norm but engage in counternormative behavior in private (Schlenker, 1986). For example, a woman may eat only a salad for dinner in the public domain of the campus dining hall but may later eat a more substantial meal in the privacy of her own room (or may eat before arriving at the dining hall). In line with this self-presentational theory, research has shown that women do moderate the amount they eat depending on the social situation they are in and will deliberately eat less in situations in which they wish to appear attractive to men (Mori, Chaiken, & Pliner, 1987; Pliner & Chaiken, 1990). For example, Mori and colleagues found that women who were interacting with a desirable male partner ate significantly fewer grams of M&Ms than those interacting with women or undesirable men. Similarly, women may actually eat less than they normally would (or would like to) in campus dining halls in an effort to present themselves as conforming to the campus thinness norm (and hence appearing more attractive) but may eat more later in a less public forum. In turn, this type of dichotomy between public and private behavior may lead to the perpetuation of a campus norm (e.g., women eat little) that few (if any) women are actually following but that all women believe others are indeed following.

Second, the prevalence of the thinness norm may lead women not only to engage in public behavior that is in line with this norm but also to express norm-congruent attitudes (Goffman, 1961; Matza, 1964; Miller & McFarland, 1987; Prentice & Miller, 1993; Schanck, 1932). Women may, for example, describe how little they have eaten, admire thinness in others, or discuss their own intention to lose weight as a way of demonstrating their conformity to the thinness norm. Moreover, because losing weight can occur through eating less or expending more calories, women also may emphasize the frequency and/or intensity of their exercise as well as their motivation to exercise to achieve the thin ideal. Once again, women may express norm-congruent attitudes that do not accurately represent their private attitudes, which can lead to feelings of discrepancy from the norm (e.g., a belief that other women support the thinness norm more than they themselves do).

In sum, we believe that women's perceptions of the campus thinness norm are anchored in insensitive sources of information that are based on the public expression of behavior (e.g., eating low calorie foods, eating small amounts of food, etc.) and attitudes (e.g., describing how little they have eaten, emphasizing their frequency of exercise) that may not represent women's true beliefs and behaviors. In turn, if public behavior does not accurately reflect women's private attitudes about the thinness norm, more exposure to the norm will lead to a greater perceived self-other discrepancy over time. Moreover, feelings of discrepancy from the thinness norm could lead women to engage in disordered eating in an attempt to conform to the perceived thin ideal.

Overview   This study examines three hypotheses regarding women's perceived discrepancy on eating and exercise attitudes and behaviors. First, we will examine whether women perceive other women's actual and ideal behaviors (body-mass index, ideal body size, exercise frequency), motivations for exercise, and attitudes toward the thinness norm as different from their own. It is hypothesized that compared to themselves, women will see other women as more focused on achieving a thin ideal (e.g., as having a smaller body-mass index, exercising more frequently, exercising specifically to lose weight, and as particularly aware of and influenced by the perceived campus thinness norm). Second, we will examine how this perceived discrepancy develops over time by assessing attitudes and behaviors related to the thinness norm in both first-year students (e.g., those in their first few weeks of college) and upper-class students.[1] Finally, we will examine the consequences of feeling discrepant from both attitudinal and behavioral norms on symptoms of eating disorders.

Methods

Participants   The study included 120 undergraduate women at Princeton University who served as participants in this research. The sample included 59 freshmen, 20 sophomores, 21 juniors, and 20 seniors (M age $= 18.88$, $SD = 1.19$).

Procedure   Participants, who were randomly selected from the university phone directory (every 10th woman was called), received a call asking them to participate in a study examining undergraduate women's health behaviors and attitudes. Each was told that she would receive $4 to complete a 30-min survey. Of those reached by phone, 78% agreed to participate. All participants completed a written survey during the first 2 weeks of classes in September. Participants were then recontacted during the first month of spring semester (approximately 5 months later) to complete the same questionnaire a second time. Eighty-seven students (43 first-year students, 44 upper-class students) completed the follow-up, for a return rate of 72.5%.[2]

Measures

Eating disorder inventory.   Two of the eight subscales of the 64-item Eating Disorder Inventory were used to assess the behavioral traits common in anorexia and bulimia (Garner, Olmstead, & Polivy, 1983). The subscales used were Drive for Thinness (e.g., "If I gain a pound, I worry that I will keep gaining"; $\alpha = .93$) and Bulimia (e.g., "I eat or drink in secrecy"; $\alpha = .89$). Although the full Eating Disorder Inventory also includes subscales assessing traits that may be associated with the development of eating disorders (e.g., interpersonal distrust, perfectionism, maturity fears), given the focus of this research on specifically identifying attitudes and/or behaviors related to eating disorders, only the two subscales directly assessing symptoms of disordered eating were included. Although participants rate whether each item applied to themselves on a 6-point scale ($1 = $ *never* to $6 = $ *always*), following instructions by Garner et al. (1983), items were recorded such that answers of 1 to 3 (*never to sometimes*) are scored as "0," 4 (*often*) is scored as "1," 5 (*usually*) is scored as "2," and 6 (*always*) is scored as "3." These scores are then summed such that higher scores indicate greater frequency of symptoms.

Pictorial body image scale.   Ratings of women's perceptions of their ideal body size and the ideal body size of the average female student were assessed using the Pictorial Body Image Scale, which consists of nine drawings of a female figure ranging ordinally from very thin to very heavy (Stunkard, Sorensen, & Schulsinger, 1983). Each figure corresponds to a number from 1 to 9 (1 = *thinnest* to 9 = *heaviest*). Participants were asked to indicate the figure that best approximated their ideal figure and the figure they thought the average undergraduate woman at Princeton University would find ideal.

Reasons for exercise inventory-self.   The 24-item Reasons for Exercise Inventory was used to assess participants' motivations for exercising (Silberstein, Striegel-Moore, & Rodin, 1988). These items represented seven general domains: weight control (e.g., "to be slim"; $\alpha = .87$), fitness (e.g., "to improve my endurance, stamina"; $\alpha = .77$), health (e.g., "to improve my overall health"; $\alpha = .75$), body tone (e.g., "to alter a specific area of my body"; $\alpha = .79$), physical attractiveness (e.g., "to be sexually desirable"; $\alpha = .93$), mood (e.g., "to cope with stress, anxiety"; $\alpha = .74$), and socialization (e.g., "to meet people"; $\alpha = .73$). Each item was answered on a 1 to 7 scale (1 = *not at all important* to 7 = *extremely important*).

Reasons for exercise inventory–other.   Participants also completed this survey once to assess their perceptions of the average Princeton University woman's motivations for exercising (e.g., "The average Princeton University woman exercises to be slim"). These items again represented seven general domains: weight control ($\alpha = .76$), fitness ($\alpha = .81$), health ($\alpha = .71$), body tone ($\alpha = .67$), physical attractiveness ($\alpha = .88$), mood ($\alpha = .66$), and socialization ($\alpha = .80$). Each item was again answered on a 1 to 7 scale (1 = *not at all important* to 7 = *extremely important*).

Attitudes toward the campus thinness norm–self.   This scale was created for use specifically in this survey and assessed participants' attitudes towards the campus thinness norm (e.g., awareness of other women's behavior, comfort with such behavior, influence by the norm, body image). Eighteen items were written, which included 13 items focusing on eating and exercise behavior and 5 distracter items focusing on other types of health behaviors (smoking, alcohol use). A principal components factor analysis with promax rotation conducted on the 13 relevant items revealed four factors with an eigenvalue greater than 1: awareness (2 items; e.g., "I am very aware of how often women at Princeton exercise," $\alpha = .66$), body image (3 items; e.g., "I am satisfied with my body," $\alpha = .80$), comfort with others' behavior (2 items; e.g., "I am comfortable with the eating habits of women at Princeton," $\alpha = .77$), and social influence (4 items; e.g., "I tend to exercise more when I see other women exercising," $\alpha = .69$).[3] Each item was answered on a 1 to 7 scale (1 = *disagree strongly* to 7 = *agree strongly*).

Attitudes toward the campus thinness norm–other.   Participants also completed this survey once to assess their perceptions of the average Princeton woman's attitudes toward the norm (e.g., "The average Princeton woman is aware of how much other women on campus eat"). This scale used the same four subscales as described previously: awareness ($\alpha = .74$), body image ($\alpha = .21$), comfort ($\alpha = .73$), and social influence ($\alpha = .62$).[4] Each item was again answered on a 1 to 7 scale (1 = *disagree strongly* to 7 = *agree strongly*).

Demographic information.   Participants completed a series of background questions, including questions on age, class year, and race. They also were asked to provide information on their own height, weight, and average number of hours exercised per week as well as estimates of the average Princeton woman's height, weight, and number of hours exercised per week.

Results

Table 1 presents means and standard deviations by class for all variables at the time of the fall questionnaire, and Table 2 presents means and standard deviations for all variables at the time of the spring questionnaire.

> *Hypotheses 1 and 2:*
> Do women feel discrepant from others in terms of their pursuit of the thinness norm, and does this perceived discrepancy increase over time?

To answer our questions about whether women feel discrepant from others on attitudes and behaviors related to the thinness norm, we conducted a series of two-way repeated measures analyses of variance (ANOVAs) with target (self vs. other) as a within-subjects factor and class (first-year vs. not) as a between-subjects factor, which allowed us to examine the presence of perceived discrepancy in general as well as perceived discrepancy over time. We also examined three distinct types of dependent variables associated with the thinness norm: actual and ideal behaviors (i.e., body-mass index [BMI], ideal body size, frequency of exercise), motivations for exercise, and attitudes toward the thinness norm.

First, analyses were conducted predicting women's actual and ideal behaviors related to the thinness norm (BMI, ideal body size, and frequency of exercise). The first analysis revealed a significant main effect of target, $F(1, 106) = 15.31$, $p < .0001$, $\eta^2 = .13$, on BMI, with own average BMI higher than the perceived average BMI of other women. However, this main effect was qualified by a significant Target $\times$ Class interaction, $F(1,103) = 5.17$, $p < .03$, $\eta^2 = .05$. Simple effects tests indicated that whereas there is no difference as a function of class

TABLE 1

Means and Standard Deviations of All Time 1 Measures

Measure	First-Year Students				Upper-Class Students			
	Own		Other		Own		Other	
	M	SD	M	SD	M	SD	M	SD
Actual and ideal behaviors								
BMI[a]	21.22	2.23	20.75	1.05	22.04	2.32	20.53	1.37
Ideal body size[b]	3.05	0.63	2.73	0.55	3.00	0.63	2.26	0.55
Exercise frequency[c]	2.80	2.40	4.30	2.33	3.91	2.66	5.46	2.43
Exercise motivations[d]								
Mood	4.64	1.18	4.33	0.70	4.93	1.27	4.56	0.95
Fitness	5.37	1.06	4.86	0.82	5.47	1.05	4.60	0.99
Health	5.36	1.11	4.74	0.71	5.64	0.97	4.65	0.98
Tone	4.89	1.46	5.55	0.97	5.00	1.51	5.95	0.77
Enjoyment	3.86	1.42	4.80	0.99	3.67	1.51	4.21	1.21
Attraction	4.93	1.44	6.04	0.89	5.10	1.57	6.36	0.70
Weight	4.57	1.71	5.71	0.93	4.90	1.53	6.17	0.64
Attitudes toward campus norms[e]								
Awareness	3.82	1.24	4.14	1.23	4.97	1.34	5.48	1.05
Comfort	4.88	1.17	4.33	0.91	3.58	1.31	3.59	1.16
Social influence	3.81	1.36	4.49	0.69	3.79	1.49	4.86	0.89
Body image	4.32	1.31	5.10	0.68	4.25	1.38	4.73	0.69
Eating disorders symptoms[f]								
Drive for thinness	0.51	0.64		—	0.73	0.90		—
Binging and purging	0.18	0.29		—	0.19	0.53		—

Note. BMI = body-mass index.

[a] Measured as weight (in kilograms) divided by height (in meters) squared.
[b] Measured on a 1 to 9 scale (1 = *thinnest* to 9 = *heaviest*).
[c] Measured in hours per week.
[d] Measured on a 1 to 7 scale (1 = *not at all important* to 7 = *extremely important*).
[e] Measured on a 1 to 7 scale (1 = *disagree strongly* to 7 = *agree strongly*).
[f] Measured on a 0 to 3 scale (0 = *never, rarely, or sometimes*, 1 = *often*, 2 = *usually*, 3 = *always*).

TABLE 2

Means and Standard Deviations of All Time 2 Measures

| | First-Year Students | | | | Upper-Class Students | | | |
| | Own | | Other | | Own | | Other | |
Measure	M	SD	M	SD	M	SD	M	SD
Actual and ideal behaviors								
BMI[a]	21.61	2.19	20.59	1.15	22.23	2.41	20.68	1.38
Ideal body size[b]	3.17	0.65	2.85	0.73	2.98	0.70	2.30	0.64
Exercise frequency[c]	2.45	2.16	4.40	2.28	3.05	2.18	5.08	2.15
Exercise motivation subscale[d]								
Mood	4.69	1.35		—	5.08	1.33		—
Fitness	5.44	0.96		—	5.56	1.16		—
Health	5.15	1.21		—	5.67	1.14		—
Tone	4.87	1.52		—	4.83	1.69		—
Enjoyment	3.52	1.31		—	3.47	1.54		—
Attraction	4.96	1.41		—	4.99	1.61		—
Weight	4.85	1.47		—	4.63	1.64		—
Attitudes toward campus norms[e]								
Awareness	4.66	1.00	4.68	0.92	3.94	1.33	5.32	0.88
Comfort	4.10	1.26	4.43	0.83	4.49	1.30	3.51	1.15
Social influence	3.80	1.17	4.72	0.82	3.81	1.38	4.82	0.81
Body image	4.35	1.25	5.09	0.58	4.27	1.53	4.68	0.73
Eating disorders symptoms[f]								
Drive for thinness	0.54	0.73		—	0.76	1.02		—
Binging and purging	0.17	0.33		—	0.22	0.47		—

Note. BMI = body-mass index.

[a] Measured as weight (in kilograms) divided by height (in meters) squared.
[b] Measured on a 1 to 9 scale (1 = *thinnest* to 9 = *heaviest*).
[c] Measured in hours per week.
[d] Measured on a 1 to 7 scale (1 = *not at all important* to 7 = *extremely important*).
[e] Measured on a 1 to 7 scale (1 = *disagree strongly* to 7 = *agree strongly*).
[f] Measured on a 0 to 3 scale (0 = *never, rarely, or sometimes*, 1 = *often*, 2 = *usually*, 3 = *always*).

between the perceived average BMI in other women, $t(106) < 1$, upper-class women have a significantly larger BMI than first-year women, $t(109) = 1.90$, $p < .06$. There was also a significant effect of target on body shape, $F(1,108) = 60.07$, $p < .0001$, $\eta^2 = .36$, indicating that women believe other women want to be thinner than they themselves do, which was in turn qualified by a significant Target $\times$ Class interaction, $F(1, 108) = 9.35$, $p < .003$, $\eta^2 = .08$. Simple effects tests indicated that whereas there is no difference in own ideal body size as a function of class, $t(109) < 1$, upper-class women believe that other women want to be thinner than do first-year women, $t(108) = 3.87$, $p < .0001$. Finally, there was a significant effect of target on exercise frequency, $F(1, 103) = 48.35$, $p < .0001$, $\eta^2 = .32$, with women believing that other women exercise more than themselves. Thus, these analyses provide evidence for a perceived discrepancy across all three dependent variables (e.g., women believe that compared to other women, they weigh more, exercise less frequently, and want to be somewhat heavier) as well as some evidence for a larger perceived discrepancy over time (e.g., the main effects of target were qualified by significant Target $\times$ Class interactions predicting BMI and ideal body size, indicating that the self versus other discrepancy on these measures is larger in upper-class than first-year women).

The next set of analyses examined motivations for exercise, again as a function of target (within-subjects) and class (between-subjects). As predicted, compared to themselves, women believe that other women exercise for more extrinsic reasons, such as toning, $F(1, 118) = 41.70$, $p = .0001$, $\eta^2 = .26$; attractiveness, $F(1, 118) = 89.49$, $p = .0001$, $\eta^2 = .43$; weight loss, $F(1, 118) = 66.83$, $p = .0001$, $\eta^2 = .36$; and socialization, $F(1, 118) = 31.12$, $p = .0001$, $\eta^2 = .21$, and less for intrinsic reasons, namely mood, $F(1, 118) = 10.41$, $p = .002$, $\eta^2 = .08$; health, $F(1, 118) = 73.49$, $p = .0001$, $\eta^2 = .38$; and fitness, $F(1, 118) = 55.10$, $p = .0001$, $\eta^2 = .32$. In sum, these analyses revealed significant effects of target on all seven subscales, with women believing other women exercise more for extrinsic reasons than they themselves do, and less for intrinsic reasons.

Finally, analyses were conducted predicting attitudes toward campus eating and exercise norms. These analyses revealed significant main effects of target on all four measures, namely, body image, $F(1, 107) = 16.71$, $p < .0001$, $\eta^2 = .14$; social influence, $F(1, 107) = 36.91$, $p < .0001$, $\eta^2 = .26$; awareness, $F(1, 107) = 13.40$, $p < .001$, $\eta^2 = .10$; and comfort, $F(1, 107) = 6.56$, $p < .01$, $\eta^2 = .06$. These analyses indicate that compared to themselves, women see other women as more positive about their bodies, more aware of and influenced by social pressures toward thinness, and less comfortable with the campus eating and exercise norms.

Hypothesis 3:

Do women who feel discrepant from the thinness norm have more symptoms of eating disorders?

To examine whether women who feel discrepant from perceived campus eating and exercise norms experience more symptoms of eating disorders, we computed perceived self-other discrepancy scores for each of the following Time 2 measures: BMI, ideal body size, frequency of exercise, and each of the four attitudes toward the campus thinness norm subscales. (Similar analyses were conducted at Time 1 and yielded virtually the same results.) Thus, positive betas indicate that women who believe they have larger scores than other women on a particular measure (e.g., have a larger BMI, exercise more frequently, are more motivated by a particular reason to exercise, are more aware of the campus thinness norm) have more symptoms of eating disorders, and negative betas indicate that women who believe they have smaller scores than other women on a particular measure have fewer symptoms. We then conducted hierarchical linear regressions predicting symptoms of eating disorders (drive for thinness, binging and purging) at the follow-up from perceived self versus other discrepancy on actual and ideal behaviors (i.e., BMI, ideal body size, frequency of exercise) and on attitudes toward the thinness norm. (Because the Exercise Motivations–Other Scale was not given to participants at the follow-up given time constraints, we could not assess the effect of perceived discrepancies on motivations for exercise.) We also controlled for upper-class status in all analyses and BMI in the analyses predicting symptoms of eating disorders from perceived discrepancy on attitudes toward the campus thinness norm. (Actual discrepancy scores were used as a substitute for perceived discrepancy scores and yielded similar results.)

First, hierarchical linear regressions were conducted predicting drive for thinness and binging and purging at the follow-up from each of the three perceived discrepancy measures on actual and ideal behaviors (BMI, ideal body size, exercise frequency), controlling for upper-class status. The analysis predicting drive for thinness revealed significant effects of perceived discrepancy on BMI and ideal body size ($\beta = .51, p < .0001$; $\beta = -.37, p < .001$, respectively), and the inclusion of the discrepancy scores added significantly to the power of the equation, $\Delta R^2 = .32$, $F_{change}(3, 72) = 11.30$, $p < .0001$. These findings demonstrated that women who believe they weigh more than other women and have a smaller ideal body size experience a stronger drive for thinness. The analysis predicting binging and purging revealed identical findings, namely, a significant effect of perceived discrepancy on BMI ($\beta = .26, p < .02$) and ideal body size ($\beta = -.25, p < .04$), $\Delta R^2 = .12$, $F_{change}(3, 72) = 3.31, p < .03$. In sum, women who believe they weigh more than other women and would like to have a smaller body size than other women have more signs of disordered eating, including binging and purging and extreme drive for thinness.

Second, hierarchical regression analyses were conducted predicting drive for thinness and binging and purging from each of the four perceived discrepancy measures on attitudes toward and awareness of the thinness norm, again controlling for BMI and upper-class status. The analysis predicting drive for thinness revealed only a significant effect of perceived discrepancy on body image ($\beta = -.49$, $p < .0001$), which added significantly to the predictive power of the equation, $\Delta R^2 = .34$, $F_{change}(4, 72) = 11.24$, $p < .0001$. Similarly, the analysis predicting binging and purging revealed a significant effect only of perceived discrepancy on body image ($\beta = -.69$, $p < .0001$), $\Delta R^2 = .40$, $F_{change}(4, 72) = 11.97$, $p < .0001$. These effects indicated that women who believed they felt less attractive and thin than other women had more symptoms of anorexia and bulimia.

Discussion

This research contributes to prior work on the power of social norms in influencing attitudes and behavior by showing that individuals often feel discrepant from the norms of their social group, that this perceived discrepancy increases over time, and that the consequences of feeling discrepant from one's social group can be quite negative. First, we have shown that people can feel discrepant from attitudinal norms (e.g., motivations for exercise, comfort with the thinness norm) as well as seemingly clear public behavioral norms (e.g., BMI, exercise frequency). As predicted, compared to themselves, women believe that other women are smaller in terms of body-mass index, have a thinner ideal body shape, and exercise more frequently. They also believe that other women are more motivated to exercise by concerns with body toning, sexual attractiveness, and weight loss, whereas they themselves are more motivated by concerns with health, fitness, and mood. Finally, they see other women as more aware of and influenced by these campus eating and exercise norms than they themselves are. Thus, women are clearly perceiving a campus norm stressing thin bodies, with exercise as one way to achieve this ideal, and they believe that other women are paying close attention to and following such a norm. These findings demonstrate that women believe in a thinness norm that individually they are not following (e.g., in terms of their own actual body size, ideal body size, exercise frequency, motivation to exercise) and that they believe other women are particularly motivated to follow such norms.

Second, there was evidence that women perceive a larger discrepancy on behavioral norms as they spend more time in the college environment. First-year women perceive a small self versus other discrepancy on BMI (.47), whereas the gap for upper-class women is 3 times as large (1.51). Moreover, upper-class women believe that other women are focused on attaining a much thinner body than they themselves are, whereas first-year women perceive only a small discrepancy on the ideal body size of the typical woman as compared to their own. These findings indicate that as women spend more time in the college environment, they increasingly perceive other women as weighing less and wanting to be even thinner than they themselves do.

Finally, our findings provide further evidence that feeling discrepant from the norms of one's social group can have undesirable, and in fact dangerous, consequences (Newcomb, 1943; Prentice & Miller, 1993). Specifically, women who believed that compared to other women, they weighed more, felt less good about their bodies, preferred a smaller body size, and had more signs of disordered eating, including binging and purging and extreme drive for thinness. Thus, our findings indicate that women who perceive they are discrepant from the campus thinness norm may go to considerable lengths to meet the perceived campus body image ideals (i.e., of excessive thinness). In fact, many of the consequences of simply believing one is discrepant from the norm are the same as accurately believing one is discrepant from the norm (e.g., alienation, discomfort, desire to change attitudes and behaviors to conform) (Newcomb, 1943; Prentice & Miller, 1993).

Limitations and future research   There are several limitations of this research that should be acknowledged. First, our participants may not have been a truly representative sample of women at that university; therefore, it is possible that they were accurately perceiving the broader campus eating and exercise norms but that these norms did not express the attitudes and behaviors of those in their particular social group. Although considerable effort was made to recruit a random sample of participants (e.g., women randomly called from the campus directory), we have no way of knowing if indeed the participants we sampled represent a broad section of the college population. For example, potential participants were told that some of the questions involved eating and exercise behavior, and hence, those who are in the midst of struggling with an eating disorder may have opted not to participate. However, we did have respondents with a full range of scores on both of the Eating Disorders Inventory subscales, and the analyses comparing those who did versus did not participate in the follow-up revealed no differences on any of our measures.

Second, our research focused only on the general campus thinness norm as opposed to the distinct norms in different groups (e.g., on athletic teams, in sororities, etc.). However, given prior research showing that eating disorders tend to run in social groups, such as cheerleading squads (Squire, 1983), athletic teams (Crago, Yates, Beutler, & Arizmedni, 1985), dance camps (Garner & Garfinkel, 1980), and sororities (Crandall, 1988), it is likely that there are specific eating and exercise norms within particular campus groups. Future research should examine how individuals form distinct representations of the norms in their particular social group, as well as whether women are more accurate about the norms within their close friendship groups than about campus norms in general. For example, Prentice and Miller (1993) found that students' perceptions of their friends' attitudes were closer to that of their own than that of the average student. It is also possible that those who identify strongly with a particular group (e.g., athletic team, sorority, friendship group) are most likely to be influenced by its perceived norms (Terry & Hogg, 1996), and hence, different people may conform to the norms of distinct (e.g., particularly valued) groups. Future research should therefore examine whether people also feel discrepant from the norms of their smaller social groups, how such norms are transmitted across time, and the consequences of feeling discrepant from the norms of one's particular social group.

Third, because the data relied entirely on self-report, it is conceivable that participants attempted to present themselves in socially desirable ways (e.g., more mature, more independent, more progressive) (Fields & Schuman, 1976; Packard & Willower, 1972). For example, first-year students, such as those who are not well established as part of the social group, may be particularly motivated to see themselves as fitting in and hence report that their own attitudes and behaviors are similar to their perception of the group norm. Upper-class students, in contrast, are likely to have formed their own distinct friendship groups and hence may have less of a need to report fitting in with the larger group norm.[5] Similarly, participants may have wanted the researcher to believe that they were more comfortable with their own body, focused on achieving a healthier (e.g., larger) body size, and less influenced by campus norms than were other women. Although this is a potential explanation for our findings showing that women perceive a discrepancy between their own attitudes and behavior and those of other women on campus, we believe it is unlikely for several reasons. First, the surveys in all cases were anonymous and the participants therefore should not have had any reason to believe they would benefit from "making themselves look good." Moreover, although it is certainly conceivable that the perceived self versus other differences we found on motivations for exercise and awareness and attitudes toward campus norms reflect biased self presentation (e.g., women report that they are more likely to exercise for the "right" reasons and less influenced by peer pressure than other women), it is difficult to explain our findings on the behavioral measures (e.g., why would women present themselves as having a larger body-mass index and exercising less than the average woman).

Finally, although our findings indicate that the mere perception of discrepancy from the thinness norm is associated with symptoms of disordered eating, these analyses demonstrate correlation as opposed to causation. It is therefore entirely possible that a third variable (e.g., depression, self-esteem, etc.) may cause both a perceived self-other discrepancy and disordered eating or that the presence of an eating disorder leads one to feel deviant from valued social norms. Although we considered trying to examine this issue of causation versus correlation by using discrepancy measures at Time 1 to predict symptoms of disordered eating at Time 2, given the amount of change women showed on both attitudes and behavior over time, such an approach was clearly inappropriate. Future research should, however, attempt to examine whether other variables are indeed associated with perceptions of discrepancy as well as patterns of disordered eating and whether individuals with eating disorders develop such perceptions over time.

Theoretical contributions and implications   Our findings replicate and extend those from prior research in several ways. First, this research is the first to our knowledge to demonstrate that as individuals spend more time in a particular social group they feel more discrepant from its norms. Although both theory and research typically suggest that greater familiarity with a social group should lead to conformity to its normative attitudes and behaviors (Bandura & Walters, 1963; Festinger, 1954; Moscovici, 1985), our findings indicate that the perceived self versus other discrepancy actually increases over time. For example, first-year women have a much smaller self versus other discrepancy on body-mass index and ideal body size than do upper-class women. We believe that this increase in the self versus other discrepancy over time is caused by the lag individuals typically show between changes in private attitudes versus the public expression of these attitudes (Miller & Prentice, 1994, 1996). In other words, individuals may come to disagree with the campus thinness norm (e.g., as they gain weight and even prefer a larger body size than they believe other women do) but fail to express these views because they are perceived as counternormative. Unfortunately, this conservative lag can lead to a situation in which the norm does not accurately represent the private attitudes of group members (Turner & Killian, 1972).

This research also extends prior work showing that men and women respond to feeling discrepant from social norms in distinct ways. Prior research has shown that men typically respond to conditions of ego threat by using externalizing defenses (e.g., projection and displacement), whereas women respond with internalization defenses (e.g., repression and reaction formation) (Cramer, 1987; Levit, 1991). Correspondingly, Prentice and Miller (1993) found that over time, men internalized the perceived campus norms on alcohol use (e.g., became more comfortable with alcohol use), whereas women felt increasingly alienated from campus norms. In turn, in this research, the greater frequency of symptoms of eating disorders found in women who feel discrepant from the campus thinness norm may be a sign of alienation (e.g., women turn against themselves in response to their perceived deviance). Another possibility, however, is that individuals respond differently to feeling discrepant from the social norm depending on how relevant the norm is for their particular group. For example, Prentice and Miller's finding that men conform to the alcohol norm, whereas women do not, may be because drinking is a more integral or central part of campus social life for men than women. In contrast, because considerable research suggests that the thinness norm is very powerful for women (Rodin et al., 1985), the pressure to conform to this norm is likely to be substantial for our participants. Future research should examine whether men and women do tend to respond to feeling discrepant from the norm in distinct ways and/or whether the response to perceived discrepancy is a function of the relative importance of the particular norm.

Finally, because social norms derive much of their influence on attitudes and behavior through the perception that they are universally held by all group members (Allport, 1924; Turner, 1991), providing individuals with information that not all group members support a particular norm should decrease its influence. For example, the power of the norm in influencing the unresponsive behavior of bystanders (Latané & Darley, 1970) and the lack of questions by confused students (Miller & McFarland, 1987) was in large part a function of the uniform behavior (i.e., inaction) coupled with the perception of an underlying uniform attitude (i.e., this is not an emergency; others have no questions). Similarly, to the extent that women are engaging in disordered patterns of eating and exercise due to their belief that other women particularly value the thinness norm (and hence weigh less, are engaging in considerable amounts of exercise to attain a thin body, and are paying close attention to other women's eating and exercise behavior), decreasing the perceived self versus other discrepancy should minimize disordered eating. Future research should therefore examine whether providing women with information about other women's attitudes and behavior relevant to the campus thinness norm would reduce feelings of discrepancy from the norm and thereby lead to corresponding decreases in symptoms of disordered eating. Dispelling the illusion of universality (Allport, 1924) may in fact go a long way toward decreasing the power of the thinness norm.

Notes

1. Although the term *upper-class* has typically been used to distinguish junior and seniors from freshmen and sophomore students, we use the term throughout this article to distinguish between students who are first-year students versus those who are sophomores, juniors, and seniors. Because we were interested in examining how new students look to others in their social groups to learn about the attitude and behavioral norms, we specifically recruited an equal sample of first-year students and non-first-year students and conducted all analyses using this distinction as our between-subjects variable.

2. Analyses testing whether participants who did versus did not complete the follow-up differed in any way (e.g., height, weight, frequency of exercise, motivations for exercise, symptoms of eating disorders, attitudes toward the campus thinness norm) revealed no differences.

3. Two items were eliminated due to inconsistent factor loadings.

4. Although the extremely low alpha for the body image subscale was unexpected, an item-by-item analysis of the three items that make up this subscale revealed an interesting pattern. The three items ("I am attractive," "I am thin," and "I am satisfied with my body") are highly correlated when considering one's own appearance, but the third item ("I am satisfied with my own body") does not correlate well with the other two items when considering one's perceptions of other women's feelings. Moreover, an inspection of the means revealed that although our participants tended to think other women believe they are both attractive and thin, they also think most women are not satisfied with their own bodies. This finding is of course in line with our general hypotheses about women's views of the campus thinness norm.

5. We thank an anonymous reviewer for raising this important point.

References

Allport, F. H. (1924). *Social psychology.* Boston: Houghton Mifflin.

Asch, S. E. (1951). Effects of group pressure upon modification and distortion of judgments. In H. Guetzkow (Ed.), *Group leadership and men* (pp. 177–190). Pittsburgh, PA: Carnegie Press.

Baer, J. S., & Carney, M. M. (1993). Biases in the perceptions of the consequences of alcohol use among college students. *Journal of Studies on Alcohol, 54,* 54–60.

Baer, J. S., Stacy, A., & Larimer, M. (1991). Biases in the perception of drinking norms among college students. *Journal of Studies on Alcohol, 52,* 580–586.

Bandura, A., & Walters, R. H. (1963). *Social learning and personality development.* New York: Holt, Rinehart & Winston.

Berscheid, E., & Walster, E. (1974). A little bit about love. In T. Huston (Ed.), *Foundations of interpersonal attraction* (pp. 355–381). New York: Academic Press.

Boskind-Lodahl, M., & Sirlin, J. (1977, March). The gorging-purging syndrome. *Psychology Today, 50–52,* 82, 85.

Breed, W., & Ktsanes, T. (1961). Pluralistic ignorance in the process of opinion formation. *Public Opinion Quarterly, 25,* 382–392.

Cantor, N., Acker, M., & Cook-Flannagan, C. (1992). Conflict and preoccupation in the intimacy life task. *Journal of Personality and Social Psychology, 63,* 644–655.

Cantril, H. (1941). *The psychology of social movement.* New York: John Wiley.

Crago, M., Yates, A., Beutler, L. E., & Arizmedni, T. G. (1985). Height-weight ratios among female athletes: Are collegiate athletics the precursors to an anorexic syndrome? *International Journal of Eating Disorders, 4,* 79–87.

Cramer, P. (1987). The development of defense mechanisms. *Journal of Personality and Social Pschology, 55,* 597–614.

Crandall, C. (1988). Social contagion and binge eating. *Journal of Personality and Social Psychology, 55,* 588–598.

Drewnowski, A., Hopkins, S., & Kessler, R. (1988). The prevalence of bulimia nervosa in the U.S. college student population. *American Journal of Public Health, 78,* 1322–1325.

Erikson, E. H. (1950). *Childhood and society.* New York: Norton.

Festinger, L. (1950). Informal social communication. *Psychological Review, 57,* 271–292.

Festinger, L. (1954). A theory of social comparison processes. *Human Relations, 7,* 117–140.

Festinger, L., Schachter, S., & Back, K. (1950). *Social pressures in informal groups.* New York: Harper & Row.

Fields, J. M., & Schuman, H. (1976). Public beliefs and the beliefs of the public. *Public Opinion Quarterly, 40,* 427–448.

Fishbein, M., & Ajzen, I. (1975). *Belief, attitude, intention and behavior.* Boston: Addison-Wesley.

Gandour, M. J. (1984). Bulimia: Clinical description, assessment, etiology, and treatment. *International Journal of Eating Disorders, 3,* 3–38.

Garner, D. M., & Garfinkel, P. E. (1980). Socio-cultural factors in the development of anorexia nervosa. *Psychological Medicine, 10,* 647–656.

Garner, D. M., Garfinkel, P. E., Schwartz, D., & Thompson, M. (1980). Cultural expectations of thinness in women. *Psychological Reports, 47,* 483–491.

Garner, D. M., Olmstead, M. A., & Polivy, J. (1983). Development and validation of a multidimensional eating disorder inventory for anorexia nervosa and bulimia. *International Journal of Eating Disorders, 2,* 12–34.

Goffman, E. (1961). *Asylums: Essays on the social situation of mental patients and other inmates.* Garden City, NJ: Anchor Books.

Goodman, W. C. (1995). *The invisible woman: Confronting weight prejudice in America.* [City], CA: Gurze.

Guy, F., Rankin, B., & Norvell, M. (1980). The relation of sex-role stereotyping to body image. *Journal of Psychology, 105,* 167–173.

Halmi, K. A., Falk, J. R., & Schwartz, E. (1981). Binge-eating and vomiting: A survey of a college population. *Psychological Medicine, 11,* 697–706.

Hatfield, E., & Sprecher, S. (1986). *Mirror, mirror . . . The importance of looks in everyday life.* Albany: State University of New York.

Hawkins, R. C., II, & Clement, P. F. (1980). Development and construct validation of a self-report measure of binge eating tendencies. *Addictive Behaviors, 5,* 219–226.

Hogg, M. A., & Abrams, D. (1988). *Social identifications: A social psychology of intergroup relations and group processes.* London: Routledge.

Johnson, C., Stuckey, M., Lewis, C., & Schwartz, D. (1982). Bulimia: A descriptive survey of 316 cases. *International Journal of Eating Disorders, 2,* 1–15.

Jones, E. E., & Pittman, T. S. (1982). Toward a general theory of strategic self-presentation. In J. Suls (Ed.), *Psychological perspectives on the self,* (Vol. 1, pp. 231–262). Hillsdale, NJ: Lawrence Erlbaum.

Latané, B., & Darley, J. (1970). *The unresponsive bystander: Why doesn't he help?* New York: Appleton-Century-Crofts.

Latane, B., & Wolf, S. (1981). The social impact of majorities and minorities. *Psychological Review, 88,* 438–454.

Levit, D. B. (1991). Gender differences in ego defenses in adolescence: Sex roles as one way to understand the differences. *Journal of Personality and Social Psychology, 61,* 992–999.

Marks, G., Graham, J. W., & Hansen, W. B. (1992). Social projection and social conformity in adolescent alcohol use: A longitudinal analysis. *Personality and Social Psychology Bulletin, 18,* 96–101.

Matza, D. (1964). *Delinquency and drift.* New York: John Wiley.

Miller, D. T., & McFarland, C. (1987). Pluralistic ignorance: When similarity is interpreted as dissimilarity. *Journal of Personality and Social Psychology, 53,* 298–305.

Miller, D. T., & Prentice, D. A. (1994). Collective errors and errors about the collective. *Personality and Social Psychology Bulletin, 20,* 541–550.

Miller, D. T., & Prentice, D. A. (1996). The construction of social norms and standards. In E. T. Higgins, & A. W. Kruglanski (Eds.), *Social Psychology: Handbook of basic principles* (pp. 799–829). New York: Guilford.

Mintz, L. B., & Betz, N. E. (1988). Prevalence and correlates of eating disordered behaviors among undergraduate women. *Journal of Counseling Psychology, 35,* 463–471.

Mori, D., Chaiken, S., & Pliner, P. (1987). "Eating lightly" and the self-presentation of femininity. *Journal of Personality and Social Psychology, 53,* 693–702.

Moscovici, S. (1985). Social influence and conformity. In G. Lindzey, & E. Aronson (Eds.), *The handbook of social psychology* (3rd ed., Vol. 2, pp. 347–412). New York: Random House.

Newcomb, T. B. (1943). *Personality and social change: Attitude formation in a student community.* Fort Worth, TX: Dryden.

O'Gorman, H. J. (1975). Pluralistic ignorance and White estimates of White support for racial segregation. *Public Opinion Quarterly, 39,* 313–330.

O'Gorman, H. J., & Garry, S. L. (1976). Pluralistic ignorance: A replication and extension. *Public Opinion Quarterly, 40,* 449–458.

Packard, J. S., & Willower, D. J. (1972). Pluralistic ignorance and pupil control ideology. *Journal of Education Administration, 10,* 78–87.

Pliner, P., & Chaiken, S. (1990). Eating, social motives, and self-presentation in women and men. *Journal of Experimental Social Psychology, 26*, 240–254.

Polivy, J., Garner, D. M., & Garfinkel, P. E. (1986). Causes and consequences of the current preference for thin female physiques. In C. P. Herman, M. P. Zanna, & E. T. Higgins (Eds.), *Physical appearance as a stigma and social behavior: The Ontario symposium* (Vol. 3, pp. 89–112). Hillsdale, NJ: Lawrence Erlbaum.

Prentice, D. A., & Miller, D. T. (1993). Pluralistic ignorance and alcohol use on campus: Some consequences of misperceiving the social norm. *Journal of Personality and Social Psychology, 64*, 243–256.

Rodin, J., Silberstein, L., & Striegel-Moore, R. (1985). Women and weight: A normative discontent. In T. B. Sonderegger (Ed.), *Nebraska symposium on motivation: Psychology and gender* (Vol. 32, pp. 267–307). Lincoln: University of Nebraska Press.

Sanderson, C. A., & Cantor, N. (1995). Social dating goals in late adolescence: Implications for safer sexual activity. *Journal of Personality and Social Psychology, 68*, 1121–1135.

Schachter, S. (1951). Deviation, rejection, and communication. *Journal of Abnormal and Social Psychology, 46*, 190–207.

Schanck, R. L. (1932). A study of community and its group institutions conceived of as behavior of individuals. *Psychological Monographs, 43*, 1–133.

Schlenker, B. R. (1986). Self-identification: Toward an integration of the private and public self. In R. Baumeister (Ed.), *Public self and private self* (pp. 21–62). New York: Springer-Verlag.

Schlesier-Stropp, B. (1984). Bulimia: A review of the literature. *Psychological Bulletin, 95*, 247–257.

Schotte, D., & Stunkard, A. (1987). Bulimia vs. bulimic behaviors on a college campus. *Journal of the American Medical Association, 258*, 1213–1215.

Seid, R. P. (1989). *Never too thin: Why women are at war with their bodies.* New York: Prentice-Hall.

Sherif, M. (1936). *The psychology of social norms.* New York: Harper.

Sherman, S. J., Presson, C. C., Chassin, L., Corty, E., & Olshavsky, R. (1983). The false consensus effect in estimates of smoking prevalence: Underlying mechanisms. *Personality and Social Psychology Bulletin, 9*, 197–207.

Silberstein, L. R., Striegel-Moore, C. T., & Rodin, J. (1988). Behavioral and psychological implications of body dissatisfaction: Do men and women differ? *Sex Roles, 19*, 219–232.

Silverstein, B., Perdue, L., Peterson, B., & Kelly, E. (1986). The role of the mass media in promoting a thin standard of bodily attractiveness for women. *Sex Roles, 14*, 519–532.

Squire, S. (1983). *The slender balance.* New York: Pinnacle.

Stewart, R. A., Tutton, S., & Steele, R. E. (1973). Stereotyping and personality: Sex differences in perception of female physiques. *Perceptual and Motor Skills, 36*, 811–814.

Striegel-Moore, R., Silberstein, L., & Rodin, J. (1986). Toward an understanding of risk factors for bulimia. *American Psychologist, 41*, 246–263.

Stunkard, A. J., Sorensen, T., & Schulsinger, F. (1983). Use of the Danish adoption register for the study of obesity and thinness. In S. Kety (Ed.), *The genetics of neurological and psychiatric disorders* (pp. 115–120). New York: Raven Press.

Tajfel, H., & Turner, J. C. (1986). The social identity theory of intergroup behavior. In S. Worchel & W. G. Austin (Eds.), *Psychology of intergroup relations* (2nd ed., pp. 7–24). Chicago: Nelson-Hall.

Terry, D. J., & Hogg, M. A. (1996). Group norms and the attitude-behavior relationship: A role for group identification. *Personality and Social Psychology Bulletin, 22,* 776–793.

Tetlock, P. E., & Manstead, A. S. R. (1985). Impression management versus intrapsychic explanations in social psychology: A useful dichotomy? *Psychological Review, 92,* 59–77.

Turner, J. C. (1982). Towards a cognitive redefinition of the social group. In H. Tajfel (Ed.), *Social identity and intergroup relations* (pp. 15–40). Cambridge, UK: Cambridge University Press.

Turner, J. C. (1985). Social categorization and the self concept: A social cognitive theory of group behavior. In E. J. Lawler (Ed.), *Advances in group processes: Theory and research* (Vol. 2, pp. 77–122). Greenwich, CT: JAI.

Turner, J. C. (1991). *Social influence.* Pacific Grove, CA: Brooks/Cole.

Turner, R., & Killian, L. (1972). *Collective behavior* (2nd ed.). Englewood Cliffs, NJ: Prentice Hall.

von Baeyer, C., Sherk, D., & Zanna, M. (1981). Impression management in the job interview: When the female applicant meets the male (chauvinist) interviewer. *Personality and Social Psychology Bulletin, 7,* 45–51.

White, K. M., Terry, D. J., & Hogg, M. A. (1994). Safer sex behavior: The role of attitudes, norms, and control factors. *Journal of Applied Social Psychology, 24,* 2164–2192.

Winslow, R. W., Franzini, L. R., & Hwang, J. (1992). Perceived peer norms, casual sex, and AIDS risk prevention. *Journal of Applied Social Psychology, 22,* 1809–1827.

Wolf, N. (1991). *The beauty myth: How images of beauty are used against women.* New York: William Morris.

Zanna, M. P., & Pack, S. J. (1975). On the self-fulfilling nature of apparent sex differences in behavior. *Journal of Experimental Social Psychology, 11,* 583–591.

Questions for Review and Discussion

1. What evidence do Sanderson et al. provide to support their contention that there is a thinness norm among college women?

2. How did women's perception of their deviance from the thinness norm relate to their symptoms of eating disorders?

3. How did Sanderson et al. assess women's perceptions of their own body size and what did they find predicted these perceptions?

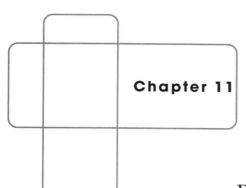

Chapter 11

Perceptions of a Fluid Consensus: Uniqueness Bias, False Consensus, False Polarization, and Pluralistic Ignorance in a Water Conservation Crisis

Benoît Monin and Michael I. Norton

When tropical storm Floyd hit the East Coast of the United States in September 1999, a sudden water short-age prompted Princeton University to ask students to limit their water usage and avoid drinking potentially contaminated water. These instructions included a ban on showering for the first 3 days of the crisis. As a result, showering suddenly went from a common behavior denoting hygiene and social grace to a rare behavior reflecting a lack of concern for the community. When the ban was lifted 3 days later, showering went back to being common and desirable. In our social world, the frequency and desirability of behaviors often fluctuates, but rarely at such a rapid pace. This situation thus provides a unique opportunity to study biases both in estimates of the prevalence of the behavior ("What proportion of my peers shower?") and in the inferences drawn from this behavior ("What kind of person would shower?") in the context of a changing consensus. This article presents the results of a field study that we conducted during these 5 consecutive days, tracking the various biases as the crisis unfolded.

From *Personality and Social Psychology Bulletin*, Vol. 29, No. 5 (May 2003), pp. 559–567. © 2003 by the Society for the Personality and Social Psychology, Inc. Reprinted by permission of Sage Publications.

Changing consensus   It is particularly important to study these biases in the context of a changing consensus because change is a staple of the social world rarely captured by laboratory experiments or punctual surveys and more often than not left to historians, sociologists, economists (e.g., Kuran, 1995), or journalists (e.g., Gladwell, 2000). With time, a behavior that was common and desirable can become rare and undesirable (e.g., smoking in late 20th-century America; see S. Katz, 1997), or vice-versa. It is not rare for behaviors to move back and forth on these dimensions. Hairstyles and hemlines go up and down as dictated by fashion. Fads regulate what restaurant to go to, what book to read, but also what theoretical bandwagon academics jump on, what health-promoting behavior people engage in, or what psychological disorder gets diagnosed in children. Watershed changes in actual consensus and desirability are the ultimate goal of the marketer, the public health advocate, and the moral crusader. Consensus changes can be brought about by an authority figure (e.g., the Surgeon General), by the publication of new scientific evidence, by a vocal minority mistakenly assumed to represent the majority, by trendsetters and the media, by a sudden crisis, and so forth. They can happen over decades or overnight. Witness the sudden frequency and desirability of displaying the American flag after the events of September 11, 2001. A behavior once suspect of jingoism suddenly became a demonstration of concern and sympathy for disaster victims. Consensus also will change for a given individual as he or she moves from one social group to another. Thus, the college freshman might encounter a culture that is much more permissive of alcohol consumption than she was accustomed to in high school (Prentice & Miller, 1996); the expatriate may soon realize that the mores of his own culture have little currency in his country of residence ("When in Rome . . .").

The current study illustrates the common case in which a resource comes to be limited and an authority figure asks group members to voluntarily limit their usage to avoid depletion. Examples abound, from the rationing of household goods in postwar Europe to energy conservation following the oil crisis in the 1970s or the current plea to avoid computer programs using inordinate amounts of bandwidth (e.g., music-sharing software) on university computer networks. Such situations are particularly dependent on perceptions of consensus because, as is illustrated in the classic "commons dilemma," if one believes that others are not engaging in conservation efforts, then one's own sacrifice is pointless and is best to be avoided (Dawes, McTavish, & Shaklee, 1977). For all of these reasons, it is crucial that we start investigating social biases in the context of a changing consensus.

Biases in the estimation of consensus   In the abundant literature on the estimation of consensus since F. H. Allport (1924) introduced the concept of social projection, two biases have been particularly pervasive: the false consensus effect and the uniqueness bias.

The *false consensus* effect refers to the tendency to estimate more support for one's own position or behavior than do people holding the opposite position or engaged in the opposite behavior (Ross, Greene, & House, 1977). The effect, defined empirically as the difference between the estimates given by people who perform the relevant behavior and those given by people who do not, has been observed in numerous studies (see Mullen & Hu, 1988, for a review). For example, when participants who agree to carry a sandwich board around campus provided estimates of the prevalence of their response, they offered higher estimates than did participants who refused to carry the sandwich board (Ross et al., 1977). In the present field study, the false consensus effect would take the form of bathers giving higher estimates of the prevalence of showering than nonbathers.

The *uniqueness bias* (Goethals, Messick, & Allison, 1991; Suls & Wan, 1987), on the other hand, is the tendency for people to underestimate the proportion of others who can or will perform desirable actions, computed by subtracting the mean estimate of prevalence of a desirable behavior from its actual reported prevalence. In practice, those who perform a desirable behavior underestimate the number of others as good as them, whereas those who perform an undesirable behavior overestimate the number of others as bad as them. For example, people underestimate the percentage of their peers who would perform moral or altruistic acts such as giving blood and overestimate the prevalence of selfish acts (Allison, Messick, & Goethals, 1989; Goethals, 1986). In the situation under investigation, the uniqueness bias would be observed if the prevalence of showering is overestimated during the shower ban but is underestimated once the ban is lifted.

As the literature on these two biases accumulated, it became apparent that their surface simplicity and the ease with which they were obtained belied their theoretical complexity and the difficulty to pinpoint a single cause for their occurrence. For example, although many of the factors originally put forward by Ross et al. (1977) were shown to impact the false consensus effect, none was shown to be necessary (Krueger, 1998; Marks & Miller, 1987). Soon, more parsimonious models that could account for both the false consensus effect and the uniqueness bias emerged. Mullen and Hu (1988) argued that both effects could be explained by the fact that, independently of desirability, majorities systematically underestimate their size, whereas minorities overestimate theirs. Because desirable behaviors tend to be more common, this results in the apparently self enhancing uniqueness bias.[1] Furthermore, because minorities overestimate more than majorities underestimate, we observe the false consensus effect. Recently, Krueger and Clement (1997; see also Krueger, 1998) argued that the simple assumption that all respondents believe they are in the majority, regardless of true majority status, can account for both the false consensus effect and the uniqueness bias. Because our central aim was to demonstrate the co-occurrence of a variety of biases in the context of fluctuating, real-world norms, our data do not speak directly to this debate: The fact that these biases may be multiply determined, of course, is part of what makes them so interesting.

Consensus estimates and psychological inferences   The other aspect of the situation we wanted to explore is people's willingness to draw attitude or personality inferences from simple behavioral labels. Implicit in the basic question of consensus estimate studies ("How many people do X?") is a question about the psychological implications of the behavior ("What kind of person does X?"). Given the logic of causal attribution (Kelley, 1972), asking how many people cheat on their taxes is tantamount to asking what it takes to cheat on one's taxes. If very few people are thought to cheat, it probably takes a very dishonest person, but if everyone does, the explanation must lie elsewhere, maybe in the incentive structure of the situation. It should therefore be instructive to study the inferences people make based on a given behavior in conjunction with how frequent people perceive that behavior to be. Individuals have a tendency to make dispositional judgments based on other people's behavior (Gilbert & Malone, 1995; Jones & Davis, 1965; Ross, 1977), to make the leap from what an actor does to what kind of person the actor is. This phenomenon has most often been studied by placing participants in the role of observers and asking them to judge a target. In real life, however, we have often had to decide beforehand whether to engage in the behavior for which we judge others. The attribution process becomes much more self-relevant, and this opens the door to a whole new class of biases. As with consensus estimates, where people exhibit predictable patterns of relationship between their choices and their estimates of other people's choices, we expect to observe systematic relationships between one's attitudes and the attitudes imputed to others on the basis of their behavior. However, whereas social projection revealed an excessive belief in self-other similarity, biases in psychological inferences tend to reveal, if anything, a failure to take into account one's experience when imagining that of others (Miller & McFarland, 1991). This leads people to take the behavior of others as more representative of their personality and attitudes than it really is. As a result, they think that behavioral differences represent wide gaps in attitudes or personalities (false polarization) and they believe that others behaving like them are more committed to the values underlying the behavior than they are (pluralistic ignorance).

Pluralistic ignorance (D. Katz & Allport, 1931) refers to the belief that one's private thoughts, feelings, and behaviors are different from those of others, even though one's public behavior is identical (Miller & McFarland, 1991). Even when individuals do not fall victim to social projection in estimating population parameters, they can still err in their inferences about the determinants of that behavior. The issue here is not that the processing or sampling of information is biased but that the information itself is misleading because public behavior is not reflective of private attitudes. As a result, individuals mistakenly believe that their attitudes differ from the attitudes of others, when in reality there is remarkable agreement within the group (Miller, Monin, & Prentice, 2000). Pluralistic ignorance is a common feature of social life and has been documented in a variety of settings (see Prentice & Miller, 1996, for a review). In the case of the water crisis, those who refrain from showering during the ban—presumably because of social pressure—would exhibit pluralistic ignorance if they failed to recognize that other non-bathers fall prey to similar pressure and if they assumed instead that other non-bathers are intrinsically more community-minded than they are. Those who shower, on the other hand, would exhibit pluralistic ignorance if they believed they cared more about the community than other bathers because they thought their behavior was exonerated by special circumstances while failing to recognize that similar factors influence others.

Pluralistic ignorance captures the personality inferences people draw about those who behave like they do, but individuals also draw inferences about those who hold opposing attitudes or make different behavioral choices, sometimes exhibiting *false polarization*. In their study of adversarial disputes such as the abortion debate, Robinson, Keltner, Ward, and Ross (1995); (see also Keltner & Robinson, 1996) found that individuals overestimate the extremity of attitudes of the people involved (see also Dawes, Singer, & Lemons, 1972), a bias that extends from inferences about one's fellow partisans (a form of pluralistic ignorance) to inferences about one's opponents. Although partisans on both sides of the debate held relatively moderate positions, they believed that others, both on their side and on the other side, held much more extreme attitudes and that the gap between the two sides was much larger than it really was. We wish to extend this false polarization effect to any situation where an attitudinal or behavioral choice is made: No matter which attitude is endorsed or behavior performed, individuals should exaggerate the difference in attitudes between the two sides. In the situation under study, both bathers and non-bathers should overestimate the difference between the two groups in terms of underlying attitudes, such as caring for the community.

The present investigation   This naturally occurring water crisis provided a rare opportunity to study consensus estimates and psychological inferences in the context of rapidly changing desirability and frequency of the target behavior. Note that the false consensus effect and the uniqueness bias have been studied conjointly in the past (e.g., Mullen & Goethals, 1990) but never in such a naturalistic and evolving environment. Furthermore, we wished to go one step further in our understanding of the psychology of consensus estimation by simultaneously looking at biases in drawing psychological inferences from the target behavior, such as pluralistic ignorance and false polarization. By using a broad array of indicators, and thus assessing a variety of social biases, we hoped to make the most of this rich naturalistic situation and capture some of the theoretical complexities of social perception.

Method

Participants   On 5 consecutive nights, we went to a different dormitory on the Princeton campus and distributed a survey titled "Water Crisis Survey" to students as they left their dining halls. All freshmen and sophomores at Princeton live and eat in one of five dormitories and are assigned to them randomly at matriculation. The study was conducted on the first week of class, so prior contact and socialization within colleges was limited. Overall, 415 respondents took a version of our survey, broken down as follows: Day 1, $n = 78$; Day 2, $n = 122$; Day 3, $n = 44$; Day 4, $n = 70$; and Day 5, $n = 101$. We chose to go to a different dormitory every night, each of which houses from 450 to 500 students, to make sure we would never survey the same respondent twice.

Materials and procedure   Figure 1 recapitulates the timeline of the study. On the night immediately following the ban (Day 1), we gave people a list of seven recommendations included in the administration's initial water conservation message. We asked them to indicate how much they had followed each instruction, on a scale from 1 to 14, with lower scores meaning they had followed it better. In this pilot survey we found that students had promptly followed the self-protective instructions (e.g., "Don't drink from water fountains or taps"), $M = 3.3$ for these items, but were more hesitant to make personal sacrifices in their water usage for the community (e.g., "Don't shower"), $M = 5.3$ for these items, $t(81) = -4.3, p < .001$. We thus used a water conservation measure— refraining from showering—in the subsequent surveys.

On Days 2 and 3, we ensured that participants were aware of the shower ban by asking them when they had heard about it and through what medium. Then we asked them how many showers they had taken since 5 p.m. the day before and what percentage of "other Princeton students" they thought had taken one or more showers since that time.

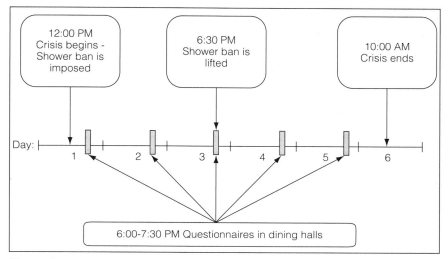

Figure 1 ■ Timeline of water crisis and questionnaire administration.

After the ban was lifted (Day 3), we modified the format of the survey on the last 2 days to include questions about showering during the ban. Thus, on Days 4 and 5, in addition to the three questions about showers taken since 5 p.m. the previous day, participants reported how many showers they had taken "from Monday [Day 2] at 5 p.m. until Tuesday [Day 3] at 5 p.m.," that is, at the height of the water crisis.

On the last 3 days, we added items specifically designed to study perceptions of behavioral stereotypes:

On Day 3, Day 4, and Day 5, we asked respondents how much they cared about the community, how much people who showered during the ban cared about the community, and how much people who did not shower during the ban cared about the community, on a 7-point scale ranging from 1 (*don't care at all about the community*) to 7 (*care very much about the community*). After the ban was lifted (Days 4 and 5), questions about caring were explicitly phrased to refer to taking showers during the ban.

Predictions

Social projection: Behavior.   When participants were required to estimate how many others took showers, we expected to observe social projection, manifested by (a) *false consensus*: bathers should estimate higher rates of showering among students than non-bathers and (b) *uniqueness bias*: showering should be over-estimated when it is undesirable and uncommon but underestimated when desirable and common again.

Social projection: Attitudes. We expected participants to rely on social projection when estimating other people's attitudes. Thus, we predicted (c) *self-other correlation*: reported caring by respondents should correlate with their estimates of how much others (bathers or non-bathers) care about the community.

Psychological inferences. Although bathers and non-bathers might differ slightly in how much they report caring about the community, we expected these differences to be vastly exaggerated in participants' perceptions. We predicted (d) *false polarization*: bathers and non-bathers should be seen as differing more in how much they care than is actually the case and (e) *pluralistic ignorance*: bathers should think they care more about the community than do other bathers because they believe that theirs are special circumstances (e.g., having engaged in strenuous exercise) and overlook similar excuses in others, whereas non-bathers should believe they care less about the community than do other non-bathers because they are aware of situational forces affecting their decision (e.g., conformity) but are oblivious to the strength of these factors on others.

Results

Social projection

False consensus. (a) We observed a clear false consensus effect. Participants who took one or more showers gave a higher estimate of students showering ($M = 72\%$ overall) than participants who did not ($M = 44\%$), $t(325) = -11.6$, $p < .001$. Table 1 shows that this phenomenon also was apparent within days (all $ps < .01$). During the crisis (Days 2 and 3), social projection was such that both bathers and non-bathers thought they were in the majority. In fact, on Day 3, although most people (53%) did not shower, bathers thought they had more consensual support (66%) than did non-bathers (53%), $t(41) = 2.5$, $p < .05$. When the ban was lifted, although we still observed the false consensus effect, non-bathers—now the minority—tempered their projection and recognized that they were in the minority (48% and 42% on Days 4 and 5).

Uniqueness bias. (b) As Figure 2 and Table 1 illustrate, the results supported our uniqueness bias prediction. During the ban, students were seen as taking more showers than was really the case [Day 2: 47% versus 33%,[2] $t(119) = 6.6$, $p < .001$; Day 3: 56% versus 47%, $t(43) = 3.1$, $p < .005$] but as soon as the ban was lifted, other students were seen as taking fewer showers than was really the case [Day 4: 70% versus 77%, $t(67) = -2.5$, $p < .05$; Day 5: 72% versus 84%, $t(98) = -5.1, p < .001$].

Self-other correlation. (c) Participants also showed social projection when trying to guess other people's attitudes. Their estimates of how much bathers and

TABLE 1									
Estimated and Actual Percentage of Students Taking a Shower, Broken Down by Day and, by Respondent's Behavior									
Estimated percentage of showers	Day 2		Day 3		Day 4		Day 5		All Days	
	P	n	P	n	P	n	P	n	P	n
By bathers	63	39	66	20	75	52	75	82	72	193
By non-bathers	39	81	47	23	52	15	58	15	44	134
False consensus	24***		19**		23***		17**		28***	
All respondents[a]	47	120	56	44	70	68	72	99	60	331
Reported percentage of showers	33		47		77		84		59	
Uniqueness bias	14***		9**		−7*		−12***		1	

$*p < .05.$ $**p < .01.$ $***p < .001.$
[a] Some of the column total ns are slightly greater than the sum of bathers and non-bathers because of the few respondents ($n = 4$) who did not report their behavior.

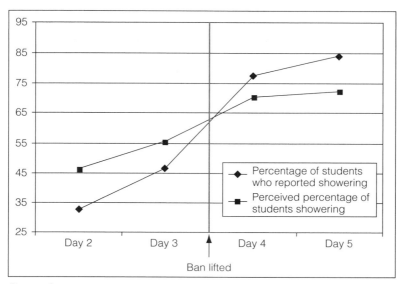

Figure 2 ■ Perceived and self-reported prevalence of showering, by day.

non-bathers cared about the community were highly significantly correlated with their own reported caring (rs = .34 and .28, respectively, both ps < .001). We report mean values for these variables below.

Psychological inferences   None of the five main variables in our "caring" data was influenced by day, as indicated by nonsignificant one-way analyses of variance, and the pattern of means was the same on all 3 days, so we collapsed our data across days. Furthermore, when separating bathers from non-bathers, we used recollections from the height of the ban, Day 3, rather than reports of the day the survey was given out on Day 4 or 5, because by that time the ban had been lifted. We found that these recollected self-reports did not differ significantly from what we actually collected on Day 3, whereas 47% reported showering on Day 3, 44% of our Day 4 sample and 58% of our Day 5 sample remembered showering on Day 3, $\chi^2(1, N = 113) = .05$ and $\chi^2(1, N = 143) = 1.6$, both *ns.*

False polarization.   (d) Figure 3 presents the caring data using Keltner and Robinson's (1996) system of representation. As predicted, showering was seen as highly diagnostic of caring about the community in others. Bathers were seen as caring little, $M = 3.5$, whereas non-bathers were seen as caring much more, $M = 5.7$, $t(211) = -20.7$, $p < .001$. However, in reality, as is apparent in Figure 3, the two groups are strikingly similar in their self-reports. Non-bathers report caring only slightly more about the community ($M = 5.2$) than do bathers ($M = 4.9$), and this difference falls short of conventional levels of significance, $t(207) = 1.6$, $p = .10$.

Furthermore, there was remarkable agreement between bathers and non-bathers as to the meaning of showering. Both bathers and non-bathers thought that not showering indicated caring about the community, $Ms = 5.8$ and 5.6, respectively, $t(207) = .28$, *ns.* They also generally agreed that showering was a sign of not caring much, but bathers still thought that bathers cared a little more, $M = 3.8$, than non-bathers were ready to give them credit for, $M = 3.3$, $t(207) = -2.6$, $p < .01$.

Pluralistic ignorance.   (e) The strong version of false polarization was upheld: People used behavior to make unwarranted inferences even about others who behaved like them. They thought that showering was more diagnostic for others than for themselves. Bathers thought they cared about the community more than other bathers, $M = 4.9$ versus 3.8, $t(105) = 8.2$, $p < .001$. This might not seem that surprising given a host of well-studied self-enhancement biases—what is more impressive is that non-bathers thought they actually cared about the community less than did other non-bathers, $M = 5.2$, versus 5.6, $t(100) = -3.6$, $p < .001$.

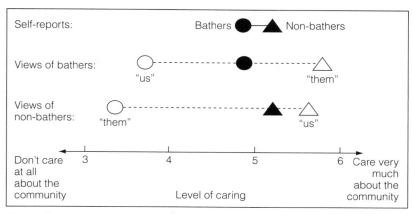

Figure 3 ■ Perceived and actual differences in level of caring about the community.

Correlations   We computed correlations between estimates of consensus and the three measures of caring (self, bathers, and non-bathers) separately for both bathers and non-bathers. Lacking a priori predictions for these six correlations, we used an adjusted alpha of (.05/6). Given this adjusted alpha, none of the correlations was significant, so we will not discuss this analysis any further.

Discussion

This field study of reactions to a naturally occurring emergency illustrates the multiple facets of the estimation of consensus in the instance of fluctuating norms. We were able to approach the situation at two levels. First, we looked at social projection, at the behavioral as well as at the psychological level. As predicted, we found that respondents gave higher estimates of showering when they themselves showered than when they did not (demonstrating false consensus) and that the more they cared about the community, the more they thought others cared. In addition, we observed that participants overestimated the prevalence of showering when it was undesirable and thus uncommon but underestimated it when it was desirable and thus common (demonstrating the uniqueness bias).

People not only misperceived what others were doing but also why they were doing it. At the level of psychological inferences, by asking respondents how much others cared about the community, we witnessed participants' willingness to use relatively innocuous behavior to make sweeping, morally loaded judgments of fellow students. Although bathers and non-bathers reported similar levels of caring about their community, bathers were perceived as much less concerned than non-bathers (demonstrating false polarization). Indeed, participants viewed the simple act of showering as so diagnostic of others' attitudes that bathers themselves assumed that other bathers cared less than they did, whereas non-bathers thought other non-bathers cared more than they did (demonstrating pluralistic ignorance). This later finding is important because it is sometimes erroneously assumed that pluralistic ignorance is merely the consequence of wanting to feel superior to others, whereas here it results in some participants feeling inferior to others on an important moral dimension.[3]

Social projection in uncertain times   Crises are particularly volatile times, when consensus is unclear and the biases that people normally harbor about what others are doing or thinking can be exacerbated. Social projection may well reach its peak in what is sometimes called the "fog of battle," when no one is sure yet where others stand. It may be particularly likely when situations and choices are ambiguous (Gilovich, 1990): Precisely when we are unsure of appropriate opinions and behavior is when we are most likely to look to others (Festinger, 1954; Hogg & Mullin, 1999) and to seek social support (Festinger, Riecken, & Schachter, 1956). Social projection is further exacerbated because consensus information is particularly difficult to obtain in uncertain times (when a new product is released, a new law is passed, or an old norm becomes obsolete), because others engaged in the same search divulge little until they know what is appropriate. Just as Latané and Darley's (1970) non-intervening bystanders kept poker faces while scrutinizing their neighbors' demeanor for the appropriate response to an emergency, individuals are unlikely to commit publicly to a behavior before they have a sense of the prevailing consensus. Before a norm coalesces, estimates of consensus should be labile and are likely to be particularly influenced by one's own reaction. In particular, during times of uncertainty, individuals should be more likely to rely solely on projection, leading to the belief that one is in the majority when one is really in the minority.[4] Indeed, we observed just that in the study presented here. During the ban, a fairly new and ambiguous situation in which norms did not have time to be established, both bathers and non-bathers believed they were in the majority. Once the ban was lifted, we still observed the false consensus effect, but by then it was clear to all that a majority of people shower every day. Now respondents, back in a familiar context, could rely on pre-existing knowledge about the world. Note that this phenomenon makes the resolution of conflicts particularly difficult in uncertain times, because each side, believing it represents the majority, is unwilling to compromise: Bridging the gap between the two sides is made even harder by the essentialist interpretations of the behavioral divide, to which we now turn.

Behavioral stereotypes   A simple behavior, showering, was seen as reflective of a deeper underlying personality trait with obvious moral undertones, caring about the community. The tendency to jump quickly from observing an actor's behavior to inferring dispositional attributes of that actor is one of the core findings in social psychology (Gilbert & Malone, 1995; Jones & Davis, 1965; Ross, 1977). The present results show that people are willing to make the same dispositional attributions more generally and infer personality traits or attitudes from behavioral labels the same way they make stereotypical judgments of others based on their membership in social categories (G. W. Allport, 1954; Fiske, 1998; D. Katz & Braly, 1933). In addition, the pluralistic ignorance observed suggests that people infer an underlying attitude from behavior, even when they performed the behavior themselves, but do not hold that attitude as strongly. "Behavioral stereotypes" of this kind are quite common in everyday social experience, as in the case of more familiar stereotypes defined merely by behavior: smokers versus nonsmokers, vegetarians versus meat-eaters, or exercisers versus non-exercisers. We hold well-formed theories about the kind of person who would fall on either side of these behavioral divides, although none of these categories form a group in the traditional sense of the term, in that they do not need to engage in any group-like activity.[5]

One possible concern in using the data in this article to explore behavioral stereotypes is that by only asking about concern for the community, we might have implied that this was the appropriate dimension by which to judge showering during the ban and therefore the most logical personality inference to draw from the behavioral labels. One could then argue that the differences observed in the perception of groups result from the demand characteristics of the situation. One way to address this problem would be to use less directed scales, such as the items of the semantic differential scales (Osgood, Suci, & Tannenbaum, 1967). We asked 107 participants to rate smokers, vegetarians, exercisers, and their behavioral counterparts on the semantic differential scales. As predicted, these behaviors were seen as highly diagnostic of the dimensions underlying the semantic differential. For example, non-smokers and exercisers were rated significantly higher than their behavioral counterparts on the evaluation, potency, and activity factors. More interestingly, vegetarians, a minority that could claim the moral high ground, were seen as significantly better on the evaluation scale but significantly weaker on the potency scale by our mostly meateating (91%) sample. This illustrates that there is a logic to behavioral stereotypes and that they are complex representations that can include positive as well as negative traits.

Casuistry   Another intriguing line of research lies in uncovering the mechanisms by which individuals performing an undesirable behavior are able to distance themselves from others who do the same, implicitly claiming that their behavior is not diagnostic of an underlying disposition. We assume that they engage in some degree of casuistry, claiming they were in special circumstances, thus following a tendency to attribute their own behavior to situational factors and others' behavior to their dispositions (Jones & Nisbett, 1976). Anecdotal evidence supports this view: In an article published by the *Daily Princetonian* on Day 3 (Esguerra, 1999), many student interviewees sympathized with the water concerns but felt that their special circumstances justified taking a shower. For example, the president of a dance group famous for its exhausting practices reported that although members were "doing their best to conserve water," the long auditions on Day 1 would have made it "fairly disgusting" not to shower afterward. This insight into the phenomenology of the shower-taker highlights one strategy that people use to justify—to themselves and others—their socially undesirable behavior. Future research should focus on the systematic study of such exculpatory strategies.

The legacy of uncertain times   Today's norms are often remnants of yesterday's fluid consensus. In the water crisis, things quickly went back to normal after a temporary, if drastic, change in both descriptive (actual consensus) and injunctive (desirability) norms. Such changes, however, are not always temporary, and when crises mark the beginning of a new era (e.g., successful revolutions), the dynamics observed in this article can have lasting consequences. Given the inertia inherent in less critical times, many of the norms and behavioral stereotypes that have currency in times of relative certainty emerged and coalesced in times of uncertainty. Thus, norms and stereotypes that emerge overnight in times of uncertainty, when social consensus is in some sense "up for grabs," may very well endure, entrenched and crystallized, and remain the ones we deal with in the relative certainty of our everyday lives.

Notes

1.   Whereas earlier writing on consensus estimates tended to privilege the role of desirability (e.g., Goethals, Messick, & Allison, 1991), more recent models emphasize the centrality of actual consensus (Krueger, 1998; Mullen & Hu, 1988). One rare attempt to disentangle these two factors was conducted by Mullen and Goethals (1990), who showed that desirability and actual consensus exert independent, additive, and noninteractive effects on social projection

(see also Krueger, 1998). In our investigation of the water crisis, as in many naturalistic settings, the natural confounding of the two factors precludes any analysis of their separate contributions, and our results should be interpreted as reflecting the impact of both desirability and frequency.

2.   This figure closely resembles that obtained by the *Daily Princetonian* (57 out of 157, or 36%) through an "informal telephone survey" conducted on Day 2 (Esguerra, 1999). Note that the publication of this figure should have worked against us, because it provides an anchor that might have limited false consensus and the uniqueness bias.

3.   Similarly, Miller and McFarland (1987) showed that pluralistic ignorance can lead to people feeling less intelligent than their peers, as exemplified by the typical classroom situation where each student attributes her peers' lack of clarification questions as evidence that she is the only one confused and as a result the whole confused class stays silent.

4.   It is important to note, however, that this extreme reliance on social projection is in most cases the optimal strategy because in the absence of other information it would be irrational not to take one's own behavior into account when making consensus estimates. Dawes and his colleagues observed that as predicted by Bayesian statistics, the more perceivers rely on projection when making estimates of consensus, the more accurate they are (Dawes, 1989; Dawes & Mulford, 1996). If there really is a bias involved in social projection, it seems to be that when other information is available, people still give too much weight to their own experience (Krueger, 1998).

5.   In a related vein, Gross and Miller (1997) note that "the groups studied in false consensus research, the majority and the minority, typically do not exist in any real interactive sense" (p. 241).

References

Allison, S. T., Messick, D. M., & Goethals, G. R. (1989). On being better but not smarter than others: The Muhammad Ali effect. *Social Cognition, 7,* 275–295.

Allport, F. H. (1924). *Social Psychology.* Cambridge, MA: Riverside Press.

Allport, G. W. (1954). *The nature of prejudice.* Reading, MA: Addison-Wesley.

Dawes, R. M. (1989). Statistical criteria for establishing a truly false consensus effect. *Journal of Experimental Social Psychology, 25,* 1–17.

Dawes, R. M., McTavish, J., & Shaklee, H. (1977). Behavior, communication, and assumptions about other people's behavior in a commons dilemma situation. *Journal of Personality and Social Psychology, 35*(1), 1–11.

Dawes, R. M., & Mulford, M. (1996). The false consensus effect and overconfidence: Flaws in judgment or flaws in how we study judgment? *Organizational Behavior and Human Decision Processes, 65*(3), 201–211.

Dawes, R. M., Singer, D., & Lemons, F. (1972). An experimental analysis of the contrast effect and its implications for intergroup communication and the indirect assessment of attitude. *Journal of Personality and Social Psychology, 21*(3), 281–295.

Esguerra, I. V. (1999, September 21). Putting cleanliness first, some students ignore restrictions. *Daily Princetonian.*

Festinger, L. (1954). A theory of social comparison processes. *Human Relations, 7,* 117–140.

Festinger, L., Riecken, H. W., & Schachter, S. (1956). *When prophecy fails: A social and psychological study of a modern group that predicted the destruction on the world.* New York: Harper & Row.

Fiske, S. T. (1998). Stereotyping, prejudice, and discrimination. In D. T. Gilbert, S. T. Fiske, & G. Lindzey (Eds.), *The handbook of social psychology* (4th ed., pp. 357–411). New York: McGraw-Hill.

Gilbert, D. T., & Malone, P. S. (1995). The correspondence bias. *Psychological Bulletin, 117*(1), 21–38.

Gilovich, T. (1990). Differential construal and the false consensus effect. *Journal of Personality and Social Psychology, 59,* 623–634.

Gladwell, M. (2000). *The tipping point: How little things can make a big difference.* Boston: Little, Brown.

Goethals, G. R. (1986). Fabricating and ignoring social reality: Self-serving estimates of consensus. In J. M. Olson, C. P. Herman, & M. P. Zanna (Eds.), *Social comparison and relative deprivation: The Ontario symposium* (Vol. 4). Hillsdale, NJ: Lawrence Erlbaum.

Goethals, G. R., Messick, D. M., & Allison, S. T. (1991). The uniqueness bias: Studies of constructive social comparison. In J. Suls & T. A. Wills (Eds.), *Social comparison: Contemporary theory and research.* Hillsdale, NJ: Lawrence Erlbaum.

Gross, S. R., & Miller, N. (1997). The "golden section" and bias in perceptions of social consensus. *Personality and Social Psychology Review, 1*(3), 241–271.

Hogg, M. A., & Mullin, B. A. (1999). Joining groups to reduce uncertainty: Subjective uncertainty reduction and group identification. In D. Abrams & M. A. Hogg (Eds.), *Social identity and social cognition* (pp. 249–279). Malden, MA: Blackwell.

Jones, E. E., & Davis, K. E. (1965). A theory of correspondent inference: From acts to dispositions. *Advances in Experimental Social Psychology, 2,* 219–266.

Jones, E. E., & Nisbett, R. E. (1976). The actor and the observer: Divergent perceptions of the causes of behavior. In J. W. Thibaut, J. T. Spence, & R. C. Carson (Eds.), *Contemporary topics in social psychology.* Morristown, NJ: General Learning Press.

Katz, D., & Allport, F. H. (1931). *Students' attitudes: A report of the Syracuse University reaction study.* Syracuse, NY: Craftsman.

Katz, D., & Braly, K. W. (1933). Racial stereotypes of 100 college students. *Journal of Abnormal Social Psychology, 28,* 280–290.

Katz, S. (1997). Secular morality. In A. M. Brandt & P. Rozin (Eds.), *Morality and health.* New York: Routledge.

Kelley, H. H. (1972). Causal schemata and the attribution process. In E. E. Jones, D. E. Kanouse, H. H. Kelley, R. E. Nisbett, S. Valins, & B. Weiner (Eds.), *Attribution:*

Perceiving the causes of behavior (pp. 151–174). Morristown, NJ: General Learning Press.

Keltner, D., & Robinson, R. J. (1996). Extremism, power, and the imagined basis of social conflict. *Current Directions in Psychological Science, 5*(4), 101–105.

Krueger, J. (1998). On the perception of social consensus. In M. P. Zanna (Ed.), *Advances in experimental social psychology* (Vol. 30). New York: Academic Press.

Krueger, J., & Clement, R. W. (1997). Estimates of social consensus by majorities and minorities: The case for social projection. *Personality and Social Psychology Review, 1*(4), 299–313.

Kuran, T. (1995). *Private truths, public lies: The social consequences of preference falsification.* Cambridge, MA: Harvard University Press.

Latané, B., & Darley, J. M. (1970). *The unresponsive bystander: Why doesn't he help?* New York: Appleton Century Crofts.

Marks, G., & Miller, N. (1987). Ten years of research on the false-consensus effect: An empirical and theoretical review. *Psychological Bulletin, 102*(1), 72–90.

Miller, D. T., & McFarland, C. (1987). Pluralistic ignorance: When similarity is interpreted as dissimilarity. *Journal of Personality and Social Psychology, 53,* 298–305.

Miller, D. T., & McFarland, C. (1991). When social comparison goes awry: The case of pluralistic ignorance. In J. Suls & T. A. Wills (Eds.), *Social comparison: Contemporary theory and research.* Hillsdale, NJ: Lawrence Erlbaum.

Miller, D. T., Monin, B., & Prentice, D. A. (2000). Pluralistic ignorance and inconsistency between private attitudes and public behaviors. In D. J. Terry & M. A. Hogg (Eds.), *Attitudes, behavior, and social context: The role of norms and group membership.* Mahwah, NJ: Lawrence Erlbaum.

Mullen, B., & Goethals, G. R. (1990). Social projection, actual consensus and valence. *British Journal of Social Psychology, 29,* 279–282.

Mullen, B., & Hu, L. (1988). Social projection as a function of cognitive mechanisms: Two meta-analytic integrations. *British Journal of Social Psychology, 27,* 333–356.

Osgood, C. E., Suci, G. J., & Tannenbaum, P. H. (1967). *The measurement of meaning.* Urbana: University of Illinois Press.

Prentice, D. A., & Miller, D. T. (1996). Pluralistic ignorance and the perpetuation of social norms and unwitting actors. *Advances in Experimental Social Psychology, 28,* 161–210.

Robinson, R. J., Keltner, D., Ward, A, & Ross, L. (1995). Actual versus assumed differences in construal: "Naive realism" in intergroup perception and conflict. *Journal of Personality and Social Psychology, 68*(3), 404–417.

Ross, L. (1977). The intuitive psychologist and his shortcomings: Distortions in the attribution process. In L. Berkowitz (Ed.), *Advances in experimental social psychology* (Vol. 10, pp. 174–221). New York: Academic Press.

Ross, L., Greene, D., & House, P. (1977). The false consensus phenomenon: An attributional bias in self-perception and social-perception processes. *Journal of Experimental Social Psychology, 13*(3), 279–301.

Suls, J., & Wan, C. K. (1987). In search of the false-uniqueness phenomenon: Fear and estimates of social consensus. *Journal of Personality and Social Psychology, 52*(1), 211–217.

Questions for Review and Discussion

1. Define the false consensus bias. What evidence did Monin and Norton find of it in their study?
2. Define the false uniqueness bias. What evidence did Monin and Norton find of it in their study?
3. How did the bathers and non-bathers in the study perceive others who responded as they did to the water shortage?

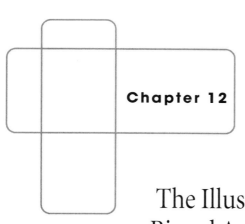

Chapter 12

The Illusion of Transparency: Biased Assessments of Others' Ability to Read One's Emotional States

Thomas Gilovich, Kenneth Savitsky, and Victoria Husted Medvec

Fans of Edgar Allan Poe will recall that the key passage in *The Tell-Tale Heart* is one in which the protagonist does his best to play it cool during a conversation with three police officers. It is a performance made more difficult by the fact that the officers happen to be standing directly above the hidden body of the protagonist's murder victim. As he becomes increasingly anxious that the officers suspect his guilt, he begins to hear what he takes to be his victim's heart beating underneath the floorboards. He becomes convinced that the sound, which in reality is the beating of his own heart, can be heard by the officers as well. Eventually, his emotions get the best of him and he gives himself away:

> Was it possible they heard it not? . . . no, no! They heard!—they suspected!—They *knew!*—they were making a *mockery* of my horror! . . . I could bear those hypocritical smiles no longer! . . . "Villains!" I shrieked, "dissemble no more! I admit the deed!—tear up the planks!—here, here!—it is the beating of his hideous heart!" (Poe, 1976, p. 262)

One element of the central character's reaction doubtless belongs more to the world of fiction than to everyday life: his conviction that the heartbeat was his victim's rather than his own. Although people sometimes project their mental states onto others, they typically recognize that their own strong physiological reactions belong to themselves and not to someone else.

In contrast, a second element of the protagonist's behavior, namely his exaggerated view of the officers' ability to read his internal reactions, may be quite common. In particular, we contend that, like Poe's character, people often overestimate the extent to which their thoughts, feelings, and sensations "leak out" and are available to others. A dinner guest may feel that her distaste over her host's atrocious cooking is more apparent than it really is, a secret admirer may believe his infatuation with a colleague is more obvious than is actually the case, or (closer to our own telltale hearts) a social psychologist conducting a deceptive experiment may overestimate the extent to which her participants can sense her apprehension and see through the cover story. Borrowing a term from Miller and McFarland (1987, 1991), we refer to this tendency to overestimate the extent to which others can read one's internal states as the *illusion of transparency.*

Why might people be susceptible to such an illusion? We contend that the bias stems primarily from the powerful impact of an individual's own phenomenology. People are typically quite aware of their own internal states and tend to focus on them rather intently when they are strong. To be sure, people recognize that others are not privy to the same information as they are, and they attempt to adjust for this fact when trying to anticipate another's perspective. Nevertheless, it can be hard to get beyond one's own perspective even when one knows that it is necessary to do so: The "adjustment" that one makes from the "anchor" of one's own internal experience is likely to be insufficient (Jacowitz & Kahneman, 1995; Quattrone, Lawrence, Finkel, & Andrus, 1984; Quattrone, 1982; Tversky & Kahneman, 1974). The net result is a residual effect of one's own phenomenology and a sense that one's internal states are leaking out and are more available to others than is actually the case.

In this regard, the illusion of transparency has much in common with the *spotlight effect,* a phenomenon we have demonstrated and discussed at length elsewhere (Gilovich, Medvec, & Savitsky, 1998; Gilovich, Kruger, Medvec, & Savitsky, 1998; Savitsky & Gilovich, 1998). The spotlight effect refers to the tendency to overestimate the extent to which others notice and attend to one's external appearance and behavior. In one study, for example, undergraduate participants who were asked to wear a T-shirt depicting the singer Barry Manilow (a figure of dubious renown among college students) drastically overestimated the likelihood that observers would take notice of their attire and recall who was pictured on the shirt (Gilovich, Medvec, et al., 1998). People appear to believe that the social spotlight shines more brightly on them than it actually does.

Like the proposed illusion of transparency, the spotlight effect appears to stem from the difficulty of getting beyond one's own phenomenological experience. Here too, people typically recognize that others are less focused on them than they are themselves, but it can be difficult to properly adjust for that realization. The adjustment people make from their own experience tends to be insufficient, causing them to overestimate the extent to which they are the object of others' scrutiny. Support for this anchoring and adjustment interpretation was obtained by showing that the spotlight effect was diminished considerably when participants made their estimates after they had had time to acclimate to wearing the embarrassing shirt. The delay led the participants to be less absorbed with their own appearance and thus to begin their estimates from a lower anchor (Gilovich, Medvec, et al., 1998). The present investigation of the illusion of transparency expands on this work by suggesting that people believe the social spotlight shines through to their internal states as well.

Indirect evidence for an illusion of transparency comes from several recent sources. In one study, participants watched a humorous videotape while their facial expressions were covertly recorded. Across a variety of experimental conditions, the participants thought they had been more expressive than observers rated them as being. Indeed, when the participants were allowed to view their own videotapes, they generally expressed surprise at how inexpressive they had been, relative to how expressive they had felt. As the authors put it, people may not know just how little they show (Barr & Kleck, 1995).

Additional support comes from research by Vorauer and Ross (1998), who found that people tend to overestimate the extent to which others can make accurate trait inferences about them from a sample of their behavior. Participants whose behavior was completely determined by the constraints of the situation nevertheless felt as though observers could discern important elements of their true nature by observing their actions. Vorauer and Ross suggest that this error occurs when individuals fail to appreciate the extent to which they are uniquely "in the know" about themselves (see also Vorauer, in press; Vorauer & Claude, 1998).

Finally, the marked discrepancy between one's own knowledge of one's internal states and one's sense of what others are able to discern is nicely illustrated by an experiment (cited by Griffin & Ross, 1991) in which participants were asked to tap a well-known melody on a tabletop and then to estimate the proportion of listeners who would be able to identify the song they had tapped. As predicted, tappers grossly overestimated the listeners' abilities.

To appreciate these results, Griffin and Ross (1991) invited the reader to consider the different subjective experiences of the participants in each of the two roles.

First, imagine yourself as the tapper. As you tap rhythmically on the table in communicating the opening bars of the catchy tune you have chosen (let's say, "Yankee Doodle" or "Auld Lang Syne") you inevitably experience much more than your own tapping. Rather than impoverished knocks on the table, you "hear" the tune and the words to the song; indeed you are apt to hear ... a full orchestration, complete with rich harmonies between strings, winds, brass, and human voice. Now imagine you are the listener. For you, there are no notes, words, chords, or instruments; you hear only an aperiodic series of taps. Indeed, you are unable even to tell how the brief, irregular moments of silence between taps should be construed—that is, whether each is a sustained note, a musical "rest" between notes, or a simple pause as the tapper contemplates the "music" to come next. (p. 335)

What is required, then, is for tappers to realize that the rich information they possess is radically different from the impoverished stimulus available to listeners. What is more, tappers must then adjust adequately to capture the perspectives of their listeners. Note, however, that these adjustments tended to be insufficient, resulting in biased intuitions of listeners' abilities. In the present research, we demonstrate that this phenomenon applies not just to musical melodies heard inside one's head, but also to internal states generally, including nervousness, disgust, alarm, and potentially many others.

The illusion of transparency also bears some resemblance to several additional established phenomena, including the hind-sight bias (Fischoff, 1975, 1982; Fischoff & Beyth, 1975), the curse of knowledge (Camerer, Lowenstein, & Weber, 1989; Keysar & Bly, 1995; Keysar, Ginzel, & Bazerman, 1995), the self-as-target bias (Fenigstein, 1984; Zuckerman, Kernis, Guarnera, Murphy, & Rappoport, 1983), and various other accounts of egocentrism and biased perspective-taking (e.g., Fenigstein & Abrams, 1993; Griffin & Ross, 1991; Piaget, 1928/1959a, 1926/1959b; L. Ross & Ward, 1995, 1996; Stephenson & Wicklund, 1983; M. Ross & Sicoly, 1979). We discuss the most pertinent examples of this work in the context of specific experiments described below and defer a treatment of more general connections to earlier research to the General Discussion.

Overview of Present Experiments

We report three sets of studies in this paper. In the first, we demonstrate that participants induced to lie overestimate the detectability of their lies. Second, we show that participants asked to sample a foul-tasting drink while trying to maintain a neutral facial expression exaggerate the extent to which their disgust leaks out and can be detected by observers. Finally, we explore the speculation originally offered by Miller and McFarland (1987, 1991) that an illusion of transparency can help explain an enduring mystery in the literature on bystander nonintervention.

Across all three sets of studies, our approach is the same: Participants' intuitions about how they will be judged by others are compared with how participants are actually rated by observers. The illusion of transparency exists, then, when participants' estimates of the extent to which observers can discern their internal states exceed observers' actual ability to do so.

Study 1a

As an initial investigation of the illusion of transparency, we put Poe's account of the telltale heart to empirical test. Do people who lie overestimate the detectability of their deception? Of course, we could not simulate the high-stakes nature of the deception in Poe's tale. Nevertheless, we suspected that participants would tend to overestimate the detectability of their lies even for fairly innocuous falsehoods told in the confines of the laboratory. Accordingly, we had groups of participants play a round-robin lie detection game in which each of them told lies and truths to the rest of the group. Within each session, each participant served as a "liar" in one round and as a truth-telling foil in all other rounds. Furthermore, when not called on to lie, each player served as an observer whose job it was to detect which player was lying. Of key interest were the intuitions of participants when they were the liars regarding the detectability of their own lies. According to our illusion of transparency hypothesis, liars should feel as though their lies are more obvious and detectable than they really are.

Method

Participants.   Thirty-nine Cornell University undergraduates participated in one of seven groups of 5 participants each, or one group of 4. Participants in this and all experiments reported in this article were recruited from a variety of courses in psychology and human development and earned extra credit for their participation.

Materials.   We created 25 personal information questions that could unambiguously be answered truthfully or deceptively (e.g., "Name a foreign country you have visited," "Name a famous person you have met," "What brand of shampoo do you typically use?"). Each question was typed onto two separate index cards—one labeled "truth" and the other labeled "lie." In addition to the particular question, each card contained a sentence fragment for the participant to complete (e.g., "The brand of shampoo I typically use is . . .").

Procedure.   After being screened to ensure that they were unacquainted with one another, the participants were escorted into a large laboratory room where they were randomly assigned to one of five chairs facing a podium. Participants each donned a name tag marked with a number from 1 to 5. The experimenter explained that the study was designed to investigate people's ability to detect lies and that they would be asked to play five rounds of a round-robin lie detection game. In each round, the players would be asked, one by one, to walk to the front of the room and receive a card from the experimenter. This card would contain a question, which they were to answer aloud in front of the assembled participants. Some of the cards, they were told, would require a true answer whereas others would require them to tell a lie.

The experimenter went on to explain that participants' main job was to be astute lie detectors. They were informed that the player correctly identifying the greatest number of liars would be awarded a prize—a coupon for a free ice cream at a campus ice-cream shop. When lying, on the other hand, their job was to appear as if they were telling the truth.

Participants were informed that there would be one liar per round of the game and that each individual would be the liar once and only once in the course of the experiment. Prior to the experimental session, the experimenter had sorted the 25 cards such that there was only one lie card (and four truth cards) in each round, and such that each participant was to be the liar in one and only one round. The particular five questions for which participants were asked to lie were counterbalanced across experimental sessions.

In each of five rounds, then, each participant received a card from the experimenter, was given a brief moment to compose his or her answer, and made a single statement to the rest of the group from the podium at the front of the room. Each round thus consisted of five statements, delivered by the participants one after another (e.g., "I spent a summer in Kamchatka," "I have met David Letterman," "I usually use extra strength Head & Shoulders shampoo").

Participants completed a brief questionnaire after each round. On their questionnaire, liars were asked to estimate the number of participants, besides themselves, who would guess correctly that they had been the liar in that round. Answers could range from 0 (*none of the other players would peg them as the liar*) to 4 (*all of the other participants would guess that they had been the liar*). Special care was taken to inform participants that one person out of four, on average, would be expected to guess the identity of the liar in each round by chance alone.[1]

At the same time as the liar was estimating his or her detectability, truth-tellers were asked to guess the identity of the liar.[2] They did this by circling the player number of the participant they suspected had lied in that round. In addition, all truth-tellers were asked "How many people do you think will guess (incorrectly) that *you* were the liar in this round?" This question was included to address an alternative interpretation for the hypothesized results, discussed below.

When all questionnaires had been completed, the experimenter collected them and began the next round. After the final round, each player "came clean" and revealed to the group what he or she had lied about. The participant who had correctly identified the greatest number of liars was then awarded his or her prize, and everyone was debriefed. The experimental session lasted approximately 30 min.

Results

Because the data within each session are highly interdependent, all analyses were conducted at the level of the experimental session rather than the individual participant.

As anticipated, liars overestimated the likelihood that their fellow participants would be able to identify them as the liar. Across the eight sessions, liars estimated that an average of 48.8% of the participants would correctly peg them as the liar when, in fact, only 25.6% did so—an accuracy rate indistinguishable from chance. The difference between liars' intuitions and the actual accuracy rate was highly statistically significant, paired $t(7) = 5.41, p < .001$.

We attribute this finding to an illusion of transparency: Liars presumably felt as if their feelings of nervousness about lying leaked out, or that others could "see right through them." There are, however, several alternative interpretations of this result. One derives from the *self-as-target bias*, or people's exaggerated judgments of the extent to which others' thoughts and actions are directed at them (Fenigstein, 1984; Zuckerman et al., 1983). Applied to the present experiment, liars' overestimations of the number of observers who would correctly identify them might not have stemmed from any feeling of transparency, but from a simple conviction that they would tend to be the target of others' guesses and suspicions more than one would expect by chance.

But note that if this alternative interpretation is true, and participants felt like the generalized targets of others' suspicions, they would have felt this way even when they were telling the truth. The illusion of transparency hypothesis, in contrast, entails elevated estimates of detectability only when an individual is lying. Our data permitted a test of this issue. Recall that in addition to asking participants to estimate their detectability when they were lying, we also asked them to estimate the number of their fellow participants who would guess that they were lying when they were telling the truth. We averaged across each participant's four truth-telling rounds and compared this average with the estimate each participant made when he or she was lying. Consistent with our expectations, but in contrast to what would be expected if our results stemmed exclusively from a self-as-target bias, participants expected significantly fewer of their fellow participants to pick them as the liar when they were telling the truth ($M = 34\%$) than when they were lying ($M = 49\%$, reported above), paired $t(7) = 6.11, p < .0005$.

Study 1b

We conducted two follow-up experiments to explore additional alternative interpretations of the results of Study 1a. First, recall that in the previous study, each participant was the liar once and only once and, moreover, that the participants were aware of this aspect of the design. One might argue that this was partly responsible for observers' low accuracy rates. Specifically, if a participant guessed a particular player as the liar in Round 1, he or she may have been reluctant to guess that player again as the liar in any subsequent round. If the original guess had been in error, the participant would thereby decrease his or her chances of correctly identifying the liar in these latter rounds. Thus, the participants' awareness that each of them was the liar once and only once might have artifactually lowered their accuracy rates.

In truth, we do not think this represents much of a challenge to our results. Because participants were given no feedback about the accuracy of their guesses until the end of the experiment, nor were they forbidden to guess the same player as the liar more than once, their overall accuracy should not have been affected. Indeed, the logic presented above could also be used to argue that our design artifactually *increased* observers' accuracy rates, making Study 1a a conservative test of our hypothesis. Still, to be certain that this aspect of our design in no way affected the observers' ability to detect deception, we conducted a replication in which participants were informed that although there was only one liar per round, repetitions were allowed. Specifically, participants were informed that a computer had randomly selected which participant was to be the liar in each round, and so any individual could be the liar once, more than once, or not at all during the course of the experiment.

In actuality, however, each player was the liar once and only once across the five rounds of the experiment. All that changed were participants' perceptions of the frequency with which each could receive a lie card.[3] Forty Cornell

University students served as participants in eight groups of 5. As before, liars substantially overestimated the detectability of their lies: They estimated that an average of 50% would correctly select them as the liar; in fact, only 27% did so, paired $t(7) = 6.56$, $p < .0005$. Once again, people's lies were less detectable than they suspected.

Study 1c

Study 1c was designed to investigate two more plausible alternative interpretations of the results observed in Studies 1a and 1b. First, liars' exaggerated fear that they would be detected may have stemmed not from an illusion of transparency but from an abstract theory that lies are easy to detect. Empirical research has repeatedly shown that people's ability to detect lies is quite modest (DePaulo, Zuckerman, & Rosenthal, 1980; Ekman, 1985; Knapp & Comadena, 1979; Kraut, 1980; Zuckerman, DePaulo, & Rosenthal, 1981)—a result that most people find surprising. Before being exposed to this evidence, people tend to believe that lies are readily detectable.

Of course, any such belief that lies are readily detectable would be aided and abetted by the illusion of transparency that we have proposed. Still, our account emphasizes the feelings of detectability that arise, in vivo, in the particular situation, rather than intuitions based on an abstract theory about human cognitive and perceptual abilities. If the liars in our experiment simply thought that lies were readily detectable, their estimates of the number of observers who would correctly select them as the liar in a particular round might have followed rather dispassionately from this abstract theory rather than from any personal feelings of transparency.

A second plausible alternative interpretation comes from research suggesting that whenever individuals possess some knowledge, they can have difficulty assuming the perspective of another individual who is not in the know. Instead, they mistakenly attribute to the other person some degree of awareness of their privileged information. This tendency has been referred to as the *curse of knowledge*—one is "cursed" by one's own knowledge in the sense that it can be difficult to set that knowledge aside when imagining how things appear to someone else (Camerer et al., 1989; Keysar & Bly, 1995; Keysar et al., 1995).

How might the curse of knowledge account for our results? Liars were (of course) well aware that they were lying and may have had difficulty getting beyond that fact when anticipating the perspective of others. As a consequence, they may have felt that others would share their knowledge, resulting in an overestimation of their own detectability. As we discuss later, this interpretation resembles our own theorizing to some degree. Even so, the curse of knowledge explanation does not require that participants perceived anything akin to the feelings of leakage that we believe underlie the illusion of transparency. Indeed, the curse of knowledge hypothesis, unlike our own speculations, makes no distinction between an individual who tells a lie and another person who merely knows for certain that a particular individual has done so. Both should be equally cursed by that knowledge.

To investigate these two alternative interpretations—the abstract theory that lies are detectable and the curse of knowledge—we ran a version of our experiment in which each of the 5 participants was yoked to his or her own personal observer. Each yoked observer received a card from the experimenter identical to the card given to the actual participant. Thus, each observer knew the question posed to his or her partner in each round at the exact moment the partner did and was also aware of whether the card called for the truth or a lie. Finally, the observers completed questionnaires analogous to those completed by their partners after every round. Thus, the observer yoked to the liar in each round also estimated the number of players who would correctly identify the liar. These estimates could then be compared with the intuitions of the liars themselves.

The yoked observers allowed us to examine simultaneously both alternative interpretations discussed above. First, the yoked observers should hold the same abstract theory about lying and lie detection as the participants, but should be immune to any in vivo feelings of transparency, as they themselves do not make statements to the rest of the group. Thus, if the results of Studies 1a and 1b stemmed from an abstract theory about the detectability of lies, the observers should overestimate the detectability of their partners' lies to the same extent as the partners themselves. If, on the other hand, our results stem from an illusion of transparency, only the liars should overestimate the detectability of their lies.

A curse of knowledge interpretation likewise predicts that the yoked observers, who are "cursed" by the same information as the liars, will overestimate the detectability of the liars' lies every bit as much as the liars themselves. According to the illusion of transparency hypothesis, in contrast, the yoked observers should not experience the sensation of leakage and, hence, should not overestimate the detectability of their partner's lies. In summary, then, to the extent that the yoked observers do not overestimate the detectability of their partner's lies, both alternative interpretations can be ruled out. Finally, the yoked observers also control for any alternative interpretation involving response bias or the particularities of the response mode (e.g., that participants ignored our statements about the level of identification accuracy that could be expected by chance).

Method

Eighty Cornell University students participated in one of eight sessions of this experiment. 40 as players, replicating our earlier design, and an additional 40 as yoked observers. The experiment followed the same basic procedure as the earlier studies, but with observers completing questionnaires after each round as well. Also, one additional item was added to these questionnaires: Liars and their partners were both asked to rate the "obviousness" of the lie on a 7-point scale ranging from *not at all obvious* (1) to *very obvious* (7).

Finally, we also included an individual difference scale, in part to explore the mechanism hypothesized to give rise to the illusion of transparency. Recall our thesis that the illusion derives from the difficulty of putting aside one's own phenomenological experience when attempting to view oneself from the perspective of another. If individuals base their estimates of leakage on their own phenomenological experience, then those for whom these internal experiences are more available should be particularly prone to believe that their internal states are leaking out.

To test this possibility, we had each participant complete an inventory of dispositional self-consciousness (Fenigstein, Scheier, & Buss, 1975; see also Carver & Glass, 1976; Fenigstein, 1987). Participants responded to each of 23 items on 5-point scales with endpoints *extremely uncharacteristic of me* (0) and *extremely characteristic of me* (4). The Self-Consciousness Scale consists of three subscales: Private Self-Consciousness, Public Self-Consciousness, and Social Anxiety. It was the first of these that was of particular interest to us. Private self-consciousness refers to an individual's tendency to focus internally, reflecting on his or her inner thoughts and feelings (e.g., "I reflect about myself a lot"). We reasoned that individuals scoring high on this subscale, who were likely to have been keenly aware of their own internal states during the course of the experiment, would be especially likely to believe that those internal states had leaked out. In our terms, when attempting to capture others' perspectives on themselves, these individuals may have begun the inferential chain from a more pronounced anchor.

Results

As before, liars overestimated the detectability of their lies: On average, they predicted that 44.3% of their fellow players would detect their deception; in fact, only 32.4% did so, paired $t(7) = 2.91$, $p < .05$. Of greater interest to the present investigation, however, is that liars' estimates diverged from those made by the yoked observers: Observers estimated that only 25.3% of the players would detect the liars' deception, far fewer than the 44.3% estimate made by the liars themselves, paired $t(7) = 4.12$, $p < .005$. Additionally, liars rated their own lies as significantly more obvious than did their yoked observers, $Ms = 3.0$ and 2.0, respectively, paired $t(7) = 3.90, p < .01$.

These results indicate that the discrepancy between liars' estimates and observers' actual accuracy cannot be attributed to participants' abstract theory that lies are easy to detect. These results also cast doubt on the curse of knowledge alternative interpretation of our results. It seems, then, that rather than deriving dispassionately from a theory of human psychology or from an inability to put one's knowledge aside when considering another person's perspective, liars' heightened estimates of the detectability of their lies are the result of an illusion of transparency.

Finally, was dispositional self-consciousness related to participants' feelings of transparency? To address this question, we correlated each of the three self-consciousness subscales with liars' estimates of the number of their fellow participants who would catch them in their lie as well as their ratings of how obvious their lie had been. As expected, neither public self-consciousness nor social anxiety was significantly correlated with liars' estimates of their own leakage, $rs = -.03$ and $-.18$, respectively, or with their obviousness ratings, both $rs = .10$.

In contrast, private self-consciousness was significantly related to liars' feelings of transparency, $r = .41, p < .01$, as well as their ratings of how obvious their lie had been, $r = .40, p < .02$. Multiple regression analyses predicting liars' detectability estimates and obviousness ratings from all three self-consciousness subscales simultaneously also revealed significant effects only for private self-consciousness: $b = .85, t(34) = 2.66, p < .02$, for detectability; $b = 1.38, t(34) = 2.70, p = .01$, for obviousness. This relationship between estimates of leakage and individuals' habitual focus on their own thoughts and feelings suggests that liars based their estimates of how detectable their lies were on their own phenomenological experiences. Those who tended to be highly aware of their own internal states apparently began from a more pronounced anchor, resulting in greater feelings of transparency.

Discussion of Studies 1a, 1b, and 1c

Across three studies, we found consistent support for an illusion of transparency. Participants induced to lie overestimated the detectability of their lies in all three experiments. Like the protagonist in *The Tell-Tale Heart*, our participants' deception was not as obvious as they thought. The three studies also diffuse the concern that the observed discrepancy between liars' estimates and the actual detectability of their lies was caused by some factor other than the hypothesized illusion of transparency. In particular, we have provided empirical evidence indicating that our findings do not derive from the self-as-target bias (Study 1a), an abstract theory that lies are easy to detect (Study 1c), the curse of knowledge (Study 1c), or a feature of our design that could have artifactually lowered actual accuracy rates (Studies 1b and 1c).

Finally, although our lie-detection studies were not designed as explicit tests of the anchoring and adjustment mechanism that we believe underlies the illusion of transparency, they nevertheless provided evidence consistent with that interpretation. First, as already discussed, the illusion was most pronounced among participants in Study 1c who had the highest private self-consciousness scores. This is consistent with the proposed mechanism in that these individuals are the ones who are most focused on their internal states and thus felt them most keenly. They doubtless recognized that the observers were not privy to the fullness and intensity of their internal experience, but the adjustments they made in light of this realization nevertheless began from a higher anchor—that is, from a richer emotional experience. The net result is that these participants gave higher estimates of the number of observers who would be able to detect their deception.

Additional evidence in support of the proposed anchoring and adjustment mechanism comes from an ancillary finding in Study 1a. Recall that participants in that study were asked to estimate how many observers would think they were lying both when they were lying and when they were telling the truth. The complement of the latter estimates, of course, represents their estimates of how many people could discern that they were telling the truth, or how much leakage they felt when they were being honest. Would these estimates yield an illusion of transparency as well? We would expect not, because when telling the truth there is no strong internal experience on which to anchor one's judgments of leakage. Lying typically generates a host of emotions that can potentially leak out (Ekman, 1985) and from which—according to our anchoring and adjustment model—the process of judgment begins. Not so for telling the truth. When there is no strong internal sensation from which to adjust, there is no illusion of transparency.

We tested this prediction by averaging each participant's implicit estimates of the number of observers in Study 1a who would be able to discern that they were telling the truth when, in fact, they were being truthful. Each participant made four such estimates. These estimates were then compared with the actual number of observers who indicated that the participant was telling the truth. As expected, this analysis yielded no evidence of an illusion of transparency.

On average, truth tellers estimated that 63% of observers would say they were telling the truth, when, in fact, 73% did so. We emphasize that these data should be interpreted with caution: They were obtained by reverse scoring participants' estimates of the number of observers who would think they were lying, and this feature of the study was not designed as an explicit test of the anchoring and adjustment mechanism. Nevertheless, the data are consistent with that mechanism and nicely complement the private self-consciousness data as support for the anchoring and adjustment interpretation.

The three studies reported thus far indicate that the illusion of transparency is robust across a variety of procedural changes—at least in the domain of lie detection. But what about other domains? Does it apply to emotional states other than those a person experiences when telling lies? Our remaining studies were designed to find out.

Study 2a

Consider the following awkward situation: You are a dinner guest at the home of a friend who takes pride in his culinary talents. You wait with the other guests in eager anticipation as your host toils away in the kitchen, preparing what you expect will be some succulent entrée. But when dinner arrives, you discover to your dismay that the meal contains a generous amount of an ingredient you find absolutely unpalatable. The very thought of it prompts revulsion.

What to do? One option is to admit the aversion up front, perhaps apologizing for your unsophisticated palate. We suspect, however, that most people would reject this course of action in favor of downing a few well-timed bites of the offensive entrée and doing their best to conceal their feelings of disgust from the host. We further suspect that people elect this course of action despite strong doubts about whether they will be able to execute it effectively. That is, people may believe that despite their best efforts to conceal their true feelings, their distaste will leak out and be apparent to others.

Are such doubts justified? Judging from the first three experiments, perhaps not. The illusion of transparency implies that a person's feelings of disgust may not be as obvious as he or she believes. There is a substantial discrepancy between the phenomenological experience of the individual, whose feelings of disgust may be quite pronounced, and the cues available to outside observers—a discrepancy that the individual may fail to appreciate fully and adjust for adequately.

To investigate this possibility, we simulated the essential components of the dinner-guest scenario. Participants were asked to conceal their feelings of disgust over a foul-tasting drink and then to estimate how successfully they had done so. These estimates were then compared with the participants' actual success at concealment. Our prediction was that participants would overestimate the extent of their leakage, believing that their disgust was more apparent than it actually was.

Method

Participants.   Twenty-five Cornell University undergraduates volunteered to participate in an experiment entitled "Neutral Expressions." Fifteen were run individually as tasters, and the remaining 10 were recruited later and served as observers.

Procedure.   In a first phase of the experiment, participants arrived individually and were greeted by an experimenter. They were then invited to sit at a table on which were placed 15 small plastic cups, each containing a small amount of red liquid. On the side of the table opposite their seat was a video camera mounted on a tripod. The experimenter informed the participant that the study was concerned with facial expressions, specifically *neutral* facial expressions, or "expressions that show no thought or emotion." To explore people's ability to maintain such blank expressions, the study called for participants to sample a variety of "special drinks" while their reactions were videotaped. In particular, the participant was to taste each drink, concealing his or her reactions, good or bad.

Participants were assured that the drinks were harmless, but were informed that 5 of the 15 cups contained a drink concocted by the experimenter to have an unpleasant taste. The remaining 10 cups were said to contain a good-tasting drink. This information was accurate: Five cups contained a small amount (approximately 5 ml) of a mixture of water, red food coloring, and the vinegar brine solution in which pickled grape leaves are packed. Pretesting revealed that it was indeed regarded as an unpleasant taste by all. The remaining 10 cups contained cherry-flavored Kool Aid, prepared as directed. The two different kinds of drinks were visually indistinguishable. The location of the foul-tasting drinks was counterbalanced across participants with two restrictions: The foul-tasting drink never appeared in the first position and two cups containing the foul-tasting drink never appeared side by side.

Before proceeding with the study, the experimenter noted that the videotape made of the taster would later be shown to a group of 10 observers, who would be told that five of the drinks had an unpleasant taste but would not be told which ones. The observers' job, then, would be to watch the videotape and try to determine which drinks had the unpleasant taste, based only on the taster's facial expressions. Tasters were told, in turn, that their job was to make the observers' task as difficult as possible.

The tasters then proceeded to taste each drink, one at a time, while looking at the camera and being videotaped. After each drink, the video-camera was paused and the taster completed a brief questionnaire. The questionnaire elicited the tasters' predictions of the accuracy of the 10 observers. In particular, the tasters were asked to estimate the number of observers who would correctly identify whether the drink was one with a pleasant or unpleasant taste. On the unpleasant-tasting trials, it was made clear to the tasters that an average of 3.33 observers could be expected to guess correctly by chance alone. On pleasant-tasting trials, it was made clear that the corresponding chance accuracy rate was 6.67.

In the second phase of the experiment, the observers were assembled in small groups and watched the videotapes made in the first phase of the study. Because the tasters were asked to predict the number of observers out of 10 who would correctly identify the foul-tasting drink, the videotape of each taster was seen by a total of 10 observers. They were given a detailed description of the first phase of the study, including the fact that five drinks had an unpleasant taste. Their job was to guess whether each drink had a pleasant or unpleasant taste, based on the taster's expressions. If they felt uncertain about the taste of a given drink, they were encouraged to guess. They were given no feedback regarding the accuracy of their responses.

Results

We predicted that tasters would fall victim to the illusion of transparency and overestimate the number of observers who could tell if they were sipping a foul-tasting drink. Because the pleasant-tasting drink did not constitute as strong an internal experience as the unpleasant drink, we did not expect participants to exhibit a similar illusion of transparency for these trials. To examine these questions, we collapsed separately across pleasant and unpleasant trials for each taster and computed the average number of observers that tasters predicted would guess correctly for each type of drink. We then computed the average number of observers who actually did guess correctly.

Both hypotheses were supported. Tasters estimated that an average of 4.91 observers would correctly identify the foul-tasting drinks, which was significantly higher than the average of 3.56 observers who actually did make correct identifications on these trials, $t(14) = 3.63$, $p < .005$. Furthermore, the tasters' estimates were significantly greater than the chance accuracy rate of 3.33, $t(14) = 3.97$, $p < .005$, whereas the observers' actual accuracy was not, $t < 1$. In contrast, tasters estimated that an average of 6.20 observers would correctly identify the good-tasting drinks, a figure that did not differ significantly from the actual accuracy rate of 6.83. For the good-tasting drinks, neither the tasters' estimates nor the accuracy of the observers was significantly different from the chance accuracy rate of 6.67.

As with the lie detection studies, we attribute these results to the illusion of transparency. Participants felt that cues to their disgust over the foul-tasting drink had leaked out and were noticed by more observers than was actually the case. As with the first lie detection study, however, there are a couple of alternative interpretations of these data. First, the results might merely reflect inaccurate abstract theories about the detectability of disgust, not any illusions about excessive leakage. Alternatively, they could reflect the curse of knowledge: Participants knew when they were tasting pleasant or unpleasant drinks and it may have been difficult for them to get beyond that knowledge when estimating what the observers were likely to know.

To test each of these alternative interpretations, we replicated the taste test study using the same yoked-partner procedure as in Study 1c. As in that study, the yoked partners had the same abstract theories as the tasters and were "cursed" by the same knowledge of whether a given drink had a pleasant or unpleasant taste. If the results of study 2a were due to faulty abstract theories or the curse of knowledge, the estimates made by the yoked partners should not differ systematically from those of the tasters themselves. If the previous results were due to the illusion of transparency, in contrast, the estimates of the tasters and yoked partners should diverge.

Study 2b

Method

Participants. Fifty-two Cornell University undergraduates served as participants. Thirty-two arrived in pairs and were randomly assigned to be either a taster or a partner; the remaining 20 were recruited later and served as observers.

Procedure. The basic procedure was the same as that in Study 2a, with two changes. One change was the addition of the yoked partner. Participants in the first phase of the experiment arrived in pairs, and one was randomly chosen by a coin flip to be the taster. The taster was seated across the table from the video camera, with the partner seated on an adjacent side, facing the taster. The partner's job, it was explained, was to observe as the taster sampled each drink and determine how well (or how poorly) the taster was able to maintain a neutral expression. Critically, the partner did so while knowing whether each drink had a pleasant or unpleasant taste. The experimenter informed the partner whether each drink was a pleasant or unpleasant drink at the exact moment the taster tasted it. To prevent this information from being recorded on the videotape, and to minimize the possibility of distracting the partner from the task of scrutinizing the taster's facial expressions, the experimenter alerted the partner as to whether each drink was pleasant or unpleasant via a subtle tap on the shoulder (one tap for a pleasant drink; two taps for unpleasant). Partners indicated that this mode of communication was sufficient and nonintrusive.

The second change involved the number of drinks the taster sampled and the way in which the estimates of both the taster and partner were elicited. Only 10 drinks were sampled. They were arranged in front of the taster in two groups, labeled "Set 1" and "Set 2," and were numbered 1–5 within each set. One of the drinks in each set contained the foul-tasting mixture of water, food color, and brine, and the other 4 contained Kool Aid. The location of the foul-tasting drink in each set was counterbalanced across participants with two restrictions: The foul-tasting drinks were never first in a set, and they never appeared in the same position in both sets.

Tasters and partners were informed that the taster would sample all the drinks in a set, at which point the experimenter would pause the video camera and administer a brief questionnaire. The questionnaire asked tasters and partners to estimate the number of observers who would correctly identify the single foul-tasting drink in the set. The experimenter explained that an average of 20%, or 2 observers out of 10, could be expected to answer correctly for each set by chance alone. Tasters and partners also rated the extent to which they thought the taster's feelings about the unpleasant drink had leaked out. These judgments were made on a 10-point scale with endpoints labeled *I [he/she] kept a perfect neutral facial expression* (1) and *I [he/she] leaked out to a great extent* (10). The dependent measures in this study were altered from those used in Study 2a to examine whether the same results could be obtained with different methods of elicitation, and thus further the generalizability of the illusion of transparency.

As before, the observers were run in a second phase of the study. Because tasters and partners were asked to predict the number of observers out of 10 who would correctly identify the foul-tasting drink, the videotape of each taster was seen by 10 observers. Observers were given a detailed description of the first phase of the study, including the fact that one drink (and only one drink) out of each set of five had an unpleasant taste. Their job was to guess the location of the foul-tasting drink in each set.

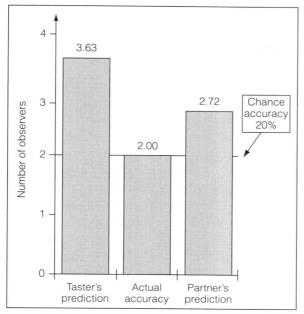

Figure 1 ▪ Mean number of observers predicted to guess the placement of the foul-tasting drink by tasters and partners, as well as observers' actual accuracy, Study 2b.

Results

We predicted that tasters would fall victim to the illusion of transparency and overestimate the number of observers who would identify the single foul-tasting drink in each set. To examine this question, we collapsed across the two sets of drinks for each taster and computed the average number of observers that tasters predicted would guess correctly and the average number who actually did guess correctly.[4] These results are presented in the two leftmost bars of Figure 1.

As can be seen from Figure 1, our prediction was supported: On average, tasters estimated that substantially more observers would correctly identify which drink had been unpleasant than actually did so, $t(15) = 5.01, p < .0005$. Figure 1 also shows that partners likewise tended to overestimate the observers' accuracy, $t(15) = 2.09, p = .05$, but not to the same extent. Indeed, the estimates made by the partners were significantly lower than those made by the tasters themselves, $t(15) = 2.11, p = .05$. This suggests that, above and beyond the curse of knowledge or the effects of any abstract theory, the tasters demonstrated an illusion of transparency. Consistent with this interpretation, tasters tended to believe that they leaked out marginally more than their partners thought they did (Ms = 3.41 and 2.53, respectively), $t(15)$ = 1.88, $p < .10$.

Discussion of Studies 2a and 2b

The findings of Studies 2a and 2b provide further support for the existence of an illusion of transparency. In both studies, participants believed that they failed to hide their reactions to an unpleasant taste. In reality, tasters were remarkably successful at concealing their distaste: Observers performed no better than chance and fell far short of tasters' estimates. We can conclude that the illusion of transparency effect is not just a manifestation of abstract theories of leakage or of the curse of knowledge because the yoked partners in Study 2b—who would have possessed all the same theories, and who were provided with factual knowledge equivalent to that possessed by the tasters themselves—did not overestimate observers' accuracy as much. As in the lie detection studies reported earlier, people can conceal their internal states better than they suspect.

Study 3a

As noted earlier, we took the term *illusion of transparency* from Miller and McFarland (1987, 1991), who proposed that such an illusion might help explain a puzzling inference on the part of participants in bystander intervention studies (Darley & Batson, 1973; Darley & Latané, 1968; Latané & Darley, 1970). Studies 3a and 3b were attempts to provide empirical support for their speculation.

When confronted with a potential emergency, people typically play it cool, adopt a look of nonchalance, and monitor the reactions of others to determine if a crisis is really at hand. No one wants to overreact, after all, if it might not be a true emergency. However, because each individual holds back, looks nonchalant, and monitors the reactions of others, sometimes everyone concludes (perhaps erroneously) that the situation is not an emergency and hence does not require intervention.

Note the inferential failure here: People witness the same behavior in others as they are engaging in themselves, but conclude that the cause of others' behavior is different than their own. Why do they fail to conclude that the nonchalance of others has the same origin and the same meaning as their own—that everyone is simply playing it cool and looking to others to define the situation for them? This is not a terribly difficult inference to make, and people's failure to make it has loomed as something of a puzzle ever since the classic bystander intervention studies were first published.

Following Miller and McFarland (1987, 1991), we propose that the illusion of transparency can help resolve this puzzle. Simply put, people may not see others' behavior as similar to their own; indeed, they may be unaware that they appear as calm and unconcerned as everyone else. If people think that their alarm over the potential emergency is leaking out more than it is, they may conclude that others—who exhibit comparatively few signs of alarm—are genuinely much less concerned about the situation than they are. They may then use this information to conclude that they were mistaken and that no real emergency exists. Thus, a person's failure to draw the right conclusion about the apparent calm of others may not reflect an inferential failure about the meaning of others' behavior so much as a failure to-recognize that how others look is precisely how one looks oneself.[5]

We examined this issue empirically in a modified version of the bystander intervention studies (Darley & Latané, 1968; Latané & Darley, 1970). Because this classic research is so widely known, we thought it would be difficult to conduct a study on a college campus involving a simulated physical or medical emergency without arousing suspicion.[6] We therefore decided to create a novel kind of laboratory emergency, one that might provoke less suspicion while still retaining the essential features of an emergency situation.

In our study, participants found themselves confronted by an individual (a confederate) who appeared to be breaking the established rules of the experiment. Indeed, it appeared to participants that the problematic individual threatened to ruin the entire experiment—and this after the experimenter had solemnly and emphatically stressed the importance of the research and the necessity that all participants follow the rules of the study precisely. Participants were thus confronted with a situation analogous to that encountered in real-life emergencies: Should they intervene (and save the threatened experiment) or not? By embedding some crucial questions amidst a variety of filler items on a questionnaire completed by participants, we were able to investigate our illusion of transparency hypothesis. In particular, we predicted that participants would rate themselves as appearing more concerned over the transgressions than they actually appeared. That is, each would tend to believe that he or she appeared more alarmed at the behavior of the confederate than others rated him or her as appearing.

Method

Participants.   Forty Cornell University students were recruited for an experiment on group problem solving and participated in 1 of 10 groups (4 participants plus 1 female confederate).

Procedure.   After being screened to ensure they were unacquainted with one another, participants were escorted into a laboratory room in which five chairs were arranged in an arc facing a chalkboard. All participants donned name tags with participant numbers (1–5).

The experimenter explained that the study was designed to investigate how various aspects of a group's working environment affect the group's problem-solving productivity. Their task in the experiment would be to unscramble as many anagrams as they could in 10 min, with the total number solved being the measure of the group's productivity. The experimenter explained that 1 participant would be randomly selected to be the "writer," and he or she would write each anagram on the chalkboard, one by one, for the group members to solve aloud. The writer would have a list of all of the anagrams and their solutions and would keep track of the number solved by the group. The experimenter then handed around a cup containing slips of paper, on one of which was ostensibly printed the word "writer." In reality, all slips said "solver." Nevertheless, when the confederate drew a slip of paper, she announced that she had drawn the writer slip.

The experimenter stressed that it was crucial that all participants follow the rules of the experiment and work at their most efficient level. Furthermore, it was important that their performance on the anagram task accurately reflect their true ability level and amount of effort expended: "If for any reason your performance level is not an accurate indication of the effort and ability you bring to the task, then the experiment will be a failure and the data will be useless to us." Then, making eye contact with each participant, the experimenter remarked, "on a personal note," that the experiment was the final component of his dissertation research, that it was almost finished, and that the data so far looked highly promising. "We just need a few more pieces to fall into place, so it's even more important than usual that everyone takes the task seriously and follows all the rules."

One such rule, the experimenter emphasized, was that the writer should refrain from giving participants any hints or assistance in solving the anagrams. For their part, solvers were restricted to offering solutions to anagrams, or uttering the word "pass" if they wished the writer to move on to the next anagram. All other "table talk," including discussions of strategy or remarks of any kind to each other or to the writer was forbidden.

After a final review of the rules, the experimenter handed the confederate the list of 30 anagrams, set the dial on a kitchen timer for 10 min, and left the room. During this time, the confederate wrote the anagrams on the chalkboard for group members to solve, as instructed. Gradually, however, despite the experimenter's admonitions, she began to offer unsolicited assistance to the solvers. She began by providing them with small hints, such as informing them which letter a particular anagram started with, or suggesting a category to which the solution belonged (e.g., "Think of things you'd find at a circus"). Soon, however, her disregard for the rules became more blatant: She provided participants with words that rhymed with an anagram's solution, she gave participants credit for anagrams that, in her eyes, they had "almost" solved, and even turned the timer back to give them a few extra minutes. We carefully pretested this portion of the experiment so that we could create maximum alarm on the part of the participants without arousing their suspicions. Within each session, moreover, the confederate was instructed to continually adjust her behavior in an attempt to keep participants alarmed at her behavior and on the verge of intervention, but never actually to elicit intervention. Nevertheless, in a few cases participants did intervene or suspect the confederate's agenda. We return to this issue later.

When the timer finally rang, the experimenter reentered the room, expressed mild surprise at the number of anagrams the group had solved, and escorted all participants (including the confederate) to individual cubicles to complete the dependent measures. When all participants had finished, they were probed for suspicion, debriefed, and dismissed.

Dependent measures. We constructed the questionnaire to fit our cover story regarding the effects of a group's working environment on productivity. Thus, for example, participants were asked to rate the extent to which they believed the laboratory setting had inhibited their group's performance, compared with how they would have performed in a more naturalistic, real-world setting. Further, we asked participants to rate the extent to which they were concerned about the laboratory setting inhibiting their performance, and also how concerned they thought they appeared to the other group members. Finally, they were also asked to rate how concerned about the laboratory setting each of the other participants had appeared.

We included these questions, and several others of the same type, to set the stage for the items of interest. Specifically, respondents were asked to indicate whether anyone had violated the rules of the experiment. If so, they were asked to circle the player number of the participant who had done so to the greatest extent. Following this, they were asked to rate how concerned they were about this individual's behavior, as well as how concerned they believed they appeared to others. These ratings were made on 7-point scales with endpoints labeled *not at all concerned* (1) and *very concerned* (7). Finally, they rated how concerned each of the other group members appeared on the same 7-point scale.

Our hypothesis involves a comparison between the participants' intuitions about how concerned they appeared about the potential emergency and how concerned they actually appeared to the other group members. By having each participant rate the appearance of every other participant, we were able to compute an average of how concerned each participant seemed to everyone else (not including the confederate). This average could then be compared with each player's self-rated appearance.

Results

Because the responses within each group were highly interdependent, all analyses reported here were conducted at the level of the experimental session rather than the individual participant.

For each group, we first checked that all participants had in fact listed the confederate as the most rule-breaking group member; all had. We then computed participants' average ratings of how concerned they were and how concerned they believed they had appeared. Next, we derived a measure of how concerned each participant had actually appeared in the eyes of his or her group members by averaging, separately for each participant, the ratings that each of the other participants made about him or her. Finally, we averaged these "actual" appearance scores across all participants within each group. The three measures are depicted in Figure 2.

Two significant findings emerged. First, participants rated themselves, on average, as moderately concerned but as appearing somewhat less concerned than they actually were, $t(9) = 4.09, p < .005$. This finding could be interpreted in several ways, of course, but note that it is consistent with the anchoring and adjustment interpretation we have proposed. Participants doubtless recognized that the full nature of their emotional experience was not available to observers, and so they adjusted their ratings of how they appeared to everyone else downward from the anchor of their own experience. Their "appearance" ratings were therefore less extreme than their ratings of how they actually felt.

But were their adjustments insufficient, as such adjustments typically are? Did participants overestimate how concerned they looked to others? A comparison of how concerned participants thought they looked with how concerned others thought they looked indicates that they did indeed. As predicted, participants believed they appeared more concerned over the rule-breaking confederate than others rated them as appearing, $t(9) = 2.84, p < .02$.

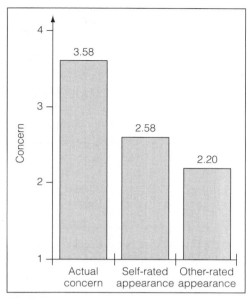

Figure 2 ■ Mean self-ratings of actual concern, mean self-ratings of the appearance of concern, and mean ratings of how concerned each participant appeared to the other members of the group, Study 3a.

Three participants, across three different experimental sessions, expressed some suspicion of either the procedures or the confederate. In addition, 2 participants engaged in some minimal form of intervention, as recorded by the confederate (e.g., "Are you supposed to be giving us hints?"). It is noteworthy that so few participants attempted to intervene and how mild the attempts at intervention were: No participant ever forcefully confronted the confederate, nor did anyone ever retrieve the experimenter to report the confederate's rule-breaking behavior.

Nevertheless, because a few participants did engage in some minimal forms of intervention or express some suspicion, we recomputed all analyses, eliminating all suspicious and interventionist individuals from the data set. Because our analyses were conducted at the group level, this could be accomplished simply by removing these individuals' data from the group averages while retaining data from all other participants in that session. These analyses again revealed support for our hypotheses: Participants believed they expressed less concern than they felt, $t(9) = 5.00$, $p < .0005$, but still believed that they appeared more concerned than they were rated by others, $t(9) = 3.09$, $p < .02$.

Discussion

This experiment provides clear support for our hypothesis. Participants felt they appeared more concerned about the confederate's problematic behavior than they actually appeared, as rated by the other members of their group. Thus, the illusion of transparency may indeed help explain why people sometimes do not intervene in emergencies: Because people think their own alarm is more apparent than it really is, they assume that others are comparatively less alarmed, leading them to conclude, in turn, that the situation is not really an emergency and that no intervention is required.

Study 3b

To ensure that the results of Study 3a were reliable, we conducted a replication that followed the same procedure, but with one exception: In an effort to boost participants' feelings of concern over the confederate's rule-breaking behavior, we adopted a procedure intended to increase participants' feelings of personal involvement in the experiment and accountability for its outcome. Specifically, in place of the "free-for-all" group effort with which participants solved the anagrams in Study 3a, we adopted a "round-robin" procedure whereby each participant functioned as the exclusive solver, one by one, for 2.5 min. During each participant's allotted 2.5 min, they alone were allowed to solve the anagrams, and the confederate escalated her rule-breaking assistance gradually. Once again, we predicted a discrepancy between participants' intuitions about how concerned they appeared and their actual appearance of concern.

Method

A total of 80 Cornell University students participated in 1 of 20 groups, each of which consisted of 4 participants and 1 confederate. Beyond the change noted above, all portions of this experiment, including the cover story and dependent measures, remained as before.

Results

Figure 3 depicts participants' average self-ratings of actual concern, their average self-ratings of how concerned they thought they appeared, and the average rating of how concerned each participant appeared to the other

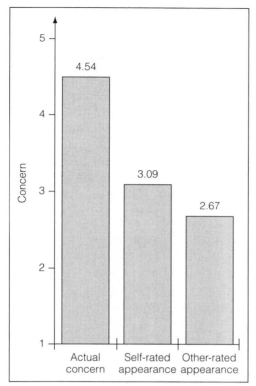

Figure 3 ▪ Mean self-ratings of actual concern,
mean self-ratings of the appearance of concern, and
mean ratings of how concerned each participant
appeared to the other members of the group, Study 3b.

members of the group. Once again, the results conform to our predictions. First, participants rated themselves as appearing less concerned than they actually were, $t(19) = 7.08$, $p < .0001$. (Note that the new procedure appears to have been successful in increasing participant's self-reported concern by approximately one scale point over the levels observed in Study 3a.) This finding, once again, fits nicely with the anchoring and adjustment interpretation of the illusion of transparency. Participants recognized that the full extent of their alarm would not be picked up by the others in the group, and so they adjusted their estimates of how concerned they appeared to others downward from how concerned they actually felt. These adjustments were insufficient, however, resulting in a significant illusion of transparency: Participants rated themselves as appearing significantly more concerned than they were rated, on average, by their fellow participants, $t(19) = 3.09$, $p < .01$.

As before, a few individuals (3 participants in three different groups) expressed some suspicion about either the procedures or the confederate, and some (11 participants in eight different groups) did intervene. Though somewhat more frequent and direct than in Study 3a (e.g., "That's cheating, don't do that!"), the interventions were, on the whole, rather mild. Also as before, an analysis that excluded suspicious and interventionist participants revealed a statistically significant illusion of transparency: Individuals believed they appeared more concerned than they were rated by others, $t(19) = 3.01, p < .01$.

Discussion

The results of Study 3b echo those observed in Study 3a: Participants confronted with a potential emergency situation were prone to an illusion of transparency, believing that their feelings of concern over a rule-breaking confederate were more observable than they actually were. In light of these results, once again, we believe that the illusion of transparency may provide one answer to the question of why people are reluctant to intervene in emergencies. Individuals may mistake the true source of others' calm exteriors not only because they fail to appreciate that others have attempted to conceal their feelings of alarm (Miller & McFarland, 1987, 1991) but also because they may underestimate their own ability to do so. Bystanders may tend to believe that their own alarm is more apparent than it really is, leading them to conclude that others are indeed comparatively less alarmed than they are. Tragically, this may lead them to infer that the situation is not an emergency and that no intervention is required.

General Discussion

We obtained consistent support for the illusion of transparency across all studies reported in this paper. In Studies 1a, 1b, and 1c, participants who were asked to tell lies overestimated the proportion of observers who would detect their deception. Their lies were far less apparent than they suspected. We ruled out several alternative interpretations of this finding, including the self-as-target bias (Fenigstein, 1984; Zuckerman et al., 1983), the curse of knowledge (e.g., Keysar & Bly, 1995), and an abstract (if mistaken) theory that lies are readily detected. In Studies 2a and 2b, participants who sampled a foul-tasting drink while attempting to maintain a blank facial expression nevertheless felt as though their feelings of disgust left telltale traces. Participants overestimated the number of observers who could identify which drinks were foul-tasting. Finally, in Studies 3a and 3b, participants who witnessed a confederate violate the rules of an experiment thought they exhibited more concern over the confederate's misbehavior than their fellow participants believed they did. That is, participants overestimated the extent to which their feelings of concern and alarm over the confederate's actions were apparent to others.

Elsewhere, we have demonstrated the illusion of transparency with respect to additional emotional states. In one set of studies (Savitsky, 1997), individuals who had to deliver public presentations overestimated how nervous they appeared. In another set (Van Boven, Medvec, & Gilovich, 1998), parties to a negotiation thought that their likes and dislikes—what they valued highly and what they could do without—were more apparent to the person with whom they wanted to strike a deal than was actually the case (see Vorauer & Claude, 1998).

It thus appears that the illusion of transparency is a robust phenomenon that applies to a host of different internal states. We attribute this illusion to an anchoring and adjustment bias. When individuals attempt to determine how apparent their internal states are to others, they begin the process of judgment from their own subjective experience. The adjustments they make from this anchor—adjustments that stem from the recognition that others are not as privy to their internal states as they are themselves—tend to be insufficient (e.g., Tversky & Kahneman, 1974). The net result, as we have shown, is a residual effect of one's own phenomenology and a feeling that one's internal states are more apparent to others than is actually the case.

Although we did not conduct an explicit test of this proposed mechanism, a variety of data that support the anchoring and adjustment interpretation was obtained from all three sets of experiments reported here. First, we found in Study 1c that participants who scored high on a measure of private self-consciousness were particularly prone to feelings of transparency. These individuals, because of their relatively inward self-focus, are likely to have a particularly keen sense of their own internal experience. Their processes of judgment should therefore begin from a higher anchor value and thus result in higher estimates, which they did. Second, we found in Studies 1a and 2a that the illusion exists only when a person is experiencing a palpable emotional state. In particular, participants exhibited an illusion of transparency when they were lying but not when telling the truth, and when they had sipped a foul-tasting drink but not a pleasant one. These findings likewise support the anchoring and adjustment interpretation because they show that when there is no pronounced internal experience to adjust from, there is no illusion of transparency. Finally, we found in Studies 3a and 3b that although participants thought they looked more alarmed over a troublesome situation than others thought they appeared, they nonetheless thought they looked less alarmed than they actually felt. This latter difference is consistent with the central premise that participants were adjusting downward from the anchor of their own experience.

Although together these findings offer substantial support for the anchoring and adjustment interpretation we have proposed, each is subject to alternative interpretation. More definitive support must thus await the outcome of experiments explicitly designed to test the role of the anchoring and adjustment processes we have proposed. There are at least two different ways to conduct such a test. One would involve manipulating the strength of the initial anchor. What would happen, for example, if one instituted a delay between, say, sipping a foul-tasting solution and estimating the number of observers who could tell it was unpleasant? By diminishing the internal representation of the foul taste, we would expect the participants' delayed estimates to begin from a lower anchor value and thus exhibit less of an illusion of transparency. The second way to test this underlying mechanism is to manipulate not the anchor but the adjustment (Gilbert, 1989; Gilbert, Pelham, & Krull, 1988). What would happen, for example, if participants were made cognitively busy while sipping the foul-tasting drink? The taste system being the way it is, we would expect the experience of the foul-tasting drink to be an automatic process but the adjustment from that experience to be more controlled. Busyness should then dampen the adjustment but not the anchor, and thus increase the magnitude of the illusion of transparency.

Of course, further studies such as these must be conducted to delineate the exact nature of the underlying causes of the illusion of transparency. Nevertheless, it is already clear from existing research that the potential consequences of this phenomenon are considerable. For example, Studies 3a and 3b lend support to the notion that the illusion of transparency may be one reason why people often fail to intervene in emergencies (Darley & Batson, 1973; Darley & Latané, 1968; Latané & Darley, 1970; see also Miller & McFarland, 1987, 1991). Each bystander may privately believe that he or she appears more concerned over the potential emergency than the others. This leads to the (sometimes tragic) conclusion that the situation is not actually an emergency and that no intervention is required.

There may be other negative consequences of the illusion of transparency as well. In particular, the illusion may play a significant role in interpersonal misunderstanding and conflict (cf. L. Ross & Ward, 1995). Among married couples, for example, the ability to read one another's nonverbal communications has been shown to be related to marital satisfaction (Gottman & Porterfield, 1981; Kahn, 1970; Noller, 1980). We suggest, further, that people's *beliefs* about how well they communicate their inner thoughts and emotions may also be important. An exaggerated view of how well one has conveyed one's inner state, or an unrealistic expectation that one's partner be able to "read one's mind," may be a source of significant interpersonal discord ("You should have known that I . . .''). Couples especially prone to an illusion of transparency may be especially prone to conflict.

Inherent in this speculation is the suggestion that the illusion of transparency applies not just when individuals attempt to conceal their inner states—as in all of the experiments reported here—but also when people attempt to communicate them. Here too, we suggest that people may succumb to an illusion of transparency, believing that they have conveyed their emotional states with greater fidelity than is actually the case. We have obtained preliminary evidence that people do indeed overestimate how clearly they can communicate their emotional states to observers via their facial expressions (Savitsky, 1997). Although one may feel emotions such as love, envy, or disappointment with great intensity, such intensity is typically not mirrored fully in one's facial expressions—a discrepancy that is easy to lose sight of when imagining how one appears to others.

Are all internal states necessarily subject to the illusion of transparency? Probably not. In many cases, people may be well calibrated regarding how much their thoughts, feelings, and emotions are apparent to others. When might individuals succumb to the illusion and when not? We believe at least two variables are important. First, as we have suggested, an individual must experience the internal state with some intensity. Many states are inherently less intense, and we suspect that such states are less conducive to an illusion of transparency. Our data from Studies 1a and 2a provide some support for this notion. Because neither the experience of telling the truth nor sampling a pleasant-tasting drink evokes a compelling phenomenological experience, these conditions yielded no illusion of transparency.

A second precondition for the illusion of transparency may be that the individual believe there is some route by which the internal state can leak out and be detected by others. The internal states we have examined—detection apprehension, disgust, and alarm, as well as speech anxiety (Savitsky, 1997)—are all states for which people have theories about the cues one can use to detect their presence (e.g., the belief, true or not, that one can tell if an individual is lying by looking him or her "straight in the eye"). For those internal states for which people do not have such theories about leakage, one would anticipate less of an illusion of transparency. People may be less likely, for example, to believe that their test-taking anxiety can be detected than to believe their anxiety over delivering a speech can be detected.

Because the illusion of transparency stems in part from people's acute awareness of their internal states, the research on self-awareness and what it suggests about the ability to take another person's perspective might also be expected to have something to say about the question of when the illusion is likely to be more or less prevalent. Unfortunately, the existing literature is mixed on this issue. According to some theorists, self-consciousness enhances an individual's ability to take another person's perspective because it focuses an individual's attention on his or her status as a social object (Duval & Wicklund, 1972; Hass, 1984; Hass & Eisenstadt, 1990; Stephenson & Wicklund, 1983; Wicklund, 1975). As Stephenson and Wicklund (1983) put it, "The impact of self-awareness . . . is one of orienting the person toward the other's point of view, with a consequent heightened sense of the differences between one's own orientation . . . and that of the other" (p. 69). Vorauer and Ross (1998), however, present evidence that self-focus does not facilitate perspective taking, and even inhibits it, when the self is the object of judgment. In this case, "the information that people need to ignore to see things from their audience's perspective is precisely the same information that is particularly salient to them" (p. 7). It seems that a clearer understanding of the impact of self-focused attention on the illusion of transparency must await the results of future research.

As mentioned earlier, the illusion of transparency bears some resemblance to a variety of established phenomena. One phenomenon that we were particularly concerned with disentangling from the illusion is the curse of knowledge. As we noted, one can be "cursed" by one's own knowledge in the sense that it can be difficult to set aside that knowledge when imagining how things appear to others (Camerer et al., 1989; Keysar, 1994; Keysar & Bly, 1995; Keysar et al., 1995). We argued that this phenomenon cannot fully account for our findings because yoked partners who were provided with all of the same knowledge as the liars in Study 1c and the tasters in Study 2b did not overestimate the leakage of those individuals' internal states as much as the individuals did themselves.[7] Note that at a deeper level, however, the two phenomena may be inextricably linked. In particular, the liars and tasters in our studies probably were cursed by their own knowledge, but it was their experiential knowledge of their own internal states, and not their abstract knowledge of which statements were lies or which drinks tasted bad, that prompted the illusion of transparency. Thus, the illusion of transparency may be something of an extreme case of the curse of knowledge, a case in which the attempt to take another person's perspective is hampered not by awareness of some pallid information but by the internal experience of one's own emotional states. In this way, our findings extend the curse of knowledge to encompass internal feelings and sensations as well as abstract, propositional knowledge.

The illusion of transparency also resembles, albeit more remotely, the self-as-target bias, or people's tendency to believe that they are the object of others' thoughts and actions more than is actually the case (Fenigstein, 1984; Zuckerman et al., 1983). Students "just know," for example, that the teacher is about to call on them—particularly if they are unprepared. The self-as-target bias appears to reflect the same difficulty in getting beyond one's own phenomenological experience that lies at the core of the illusion of transparency. In many situations, one's conscious attention is largely devoted to imagining what would happen or what one would do if another's actions were directed at the self. Because people are reluctant to view their thoughts as random or unwarranted, they use a bit of heuristic reasoning and conclude that "if I am so preoccupied with this concern, there must be a reason for it" (Savitsky, Medvec, Charlton, & Gilovich, 1998; Schwarz, 1990; Schwarz & Clore, 1983). Threats that one prepares for are threats that seem real.

The two phenomena are particularly similar when a person's thoughts are devoted to his or her shortcomings that the other person might exploit. Consider the student who is unprepared for class, or the Little Leaguer who is positioned in right field to minimize a fielding liability. Both are intensely focused on their own shortcomings, and both may believe that their fear is leaking out and can be picked up, either by a sadistic teacher or an opportunistic batter. In cases such as these, the self-as-target bias and illusion of transparency blend together considerably.

In summary, we have presented evidence that people are subject to an illusion of transparency. One (unsettling) conclusion that follows from this is that people are more skilled at dissembling than they suppose. We are better liars than we realize. So whether we are trying to get away with murder, like Poe's protagonist, or attempting to pull off the lesser feat of choking down a meal without our host detecting our feelings of disgust, we may be wise to remember that our hearts are not as telltale as we think.

Notes

1. In the single group of 4, participants donned name tags numbered 1–4, played four rounds of the lie detection game, and were told that 1 participant out of 3 could be expected to guess the identity of the liar by chance alone. All other procedural details were consistent with the other sessions.
2. To eliminate any ancillary cues to the identity of the liar, all participants received identical questionnaires but were instructed to answer different questions, depending on whether they had been a liar or a truth-teller in that particular round.

3. We did not include the self-as-target control question on the questionnaires used in Studies 1b or 1c.

4. Examining each of the two sets separately produced results virtually identical to those reported above.

5. It should be noted that Miller and McFarland (1987, 1991) offer a different resolution to this puzzle—that people, on average, tend to believe that they are more embarrassable than others. A person's own inaction, then, is explained by something (fear of embarrassment) not believed to be as significant a determinant of others' behavior. This explanation for bystander nonintervention bears some similarity to the illusion of transparency explanation in that both suggest that conclusions about the self can diverge from conclusions about others in part because certain information is more available to an individual about him- or herself than about others.

    Still, the explanations are distinct, and Miller and McFarland (1991) have noted that some of their experimental results that are consistent with their own approach are not open to reinterpretation in terms of an illusion of transparency. We agree, and we propose the illusion of transparency as one mechanism among several that jointly account for people's behavior in such complicated and multifaceted social situations.

6. Indeed, as we were planning our experiment, several students, citing lessons learned about bystander nonintervention in their introductory psychology course, thwarted an actual suicide attempt, saving a student who had intended to leap into one of the gorges that border Cornell's campus (Carmona, 1993). The publicity surrounding this event made us even more dubious about pulling off a suspicion-free medical emergency.

7. Note that we observed no curse-of-knowledge effect in our lie-detection paradigm—that is, observers who were cursed with the same abstract knowledge as the liars did not overestimate the likelihood of the lies being detected. We did, however, observe a significant curse of knowledge in our tasting study: Observers overestimated the audience's ability to detect the foul-tasting drink, though not to the same extent as the tasters themselves did. This may be because the yoked partners in the tasting study knew everything the tasters did (i.e., they knew when a drink was foul-tasting and, because they sampled the drink themselves, they knew how foul-tasting it was). In the lie-detection paradigm, on the other hand, the yoked partners knew that a lie was being told, but not how much of a lie—whether it was a mild distortion or a real whopper.

References

Barr, C. L., & Kleck, R. E. (1995). Self–other perception of the intensity of facial expressions of emotion: Do we know what we show? *Journal of Personality and Social Psychology, 68,* 608–618.

Camerer, C., Lowenstein, G., & Weber, M. (1989). The curse of knowledge in economic settings: An experimental analysis. *Journal of Political Economy, 97*, 1232–1253.

Carmona, J. (1993, September 7). Bystanders stop suicide attempt. *The Cornell Daily Sun*, pp. 1, 8.

Carver, C. S., & Glass, D. C. (1976). The self-consciousness scale: A discriminant validity study. *Journal of Personality Assessment, 40*, 169–172.

Darley, J. M., & Batson, C. D. (1973). "From Jerusalem to Jericho": A study of situational and dispositional variables in helping behavior. *Journal of Personality and Social Psychology, 27*, 100–108.

Darley, J. M., & Latané, B. (1968). Bystander intervention in emergencies: Diffusion of responsibility. *Journal of Personality and Social Psychology, 8*, 377–383.

DePaulo, B. M., Zuckerman, M., & Rosenthal, R. (1980). Humans as lie detectors. *Journal of Communication, 30*, 129–139.

Duval, S., & Wicklund, R. A. (1972). *A theory of objective self-awareness*. New York: Academic Press.

Ekman, P. (1985). *Telling lies: Clues to deceit in the marketplace, marriage, and politics*. New York: Norton.

Fenigstein, A. (1984). Self-consciousness and the overperception of self as a target. *Journal of Personality and Social Psychology, 47*, 860–870.

Fenigstein, A. (1987). On the nature of public and private self-consciousness. *Journal of Personality, 55*, 543–553.

Fenigstein, A., & Abrams, D. (1993). Self-attention and the egocentric assumption of shared perspectives. *Journal of Experimental Social Psychology, 29*, 287–303.

Fenigstein, A., Scheier, M. F., & Buss, A. H. (1975). Public and private self-consciousness: Assessment and theory. *Journal of Consulting and Clinical Psychology, 43*, 522–527.

Fischoff, B. (1975). Hindsight ≠ foresight: The effect of outcome knowledge on judgment under uncertainty. *Journal of Experimental Psychology: Human Perception and Performance, 1*, 288–299.

Fischoff, B. (1982). For those condemned to study the past: Heuristics and biases in hindsight. In D. Kahneman, P. Slovic, & A. Tversky (Eds.), *Judgment under uncertainty: Heuristics and biases* (pp. 335–354). New York: Cambridge University Press.

Fischoff, B., & Beyth, R. (1975). "I knew it would happen"—Remembered probabilities for once-future things. *Organizational Behavior and Human Performance, 13*, 1–16.

Gilbert, D. T. (1989). Thinking lightly about others: Automatic components of the social inference process. In J. S. Uleman & J. A. Bargh (Eds.), *Unintended thought* (pp. 189–211). New York: Guilford Press.

Gilbert, D. T., Pelham, B. W., & Krull, D. S. (1988). On cognitive busyness: When person perceivers meet persons perceived. *Journal of Personality and Social Psychology, 54*, 723–740.

Gilovich, T., Kruger, J., Medvec, V. H., & Savitsky, K. (1998). *Those bad hair days: Biased estimates of how variable we look to others*. Unpublished manuscript, Cornell University.

Gilovich, T., Medvec, V. H., & Savitsky, K. (1998). *The spotlight effect in social judgment: An egocentric bias in estimates of the salience of one's own action.* Unpublished manuscript, Cornell University.

Gottman, J. M., & Porterfield, A. L. (1981). Communicative competence in the nonverbal behavior of married couples. *Journal of Marriage and the Family, 43,* 817–824.

Griffin, D. W., & Ross, L. (1991). Subjective construal, social inference, and human misunderstanding. In M. P. Zanna (Ed.), *Advances in experimental social psychology* (Vol. 24, pp. 319–359). San Diego, CA: Academic Press.

Hass, R. G. (1984). Perspective taking and self-awareness: Drawing an E on your forehead. *Journal of Personality and Social Psychology, 46,* 788–798.

Hass, R. G., & Eisenstadt, D. (1990). The effects of self-focused attention on perspective-taking and anxiety. *Anxiety Research, 2,* 165–176.

Jacowitz, K. E., & Kahneman, D. (1995). Measures of anchoring in estimation tasks. *Personality and Social Psychology Bulletin, 21,* 1161–1166.

Kahn, M. (1970). Nonverbal communication and marital satisfaction. *Family Process, 9,* 449–456.

Keysar, B. (1994). The illusory transparency of intention: Linguistic perspective taking in text. *Cognitive Psychology, 26,* 165–208.

Keysar, B., & Bly, B. (1995). Intuitions of the transparency of idioms: Can one keep a secret by spilling the beans? *Journal of Memory and Language, 34,* 89–109.

Keysar, B., Ginzel, L. E., & Bazerman, M. H. (1995). States of affairs and states of mind: The effect of knowledge on beliefs. *Organizational Behavior and Human Decision Processes, 64,* 283–293.

Knapp, M. L., & Comadena, M. E. (1979). Telling it like it isn't: A review of theory and research on deceptive communications. *Human Communication Research, 5,* 270–285.

Kraut, R. E. (1980). Humans as lie detectors: Some second thoughts. *Journal of Communications, 30,* 209–216.

Latané, B., & Darley, J. (1970). *The unresponsive bystander: Why doesn't he help?* New York: Appleton-Century-Crofts.

Miller, D. T., & McFarland, C. (1987). Pluralistic ignorance: When similarity is interpreted as dissimilarity. *Journal of Personality and Social Psychology, 53,* 298–305.

Miller, D. T., & McFarland, C. (1991). When social comparison goes awry: The case of pluralistic ignorance. In J. Suls & T. Wills (Eds.), *Social comparison: Contemporary theory and research* (pp. 287–313). Hillsdale, NJ: Erlbaum.

Noller, P. (1980). Misunderstandings in marital communication: A study of couples' nonverbal communication. *Journal of Personality and Social Psychology, 39,* 1135–1148.

Piaget, J. (1959a). *Judgment and reasoning in the child.* Paterson, NJ: Littlefield, Adams, & Co. (Original work published 1928)

Piaget, J. (1959b). *The language and thought of the child.* New York: Humanities Press. (Original work published 1926)

Poe, E. A. (1976). The tell-tale heart. In S. Levine & S. Levine (Eds.), *The short fiction of Edgar Allan Poe* (pp. 259–262). Indianapolis, IN: Bobbs-Merrill.

Quattrone, G. A. (1982). Overattribution and unit formation: When behavior engulfs the person. *Journal of Personality and Social Psychology, 42,* 593–607.

Quattrone, G. A., Lawrence, C. P., Finkel, S. E., & Andrus, D. C. (1984). *Explorations in anchoring: The effects of prior range, anchor extremity, and suggestive hints.* Unpublished manuscript, Stanford University.

Ross, L., & Ward, A. (1995). Psychological barriers to dispute resolution. In M. P. Zanna (Ed.), *Advances in experimental social psychology* (Vol. 27, pp. 255–304). San Diego, CA: Academic Press.

Ross, L., & Ward, A. (1996). Naive realism in everyday life: Implications for social conflict and misunderstanding. In T. Brown, E. Reed, & E. Turiel (Eds.), *Values and knowledge* (pp. 103–135). Hillsdale, NJ: Erlbaum.

Ross, M., & Sicoly, F. (1979). Egocentric biases in availability and attribution. *Journal of Personality and Social Psychology, 37,* 322–336.

Savitsky, K. (1997). *Perceived transparency and the leakage of emotional states: Do we know how little we show?* Unpublished doctoral dissertation, Cornell University.

Savitsky, K., & Gilovich, T. (1998). *Is our absence as conspicuous as we think?* Unpublished manuscript, Cornell University.

Savitsky, K., Medvec, V. H., Charlton, A. E., & Gilovich, T. (1998). "What, me worry?": Arousal, misattribution, and the effect of temporal distance on confidence. *Personality and Social Psychology Bulletin, 24,* 529–536.

Schwarz, N. (1990). Feelings as information: Informational and motivational functions of affective states. In E. T. Higgins & R. Sorrentino (Eds.), *Handbook of motivation and cognition: Foundations of social behavior* (Vol. 2, pp. 527–561). New York: Guilford Press.

Schwarz, N., & Clore, G. L. (1983). Mood, misattribution, and judgments of well-being: Informative and directive functions of affective states. *Journal of Personality and Social Psychology, 45,* 513–523.

Stephenson, B., & Wicklund, R. A. (1983). Self-directed attention and taking the other's perspective. *Journal of Experimental Social Psychology, 19,* 58–77.

Tversky, A., & Kahneman, D. (1974). Judgment under uncertainty: Heuristics and biases. *Science, 185,* 1124–1131.

Van Boven, L., Medvec, V. H., & Gilovich, T. (1998). *The illusion of transparency in negotiations.* Unpublished manuscript, Cornell University.

Vorauer, J. D. (in press). The other side of the story: Transparency estimation in social interaction. In G. B. Moskowitz (Ed.), *Future directions in social cognition.* Mahwah, NJ: Erlbaum.

Vorauer, J. D., & Claude, S. D. (1998). Perceived versus actual transparency of goals in negotiation. *Personality and Social Psychology Bulletin, 24,* 371–385.

Vorauer, J. D., & Ross, M. (1998). *Self-awareness and feeling transparent: Failing to suppress one's self.* Unpublished manuscript, University of Manitoba, Winnipeg, Manitoba, Canada.

Wicklund, R. A. (1975). Objective self-awareness. In L. Berkowitz (Ed.), *Advances in experimental social psychology* (Vol. 8, pp. 233–275). New York: Academic Press.

Zuckerman, M., DePaulo, B. M., & Rosenthal, R. (1981). Verbal and nonverbal com-
    munication of deception. In L. Berkowitz (Ed.), *Advances in experimental social
    psychology* (Vol. 14, pp. 1–59). New York: Academic Press.
Zuckerman, M., Kernis, M. H., Guarnera, S. M., Murphy, J. F., & Rappoport, L. (1983).
    The egocentric bias: Seeing oneself as cause and target of others' behavior. *Journal
    of Personality, 51*, 621–630.

Questions for Review and Discussion

1. Define the illusion of transparency.
2. Why did Gilovich et al. propose that an anchoring and adjustment process
    accounted for their finding (Studies 1a, 1b, and 1c) that participants induced
    to lie overestimated the detectability of their lies?
3. What relationship did Gilovich et al.'s Studies 3a and 3b find between (a) par-
    ticipants' ratings of their own private concern, (b) their ratings of how
    concerned they appeared to others, and (c) how concerned they actually
    seemed to others?

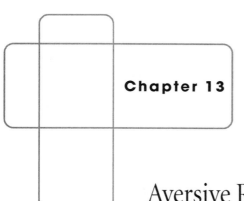

Chapter 13

Aversive Racism and Selection Decisions: 1989 and 1999

John F. Dovidio and Samuel L. Gaertner

In part because of changing norms and the Civil Rights Act and other legislative interventions that have made discrimination not simply immoral but also illegal, overt expressions of prejudice have declined significantly over the past 35 years (Schuman, Steeh, Bobo, & Krysan, 1997). Discrimination, however, continues to exist and affect the lives of people of color and women in significant ways (Hacker, 1995). What accounts for this discrepancy? One possibility is that it represents a change in the nature of racial prejudice. Contemporary forms of prejudice may be less conscious and more subtle than the overt, traditional form (Gaertner & Dovidio, 1986; Sears, van Laar, Carillo, & Kosterman, 1997). For these more subtle forms of prejudice, discrimination is expressed in indirect and rationalizable ways, but the consequences of these actions (e.g., the restriction of economic opportunity) may be as significant for people of color and as pernicious as the consequences of the traditional, overt form of discrimination (Dovidio & Gaertner, 1998).

In the present research, we examined the issue of changes in expressed prejudice and discrimination from the perspective of one modern form of prejudice, aversive racism. Aversive racism (see Gaertner & Dovidio, 1986) is hypothesized to characterize the racial attitudes of many whites who endorse egalitarian values, who regard themselves as nonprejudiced, but who discriminate in subtle,

From *Psychological Science*, Vol. 11, No. 2 (July 2000). © 2000 American Psychological Society.

rationalizable ways. Specifically, the present research explored both the overt expression of racial attitudes and discrimination in simulated employment decisions for two samples across a 10-year period, from 1988–1989 to 1998–1999.

According to the aversive-racism perspective, many people who explicitly support egalitarian principles and believe themselves to be nonprejudiced also unconsciously harbor negative feelings and beliefs about blacks and other historically disadvantaged groups. Aversive racists thus experience ambivalence between their egalitarian beliefs and their negative feelings toward blacks. In contrast to the traditional emphasis on the psychopathological aspects of prejudice, the aversive-racism framework suggests that biases related to normal cognitive, motivational, and sociocultural processes may predispose a person to develop negative racial feelings (see Gaertner & Dovidio, 1986). Nevertheless, egalitarian traditions and norms are potent forces promoting racial equality (e.g., Kluegel & Smith, 1986). As a consequence of these widespread influences promoting both negative feelings and egalitarian beliefs, aversive racism is presumed to characterize the racial attitudes of a substantial portion of well-educated and liberal whites in the United States (Gaertner & Dovidio, 1986).

The aversive-racism framework further suggests that contemporary racial bias is expressed in indirect ways that do not threaten the aversive racist's nonprejudiced self-image. Because aversive racists consciously recognize and endorse egalitarian values, they will not discriminate in situations in which they recognize that discrimination would be obvious to others and themselves—for example, when the appropriate response is clearly dictated. However, because aversive racists do possess negative feelings, often unconsciously, discrimination occurs when bias is not obvious or can be rationalized on the basis of some factor other than race. We have found support for this framework across a range of experimental paradigms (see Dovidio & Gaertner, 1998; Gaertner & Dovidio, 1986).

Because the negative consequences of aversive racism are expressed in ways that are not easily recognizable (by oneself, as well as by others) as racial bias, traditional techniques for eliminating bias by emphasizing the immorality of prejudice and illegality of discrimination are not effective for combating contemporary racism: "Aversive racists recognize prejudice is bad, but they do not recognize that they are prejudiced. . . . Like a virus that has mutated, racism has also evolved into different forms that are more difficult not only to recognize but also to combat" (Dovidio & Gaertner, 1998, p. 25). Thus, direct and overt expressions of prejudice, such as self-reported attitudes, are more amenable to change and pressures of increasingly egalitarian norms (Kluegel & Smith, 1986) than are indirect manifestations of racism because they are more easily recognized as racial biases.

The present research was designed to extend the research on aversive racism by exploring changes, over a 10-year period, in expressed racial attitudes and patterns of discrimination in hiring recommendations for a black or white candidate for a position as a peer counselor. Two measures were taken from two comparable student samples 10 years apart. One measure was self-reported racial prejudice. The other measure involved decisions in a simulated employment context. Participants were asked to use interview excerpts to evaluate candidates for a new program for peer counseling at their university. Three profiles were developed: One reflected clearly strong qualifications (pretested as being accepted 85–90% of the time across two samples), one represented clearly weak qualifications (pretested as being accepted 10–20% of the time), and the third involved marginally acceptable but ambiguous qualifications (pretested as being accepted about 50–65% of the time). Participants evaluated a single candidate who was identifiable as black or white from information in the excerpt.

With respect to expressed racial attitudes, we predicted, on the basis of continued emphasis on egalitarian values in the United States (Schuman et al., 1997), that the general trend toward the expression of less prejudiced attitudes (Dovidio & Gaertner, 1998; Schuman et al., 1997) would be reflected across our two samples. Whereas expressed prejudice was expected to decline, we hypothesized that subtle, covert forms of discrimination would persist. Specifically, we predicted, on the basis of previous work on aversive racism as well as work showing that racial stereotypes are most influential in ambiguous situations (see Fiske, 1998), that discrimination against black applicants would occur when the match between the candidate's qualifications and the position criteria was unclear—in the ambiguous-qualifications condition—but not when candidates were clearly well qualified or unqualified for the position.

Method

Participants

Participants were 194 undergraduates at a Northeastern liberal arts college during the 1988–1989 academic year ($n = 112$; 48 white male and 64 white female undergraduates) or the 1998–1999 academic year ($n = 82$; 34 white male and 48 white female undergraduates). Participants were enrolled in the university's introductory psychology class, and admissions data indicated that the student populations were scholastically (e.g., standardized-test scores, high school grades) and demographically (e.g., geographical, sex, and racial distributions; socioeconomic status) comparable across the two time periods. Involvement in the study partially satisfied one option for a course requirement. Self-reported prejudice scores were available for 77% ($n = 86$) of participants in 1988–1989 and 87% ($n = 71$) of participants in 1998–1999.

Procedure

During mass pretesting sessions, participants were administered, along with several other surveys, questionnaires assessing their racial attitudes. For the present study, we examined responses to three racial-attitude items (Weigel & Howes, 1985) that were the same at both testing periods: "Blacks shouldn't push themselves where they are not wanted," "I would probably feel somewhat self-conscious dancing with a black person in a public place," and "I would mind it if a black family with about the same income and education as my own would move next door to my home." Responses were on a scale from 1 (*disagree strongly*) to 5 (*agree strongly*) (Cronbach's alpha = .71 overall).

Later, during an experimental session, participants (from 1 to 8 per session) were informed that they would be asked questions about "the desirability and feasibility of a peer counseling program and the qualities of personnel." They were randomly assigned to one of six conditions in a 3 (qualifications: clearly strong, ambiguous, clearly weak) $\times$ 2 (race of candidate) design. Thirty to 34 participants were assigned to each condition. After reading a 120-word description of an ostensibly new program, each participant was asked to evaluate a candidate from a previous round of applicants on the basis of interview excerpts. These excerpts were systematically varied to manipulate the strength of the candidate's qualifications. For the candidate with strong qualifications, leadership experiences included being co-captain of the swim team in high school and being a member of the disciplinary board in college; his self-description was "sensitive, intelligent, and relaxed." In response to the question "If a female student came to you because she was pregnant, what would you do?" this candidate was quoted as saying, "Explain options to her and ask her if she would like the telephone number of the health center." For the candidate with ambiguous qualifications, the candidate's leadership experiences included only being co-captain of the swim team in high school; his self-description was "sensitive, intelligent, and emotional." In response to the question about the female student who might be pregnant, this candidate said, "Ask her if she would like the telephone number of the health center." For the candidate with weak qualifications, the leadership experiences included being co-captain of the chess team in high school; his self-description was "independent, forthright, and intense." This candidate's response to the question about the student's pregnancy was, "Tell her that is too personal and that she must talk with her parents."

The race of the applicant was varied by the list of his activities. Black candidates listed membership in the Black Student Union, whereas white students listed fraternity membership (which was almost exclusively white on campus).

The final versions of the three "interview excerpts" were pretested with 20 undergraduate students from each time period. They were given all three excerpts, in random order and without racially identifying information. Undergraduates at both time periods clearly distinguished among strong, ambiguous, and weak qualifications. The strongly qualified candidate was recommended for the peer counselor program by 85% and 90% of the pretest participants at the two time periods, respectively; the candidate with ambiguous qualifications was recommended by 50% and 65% of these participants; and the candidate with weak qualifications was recommended by 20% and 10% of these students.

In the main study, students evaluated the candidates by rating them on a series of scales. The first item assessed perceptions of whether the candidate was qualified for the position, on a scale from 1 (*not at all*) to 10 (*extremely*); this item served as a check on the manipulation of the interview excerpts. The last two items represented the primary dependent measures. They asked whether participants would recommend the candidate for the position (yes or no) and how strongly they would recommend the candidate (on a scale from 1, *not at all*, to 10, *very strongly*). On the last page of the booklet, participants read, "When reading a resumé or transcript, people often form a visual image of a person. Based on the information provided, what image of the applicant have you formed?" A question about the candidate's race was included among other items about his imagined physical characteristics.

Results

The manipulations of race and qualifications were effective. Participants identified the candidate as being white 100% of the time in the white-candidate condition and as being black 97% of the time in the black-candidate condition. Preliminary analyses of the yes/no recommendations and their strength revealed no systematic effects for the sex of the participant. Consequently, this factor was not included in subsequent analyses. A 3 (qualifications: clearly strong, ambiguous, clearly weak) $\times$ 2 (race of candidate) $\times$ 2 (time: 1988–1989, 1998–1999) analysis of variance demonstrated the expected main effect of manipulated qualifications on perceived qualifications, $F(1, 182) = 62.92$, $p < .001$ ($Ms = 7.21$ vs. 6.38 vs. 3.98; see Table 1). This main effect was uncomplicated by any interactions. Each of the three qualifications conditions differed significantly from the other two according to Scheffé post hoc tests.

TABLE 1

Perceived Qualifications and Candidate Recommendations as a Function of the Candidate's Qualifications and Race

Condition	Perceived qualifications[a]			Strength of recommendation[a]			Percentage recommended		
	1988–1989	1998–1999	Both	1988–1989	1998–1999	Both	1988–1989	1998–1999	Both
Clearly strong qualifications									
White candidate	7.32 (1.46)	6.93 (2.06)	7.15 (1.72)	6.74 (1.41)	6.21 (2.09)	6.52 (1.72)	89	79	85
Black candidate	7.79 (1.23)	6.60 (1.77)	7.27 (1.58)	7.32 (1.67)	7.00 (1.60)	7.18 (1.62)	95	87	91
Ambiguous qualifications									
White candidate	6.45 (1.11)	5.85 (1.68)	6.21 (1.36)	6.05 (1.73)	5.69 (1.60)	5.91 (1.67)	75	77	76

T A B L E 1 (*continued*)

Perceived Qualifications and Candidate Recommendations as a Function of the Candidate's Qualifications and Race

Condition	Perceived qualifications[a]			Strength of recommendation[a]			Percentage recommended		
	1988–1989	1998–1999	Both	1988–1989	1998–1999	Both	1988–1989	1998–1999	Both
Black candidate	6.72 (1.32)	6.33 (1.59)	6.55 (1.44)	5.06 (1.39)	4.53 (1.64)	4.82 (1.51)	50	40	45
Clearly weak qualifications									
White candidate	3.90 (2.00)	3.67 (2.27)	3.81 (2.07)	3.05 (1.65)	2.42 (1.68)	2.81 (1.66)	5	8	6
Black candidate	4.24 (1.75)	4.08 (2.06)	4.17 (1.86)	3.29 (1.69)	3.77 (1.69)	3.50 (1.68)	12	15	13

[a] Table entries are means, with standard deviations in parentheses. Responses were on a scale from 1 (*not at all qualified or not at all recommended*) to 10 (*extremely qualified or very strongly recommended*).

The 3 × 2 × 2 analysis of variance performed on the strength of recommendations revealed the anticipated main effect for qualifications, $F(1, 182) = 81.15$, $p < .001$ (see Table 1). Participants recommended candidates in the strong-qualifications condition most highly ($M = 6.85$), candidates in the ambiguous-qualifications condition next most highly ($M = 5.36$), and those in the weak-qualifications condition least highly ($M = 3.15$). Scheffé tests demonstrated that these means differed significantly from each other. There was no main effect for the candidate's race ($F < 1$), but the predicted Qualifications × Race of Candidate interaction was obtained, $F(2, 182) = 6.08$, $p < .003$. Planned comparisons revealed no significant difference in the strength of recommendations for black and white candidates who had strong qualifications ($Ms = 7.18$ vs. 6.52, $p > .10$) or who had weak qualifications ($Ms = 3.50$ vs. 2.81, $p > .10$). However, as predicted, ambiguously qualified black candidates were recommended significantly less strongly than were comparable white candidates ($Ms = 4.82$ vs. 5.91), $t(64) = 2.79$, $p < .001$. In addition, Scheffé tests comparing the strengths of participants' recommendations revealed that when the applicant was white, participants responded to ambiguous qualifications more as if these qualifications were strong (difference between means = 0.61, n.s.; Table 1) than as if they were weak (difference = 3.10, $p < .05$). When the applicant was black, however, participants reacted to ambiguous qualifications more like weak qualifications (difference between means = 1.32, n.s.) than like strong qualifications (difference = 2.36, $p < .05$).

Moreover, the Qualifications × Race of Candidate interaction was comparable across participants in the 1988–1989 and the 1998–1999 samples: The Qualifications × Race of Candidate × Time interaction did not approach significance, $F(2, 182) = 0.61$, $p > .54$. The Qualifications × Race of Candidate interaction was marginally significant for participants in 1988–1989, $F(2, 106) = 2.54$, $p < .083$; it was significant for participants in the 1998–1999 sample alone, $F(2, 76) = 3.94$, $p < .024$ (see Table 1).

Log-linear analyses, paralleling those for the strength of recommendations, were conducted on the dichotomous (yes/no) recommendation measure. These analyses yielded the same pattern of results. Overall, candidates in the strong-qualifications condition were recommended most frequently (88%), those in the ambiguous-qualifications condition were recommended next most frequently (61%), and those in the weak-qualifications condition were recommended least frequently (10%), $\chi^2(2, N = 194) = 80.37$, $p < .001$. The Qualifications × Race of Candidate interaction was also obtained, $\chi^2(2, N = 194) = 6.75$, $p < .035$. Black and white candidates were recommended equivalently often in the strong-qualifications (91% vs. 85%) and weak-qualifications (13% vs. 6%) conditions ($ps > .50$), but blacks were recommended less often than whites in the ambiguous-qualifications condition (45% vs. 76%), $\chi^2(1, N = 66) = 6.35$, $p < .012$. Again, the interaction was not moderated by the time period in which the data were collected; the three-way interaction did not approach significance ($p > .50$). Taken together, the results for the strength of recommendations and the yes/no measure offer support for the hypotheses.

For the participants for whom prejudice scores were available, the 3 (qualifications) $\times$ 2 (race of candidate) $\times$ 2 (time: 1988–1989, 1998–1999) analysis of variance demonstrated only a main effect for time, $F(1, 145) = 8.31, p < .005$. As expected, participants in 1988–1989 had higher prejudice scores than those in 1998–1999 ($Ms = 1.84$ vs. 1.54). In addition, for both ratings of qualifications and recommendations, $3 \times 2 \times 2 \times 2$ (prejudice) analyses of variance, classifying participants in the two samples as high or low in prejudice on the basis of median splits, were performed. There were no significant effects for prejudice qualifying the results reported earlier. However, overall, participants higher in prejudice (as a continuous variable) recommended black candidates less strongly than participants lower in prejudice, $r(79) = -.24, p < .05$. The correlation between prejudice and strength of recommendation was nonsignificant for white applicants, $r(74) = .05, p > .50$.

Discussion

Overall, the pattern of results supports the hypothesis derived from the aversive-racism framework. As predicted from that framework, and consistent with other theories of modern racism (e.g., McConahay, 1986) and the influence of stereotyping (Fiske, 1998), bias against blacks in simulated hiring decisions was manifested primarily when a candidate's qualifications for the position were ambiguous. When a black candidate's credentials clearly qualified him for the position, or when his credentials clearly were not appropriate, there was no discrimination against him. Moreover, as expected, self-reported expressions of prejudice declined significantly across the 10-year period. Taken together, these contrasting trends for self-reported prejudice and discrimination in simulated employment decisions support our hypothesis that the development of contemporary forms of prejudice, such as aversive racism, may account—at least in part—for the persistence of racial disparities in society despite significant decreases in expressed racial prejudice and stereotypes. However, this finding does not imply that old-fashioned racism is no longer a problem. In fact, the overall negative correlation between expressed prejudice and recommendations for black candidates suggests that traditional racism is a force that still exists and that can operate independently of contemporary forms of racism.

One potential alternative explanation for the results of the employment decision is that the credentials in the clear-qualifications condition were so extreme that ceiling and floor effects suppressed the variance in responses and reduced the likelihood of obtaining differences as a function of the candidate's race. Although plausible, this explanation is not supported empirically. The strength-of-recommendation measure could range from 1 to 10, and the means in the strong-qualifications condition (6.52 for white candidates and 7.18 for black candidates) and the weak-qualifications condition (2.81 for white candidates and 3.50 for black candidates) did not closely approach these scale endpoints. This restricted-range interpretation would also suggest that the within-condition standard deviations would be substantially lower in the clear-qualifications conditions than in the ambiguous-qualifications condition. As illustrated in Table 1, this was not the case. The standard deviations were similar for both white candidates (1.72 and 1.66 vs. 1.67) and black candidates (1.62 and 1.68 vs. 1.51); there was no statistical evidence of heterogeneity of within-group variances. Thus, this extremity explanation cannot readily account for the obtained pattern of results.

In addition, although we had predicted, on the basis of the ambiguity versus clarity of appropriate decisions, that discrimination against blacks would be unlikely to occur when qualifications were either clearly weak or clearly strong, other perspectives could suggest that bias would occur in these conditions. In the weak-qualifications condition, the black candidate's clear lack of credentials could have provided an ostensibly nonracial justification for particularly negative evaluations. Although a floor effect offers one potential explanation for the lack of difference in this condition, as we noted earlier, the within-cell standard deviations do not readily support this interpretation. Another possibility is that because the black candidate did not display obviously negative qualities, but rather insufficiently positive ones, excessive devaluation of this candidate was difficult to rationalize. Contemporary racism is hypothesized to involve sympathy for blacks (Katz, Wackenhut, & Hass, 1986), as well as cautiousness by whites about being too negative in evaluations of blacks (and thus appearing biased); either or both of these factors could have limited the negativity of response to blacks when qualifications were weak and could account for the slightly more positive response to black than to white candidates in this condition (see Table 1). In addition, sympathy and concerns about being too harsh in evaluations are particularly likely to occur when the relevance to the evaluator and the challenge to the status quo are minimal (see Dovidio & Gaertner, 1996; McConahay, 1986). Participants were not led to believe that their responses would directly influence the outcome of the particular candidate's application in the current study. Under conditions of greater relevance to the evaluator, greater bias toward either highly qualified or underqualified blacks may occur as a function of direct or symbolic threats (Dovidio & Gaertner, 1996).

The overall pattern of results obtained in the present study also helps to illuminate some of the processes underlying the effects of aversive racism. In particular, participants' ratings of the candidates' qualifications were not directly influenced by race: Participants rated the objective qualifications of blacks and whites equivalently. The effect of race seemed to occur not in how the qualifications were perceived, but in how they were considered and weighed in the recommendation decisions. We (Gaertner et al., 1997) have proposed, for example, that the effects of aversive racism may be rooted substantially in intergroup biases based on social categorization processes. These biases reflect in-group favoritism as well as out-group derogation. Along these lines, Hewstone (1990) found that people tend to judge a potentially negative behavior as more negative and intentional, and are more likely to attribute the behavior to the person's personality, when the behavior is performed by an out-group member than when it is performed by an in-group member. Thus, when given latitude for interpretation, as in the ambiguous-qualifications condition, whites may give white candidates the "benefit of the doubt," a benefit that is not extended to out-group members (i.e., to black candidates). As a consequence, as demonstrated in the present study, moderate qualifications are responded to as if they were strong qualifications when the candidate is white, but as if they were weak qualifications when the candidate is black.

The subtle, rationalizable type of bias demonstrated in the present study, which is manifested in terms of in-group favoritism, can pose unique challenges to the legal system. As Krieger (1998) observed, "Title VII is poorly equipped to control prejudice resulting from ingroup favoritism" (p. 1325). Identifying the existence and persistence of subtle bias associated with aversive racism can thus help to demonstrate that discriminations is not "a thing of the past" and can encourage renewed efforts to develop techniques to combat contemporary racial bias.

References

Dovidio, J. F., & Gaertner, S. L. (1996). Affirmative action, unintentional racial biases, and intergroup relations. *Journal of Social Issues, 52*(4), 51–75.

Dovidio, J. F., & Gaertner, S. L. (1998). On the nature of contemporary prejudice: The causes, consequences, and challenges of aversive racism. In J. Eberhardt & S. T. Fiske (Eds.), *Confronting racism: The problem and the response* (pp. 3–32). Newbury Park, CA: Sage.

Fiske, S. (1998). Stereotyping, prejudice, and discrimination. In D. Gilbert, S. Fiske, & G. Lindzey (Eds.), *The handbook of social psychology* (4th ed., Vol. 2, pp. 357–411). New York: McGraw-Hill.

Gaertner, S. L., & Dovidio, J. F. (1986). The aversive form of racism. In J. F. Dovidio & S. L. Gaertner (Eds.), *Prejudice, discrimination, and racism* (pp. 61–89). Orlando, FL: Academic Press.

Gaertner, S. L., Dovidio, J. F., Banker, B., Rust, M., Nier, J., Mottola, G., & Ward, C. (1997). Does racism necessarily mean anti-blackness? Aversive racism and pro-whiteness. In M. Fine, L. Powell, L. Weis, & M. Wong (Eds.), *Off white* (pp. 167–178). London: Routledge.

Hacker, A. (1995). *Two nations: Black and White, separate, hostile, unequal.* New York: Ballantine Books.

Hewstone, M. (1990). The "ultimate attribution error"? A review of the literature on intergroup attributions. *European Journal of Social Psychology, 20,* 311–335.

Katz, I., Wackenhut, J., & Hass, R. G. (1986). Racial ambivalence, value duality, and behavior. In J. F. Dovidio & S. L. Gaertner (Eds.), *Prejudice, discrimination, and racism* (pp. 35–59). Orlando, FL: Academic Press.

Kluegel, J. R., & Smith, E. R. (1986). *Beliefs about inequality: America's views of what is and what ought to be.* New York: Aldine de Gruyter.

Krieger, L. H. (1998). Civil rights perestroika: Intergroup relations after affirmative action. *California Law Review, 86,* 1251–1333.

McConahay, J. B. (1986). Modern racism, ambivalence, and the modern racism scale. In J. F. Dovidio & S. L. Gaertner (Eds.), *Prejudice, discrimination, and racism* (pp. 91–125). Orlando, FL: Academic Press.

Schuman, H., Steeh, C., Bobo, L., & Krysan, M. (1997). *Racial attitudes in America: Trends and interpretations.* Cambridge, MA: Harvard University Press.

Sears, D. O., van Laar, C., Carillo, M., & Kosterman, R. (1997). Is it really racism? The origin of white Americans' opposition to race-targeted policies. *Public Opinion Quarterly, 61,* 16–53.

Weigel, R. H., & Howes, P. W. (1985). Conceptions of racial prejudice: Symbolic racism reconsidered. *Journal of Social Issues, 41*(3), 117–138.

Questions for Review and Discussion

1. How do the authors define aversive racism and why do they term it a modern form of racism?
2. What changes in self-reported expressions of prejudice occurred over the 10-year period of this study?
3. Why did the researchers expect white participants to discriminate most against those black employment candidates whose credentials were ambiguous?

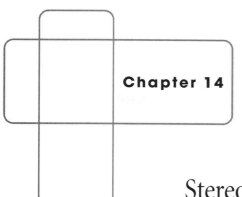

Chapter 14

Stereotypes and Prejudice: Their Automatic and Controlled Components

Patricia G. Devine

Social psychologists have long been interested in stereotypes and prejudice, concepts that are typically viewed as being very much interrelated. For example, those who subscribe to the tripartite model of attitudes hold that a stereotype is the cognitive component of prejudiced attitudes (Harding, Proshansky, Kutner, & Chein, 1969; Secord & Backman, 1974). Other theorists suggest that stereotypes are functional for the individual, allowing rationalization of his or her prejudice against a group (Allport, 1954; LaViolette & Silvert, 1951; Saenger, 1953; Simpson & Yinger, 1965).

In fact, many classic and contemporary theorists have suggested that prejudice is an inevitable consequence of ordinary categorization (stereotyping) processes (Allport, 1954; Billig, 1985; Ehrlich, 1973; Hamilton, 1981; Tajfel, 1981). The basic argument of the *inevitability of prejudice* perspective is that as long as stereotypes exist, prejudice will follow. This approach suggests that stereotypes are automatically (or heuristically) applied to members of the stereotyped group. In essence, knowledge of a stereotype is equated with prejudice toward the group. This perspective has serious implications because, as Ehrlich (1973) argued, ethnic attitudes and stereotypes are part of the social heritage of a society and no one can escape learning the prevailing attitudes and stereotypes assigned to the major ethnic groups.

From *Journal of Personality and Social Psychology*, Vol. 56, No. 1, pp. 5–18. Copyright © 1989 by the American Psychological Association. Reproduced with permission.

The inevitability of prejudice approach, however, overlooks an important distinction between knowledge of a cultural stereotype and acceptance or endorsement of the stereotype (Ashmore & Del Boca, 1981; Billig, 1985). That is, although one may have *knowledge of a stereotype*, his or her *personal beliefs* may or may not be congruent with the stereotype. Moreover, there is no good evidence that knowledge of a stereotype of a group implies prejudice toward that group. For example, in an in-depth interview study of prejudice in war veterans, Bettleheim and Janowitz (1964) found no significant relation between stereotypes reported about Blacks and Jews and the degree of prejudice the veterans displayed toward these groups (see also Brigham, 1972; Devine, 1988; Karlins, Coffman, & Walters, 1969).

Although they may have some overlapping features, it is argued that stereotypes and personal beliefs are conceptually distinct cognitive structures. Each structure represents part of one's entire knowledge base of a particular group (see Pratkanis, in press, for a supporting argument in the attitude domain). Beliefs are propositions that are endorsed and accepted as being true. Beliefs can differ from one's knowledge about an object or group or one's affective reaction toward the object or group (Pratkanis, in press). To the extent that stereotypes and personal beliefs represent different and only potentially overlapping subsets of information about ethnic or racial groups, they may have different implications for evaluation of and behavior toward members of the ethnic and racial groups. Previous theorists have not adequately captured this distinction and explored its implications for responding to stereotyped group members. The primary goal of the three studies reported here was to examine how stereotypes and personal beliefs are involved in responses toward stereotyped groups.

This work challenges the inevitability of prejudice framework and offers a model of responses to members of stereotyped groups that is derived largely from work in information processing that distinguishes between automatic (mostly involuntary) and controlled (mostly voluntary) processes (e.g., Posner & Snyder, 1975; Schneider & Shiffrin, 1977; Shiffrin & Schneider, 1977). Automatic processes involve the unintentional or spontaneous activation of some well-learned set of associations or responses that have been developed through repeated activation in memory. They do not require conscious effort and appear to be initiated by the presence of stimulus cues in the environment (Shiffrin & Dumais, 1981). A crucial component of automatic processes is their inescapability; they occur despite deliberate attempts to bypass or ignore them (Neely, 1977; Shiffrin & Dumais, 1981). In contrast, controlled processes are intentional and require the active attention of the individual. Controlled processes, although limited by capacity, are more flexible than automatic processes. Their intentionality and flexibility makes them particularly useful for decision making, problem solving, and the initiation of new behaviors.

Previous theoretical and empirical work on automatic and controlled processes suggests that they can operate independently of each other (Logan, 1980; Logan & Cowan, 1984; Neely, 1977; Posner & Snyder, 1975). For example, by using a semantic priming task, Neely demonstrated that when automatic processing would produce a response that conflicted with conscious expectancies (induced through experimenter instructions), subjects inhibited the automatic response and intentionally replaced it with one consistent with their conscious expectancy.

For example, Neely (1977) examined the influence of a single-word prime on the processing of a single-word target in a lexical decision task (i.e., whether the target was a word). The prime was either semantically related to the target (e.g., *body*–arm) or related to the target through experimenter instructions (e.g., subjects were told that *body* would be followed by a bird name such as sparrow). In this latter condition, subjects had a conscious expectancy for a bird name when they saw the *body* prime, but *body* should also have automatically primed its semantic category of body parts.

Neely (1977) found that with brief intervals between the prime and target (i.e., 250 ms), the prime facilitated decisions for semantically related targets regardless of experimenter instructions. Neely argued that this facilitation was a function of automatic processes. At longer delays (i.e., 2,000 ms), however, experimenter-induced expectancies produced both facilitation for expected targets and inhibition for unexpected targets regardless of their semantic relation to the prime. Before such inhibition of automatically activated responses can occur, there has to be enough *time* and *cognitive capacity* available for the conscious expectancy to develop and inhibit the automatic processes.

Automatic and Controlled Processes: Implications for Activation of Stereotypes and Personal Beliefs

The dissociation of automatic and controlled processes may provide some theoretical leverage for understanding the role of stereotypes and personal beliefs in responses to members of racial or ethnic groups. In the model proposed, interest centers on the conditions under which stereotypes and personal beliefs are activated and the likelihood that personal beliefs overlap with the cultural stereotype. There is strong evidence that stereotypes are well established in children's memories before children develop the cognitive ability and flexibility to question or critically evaluate the stereotype's validity or acceptability (Allport, 1954; P. Katz, 1976; Porter, 1971; Proshansky, 1966). As a result, personal beliefs (i.e., decisions about the appropriateness of stereotypic ascriptions) are necessarily newer cognitive structures (Higgins & King, 1981). An additional consequence of this developmental sequence is that stereotypes have a longer history of activation and are therefore likely to be more accessible than are personal beliefs. To the extent that an individual rejects the stereotype, he or she experiences a fundamental conflict between the already established stereotype and the more recently established personal beliefs.

The present model assumes that primarily because of common socialization experiences (Brigham, 1972; Ehrlich, 1973; P. Katz, 1976; Proshansky, 1966), high- and low-prejudice persons are equally knowledgeable of the cultural stereotype of Blacks. In addition, because the stereotype has been frequently activated in the past, it is a well-learned set of associations (Dovidio, Evans, & Tyler, 1986) that is *automatically* activated in the presence of a member (or symbolic equivalent) of the target group (Smith & Branscombe, 1985). The model holds that this unintentional activation of the stereotype is equally strong and equally inescapable for high- and low-prejudice persons.

A major assumption of the model is that high- and low-prejudice persons differ with respect to their personal beliefs about Blacks (Greeley & Sheatsley, 1971; Taylor, Sheatsley, & Greeley, 1978). Whereas high-prejudice persons are likely to have personal beliefs that overlap substantially with the cultural stereotype, low-prejudice persons have *decided* that the stereotype is an inappropriate basis for behavior or evaluation and experience a conflict between the automatically activated stereotype and their personal beliefs. The stereotype conflicts with their nonprejudiced, egalitarian values. The model assumes that the low-prejudice person must create a cognitive structure that represents his or her newer beliefs (e.g., belief in equality between the races, rejection of the stereotype, etc.). Because the stereotype has a longer history of activation (and thus greater frequency of activation) than the newly acquired personal beliefs, overt nonprejudiced responses require intentional inhibition of the automatically activated stereotype and activation of the newer personal belief structure. Such inhibition and initiation of new responses involves controlled processes.

This analysis suggests that whereas stereotypes are automatically activated, activation of personal beliefs require conscious attention. In addition, nonprejudiced responses require both the inhibition of the automatically activated stereotype and the intentional activation of nonprejudiced beliefs (see also Higgins & King, 1981). This should not be surprising because an individual must overcome a lifetime of socialization experiences. The present model, which suggests that automatic and controlled processes involved in stereotypes and prejudice can be dissociated, posits that the inevitability of prejudice arguments follow from tasks that are likely to engage automatic processes on which those high and low in prejudice are presumed not to differ (i.e., activation of a negative stereotype in the absence of controlled stereotype-inhibiting processes). Interestingly, the model implies that if a stereotype is automatically activated in the presence of a member of the target group and those who reject the cultural stereotype do not (or perhaps cannot) monitor consciously this activation, information activated in the stereotype could influence subsequent information processing. A particular strength of the model, then, is that it suggests how knowledge of a stereotype can influence responses even for those who do not endorse the stereotype or have changed their beliefs about the stereotyped group.

Higgins and King (1981) presented a similar analysis with respect to the effect of gender stereotypes on memory. They demonstrated that when gender was not salient, subjects' descriptions of self and others reflected traditional views of gender-linked attributes. They suggested that under such conditions traditional gender stereotypes, with their longer history (i.e., greater frequency) of activation, are passively (automatically) activated and influence recall. When gender was made salient, however, subjects apparently inhibited the traditional stereotype and descriptions were more consistent with their more recently developed, modern views of gender-linked attributes.

In summary, the present model suggests that a target's group membership activates, or primes, the stereotype in the perceiver's memory (Smith, 1984; Wyer & Srull, 1981), making other traits or attributes associated with the stereotype highly accessible for future processing (Dovidio et al., 1986; Gaertner & McLaughlin, 1983; Smith & Branscombe, 1985). The implications of this automatic stereotype activation may be serious, particularly when the content of the stereotype is predominately negative, as is the case with racial stereotypes. For example, Duncan (1976) found that Whites interpreted the same ambiguous shove as hostile or violent when the actor was Black and as playing around or dramatizing when the actor was White. Duncan assumed that the presence of the Black actor automatically primed the stereotype of Blacks and because the stereotype associates Blacks with violence, the violent behavior category was more accessible when viewing a Black compared with a White actor. Sager and Schofield (1980) replicated these findings with schoolchildren. Both Black and White children rated ambiguously aggressive behaviors (e.g., bumping in the hallway) of Black actors as being more mean or threatening than the same behaviors of White actors.

In only one of these studies (Gaertner & McLaughlin, 1983) was prejudice assessed and responses of high- and low-prejudice subjects compared. Thus, the extent to which high- and low-prejudice persons differ or are similar in their automatic and controlled responses to target group members remains unclear. The present studies were designed to test implications of the dissociation of automatic and controlled processes in prejudice. Study 1 examined the validity of the assumption that high- and low-prejudice subjects are equally knowledge-able of the cultural stereotype. Study 2 explored the implications of automatic racial stereotype priming on the evaluation of ambiguous stereotype-relevant behaviors. This task permitted examination of the effects of automatic stereo-type activation independently of controlled processes relevant to the stereotype. Finally, Study 3 examined the likelihood that high- and low-prejudice subjects will engage in controlled processes to inhibit prejudiced responses in a con-sciously directed thought-listing task.

Study 1: Stereotype Content and Prejudice Level

Historically, little attention has focused on individual differences in prejudice when assessing the content of stereotypes. Although implicit in the stereotype assessment literature (Brigham, 1971), the assumption that high- and low-prejudice subjects are equally knowledgeable of the cultural stereotype has not been documented. The first step in validating the present model was to exam-ine directly high- and low-prejudice subjects' knowledge of the content of the cultural stereotype of Blacks.

In contrast to the typical adjective checklist assessment of stereotype con-tent (Gilbert, 1951; Karlins et al., 1969; D. Katz & Braly, 1933), a free response task was used in the present study. This task provides a more sensitive test of subjects' knowledge of the stereotype because no cues (e.g., a list of possible characteristics) regarding possible content are provided. Thus, high- and low-prejudice subjects were asked to list the content of the cultural stereotype of Blacks regardless of their personal beliefs.

Method

Subjects and procedure.   Forty White introductory psychology students partici-pated in groups of 4–6 for course credit. To ensure anonymity, subjects were isolated from each other and the experimenter left the room after giving gen-eral instructions. Written instructions told subjects that the questionnaire was designed to help researchers better understand social stereotypes and that interest centered on the cultural stereotype of Blacks. The experimenter informed them that she was not interested in their personal beliefs but in their knowledge of the content of the cultural stereotype. Subjects were provided with a page with several blank lines on which to list the components of the stereotype and were asked not to write any identifying marks on the booklet.

After listing the components of the stereotype, subjects completed the seven-item Modern Racism Scale (McConahay, Hardee, & Batts, 1981). The Modern Racism Scale is designed to measure subjects' anti-Black attitudes in a nonreactive fashion. The Modern Racism Scale has proven to be useful in predicting a variety of behaviors including voting patterns and reactions to busing (Kinder & Sears, 1981; Sears & Kinder, 1971; Sears & McConahay, 1973). Subjects indicated their agreement with each of the items on the 5-point rating scale that ranged from -2 (*disagree strongly*) to $+2$ (*agree strongly*). Subjects put the completed booklet into an unmarked envelope and dropped it into a large box containing several envelopes. Finally, subjects were debriefed and thanked for their participation. The Modern Racism Scale ranges from -14 (*low prejudice*) to $+14$ (*high prejudice*). The scale had good reliability (Cronbach's alpha $= .83$). Subjects were assigned to a high-prejudice ($N = 21$) or a low-prejudice ($N = 19$) group on the basis of a median split of scores on the scale.

Results and discussion The coding scheme, based primarily on the previous stereotype assessment literature, included traits such as lazy, poor, athletic, rhythmic, ostentatious, and so on. In addition, a category was included for themes related to hostility, violence, or aggressiveness. Although these terms have not been included in the traditional assessment literature, the assumption that Blacks are hostile or aggressive has guided much of the research on the effect of racial stereotypes on perception and behavior (Donnerstein & Donnerstein, 1972; Donnerstein, Donnerstein, Simon, & Ditrichs, 1972; Duncan, 1976; Sager & Schofield, 1980). Trait listings, however, do not completely capture the components of cultural stereotypes. For example, subjects also listed descriptive features (e.g., afro, brown eyes) and family characteristics (e.g., many children, single-parent homes). Coding categories for these components and a miscellaneous category for components listed that did not clearly fit into the existing categories were included. In all, there were 16 coding categories (see Table 1).

Two judges, blind to subjects' prejudice level, were provided with the coding instructions and the 40 protocols in different random orders. Each characteristic listed received one classification by each judge; the judges agreed on 88% of their classifications.

Table 1 shows coding categories and the proportion of high- and low-prejudice subjects who used the coding category in describing the stereotype. There are several noteworthy aspects of these data. First, the most striking aspect of these data is that the most common theme in subjects' protocols was that Blacks are aggressive, hostile, or criminal-like (see Table 1). All subjects listed either the aggressive or criminal categories and many listed both categories. This finding is important because, as was suggested earlier, much of the intergroup perception literature has

	TABLE 1	
Proportion of Thoughts Listed in Each of the Coding Categories as a Function of Prejudice Level		
Category	High prejudice	Low prejudice
Poor	.80	.75
Aggressive/tough	.60	.60
Criminal	.65	.80
Low intelligence	.50	.65
Uneducated	.50	.50
Lazy	.55	.75
Sexually perverse	.50	.70
Athletic	.75	.50
Rhythmic	.50	.40
Ostentatious	.50	.40
Inferior	.20	.30
Food preferences	.25	.35
Family characteristic	.25	.30
Dirty/smelly	.20	.30
Descriptive terms	.55	.50

Note.   None of these differences is significant.

been predicated on the assumption that Blacks are hostile and aggressive. Second, consistent with the stereotype assessment literature, the protocols were dominated by trait listings and were predominately negative. Third, there appeared to be few differences in the content reported by high- and low-prejudice subjects.

The prediction of no difference between the high- and low-prejudice subjects' knowledge of the cultural stereotype was tested in two different ways. First, none of the differences in Table 1 was statistically reliable. Second, two separate judges were given subjects' protocols and were instructed to read the content listed and to separate the protocols into high- and low-prejudice groups. The judges could not reliably predict the subjects' prejudice level from the content of their protocols. These data validate Ehrlich's (1973) assumption as well as the first assumption of the present model: High- and low-prejudice persons are indeed equally knowledgeable of the cultural stereotype.

Study 2: Automatic Priming, Prejudice Level, and Social Judgment

Study 1 showed that prejudice has little effect on direct reports of stereotype content. However, the free response task directly involved controlled processes. Subjects were explicitly instructed to be bias-free when making these reports. These data, then, are not necessarily informative regarding the implicit cognitive structures that are accessed during automatic processing. What is needed is a task in which the controlled processes do not provide an alternative explanation for the automatic processes. Thus, the goal of the Study 2 was to examine automatic stereotype priming effects for both high- and low-prejudice subjects.

Several studies have demonstrated that increasing the temporary accessibility of trait categories available in memory influences subsequent evaluations of a target person who performs ambiguous trait-relevant behaviors. These findings have been produced with conscious processing of the primes (Carver, Ganellin, Froming, & Chambers, 1983; Srull & Wyer, 1979, 1980) and with priming that is reported to be nonconscious (Bargh, Bond, Lombardi, & Tota, 1986; Bargh & Pietromonaco, 1982). That is, Bargh and Pietromonaco (1982) demonstrated that even when subjects were unaware of the content of the primes, priming increased the likelihood that the primed category was used to interpret subsequently presented ambiguous category-related information.

Nonconscious priming was of particular interest in this research because it is this type of processing that would allow the clearest dissociation of automatic and controlled processes involved in responses to members of a stereotyped group. Thus, the priming technique developed by Bargh and Pietromonaco (1982) was used in this study to automatically or passively prime the racial stereotype. Because the priming task activates the stereotype without conscious identification of the primes, the effects of stereotype activation can be studied independently of controlled stereotype-related processes. Specifically, interest centered on the effect of automatic racial stereotype activation on the interpretation of ambiguous stereotype-related behaviors performed by a race-unspecified target person.

In this study, evaluation of ambiguously hostile behaviors was examined because the assumption that Blacks are hostile is part of the racial stereotype (Brigham, 1971; Study 1) and because it has guided research in intergroup perception (Duncan, 1976; Sager & Schofield, 1980; Stephan, 1985). Because interest centered on the effects of activation of the stereotype on the ratings of a target person's hostility, no words directly related to hostility were used in the priming task. This study explicitly examined Duncan's (1976) hypothesis that the activation of the racial stereotype, which presumably activates a link between Blacks and hostility, explains why ambiguously aggressive behaviors were judged as being more aggressive when performed by a Black than a White actor.

According to the assumptions of the present model, priming will automatically activate the cultural stereotype for both those high and low in prejudice. Because hostility is part of the racial stereotype, increased priming should lead to more extreme ratings on the hostility-related scales for both high- and low-prejudice subjects.

Thus, following Bargh and Pietromonaco (1982), during an initial perceptual vigilance task, subjects were asked to identify the location of stimuli, which were actually words, presented rapidly in subjects' parafoveal visual field. These strategies were used to prevent subjects from consciously identifying the content of the primes. During the vigilance task either 20% or 80% of the words presented were related to the racial stereotype. Then, during an ostensibly unrelated impression-formation task, subjects read a paragraph describing a race-unspecified target person's ambiguously hostile behaviors and rated the target person on several trait scales. Half of the trait scales were related to hostility and thus allowed a test of the effect of stereotype activation on ratings of the target person's hostility. The remaining trait scales were not related to hostility and provided the opportunity to examine the possibility that stereotype activation led to a global negative evaluation that generalized beyond hostility ratings.

The data from this study could have important theoretical implications regarding the role of controlled processes and automatic processes involved in prejudice. However, the criteria required to establish automatic activation have been debated (see Holender, 1986, and Marcel, 1983b, for reviews). Greenwald, Klinger, and Liu (in press) recently suggested that automatic activation can be achieved through either *detectionless processing* or *attentionless processing*, both of which have been shown to produce reliable priming effects. Detectionless processing involves presenting stimuli below subjects' threshold level for reliable detection (Bolota, 1983; Fowler, Wolford, Slade, & Tassinary, 1981; Greenwald et al., in press; Marcel, 1983a). Attentionless processing involves processing stimuli that, although detectable, cannot be recalled or recognized (Klatzky, 1984).

In this study attentionless processing was accomplished by presenting the primes parafoveally (Bargh & Pietromonaco, 1982) followed immediately with a pattern mask. With phenomenal awareness of the semantic content of the primes as the criterion for conscious processing (Marcel, 1983a, 1983b), any effects of priming in this study without immediate conscious identification of the primes or recognition for them will be taken as evidence of attentionless automatic processing effects.

Method

Subjects and selection criteria.   Data were collected over two academic quarters. Introductory psychology students were pretested on the seven-item Modern Racism Scale embedded in a number of political, gender, and racial items. This was done to minimize the likelihood that subjects would identify the scale as a measure of prejudice. The experimenter told subjects that completion of the questionnaire was voluntary and that responses would be kept confidential. Subjects were also provided with a form concerning participation in subsequent experiments and provided their names and phone numbers if they were willing to be contacted for a second study for which they could earn extra credit.

Over the two quarters a total of 483 students filled out the Modern Racism Scale. Participants from the upper and lower third of the distribution of scores were identified as potential subjects ($N = 323$). When contacted by phone, potential subjects were asked about their vision, and only subjects with perfect vision or corrected perfect vision were considered eligible. High-prejudice subjects' scores on the Modern Racism Scale fell within the upper third of scores (between $+2$ and $+14$), and low-prejudice subjects' scores fell within the lower third of scores (between -9 and -14). The scale had good reliability (Cronbach's alpha = .81). From this sample of 323 subjects, 129 who agreed and had good vision participated in the experiment. After replacing 3 Black subjects, 1 subject who reported having dyslexia following the vigilance task, and 3 subjects who failed to follow instructions, the sample consisted of 78 White subjects in the judgment condition, 32 White subjects in the recognition condition, and 12 White subjects in the guess condition.

The experimenter remained blind to subjects' prejudice level, priming condition, and stimulus replication condition. Subjects were telephoned by one experimenter, who prepared the materials (with no treatment information) for the second experimenter, who conducted the experiment.

The method and procedure for this study were modeled after Bargh and Pietromonaco (1982). The only difference between their procedure and the one in this study was that in this study, stimuli were presented tachistoscopically rather than on a computer monitor. The experimental room contained a Scientific Prototype two-channel tachistoscope connected to an experimenter-controlled panel for presenting stimuli. Subjects placed their heads against the eyepiece such that the distance from subjects' eyes to the central fixation point was constant. The presentation of a stimulus activated a Hunter Model 120 Klockounter on which the interval between stimulus onset and the response was recorded to the nearest millisecond. Subjects indicated their responses by pushing one of two buttons (labeled *left* or *right*) on a response box. The experimenter recorded each response and its latency.

The stimuli were black and presented on a white background. Each stimulus was presented for 80 ms and was immediately followed by a mask (a jumbled series of letters). In addition, following Bargh and Pietromonaco (1982), the interstimulus interval was 2–7 s. The stimuli (words) were centered in each quadrant, with the center of each word being approximately 2.3 in. (0.06 m) from the central fixation point. The eye-to-dot distance was 31 in. (0.79 m) for the Scientific Prototype tachistoscope. As a result, to keep the stimulus within the parafoveal visual field (from 2° to 6° of visual angle), words could not be presented closer than 1.08 in. (0.03 m) or farther than 3.25 in. (0.08 m) from the fixation point. Twenty-five of the 100 trials within each replication were randomly assigned to each quadrant.

Stimulus materials.   Words that are labels for the social category *Blacks* (e.g., Blacks, Negroes, niggers) or are stereotypic associates (e.g., poor, lazy, athletic) were the priming stimuli. Twenty-four primes were used to generate two stimulus replications. Efforts were made to produce roughly equivalent content in the two replications. Replication 1 primes included the following: nigger, poor, afro, jazz, slavery, musical, Harlem, busing, minority, oppressed, athletic, and prejudice. Replication 2 primes included the following: Negroes, lazy, Blacks, blues, rhythm, Africa, stereotype, ghetto, welfare, basketball, unemployed, and plantation. Twelve neutral words (unrelated to the stereotype) were included in each replication. All neutral words were high-frequency words (Carrol, Davies, & Richman, 1971) and were matched in length to the stereotype-related words. Neutral words for Replication 1 included the following: number, considered, what, that, however, remember, example, called, said, animal, sentences, and important. Replication 2 neutral words included the following: water, then, would, about, things, completely, people, difference, television, experience, something, and thought. Ten additional neutral words were selected and used during practice trials.

Within each stimulus replication, the stereotype-related and neutral words were used to generate two separate 100-word lists. One list contained 80 stereotype-related words (the rest were neutral words) and the other contained 20 stereotype-related words (the rest were neutral words). The lists were organized into blocks of 20 words. In the 80% stereotype-priming condition, each block contained 16 stereotype-related words and 4 neutral words. Within each block, to make 16 stereotype-related words, 4 of the 12 stereotype-related words were randomly selected and presented twice.

For both stimulus replications, the words within each block were randomly ordered with the restriction that the first stereotype-related word was a label for the group (e.g., Negro or nigger). The positions of the minority items (stereotype-related words in the 20% priming list and neutral words in the 80% priming list) were the same for the 20% and 80% priming lists. Each of the 12 stereotype-related and the 12 control words appeared approximately the same number of times as the other stereotype-related and neutral words, respectively.

Judgment condition.   The experimenter told subjects that they would participate in two separate tasks. First, they were seated at the tachistoscope and then provided with a description of the vigilance task. The experimenter told subjects that the vigilance task involved identifying the location of stimuli presented for brief intervals. Subjects also learned that stimuli could appear in one of the four quadrants around the dot in the center of the screen. They were to identify as quickly and as accurately as possible whether the stimulus was presented to the left or the right of the central dot. Subjects indicated their responses by pressing the button labeled *left* or *right* on the response panel. The experimenter informed subjects that the timing and the location of the stimuli were unpredictable. Because both speed and accuracy were emphasized, subjects were encouraged to concentrate on the dot, as this strategy would facilitate detection performance. All subjects first completed 10 practice trials and then 100 experimental trials. Overall, the vigilance task took 11–13 min to complete.

Following the vigilance task, the second task was introduced. Subjects were told that the experimenter was interested in how people form impressions of others. They were asked to read a paragraph describing the events in the day of the person about whom they were to form an impression. This paragraph is the now familiar "Donald" paragraph developed by Srull and Wyer (1979, 1980; see also Bargh & Pietromonaco, 1982, and Carver et al., 1983). This 12-sentence paragraph portrays Donald engaging in a series of empirically established ambiguously hostile behaviors. For example, Donald demands his money back from a store clerk immediately after a purchase and refuses to pay his rent until his apartment is repainted.

After reading the paragraph, subjects were asked to make a series of evaluative judgments about Donald. Subjects rated Donald on each of 12 randomly ordered trait scales that ranged from 0 (*not at all*) to 10 (*extremely*). Six of the scales were descriptively related to hostility; 3 of these scales were evaluatively negative (hostile, dislikeable, and unfriendly) and 3 were evaluatively positive (thoughtful, kind, and considerate). The remaining 6 scales were not related to hostility; 3 of these scales were evaluatively negative (boring, narrow-minded, and conceited) and 3 were evaluatively positive (intelligent, dependable, and interesting).

After completing the rating scales, the experimenter questioned subjects about whether they believed that the vigilance task and the impression-formation task were related. No subject reported thinking the tasks were related or indicated any knowledge of why the vigilance task would have affected impression ratings. The experimenter then explained the nature of priming effects to the subjects. During this debriefing, however, the fact that subjects had been selected for participation on the basis of their Modern Racism Scale scores was not revealed. Subjects were then thanked for their participation.

Recognition test condition.   Up through completion of the vigilance task, recognition test subjects were treated exactly the same as the judgment subjects. Subjects in this condition were exposed to either the 80% or 20% priming lists of Replication 1 or Replication 2. Following the vigilance task, however, the experimenter explained that the stimuli were actually words and that subjects would be asked to try to recognize the words previously presented. The recognition test was distributed and subjects were instructed to check off the items that they believed had been presented. The experimenter told them that only half of the words on the list had been presented during the vigilance task.

The 48 items of this test consisted of the 24 words in Replication 1 (12 stereotype-related and 12 neutral words) and the 24 words in Replication 2 (12 stereotype-related and 12 neutral words). Words in Replication 2 served as distractors (words not presented) for Replication 1 targets (words actually presented), and Replication 1 words were used as distractors for Replication 2 targets during the recognition test. The recognition test items were randomly ordered.

Guess condition.   The experimenter told subjects in this condition that the words would be presented quickly in one of four locations around the central fixation point. Their task was to guess each word immediately following its presentation. The experimenter instructed subjects to maintain their gaze on the fixation point, as this was the best strategy for guessing words given their unpredictable location and timing. Subjects saw either the 80% list of Replication 1 or the 80% list of Replication 2. Subjects were to make a guess for each word presented, even making blind guesses if necessary, and were prompted to guess if they failed to do so spontaneously. This requirement was introduced to lower subjects' guessing criterion so as to provide a fair test of their immediate awareness of the stimuli (Bargh & Pietromonaco, 1982).

Results

Several checks on subjects' awareness of the content of primes were included in this study. Attentionless processing should allow detection but not immediate or delayed recognition of the stimuli.

Guess condition.   A check on immediate awareness.   Six high- and 6 low-prejudice subjects were run in this condition. Half of each group were presented with the 80% list of Replication 1 and half with the 80% list of Replication 2. If word content were truly not available to consciousness under the viewing conditions of this study, then subjects should not have been able to guess the content of the stereotype-related or neutral words. Subjects reported that this was a difficult task and that they had no idea of the content of the stimuli. Overall, they made few accurate guesses.

Of the 1,200 guesses, subjects guessed 20 words accurately, a hit rate of 1.67%. Overall, subjects guessed 1.4% of the stereotype-related words and 3.33% of the neutral words. Replicating Bargh and Pietromonaco (1982), the neutral word hit rate was appreciably higher than that for stereotype-related words. The neutral words were high-frequency words and thus would presumably be more easily detectable under the viewing conditions in this study.

Incorrect guesses were examined for their relatedness to the racial stereotype. Only three of the incorrect guesses could be interpreted as being related to the stereotype. Twice *Black* appeared as a guess, once from a high-prejudice subject and once from a low-prejudice subject. These data suggest that neither high- nor low-prejudice subjects were able to identify the content of the priming words at the point of encoding, thus satisfying one criterion for attentionless processing.

Recognition condition.   A check on memory for primes.   Although subjects could not guess the content of the words at the point of stimulus presentation, it is possible that a recognition test would provide a more sensitive test of subjects' awareness of the content primes. On the basis of their performance on the recognition test, subjects were assigned a hit (correct recognition of presented items) and a false alarm (incorrect recognition of new items) score for both stereotype-related and neutral words.

The hits and false alarms were used to generate d' scores for both stereotype-related and neutral words, which corresponded to subjects' ability to correctly identify previously presented information. Green and Swets (1966) have tabled d' scores for all possible combinations of hits and false alarms. The primary analysis concerned whether subjects performed the recognition task better than would be expected by chance. Over all subjects, neither d' for stereotype-related words ($M = .01$) nor for neutral words ($M = .07$) differed significantly from zero ($ps > .42$). These same comparisons were also done separately for high- and low-prejudice subjects. These analyses, like the overall analysis, suggest that subjects could not reliably recognize the primes. High-prejudice subjects' mean d' scores for stereotyped-related and neutral words were .02 and .12, respectively

($ps > .40$). Low-prejudice subjects' mean d' scores for stereotype-related and neutral words were .01 and .02, respectively ($ps > .84$).

In addition, the d' scores were submitted to a four-way mixed-model analysis of variance (ANOVA)—Prejudice Level × Priming × Replication × Word Type—with word type (stereotype-related vs. neutral) as a repeated measure.[1] Interest centered on whether (a) high- and low-prejudice subjects were differentially sensitive to stereotype-related and neutral words on the recognition test and (b) priming affected recognition performance. The analysis revealed that prejudice level did not affect subjects' overall performance, $F(1, 24) = 0.07$, $p = .78$, and that it did not interact with word type, $F(1, 24) = 0.04$, $p = .84$.

The second crucial test concerned whether increasing the number of primes interacted with recognition of the word type or subjects' prejudice level to affect performance on the recognition test. None of these tests was significant. Priming did not interact with word type, $F(1, 24) = 0.47$, $p = .50$, or affect the Prejudice × Word Type interaction, $F(1, 24) = 0.32$, $p < .56$. The analysis revealed no other significant main effects or interactions. Subjects were not able to reliably recognize either stereotype-related or neutral words, suggesting that subjects did not have conscious access to the content of the primes, thus establishing the second criterion for attentionless processing.

Automatic stereotype activation and hostility ratings.   The major issue concerned the effect of automatic stereotype activation on the interpretation of ambiguous stereotype-congruent (i.e., hostile) behaviors performed by a race-unspecified target person. Following Srull and Wyer (1979) and Bargh and Pietromonaco (1982), two subscores were computed for each subject. A hostility-related subscore was computed by taking the mean of the six traits denotatively related to hostility (hostile, dislikeable, unfriendly, kind, thoughtful, and considerate). The positively valenced scales (thoughtful, considerate, and kind) were reverse scored so that higher mean ratings indicated higher levels of hostility. Similarly, an overall hostility-unrelated subscore was computed by taking the mean of the six hostility-unrelated scales. Again, the positive scales were reverse scored.

The mean ratings were submitted to a mixed-model ANOVA, with prejudice level (high vs. low), priming (20% vs. 80%), and replication (1 vs. 2) as between-subjects variables and scale (hostility related vs. hostility unrelated) as a within-subjects variable. The analysis revealed that the Priming × Scale interaction was significant, $F(1, 70) = 5.04$, $p < .03$. Ratings on the hostility-related scales were more extreme in the 80% ($M = 7.52$) than in the 20% ($M = 6.87$) priming condition.[2] The hostility-unrelated scales, however, were unaffected by priming ($Ms = 5.89$ and 6.00 for the 20% and 80% priming conditions, respectively). Moreover, the three-way Prejudice Level × Priming × Scale interaction was not significant, $F(1, 70) = 1.19$, $p = .27$. These results were consistent with the present model and suggest that the effects of automatic stereotype priming were equally strong for high- and low-prejudice subjects. Activating the stereotype did not, however, produce a global negative evaluation of the stimulus person, as only trait scales related to the behaviors in the ambiguous passage were affected by priming.

These analyses suggest that the automatic activation of the racial stereotype affects the encoding and interpretation of ambiguously hostile behaviors for both high- and low-prejudice subjects. To examine this more closely, separate tests on the hostility-related and hostility-unrelated scales were conducted. If high- and low-prejudice subjects are equally affected by the priming manipulation, then prejudice level should not interact with priming in either analysis. The analysis on hostility-related scales revealed only a significant priming main effect, $F(1, 70) = 7.59, p < .008$. The Prejudice Level $\times$ Priming interaction was nonsignificant, $F(1, 70) = 1.19, p = .28$. None of the other main effects or interactions was significant. In the analysis of the hostility-unrelated scales, neither the priming main effect, $F(1, 70) = 0.23, p = .63$, nor the Prejudice Level $\times$ Priming interaction, $F(1, 70) = 0.02, p = .88$, reached significance.

Subjects' prejudice level did enter into several higher order interactions. The Prejudice Level $\times$ Priming $\times$ Replication interaction, $F(1, 70) = 4.69, p < .03$, indicated that the priming effect was slightly reversed for low-prejudice subjects exposed to Replication 1. A Prejudice Level $\times$ Scale Relatedness $\times$ Replication interaction, $F(1, 70) = 4.42, p < .04$, suggested that the difference between scores on hostility-related and hostility-unrelated scales was greater for low-prejudice subjects in Replication 1 and high-prejudice subjects in Replication 2.

Discussion

Study 2 examined the effects of prejudice and automatic stereotype priming on subjects' evaluations of ambiguous stereotype-related behaviors performed by a race-unspecified target person under conditions that precluded the possibility that controlled processes could explain the priming effect. The judgment data of this study suggest that when subjects' ability to consciously monitor stereotype activation is precluded, both high- and low-prejudice subjects produce stereotype-congruent or prejudice-like responses (i.e., stereotype-congruent evaluations of ambiguous behaviors).

These findings extend those of Srull and Wyer (1979, 1980), Bargh and Pietromonaco (1982), Bargh et al. (1986), and Carver et al. (1983) in demonstrating that in addition to trait categories, stereotypes can be primed and can affect the interpretation of subsequently encoded social information. Moreover, it appears that stereotypes can be primed automatically by using procedures that produce attentionless processing of primes (Bargh & Pietromonaco, 1982). The effects of stereotype priming on subjects' evaluation of the target person's hostility are especially interesting because no hostility-related traits were used as primes. The data are consistent with Duncan's (1976) hypothesis that priming the racial stereotype activates a link between Blacks and hostility. Unlike Duncan's research, however, stereotype activation was achieved through attentionless priming with stereotype-related words and not by the race of the target person.

In summary, the data from Studies 1 and 2 suggest that both those high and low in prejudice have cognitive structures (i.e., stereotypes) that can support prejudiced responses. These data, however, should not be interpreted as suggesting that all people are prejudiced. It could be argued that neither task allowed for the possibility of nonprejudiced responses. Study 1 encouraged subjects not to inhibit prejudiced responses. Study 2 suggested that when the racial category is activated and subjects' ability to consciously monitor this activation is bypassed, their responses reflect the activation of cognitive structures with a longer history (i.e., greater frequency) of activation. As previously indicated, it appears that these structures are the culturally defined stereotypes (Higgins & King, 1981), which are part of people's social heritage, rather than necessarily part of subjects' personal beliefs.

This analysis suggests that the effect of automatic stereotype activation may be an inappropriate criterion for prejudice because to use it as such equates knowledge of a stereotype with prejudice. People have knowledge of a lot of information they may not endorse. Feminists, for example, may be knowledgeable of the stereotype of women. Blacks and Jews may have knowledge of the Black or Jewish stereotype.[3] In none of these cases does knowledge of the stereotype imply acceptance of it (see also Bettleheim & Janowitz, 1964). In fact, members of these groups are likely to be motivated to reject the stereotype corresponding to their own group. In each of these cases, however, the stereotypes can likely be intentionally or automatically accessed from memory.

The present data suggest that when automatically accessed the stereotype may have effects that are inaccessible to the subject (Nisbett & Wilson, 1977). Thus, even for subjects who honestly report having no negative prejudices against Blacks, activation of stereotypes can have automatic effects that if not consciously monitored produce effects that resemble prejudiced responses. Study 3 examined the responses of high- and low-prejudice subjects to a task designed to focus attention on and thus activate subjects' personal beliefs about Blacks (in addition to the automatically activated stereotype).

Study 3: Controlled Processes and Prejudice Level

The present model suggests that one feature that differentiates low- from high-prejudice persons is the effort that they will put into stereotype-inhibition processes. When their nonprejudiced identity is threatened, low-prejudice persons are motivated to reaffirm their nonprejudiced self-concepts (Dutton, 1976; Dutton & Lake, 1973). Thus, when the conflict between their nonprejudiced personal beliefs and the stereotype of Blacks is made salient, low-prejudiced persons are likely to resolve the conflict by denouncing the stereotype and expressing their nonprejudiced beliefs. To express stereotype-congruent ideas would be inconsistent with and perhaps threaten their nonprejudiced identities.

Study 3 tested this hypothesis by asking high- and low-prejudice subjects to list their thoughts about the racial group *Blacks* under anonymous conditions. This type of task is likely to make the stereotype-personal belief conflict salient for low-prejudice subjects. The model suggests that under these conditions, high- and low-prejudice subjects will write different thoughts about Blacks. High-prejudice subjects, because their beliefs overlap with the stereotype, are expected to list stereotype-congruent thoughts. Low-prejudice subjects, it is argued, will take this opportunity to demonstrate that they do not endorse the cultural stereotype; they are likely to inhibit stereotype-congruent thoughts and intentionally replace them with thoughts consistent with their nonprejudiced personal beliefs. According to the model, resolution of the conflict between personal beliefs and the cultural stereotype in the form of nonprejudiced responses requires controlled inhibition (Logan & Cowan, 1984; Neely, 1977) of the automatically activated stereotype.

Method

Subjects.   Subjects were 67 White introductory psychology students who participated for course credit.[4] Subjects were run in groups of 3–6 and were seated at partitioned tables so that subjects were isolated from each other. These procedures were used to enhance anonymity so that subjects would not feel inhibited and would write whatever came to mind.

An additional precaution was taken to ensure anonymity. Before subjects were given instructions regarding the thought-listing task, their experimental participation cards were collected, signed, and left in a pile in the front of the room for subjects to pick up after the study. The experimenter asked subjects not to put any identifying information on their booklets. These procedures were followed so that it would be clear that subjects' names could not be associated with their booklets and that they would receive credit regardless of whether they completed the booklet. No subject refused to complete the measures.

Procedure.   After subjects' cards were signed the experimenter asked them to turn over and read the general instructions on the first page of the booklet. Subjects' first task was to list as many alternate labels as they were aware of for the social group *Black Americans.* They were told that the experimenter was interested in how people think about and talk informally about social groups. As such, the experimenter told them that slang or other unconventional group labels were acceptable. Subjects were allowed 1 min to complete this task. The purpose of this task was to encourage activation of subjects' cognitive representation of Blacks. If, for example, high- and low-prejudice persons refer to the social group with different labels (i.e., pejorative vs. nonpejorative) and the labels have different associates, this could provide a basis for explaining any potential differences in content between high- and low-prejudice subjects.

Following the label-generation task, subjects read the thought-listing instructions that asked them to list all of their thoughts in response to the social group *Black Americans* and to the alternate labels they generated. The experimenter told them that any and all of their thoughts (e.g., beliefs, feelings, expectations), flattering or unflattering, were acceptable. Subjects were encouraged to be honest and forthright. The experimenter provided them with two pages of 10 thought-listing boxes in which to record their thoughts and asked them to put only one thought in each box. They were allowed 10 min to complete the task. Finally, subjects completed the seven-item Modern Racism Scale and read through a debriefing document that described the goals of the research and thanked them for their participation.

Results

Coding scheme.   On the basis of a pilot study[5] a scheme for coding the types of thoughts generated was developed. Two judges, blind to subjects' prejudice level, were provided with the coding scheme instructions. A statement or set of statements listed in a box was considered one thought and was assigned one classification by each judge. Each judge rated the 67 protocols in different random orders. The judges agreed on 92% of their classifications. A third judge resolved discrepancies in scoring.

The major interest in this study was in whether the content of thoughts generated would differ as a function of prejudice level.[6] Before examining those data, however, the alternate labels subjects generated for Black Americans were examined. If high-prejudice subjects generate more negative labels (e.g., nigger, jigaboo, etc.) than low-prejudice subjects and pejorative labels are more strongly associated with stereotype-congruent information, this could explain possible differences between high- and low-prejudice subjects. Subjects were divided into high-prejudice ($N = 34$) and low-prejudice ($N = 33$) groups on the basis of a median split of scores on the Modern Racism Scale.

The proportion of pejorative and nonpejorative labels generated was calculated for each subject. Pejorative labels included terms such as the following: niggers, coons, spades, spear-chuckers, jungle bunnies, and jigs. Nonpejorative labels included the following: Blacks, Afro Americans, Brothers, and colored people. One high-prejudice subject was eliminated from this comparison because she failed to generate any alternate labels. The comparison indicated that the proportion of pejorative alternate labels did not differ between high-prejudice ($M = .53$) and low-prejudice ($M = .44$) subjects, $t(64) = .68, p > .10$. It appears, then, that high- and low-prejudice subjects were aware of the various pejorative labels.

Examination of the thought-listing protocols, however, revealed important differences between high- and low-prejudice subjects. The important differences appeared to be associated with the belief and trait categories.[7] Negative beliefs included thoughts such as "Blacks are free loaders"; "Blacks cause problems (e.g., mugging, fights)"; "Affirmative action sucks"; and so on. Positive-belief thoughts included "Blacks and Whites are equal"; "Affirmative action will restore historical inequities"; "My father says all Blacks are lazy, I think he is wrong" (e.g., negation of the cultural stereotype); "It's unfair to judge people by their color—they are individuals"; and so on. The positive and negative traits were typically listed as single words rather than being written in complete sentences. Negative traits included hostile, lazy, stupid, poor, dirty, and so on. The positive traits included musical, friendly, athletic, and so on.

The frequency of these positive-belief, negative-belief, and trait thoughts listed in subjects' protocols were submitted to a Prejudice Level (high vs. low) × Valence (positive vs. negative) × Thought Type (trait vs. belief) mixed-model ANOVA. Prejudice level was a between-subjects variable, and valence and thought type were within-subjects variables. The analysis revealed the expected Prejudice Level × Valence interaction, $F(1, 65) = 28.82, p < .0001$. High-prejudice subjects listed more negative ($M = 2.06$) than positive ($M = 1.48$) thoughts, and low-prejudice subjects listed more positive ($M = 2.28$) than negative ($M = 1.10$) thoughts. In addition, there was a Prejudice Level × Type interaction, $F(1, 65) = 18.04, p < .0001$. This interaction suggested that high-prejudice subjects were more likely to list trait ($M = 2.56$) than belief ($M = 1.52$) thoughts. In contrast, low-prejudice subjects were more likely to list belief ($M = 2.86$) than trait ($M = 1.12$) thoughts. These interactions are important because the Black stereotype traditionally has been largely negative and composed of traits (Brigham, 1971). Ascription of negative components of the stereotype was verified in these data only for high-prejudice subjects.

These two-way interactions were qualified, however, by a significant Prejudice Level × Valence × Thought Type interaction, $F(1, 65) = 4.88$, $p < .03$. High-prejudice subjects most often listed negative traits ($M = 3.32$). A post hoc Duncan test ($p = .05$) revealed that for high-prejudice subjects, the frequency of negative trait thoughts differed significantly from each of the other three thought types but that the frequency of positive-belief ($M = 1.17$), negative-belief ($M = 1.18$), and positive trait ($M = 1.79$) thoughts did not differ from each other. In contrast, low-prejudice subjects most frequently listed positive-belief thoughts ($M = 4.52$). This mean differed significantly (Duncan test, $p = .05$) from the negative-belief ($M = 1.21$), positive trait ($M = 1.24$), and negative trait ($M = 1.00$) means, but the latter three means did not differ from each other.

It was argued earlier that this type of task would encourage subjects to intentionally access and report thoughts consistent with their personal beliefs. Trait ascriptions are part of high-prejudice, but not low-prejudice, subjects' beliefs according to the present model. It appears that in this task, both high- and low-prejudice subjects' thoughts reflected their beliefs. High-prejudice subjects reported primarily traits and low-prejudice subjects reported beliefs that contradicted the cultural stereotype and emphasized equality between the races.

To follow up implications from the previous studies, subjects' protocols were examined to determine whether the themes of hostility, aggressiveness, or violence were present. Statements such as "They are hostile," "Blacks are violent," "Blacks are aggressive," and so on were considered to reflect this theme. Non-trait-based thoughts such as "They rape women" or "I'm scared of them" were less frequent but were also considered to reflect the general theme. Sixty percent of the high-prejudice subjects directly included such themes in their thought-listing protocols. In contrast, only 9% of the subjects scoring low in prejudice included hostility themes in their protocols. A z test on proportions indicated that this difference was reliable ($z = 4.41, p < .01$).

Discussion

Taken together, these sets of analyses indicate that high- and low-prejudice subjects were willing to report different thoughts about Blacks. In addition, these analyses suggested that there were sufficient levels of variability in prejudice levels among the subjects to detect the effects of prejudice in the previous studies should those effects exist. The thought-listing task was one in which subjects were likely to think carefully about what their responses implied about their prejudice-relevant self-concepts. For those who valued a nonprejudiced identity, writing stereotype-congruent thoughts would have been inconsistent with and perhaps would have threatened their nonprejudiced identity.

Thus, even under anonymous conditions, low-prejudice subjects apparently censored and inhibited (Neely, 1977) the automatically activated negative stereotype-congruent information and consciously replaced it with thoughts that expressed their nonprejudiced values. Low-prejudice subjects wrote few pejorative thoughts. Their thoughts were more likely to have reflected the importance of equality or the negation of the cultural stereotype. Moreover, low-prejudice subjects appeared reluctant to ascribe traits to the group as a whole. In contrast, the protocols of high-prejudice subjects seemed much more consistent with the cultural stereotype of Blacks. Their thoughts were primarily negative, and they seemed willing to ascribe traits to the group (especially negative traits).

A most important comparison for the present three studies, and for the intergroup perception literature more generally, concerns the likelihood of subjects reporting thoughts reflecting the theme of hostility. Much of the intergroup perception literature has assumed that the hostility component of the stereotype influences perceptions of Blacks (Donnerstein et al., 1972; Duncan, 1976; Sager & Schofield, 1980), and Studies 1 and 2 suggested that hostility is strongly associated with Blacks for both high- and low-prejudice subjects. Study 2 in particular suggested that hostility is automatically activated when the category label and associates are presented. The present data, however, suggest that high- and low-prejudice subjects differ in their willingness to attribute this characteristic to the entire group. High-prejudice subjects included thoughts suggesting that Blacks are hostile and aggressive much more frequently than did low-prejudice subjects. The present framework suggests that this difference likely reflects low-prejudice subjects engaging in controlled, stereotype-inhibiting processes. Low-prejudice subjects apparently censored negative, what they considered inappropriate, thoughts that came to mind.

General Discussion

The model examined in these studies makes a clear distinction between knowledge of the racial stereotype, which Study 1 suggested both high- and low-prejudice persons possess, and personal beliefs about the stereotyped group. Study 2 suggested that automatic stereotype activation is equally strong and equally inescapable for high- and low-prejudice subjects. In the absence of controlled stereotype-related processes, automatic stereotype activation leads to stereotype-congruent or prejudice-like responses for both those high and low in prejudice. Study 3, however, provided evidence that controlled processes can inhibit the effects of automatic processing when the implications of such processing compete with goals to establish or maintain a nonprejudiced identity.

The present model suggests that a change in one's beliefs or attitude toward a stereotyped group may or may not be reflected in a change in the corresponding evaluations of or behaviors toward members of that group. Consider the following quote by Pettigrew (1987):

> Many southerners have confessed to me, for instance, that even though in their minds they no longer feel prejudice toward blacks, they still feel squeamish when they shake hands with a black. These feelings are left over from what they learned in their families as children. (p. 20)

It would appear that the automatically activated stereotype-congruent or prejudice-like responses have become independent of one's current attitudes or beliefs. Crosby, Bromley, and Saxe (1980) argued that the inconsistency sometimes observed between expressed attitudes and behaviors that are less consciously mediated is evidence that (all) White Americans are prejudiced against Blacks and that nonprejudiced responses are attempts at impression management (i.e., efforts to cover up truly believed but socially undesirable attitudes). (See also Baxter, 1973; Gaertner, 1976; Gaertner & Dovidio, 1977; Linn, 1965; Weitz, 1972.) Crosby et al. argued that nonconsciously monitored responses are more trustworthy than are consciously mediated responses.

In the context of the present model in which automatic processes and controlled processes can be dissociated, I disagree fundamentally with this premise. Such an argument denies the possibility for change in one's attitudes and beliefs, and I view this as a severe limitation of the Crosby et al. (1980) analysis. Crosby and her colleagues seem to identify the flexibility of controlled processes as a limitation. In contrast, the present framework considers such processes as the key to escaping prejudice. This statement does not imply that change is likely to be easy or speedy (and it is certainly not all or nothing). Nonprejudiced responses are, according to the dissociation model, a function of intentional, controlled processes and require a conscious decision to behave in a nonprejudiced fashion. In addition, new responses must be learned and well practiced before they can serve as competitive responses to the automatically activated stereotype-congruent responses. What is needed now is a fully articulated model of controlled processes that delineates the cognitive mechanisms involved in inhibition. Logan and Cowan (1984; see also Bargh, 1984) have developed a model of controlled processes that may provide valuable insights into the inhibition process.

Thus, in contrast to the pessimistic analysis by Crosby et al. (1980), the present framework suggests that rather than all people being prejudiced, all are victims of being limited capacity processors. Perceivers cannot attend to all aspects of a situation or their behavior. In situations in which controlled processes are precluded or interfered with, automatic processing effects may exert the greatest influence on responses. In the context of racial stereotypes and attitudes, automatic processing effects appear to have negative implications.

Inhibiting stereotype-congruent or prejudice-like responses and intentionally replacing them with nonprejudiced responses can be likened to the breaking of a bad habit. That is, automatic stereotype activation functions in much the same way as a bad habit. Its consequences are spontaneous and undesirable, at least for the low-prejudice person. For those who have integrated egalitarian ideals into their value system, a conflict would exist between these ideals and expressions of racial prejudice. The conflict experienced is likely to be involved in the initiation of controlled stereotype-inhibiting processes that are required to eliminate the habitual response (activation). Ronis, Yates, and Kirscht (in press) argued that elimination of a bad habit requires essentially the same steps as the formation of a habit. The individual must (a) initially decide to stop the old behavior, (b) remember the resolution, and (c) try repeatedly and decide repeatedly to eliminate the habit before the habit can be eliminated. In addition, the individual must develop a new cognitive (attitudinal and belief) structure that is consistent with the newly determined pattern of responses.

An important assumption to keep in mind in the change process, however, is that neither the formation of an attitude from beliefs nor the formation of a decision from attitudes or beliefs entails the elimination of earlier established attitudinal or stereotype representations. The dissociation model holds that although low-prejudiced persons have changed their beliefs concerning stereotyped group members, the stereotype has not been eliminated from the memory system. In fact, it remains a well-organized, frequently activated knowledge structure. During the change process the new pattern of ideas and behaviors must be consciously activated and serve as the basis for responses or the individual is likely to fall into old habits (e.g., stereotype-congruent or prejudice-like responses).

The model suggests that the change process involves developing associations between the stereotype structure and the personal belief structure. For change to be successful, each time the stereotype is activated the person must activate and think about his or her personal beliefs. That is, the individual must increase the frequency with which the personal belief structure is activated when responding to members of the stereotyped group. To the extent that the personal belief structure becomes increasingly accessible, it will better provide a rival response to the responses that would likely follow from automatic stereotype activation. In cognitive terms, before the newer beliefs and attitudes can serve as a rival, the strong association between the previously learned negative attitude and Blacks will have to be weakened and the association of Blacks to the new nonprejudiced attitudes and beliefs will have to be made stronger and conscious.

In summary, at minimum, the attitude and belief change process requires intention, attention, and time. During the change process an individual must not only inhibit automatically activated information but also intentionally replace such activation with nonprejudiced ideas and responses. It is likely that these variables contribute to the difficulty of changing one's responses to members of stereotyped groups. In addition, these variables probably contribute to the often observed inconsistency between expressed attitudes and behavior. The nonprejudiced responses take time, attention, and effort. To the extent that any (or all) of these are limited, the outcome is likely to be stereotype-congruent or prejudice-like responses.

In conclusion, it is argued that prejudice need not be the consequence of ordinary thought processes. Although stereotypes still exist and can influence the responses of both high- and low-prejudice subjects, particularly when those responses are not subject to close conscious scrutiny, there are individuals who actively reject the negative stereotype and make efforts to respond in nonprejudiced ways. At least in situations involving consciously controlled stereotype-related processes, those who score low in prejudice on an attitude scale are attempting to inhibit stereotypic responses (e.g., Study 3, Greeley & Sheatsley, 1971; Taylor et al., 1978; see also Higgins & King, 1981). The present framework, because of its emphasis on the possible dissociation of automatic and controlled processes, *allows for the possibility* that those who report being nonprejudiced are in reality low in prejudice.

This analysis is not meant to imply that prejudice has disappeared or to give people an excuse for their prejudices. In addition, it does not imply that only low-prejudice persons are capable of controlled stereotype inhibition. High-prejudice persons could also consciously censor their responses to present a non-prejudiced identity (probably for different reasons than low-prejudice persons, however). What this analysis requires is that theoreticians be more precise on the criteria established for labeling behavior as prejudiced or nonprejudiced. The present model and set of empirical studies certainly does not resolve this issue. However, the present framework highlights the potential for nonprejudiced behaviors when social desirability concerns are minimal (Study 3) and invites researchers to explore the variables that are likely to engage controlled stereotype-inhibiting processes in intergroup settings. At present, it seems productive to entertain and systematically explore the possibility that being low in prejudice reflects more than impression-management efforts and to explore the conditions under which controlled stereotype-inhibition processes are engaged.

Notes

1. The overall hit and false alarm rates for stereotype-related and neutral words were also examined as a function of prejudice level, priming, and replication. These data were submitted to a five-way mixed-model analysis of variance. Prejudice level, priming, and replication were between-subjects variables; word type (stereotype-related vs. neutral) and response type (hits vs. false alarms) were within-subject variables. This analysis, like the d' analysis, revealed no significant main effects or interactions.

2. The primary analysis was repeated for high- and low-prejudice subjects separately. The two-way Priming × Scale Related interaction was obtained for both high- and low-prejudice subjects (both $ps < .05$), thus supporting the primary analysis.

3. Data from 4 Black subjects who participated in Study 1, but who were not included in the analyses, suggest that Blacks are at least knowledgeable of the cultural stereotype. That is, there was considerable overlap between the content reported by the Black and White subjects. Two independent raters could not reliably predict the race of subjects from the protocols. In addition, Sager and Schofield (1980) found that Black and White children interpreted the same ambiguously hostile behaviors as being more aggressive or hostile when performed by a Black than a White actor. Sager and Schofield argued that subjects were making stereotype-congruent judgments of the Black actor.

4. Four Black students signed up to participate. These students did not fill out the thought-listing or Modern Racism measure but were given credit for showing up to participate. The nature of the study was described to them, and they were told why interest centered on the responses of White subjects.

5. The coding scheme was developed and pretested in a pilot study, the goal of which was to demonstrate that subjects' cognitive representations of social groups are richer and more complex than simple trait-based structures. The coding scheme was developed on the basis of considerations of the stereotype assessment, prejudice, attitude, and cognitive organization literature. The stereotype literature, for example, led to an examination of the types of traits (i.e., positive or negative) listed in response to the category label. The prejudice and attitude measurement literature, however, led to examination of whether positive (e.g., statements of equality, recognition of Blacks' plight historically, etc.) or negative (resentment of affirmative action, avoid interactions with Blacks) belief thoughts would be elicited by the label.

The cognitive organization literature (Collins & Quillian, 1969; Rips, Shoben, & Smith, 1973) suggested that both criterial (e.g., physical descriptors) as well as noncriterial (e.g., associated terms) should be examined. On the basis of Rosch's (1978) categorization model, the coding scheme included a category for basic (e.g., athletes) and subordinate (e.g., Richard Pryor) level exemplars of the social category. Superordinate labels were not included because subjects had been asked to generate alternate labels prior to the thought-listing task. Strong support for the coding scheme was found in the pilot study. The pilot study did not examine the complexity of thought listings as a function of subjects' prejudice level. That was the goal of this study.

6. As a prerequisite to examining the content of the protocols, an analysis on the number of thoughts and the number of alternate labels generated by high- and low-prejudice subjects was performed to examine whether prejudice level affected these tasks. Although it was expected that subjects would generate more thoughts than alternate labels, the key tests of interest were provided by the prejudice-level main effect (whether one group listed more items than the other) and the Prejudice Level × Task interaction (whether prejudice level differentially affected the tasks). These data were submitted to a Prejudice Level (high vs. low) × Task (label generation vs. thought generation) mixed-model analysis of variance. The analysis revealed that subjects generated a greater number of thoughts ($M = 12.67$) than labels ($M = 4.72$), $F(1, 65) = 156.83$, $p < .0001$. However, neither the prejudice main effect, $F(1, 65) = 0.66$, $p < .42$, nor the Prejudice Level × Task interaction, $F(1, 65) = 0.01$, $p < .94$, was significant.

7. A canonical discriminant function analysis in which subjects' prejudice level was predicted as a function of the best linear combination of the 10 coding categories revealed a single canonical variable (Wilks's lambda $= 0.63$), $F(10, 56) = 3.25$, $p < .002$. The canonical squared multiple correlation was 0.37. Positive-belief thoughts were located at one extreme of the canonical structure (-0.88) and negative trait thoughts at the other (0.78). None of the other categories discriminated significantly between high- and low-prejudice groups.

References

Allport, G. W. (1954). *The nature of prejudice*. Reading, MA: Addison-Wesley.

Ashmore, R. D., & Del Boca, F. K. (1981). Conceptual approaches to stereotypes and stereotyping. In D. L. Hamilton (Ed.), *Cognitive processes in stereotyping and intergroup behavior* (pp. 1–35). Hillsdale, NJ: Erlbaum.

Bargh, J. A. (1984). Automatic and conscious processing of social information. In R. S. Wyer Jr., & T. K. Srull (Eds.), *The handbook of social cognition* (Vol. 3, pp. 1–43). Hillsdale, NJ: Erlbaum.

Bargh, J. A., Bond, R. N., Lombardi, W. J., & Tota, M. E. (1986). The additive nature of chronic and temporary sources of construct accessibility. *Journal of Personality and Social Psychology, 50,* 869–878.

Bargh, J. A., & Pietromonaco, P. (1982). Automatic information processing and social perception: The influence of trait information presented outside of conscious awareness on impression formation. *Journal of Personality and Social Psychology, 43,* 437–449.

Baxter, G. W. (1973). Prejudiced liberals? Race and information effects in a two person game. *Journal of Conflict Resolution, 17,* 131–161.

Bettleheim, B., & Janowitz, M. (1964). *Social change and prejudice.* New York: Free Press of Glencoe.

Bolota, D. A. (1983). Automatic semantic activation and episodic memory encoding. *Journal of Verbal Learning and Verbal Behavior, 22,* 88–104.

Billig, M. (1985). Prejudice, categorization, and particularization: From a perceptual to a rhetorical approach. *European Journal of Social Psychology, 15,* 79–103.

Brigham, J. C. (1971). Ethnic stereotypes. *Psychological Bulletin, 76,* 15–33.

Brigham, J. C. (1972). Racial stereotypes: Measurement variables and the stereotype-attitude relationship. *Journal of Applied Social Psychology, 2,* 63–76.

Carrol, J. B., Davies, P., & Richman, B. (1971). *The American Heritage word frequency book.* New York: Houghton Mifflin.

Carver, C. S., Ganellin, R. J., Froming, W. J., & Chambers, W. (1983). Modeling: An analysis in terms of category accessibility. *Journal of Experimental Social Psychology, 19,* 403–421.

Collins, A. M., & Quillian, M. R. (1969). Retrieval time from semantic memory. *Journal of Verbal Learning and Verbal Behavior, 8,* 240–247.

Crosby, F., Bromley, S., & Saxe, L. (1980). Recent unobtrusive studies of black and white discrimination and prejudice: A literature review. *Psychological Bulletin, 87,* 546–563.

Devine, P. G. (1988). *Stereotype assessment: Theoretical and methodological issues.* Unpublished manuscript, University of Wisconsin—Madison.

Donnerstein, E., & Donnerstein, M. (1972). White rewarding behavior as a function of the potential for black retaliation. *Journal of Personality and Social Psychology, 24,* 327–333.

Donnerstein, E., Donnerstein, M., Simon, S., & Ditrichs, R. (1972). Variables in interracial aggression: Anonymity, expected retaliation, and a riot. *Journal of Personality and Social Psychology, 22,* 236–245.

Dovidio, J. F., Evans, N. E., & Tyler, R. B. (1986). Racial stereotypes: The contents of their cognitive representations. *Journal of Experimental Social Psychology, 22,* 22–37.

Duncan, B. L. (1976). Differential social perception and attribution of intergroup violence: Testing the lower limits of stereotyping of blacks. *Journal of Personality and Social Psychology, 34,* 590–598.

Dutton, D. G. (1976). Tokenism, reverse discrimination, and egalitarianism in interracial behavior. *Journal of Social Issues, 32,* 93–107.

Dutton, D. G., & Lake, R. A. (1973). Threat of own prejudice and reverse discrimination in interracial situations. *Journal of Personality and Social Psychology, 28,* 94–100.

Ehrlich, H. J. (1973). *The social psychology of prejudice.* New York: Wiley.

Fowler, C. A., Wolford, G., Slade, R., & Tassinary, L. (1981). Lexical access with and without awareness. *Journal of Experimental Psychology: General, 110,* 341–362.

Gaertner, S. L. (1976). Nonreactive measures in racial attitude research: A focus on "liberals." In P. A. Katz (Ed.), *Towards the elimination of racism* (pp. 183–211). New York: Pergamon Press.

Gaertner, S. L., & Dovidio, J. F. (1977). The subtlety of white racism, arousal, and helping. *Journal of Personality and Social Psychology, 35,* 691–707.

Gaertner, S. L., & McLaughlin, J. P. (1983). Racial stereotypes: Associations and ascriptions of positive and negative characteristics. *Social Psychology Quarterly, 46,* 23–30.

Gilbert, G. M. (1951). Stereotype persistence and change among college students. *Journal of Abnormal and Social Psychology, 46,* 245–254.

Greeley, A., & Sheatsley, P. (1971). Attitudes toward racial integration. *Scientific American, 222,* 13–19.

Green, D. M., & Swets, J. A. (1966). *Signal detection theory and psycho-physics,* New York: Wiley.

Greenwald, A. G., Klinger, M., & Liu, T. J. (in press). Unconscious processing of word meaning. *Memory & Cognition.*

Hamilton, D. L. (1981). Stereotyping and intergroup behavior: Some thoughts on the cognitive approach. In D. L. Hamilton (Ed.), *Cognitive processes in stereotyping and intergroup behavior* (pp. 333–353). Hillsdale, NJ: Erlbaum.

Harding, J., Proshansky, H., Kutner, B., & Chein, I. (1969). Prejudice and ethnic relations. In G. Lindzey (Ed.), *Handbook of social psychology* (Vol. 5). Reading, MA: Addison-Wesley.

Higgins, E. T., & King, G. (1981). Accessibility of social constructs: Information-processing consequences of individual and contextual variability. In N. Cantor & J. F. Kihlstrom (Eds.), *Personality and social interaction* (pp. 69–121). Hillsdale, NJ: Erlbaum.

Holender, D. (1986). Semantic activation without conscious identification in dichotic listening, parafoveal vision, and visual masking: A survey and appraisal. *Behavioral and Brain Sciences, 9,* 1–66.

Karlins, M., Coffman, T. L., & Walters, G. (1969). On the fading of social stereotypes: Studies in three generations of college students. *Journal of Personality and Social Psychology, 13,* 1–16.

Katz, D., & Braly, K. (1933). Racial stereotypes in one hundred college students. *Journal of Abnormal and Social Psychology, 28,* 280–290.

Katz, P. A. (1976). The acquisition of racial attitudes in children. In P. A. Katz (Ed.), *Towards the elimination of racism* (pp. 125–154). New York: Pergamon Press.

Kinder, D. R., & Sears, D. O. (1981). Prejudice and politics: Symbolic racism versus racial threats to the good life. *Journal of Personality and Social Psychology, 40*, 414–431.

Klatzky, R. L. (1984). *Memory and awareness.* San Francisco: Freeman.

LaViolette, F., & Silvert, K. H. (1951). A theory of stereotypes. *Social Forces, 29*, 237–257.

Linn, L. S. (1965). Verbal attitudes and overt behavior: A study of racial discrimination. *Social Forces, 43*, 353–364.

Logan, G. D. (1980). Attention and automaticity in Stroop and priming tasks: Theory and data. *Cognitive Psychology, 12*, 523–553.

Logan, G. D., & Cowan, W. G. (1984). On the ability to inhibit thought and action: A theory of act control. *Psychological Review, 91*, 295–327.

Marcel, A. J. (1983a). Conscious and unconscious perception: Experiments on visual masking and word recognition. *Cognitive Psychology, 15*, 197–237.

Marcel, A. J. (1983b). Conscious and unconscious perception: An approach to the relations between phenomenal experience and perceptual processes. *Cognitive Psychology, 15*, 238–300.

McConahay, J. B., Hardee, B. B., & Batts, V. (1981). Has racism declined? It depends upon who's asking and what is asked. *Journal of Conflict Resolution, 25*, 563–579.

Neely, J. H. (1977). Semantic priming and retrieval from lexical memory: Roles of inhibitionless spreading activation and limited-capacity attention. *Journal of Experimental Psychology, 106*, 226–254.

Nisbett, R. E., & Wilson, T. D. (1977). Telling more than we can know: Verbal reports on mental processes. *Psychological Review, 84*, 231–259.

Pettigrew, T. (1987, May 12). "Useful" modes of thought contribute to prejudice. *New York Times*, pp. 17, 20.

Porter, J. D. R. (1971). *Black child, white child: The development of racial attitudes.* Cambridge, MA: Harvard University Press.

Posner, M. I., & Snyder, C. R. R. (1975). Attention and cognitive control. In R. L. Solso (Ed.), *Information processing and cognition: The Loyola Symposium.* Hillsdale, NJ: Erlbaum.

Pratkanis, A. R. (in press). The cognitive representation of attitudes. In A. R. Pratkanis, S. J. Breckler, & A. G. Greenwald (Eds.), *Attitude structure and function.* Hillsdale, NJ: Erlbaum.

Proshansky, H. M. (1966). The development of intergroup attitudes. In L. W. Hoffman & M. L. Hoffman (Eds.), *Review of child development research* (Vol. 2, pp. 311–371). New York: Russell Sage Foundation.

Rips, L. J., Shoben, E. J., & Smith, E. E. (1973). Semantic distance and the verification of semantic relations. *Journal of Verbal Learning and Verbal Behavior, 12*, 1–20.

Ronis, D. L., Yates, J. F., & Kirscht, J. P. (in press). Attitudes, decisions, and habits as determinants of repeated behavior. In A. R. Pratkanis, S. J. Breckler, & A. G. Greenwald (Eds.), *Attitude structure and function.* Hillsdale, NJ: Erlbaum.

Rosch, E. (1978). Principles of categorization. In E. Rosch and B. B. Lloyd (Eds.), *Cognition and categorization* (pp. 28–48). Hillsdale, NJ: Erlbaum.

Saenger, G. (1953). *The social psychology of prejudice.* New York: Harper.

Sager, H. A., & Schofield, J. W. (1980). Racial and behavioral cues in black and white children's perceptions of ambiguously aggressive acts. *Journal of Personality and Social Psychology, 39,* 590–598.

Schneider, W., & Shiffrin, R. M. (1977). Controlled and automatic human information processing: I. Detection, search, and attention. *Psychological Review, 84,* 1–66.

Sears, D. O., & Kinder, D. R. (1971). Racial tensions and voting in Los Angeles. In W. Z. Hirsch (Ed.), *Los Angeles: Viability and prospects for metropolitan leadership* (pp. 51–88). New York: Praeger.

Sears, D. O., & McConahay, J. B. (1973). *The politics of violence: The new urban blacks and the Watts riot.* Boston: Houghton Mifflin.

Secord, P. F., & Backman, C. W. (1974). *Social psychology.* New York: McGraw-Hill.

Shiffrin, R. M., & Dumais, S. T. (1981). The development of automatism. In J. R. Anderson (Ed.), *Cognitive skills and their acquisition* (pp. 111–140). Hillsdale, NJ: Erlbaum.

Shiffrin, R. M., & Schneider, W. (1977). Controlled and automatic human information processing: II. Perceptual learning, automatic attending, and a general theory. *Psychological Review, 84,* 127–190.

Simpson, G. E., & Yinger, J. M. (1965). *Racial and cultural minorities* (rev. ed.) New York: Harper & Row.

Smith, E. R. (1984). Model of social inference processes. *Psychological Review, 91,* 392–413.

Smith, E. R., & Branscombe, N. R. (1985). *Stereotype traits can be processed automatically.* Unpublished manuscript, Purdue University, West Lafayette, IN.

Srull, T. K., & Wyer, R. S., Jr. (1979). The role of category accessibility in the interpretation of information about persons: Some determinants and implications. *Journal of Personality and Social Psychology, 37,* 1660–1672.

Srull, T. K., & Wyer, R. S., Jr. (1980). Category accessibility and social perception: Some implications for the study of person memory and interpersonal judgments. *Journal of Personality and Social Psychology, 38,* 841–856.

Stephan, W. G. (1985). Intergroup relations. In G. Lindzey & E. Aronson (Eds.), *The handbook of social psychology* (3rd ed., Vol. 2, pp. 559–658). Hillsdale, NJ: Erlbaum.

Tajfel, H. (1981). *Human groups and social categories: Studies in social psychology.* Cambridge, England: Cambridge University Press.

Taylor, D. G., Sheatsley, P. B., & Greeley, A. M. (1978). Attitudes toward racial integration. *Scientific American, 238,* 42–49.

Weitz, S. (1972). Attitude, voice, and behavior: A repressed affect model of interracial interaction. *Journal of Personality and Social Psychology, 24,* 14–21.

Wyer, R. S., Jr., & Srull, T. K. (1981). Category accessibility: Some theoretical and empirical issues concerning the processing of social stimulus information. In E. T. Higgins, C. P. Herman, & M. P. Zanna (Eds.), *Social cognition: The Ontario Symposium* (Vol. 1, pp. 161–197). Hillsdale, NJ: Erlbaum.

Questions for Review and Discussion

1. According to Devine, how do low- and high-prejudice people differ in (a) their cultural stereotypes and (b) their personal beliefs?
2. What does nonconscious priming involve?
3. According to Devine, is it more appropriate to define low-prejudice individuals as not having stereotype-related thoughts or as inhibiting them once they arise?

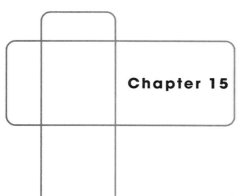

Chapter 15

Relations among the Implicit Association Test, Discriminatory Behavior, and Explicit Measures of Racial Attitudes

Allen R. McConnell and Jill M. Leibold

Since LaPiere's (1934) classic demonstration of attitude–behavior inconsistency toward a Chinese couple traveling across the United States, social psychologists have invested a great deal of energy into developing techniques to assess group attitudes in ways that circumvent problems resulting from limited introspective access, experimenter effects, and social desirability concerns. Recently, researchers have employed various social cognition approaches to assess prejudice that minimize the problems involved with explicit reports of attitudes (e.g., Devine, 1989; Dovidio, Kawakami, Johnson, Johnson, & Howard, 1997; Fazio, Jackson, Dunton, & Williams, 1995; Greenwald, McGhee, & Schwartz, 1998; Wittenbrink, Judd, & Park, 1997). The current work focuses on the most recent of these techniques, the Implicit Association Test (IAT), to examine the extent to which it relates to intergroup behavior and to explicit measures of racial attitudes.

The IAT has become a widely used instrument to measure attitudes in general, and prejudices toward groups in particular. It assesses attitudes by having

Reprinted from *Journal of Experimental Social Psychology*, Vol. 37, pp. 435–422, © 2001, with permission from Elsevier.

people quickly categorize stimulus words using two response keys. In racial IAT studies, the stimulus words are names that are racially stereotyped (e.g., Jamal and Sue Ellen) or adjectives that have evaluative connotations (e.g., wonderful and disgusting). In critical trial blocks, participants categorize these words using two keys, each of which has two response options mapped to it. Typically, White participants categorize the words more quickly when "Black or undesirable" is mapped onto one key response and "White or desirable" is mapped onto the other key response than when the opposite set of key mappings (i.e., "Black or desirable" and "White or undesirable") are used (Greenwald et al., 1998). The difference in the average response latency between these two sets of key mappings is known as the IAT effect. Presumably, larger IAT effects reflect stronger associations in memory between the concept pairings (i.e., those responses that shared the same response key) that facilitated judgment.

Social psychologists who study group prejudice have been drawn to the IAT because of its large effect size (Greenwald et al., 1998; Nosek, Banaji, & Greenwald, 2000) and because even people who know that the IAT assesses group prejudice still reliably produce the IAT effect, indicating its robustness and apparent imperviousness. As a result, the IAT appears to circumvent many of the problems of traditional, explicit measures of prejudice. Researcher enthusiasm and large effect sizes notwithstanding, the IAT effect has not been demonstrated to be related to behavior toward group members. Although strong between-group differences have revealed favoritism for religious, ethnic, age-related, and racial ingroups (Greenwald et al., 1998; Rudman, Greenwald, Mellott, & Schwartz, 1999), meaningful variability in the strength of the IAT effect has not been shown to be related to one's discriminatory behavior.

Other implicit measures of prejudice, for example, have been shown to relate to intergroup behavior (Dovidio et al., 1997; Fazio et al., 1995). Indeed, the current research married the methodologies of this previous research to examine whether the IAT predicts intergroup discrimination. Thus, the primary goal of the current study was to explore whether this relation exists, which would help substantiate the predictive utility of the IAT.

In addition, the current work also examined whether the IAT relates to explicit measures of prejudice. It has been argued that implicit and explicit measures of attitudes tap into different knowledge and thus should be unrelated (Greenwald & Banaji, 1995; Greenwald et al., 1998), whereas others have found relations between the two (Dovidio et al., 1997, Experiment 2; Wittenbrink et al., 1997; cf., Dovidio et al., 1997, Experiment 3). To the extent that explicit measures of prejudice are reactive and subject to normative pressures, a lack of correspondence between implicit and explicit measures of prejudice is not surprising (Dunton & Fazio, 1997; Fazio et al., 1995). Although other factors, such as desire to avoid discriminatory responses because they are inconsistent with one's values (e.g., Plant & Devine, 1998), can influence behavior toward group members, minimizing self-presentation concerns should, at least, increase the likelihood of observing attitude–behavior consistency (Fazio, 1990). With respect to the IAT, Greenwald et al. (1998) did not find a correlation between the IAT and explicit measures of prejudice (i.e., feeling thermometer and semantic differential scales). The current work examined whether a relation between the IAT and explicit measures would be revealed under conditions designed to minimize self-presentation concerns.

In sum, the current study explored the relations among the IAT, inter-group behavior, and explicit reports of prejudice. Participants met with a White experimenter, and later with a Black experimenter, in structured social interactions. These interactions were videotaped and later assessed by trained judges. Also, the Black and White experimenters independently assessed their interaction during the course of the experiment. Thus, a within-subjects design allowed us to examine how each participant behaved toward a Black experimenter relative to a White experimenter. Before interacting with the Black experimenter, participants privately completed a series of questionnaires to assess their attitudes toward Blacks and Whites in a minimally reactive situation. Afterward, they completed a race IAT before having an unanticipated social interaction with a Black experimenter. It was predicted that those who revealed relatively more negative attitudes toward Blacks on the IAT would behave in a relatively less friendly fashion toward the Black experimenter. This finding would substantiate the predictive validity of the IAT and suggest that it assesses individuals' idiosyncratic attitudes.

Two other empirical questions were also examined. First, would the IAT relate to explicit reports of prejudice? Previous research on implicit measures has yielded mixed results. Second, would explicit reports of prejudice relate to behavior toward the Black experimenter? It was our belief that the likelihood of observing significant relations between explicit measures of prejudice and other outcomes (i.e., IAT, behavior) would be improved under conditions in which participants felt minimal presentational concerns.

Method

Participants

At Michigan State University, 42 White undergraduates enrolled in introductory psychology courses participated in exchange for extra credit.

Block(s)	Type of judgment	Left key	Right key
\multicolumn{4}{c}{**TABLE 1**}
\multicolumn{4}{c}{Trial Blocks Used in the IAT Task}
1	Name discrimination	Black	White
2	Adjective discrimination	Undesirable	Desirable
3 and 4	Prejudice consistent combination	Black or Undesirable	White or Desirable
5	Reversed name discrimination	White	Black
6 and 7	Prejudice inconsistent combination	White or Undesirable	Black or Desirable

Note. Left key refers to categories associated with the "D" response, and right key refers to categories associated with the "K" key response.

Measures

Explicit measures of prejudice. Participants completed semantic differential scales for Blacks, semantic differential scales for Whites, a feeling thermometer for Blacks, and a feeling thermometer for Whites (in that order). Each measure was completed on a separate page in a questionnaire booklet. Seven-point scales were used for the semantic differential word pairings: beautiful–ugly, good–bad, pleasant–unpleasant, honest–dishonest, and nice–awful. Participants also reported their attitudes toward Blacks and Whites using a feeling thermometer, which ranged from 0° (*extremely unfavorable*) to 100° (*extremely favorable*).

IAT task. Participants completed a word-based IAT task, which presented 96 stimulus words: 24 Black-associated names (e.g., Jamal and Yolanda), 24 White-associated names (e.g., Fred and Mary Ann), 24 desirable words (e.g., wonderful and awesome), and 24 undesirable words (e.g., offensive and disgusting). Names were always presented in uppercase letters, and adjectives were always presented in lowercase letters.

The IAT task was based on Greenwald et al. (1998), using a computer program written by the first author. As Table 1 reports, participants encountered five types of trial blocks across seven different blocks, with each block being composed of 48 trials. For half of the participants, Blocks 3 and 4 presented the prejudice-inconsistent combination and Blocks 6 and 7 presented the prejudice-consistent combination (the left key and right key response options for Blocks 1 and 5 were also reversed). This block order manipulation did not produce any effects and thus receives no further discussion. In Blocks 1, 2, and 5, each of the 48 relevant stimulus words was presented once based on a randomly determined order. In each of the combination blocks, the word types were alternated across trials (i.e., name, adjective, name, adjective, and so forth) with individual stimulus words selected at random from their respective lists until each of the 48 relevant items had been presented once across the two blocks.

Participants were told that they would be making a series of category judgments. On each trial, a stimulus word was displayed in the center of a computer window (24-point black serif text on a gray background), and participants used the "D" or "K" key on the keyboard for their responses. Category label reminders were displayed in blue text on the left and right sides of the window. Participants were told, "Make your judgments as rapidly as possible, but don't respond so fast that you make many errors. Occasional errors are okay. If you do make a mistake, a red X will appear on the screen below the target word. Please press the correct category key to continue. You cannot continue until you make the correct response." Participants were told to keep their index fingers on the "D" and "K" keys throughout the experiment to minimize delays in responding. A 250-ms gray-screen intertrial interval was used. In between blocks, participants were given a self-paced break and instructions for the next block.

Procedure

Participants arrived at the laboratory for an experiment on "word perception" and were greeted by a White female experimenter.[1] They were run individually. Unbeknown to the participant, a hidden video camera was positioned to record the participants' and experimenters' full bodies and their entire range of movements during scripted social interactions. A hidden unidirectional microphone recorded their discussions. They were directed to a rolling desk chair initially positioned 120 cm away from the experimenter's chair, allowing participants to establish a preferred distance from the experimenter. The experimenter explained that because the experiment was brief, the participant would complete four unrelated tasks. For the first task, they were told that the Department of Psychology had asked experimenters to interview students about their experiences in psychology. The experimenter asked the participant four innocuous questions (e.g., "What would you change to improve psychology classes?"), pausing for the participant's response between each question and recording the responses on a report form. The experimenter also told a scripted joke following the second question. This interaction took about 3 min.

Next, participants completed a booklet of questionnaires that purportedly were being used to develop future experiments. They were told that it was important for them to answer honestly in order for the future research projects to be successful. The privacy of their responses was stressed by explaining that they would complete the booklet in a private room, place the completed booklet in a sealed envelope, and drop it into a covered box without any experimenter interaction. The booklet contained several questionnaires, only some of which were relevant to the current study. After completing several pages of the booklet, participants completed the semantic differential scales and the feeling thermometer measures. It took participants about 15–20 min to complete the booklet.

While the participant was completing the booklet, the White experimenter assessed her interaction with the participant (details forthcoming). After completing the booklet, participants inserted the sealed survey into a covered box in the laboratory's waiting area. They then found the experimenter, who took them to a private computer workstation to begin the "word perception" experiment (i.e., the IAT). The experimenter then looked at the clock and mentioned that her shift was almost over and that a new experimenter would assist in completing the fourth task following the word perception experiment. At that point, the White experimenter started the IAT program and excused herself. Participants required about 10 min to complete the IAT.

While participants completed the IAT, a Black female experimenter replaced the White experimenter and greeted participants after they returned from their room after completing the IAT. Once again, the participant was directed to a chair positioned 120 cm from the experimenter's chair, allowing the participant to establish a preferred seating distance. The Black experimenter asked the participant seven questions about the experiment (e.g., "What did you think about the difficulty level of the computer task?" and "Were the instructions clear?"), pausing for the participant's response between each question and recording the responses on an interview form. She also told a scripted joke after the fourth question. Afterward, the experimenter explained that both social interactions had been videotaped, and she asked for the participant's permission to use the videotape for data analyses. One participant refused, and her videotape was erased in her presence, leaving 41 participants for data analyses. Finally, participants were debriefed and thanked for their participation.

Coding of Social Interactions

Trained judges' ratings of participants' behavior.   Based on the existing literature documenting behavior cues that convey emotions and attitudes (Crosby, Bromley, & Saxe, 1980; DePaulo, 1992; DePaulo & Friedman, 1998; Duncan, 1969; Eckman & Friesen, 1967; Hendricks & Bootzin, 1976; Kleinke, 1986; Word, Zanna, & Cooper, 1974), 16 behaviors were coded by two trained judges who were unaware of participants' attitudes. Using a scale from 1 (*none*) to 9 (*very much*), judges rated the participant's friendliness during the interaction, the abruptness or curtness of the participant's responses to questions, the participant's general comfort level, how much the participant laughed at the experimenter's joke, and the amount of participant's eye contact with the experimenter. On 5-point scales, they assessed the participant's forward body lean toward the experimenter (vs leaning away), the extent to which the participant's body faced the experimenter (vs facing away), the openness of the participant's arms (vs crossed arms), and the expressiveness of the participant's arms (vs not moving at all). Judges also calculated the distance between the experimenter and the participant's chair at the end of the interaction to gauge social distance. Judges also recorded the participant's speaking time, number of smiles, number of speech errors, number of speech hesitations (e.g., "um"), number of fidgeting body movements (e.g., swinging feet and shifting positions), and number of extemporaneous social comments made by the participant.[2] The judges rated each participant's interaction with the White experimenter and with the Black experimenter separately. The videotape showed both the participant and the experimenter, and the judges were instructed to only attend to the audio for ratings associated with the interaction dialogue (e.g., curtness of responses).

Experimenters' ratings.   Each experimenter completed a 5-item inventory after their interaction with the participant. Using a scale ranging from 1 (*not at all*) to 9 (*extremely*), experimenters recorded their assessment of the participant's degree of eye contact, the abruptness or curtness of the participant's responses, the participant's friendliness, the participant's perceived comfort level during the interaction, and the experimenter's own comfort level during the interaction.

Results

Data Reduction

Overview.   The data analytic strategy was to transform all measures, implicit and explicit, into difference scores that reflected the relative degree of prejudice against Blacks (i.e., relatively more positive attitudes toward Whites than Blacks and relatively more positive behaviors toward Whites than Blacks). Thus for *all measures*, larger positive scores reflected greater negativity toward Blacks than Whites.

IAT.   To reduce the positive skew inherent in response latency data (Greenwald et al., 1998; Ratcliff, 1993), a log transformation was applied to each response latency. IAT effect scores were computed by comparing mean response latency of trials in Blocks 3 and 4 to trials in Blocks 6 and 7. The accuracy of any given trial was ignored, and extreme latencies were recoded such that those less than 300 ms were scored as 300 ms and those greater than 3000 ms were scored as 3000 ms.[3] The mean response latency for the prejudice-consistent block trials was subtracted from the mean response latency for the prejudice-inconsistent block trials. Thus, larger positive IAT effect scores reflected relatively stronger negative Black attitudes and relatively stronger positive White attitudes.

Explicit measures of prejudice.   The five semantic differential scales revealed good reliability for Blacks ($\alpha = .91$) and for Whites ($\alpha = .89$). Thus, the mean of each set of scales was calculated, and a difference score was computed such that larger scores reflected holding more positive attitudes toward Whites than Blacks. A difference score was also computed for the feeling thermometer (subtracting the Black thermometer from the White thermometer). Because both of these difference scores were strongly related, $r = .45$, $p < .01$, each difference score was standardized and the two z scores were added to create the explicit measure of prejudice score, which reflected the overall relative degree to which participants held more positive attitudes toward Whites than Blacks.

Experimenters' ratings of the interaction.   The White and Black experimenters' ratings of their social interactions were examined. Difference scores were computed for each assessment, whereby larger scores reflected more positive behavior being perceived by the White experimenter than by the Black experimenter. These five difference scores showed good reliability ($\alpha = .81$), thus an experimenters' rating score was calculated based on the sum of the five (standardized) difference scores. Thus, positive values on this experimenters' rating score represented the extent to which the White experimenter, compared to the Black experimenter, reported a more positive social interaction.

Judges' ratings of the interaction.   Two trained judges assessed the videotapes for positive and negative behaviors revealed by the participants, independently assessing each participant's interaction with both the Black and the White experimenter. Difference scores were calculated such that positive values always reflected relatively greater positivity being exhibited toward the White experimenter than toward the Black experimenter. These 16 difference score ratings were divided into two categories: molar judgments that captured overall interaction quality and specific social behaviors.

The molar judgments (interjudge agreement in parentheses) included abruptness or curtness of participant's responses ($r = .48$, $p < .01$), participant friendliness ($r = .43$, $p < .01$), and participant's general comfort level ($r = .53$,

TABLE 2			
Implicit and Explicit Measures of Prejudice Means, Effect Sizes, and Comparisons to Zero (i.e., No Group Preference)			
Measure	M	Cohen's d	$t(40)$
IAT effect	162.81 ms	0.88	11.47**
Explicit prejudice measure difference scores			
Semantic differential	0.22	0.27	2.58*
Feeling thermometer	11.34°	0.63	4.52**

Note. Larger, positive values reflect relatively more positive attitudes toward Whites than Blacks. IAT effect size and inferential statistics were performed on log-transformed values, but the IAT effect mean is reported in a real-time metric. $N = 41$.

*$p < .05$. **$p < .001$.

$p < .01$). Because of the good interjudge agreement, the mean of the judges' (standardized) differences scores were computed. These three difference scores revealed good reliability ($\alpha = .78$), thus a judges' molar rating was computed by taking the sum of the three difference scores. Therefore, more positive values reflected relatively more positive behaviors being exhibited toward the White experimenter than toward the Black experimenter.

In addition to the molar ratings, the judges also assessed specific participant behaviors for evidence of bias between the experimenters. Each judge's rating was standardized and a difference score was computed whereby larger scores reflected more positive behavior being revealed to the White experimenter than to the Black experimenter. The judges showed good interjudge agreement in their difference scores (see Table 3), thus the mean of their difference scores was computed for each of the 13 specific behaviors.

Descriptive Analyses

As Table 2 reveals, significant racial bias was exhibited in participants' implicit and explicit measures of prejudice. That is, participants revealed more positive attitudes toward Whites than Blacks on the IAT, semantic differential, and feeling thermometer measures. The effect size was large for the IAT, moderate for the feeling thermometer, and small for the semantic differential (Cohen, 1988). The IAT effect size observed is consistent with previous research (Greenwald et al., 1998). In contrast, Greenwald et al. only found significant racial bias for one of two explicit measures of prejudice (i.e., feeling thermometer), whereas significant prejudice was found in both explicit measures in the current study.

Correlational Analyses

Zero-order correlations between the IAT effect, the explicit measure of prejudice score (i.e., the combination of the feeling thermometer and semantic differential difference scores), the experimenters' ratings, the judges' molar ratings, and the judges' ratings of 13 specific biased social behaviors were calculated. With respect to the primary hypothesis, Table 3 reveals that there were significant correlations between the IAT and the experimenters' rating of social interaction bias and between the IAT and the judges' molar ratings of social interaction bias. Specifically, as participants' IAT scores reflected relatively more positive attitudes toward Whites than Blacks, social interactions were more positive toward the White experimenter than the Black experimenter as assessed both by trained judges and by the experimenters themselves. In addition to finding evidence that the IAT related to the experimenters' and judges' molar assessments, larger IAT effect scores predicted greater speaking time, more smiling, more extemporaneous social comments, fewer speech errors, and fewer speech hesitations in interactions with the White (vs Black) experimenter.

In addition to providing strong support for the primary hypothesis, the correlational analyses addressed the two empirical questions raised in the introduction as well. First, a significant correlation between the IAT and explicit reports of prejudice was observed. Specifically, as participants revealed relatively more positive attitudes toward Whites than Blacks on the IAT, they reported more positive evaluations of Whites than Blacks on the explicit measures of prejudice. The second empirical question received mixed support. That is, the explicit measures of prejudice score was positively related to experimenters' ratings of biased interactions, indicating that participants who reported relatively more positive attitudes toward Whites on explicit measures were perceived as more positive in social interactions by the White experimenter than by the Black experimenter. However, the explicit measures of prejudice score was unrelated to any of the judges' ratings (molar or specific social behaviors).

Finally, the remaining correlations addressed what was related to the judges' ratings. For instance, the experimenters' ratings of biased social interaction were positively related to the judges' molar ratings, indicating significant agreement between the experimenters' ratings and the judges' molar ratings of social interaction bias. The experimenters' judgments also corresponded (all in the expected direction) with judges' ratings of bias in terms of facing the experimenter, seating distance, and speaking time. In other words, the experimenters appeared to be especially sensitive to facing the experimenter, social distance cues, and speaking time as factors that

	Prejudice measures	Social interaction bias ratings		
	IAT	Explicit	Experimenters'	Judges' molar
Explicit measure of prejudice	.42**			
Experimenters' ratings	.39*	.33*		
Judges' molar ratings	.34*	.26	.41**	
Biased participant social behaviors				
Forward leaning (.64***)	−.26	.12	.05	−.08
Facing experimenter (.77***)	−.03	−.08	.31*	−.03
Body openness (.47**)	.17	.02	.20	.43**
Expressiveness (.60***)	.09	−.20	.00	.25
Eye contact (.35*)	.25	.20	.20	.55***
Seating distance (.69***)	.26	.14	.31*	.15
Speaking time (.85***)	.51** ·	.18	.41**	.30
Smiling (.71***)	.39*	.21	.15	.28
Speech errors (.53***)	.42*	.05	.14	−.03
Speech hesitation (.53***)	.35*	.13	−.07	.11
Fidgeting (.42**)	−.06	−.15	.00	.02
Laughter at joke (.56***)	.19	.03	.27	.35*
Social comments (.46**)	.32*	.02	.12	.44**

TABLE 3

Correlations between IAT, Explicit Measures of Prejudice, Experimenters' Ratings, and Judges' Molar Ratings and Assessments of Biased Participant Social Behavior

Note.   All measures are coded such that larger, positive values reflect relatively more positive attitudes and behaviors toward Whites in comparison to Blacks. Values in parentheses indicate interjudge correlations. $N = 41$.

$*p < .05.$ $**p < .01.$ $***p < .001.$

related to their perceptions of biased social interaction. Finally, the judges' molar ratings were in correspondence with their specific ratings of body openness, eye contact, laughter at the scripted jokes, and extemporaneous social comments (all in the expected direction).

Discussion

The current work is the first study to demonstrate relations among the IAT, intergroup discrimination, and explicit measures of prejudice. Although the IAT has become popular because of its large effect size and difficulty to inhibit, any psychological tool is only as good as its ability to predict human behavior. Indeed, it was found that the IAT was related to biases in intergroup social interactions. Therefore, researchers can be confident that attitudes assessed by the IAT do relate to intergroup behavior. These findings also suggest that the IAT does assess personal attitudes in that idiosyncratic variability in implicit measures of prejudice was related to behavior. Moreover, the ability of the IAT (unlike explicit measures of prejudice) to predict several specific biased social behaviors as assessed by independent observers is consistent with the claim that implicit measures of attitudes are especially predictive of behavioral leakage (Dovidio et al., 1997).

In addition to establishing a link between the IAT and discriminatory behavior, the current study also found a relation between the IAT and explicit measures of prejudice. Previous work by Greenwald et al. (1998) found no such relation. Further, those researchers did not observe as strong of evidence of racial prejudice in their explicit measures. The current experiment, in contrast, found reliable evidence of both. In the Greenwald et al. study, participants completed explicit measures of racial prejudice *after* completing the IAT. Because of the transparency of the IAT, it is conceivable that their methodology sensitized participants to the overall purpose of the entire study, increasing the likelihood that their subsequent explicit reports were influenced by social desirability concerns more so than by their personal attitudes. The current study, in contrast, attempted to minimize these concerns by having participants complete the IAT after the explicit measures. Accordingly, strong prejudice was found on explicit measures and it was related to IAT scores. Whether methodological differences between the current study and Greenwald et al. account for this outcome is unclear because task order was not manipulated in this study. However, the current findings suggest that implicit and explicit measures may tap the same attitude representation, though clearly correlational evidence is far from unequivocal. Yet, to the extent that parsimony is desirable, the position that implicit and explicit attitude measures tap similar knowledge has considerable appeal.

Although the current work found that the IAT predicted discrimination and explicit measures of prejudice, some potential limitations should be acknowledged. For example, the sequence of events that participants experienced was fixed in order to minimize suspicion about the purpose of the study. Therefore, it would be desirable to manipulate the order of events in future research to ensure that the fixed order did not produce unintended consequences. Also, the design of the study resulted in participants having completed the explicit measures of prejudice and the IAT just before interacting with the Black experimenter. Because these tasks would result in the conscious activation of racial attitudes, accessibility of these attitudes would be quite high when they encountered the Black experimenter. This greater accessibility makes it more likely that attitude–behavior consistency would be exhibited (e.g., Fazio, Powell, & Williams, 1989; Fazio & Williams, 1986; Snyder & Kendzierski, 1982; Snyder & Swann, 1976). Also, greater attitude accessibility might increase the likelihood that the experimenter would be categorized as "Black" rather than as a member of another applicable social category (Smith, Fazio, & Cejka, 1996), making it more likely that participants' racial attitudes would predict their behavior toward the experimenter. It seems reasonable to assume that such attitude–behavior consistency and categorization effects would naturally occur for those who chronically have highly accessible racial attitudes, but the question remains open as to the implications of attitude expression for individuals whose attitudes are, typically, not highly accessible. Future research should explore whether the expression of group attitudes and its subsequent effects on activation results in different behavior being exhibited from those who vary in attitude accessibility.

The current study also provides insights for researchers considering how to assess intergroup interactions. Our approach was to rely both on experimenters' perceptions (Fazio et al., 1995) and trained judges' assessments of videotapes (Dovidio et al., 1997) to examine behavior. In the current study, many more participant social behaviors were coded than were examined by Dovidio et al., who only reported examining time talking, eye contact with the experimenter, and number of eye blinks. Although both the judges and experimenters assessed the same interactions and showed reliable agreement in their reports, the two groups differed in some respects. For instance, experimenters used naive theories for assessing behavior while engaging in a demanding social interaction, whereas the judges had the benefit of more cognitive resources, the opportunity to replay the interactions, and exposure to the scientific literature on assessing social behavior.

In one sense, the correlation between our experimenters' reports and our judges' molar ratings suggests that the labor-intensive effort required to code specific social behaviors may not be necessary. However, the judges' ratings of specific social behaviors revealed five relations with the IAT but none with the explicit measures of attitudes. This is consistent with Dovidio et al. (1997), who found that only implicit measures of prejudice related to nonverbal behavior. Without collecting the judges' ratings in the current study, this asymmetry between implicit and explicit measures would have gone undetected. Another interesting finding was the discrepancy between the experimenters' ratings and the judges' molar ratings with respect to how each related to the specific behaviors coded by the judges. At the present time, we are far from a complete understanding of what leads to differences between the experimenters' and judges' assessments of social interactions. Future work needs to address this issue, however, because it is clear that each approach to assessing intergroup behavior is capturing something slightly different. Despite this uncertainty, we feel quite confident about the demonstration of the predictive validity of the IAT in the current study because it was reliably related to the independent assessments of social interactions offered by the experimenters and by the trained judges.

Finally, the current study reiterates the importance of making behavior the ultimate criterion for the value of psychological methods. Across the history of social psychology, the value of studying attitudes has been called into question because of concerns that attitudes do not predict behavior (e.g., LaPiere, 1934; Wicker, 1969), are beyond one's introspective capability (e.g., Nisbett & Wilson, 1977; Wilson, Hodges, & LaFleur, 1995), or are often influenced by normative pressures (e.g., Ajzen & Fishbein, 1973, 1980). More recent treatments of attitudes have recognized that cognitive associations, often those beyond our awareness, greatly influence our behavior (Bargh & Chartrand, 1999; Wegner & Bargh, 1998), especially when normative pressure is minimal (Fazio, 1990). The thrust of this emerging perspective is that indirect assessment of attitudes may not only be valuable to circumvent problems such as social desirability, but may be crucial to assess the mechanisms that often direct behavior. It is clear that the IAT holds much promise as a tool to assess attitudes, and the current work demonstrates its predictive utility. However, future work will be required to better understand the mechanisms that underlie the IAT and to predict when it will, and will not, relate to explicit measures of attitudes. At the very least, the current work suggests that such efforts can proceed with the assurance that the IAT assesses personal attitudes that relate to social behavior in meaningful ways.

Notes

1. The sequence of events that participants experienced in the experiment was fixed to minimize suspicion about the overall goals of the study (e.g., initially encountering a Black experimenter may have raised immediate concerns that the study was about racism). Although it is possible that exposure to one's own responses on the IAT or the explicit prejudice measures might affect subsequent behavior toward the Black experimenter, we reasoned that because the interaction with the Black experimenter was unexpected, participants would find it difficult to control their subtle behavioral cues toward her in an extemporaneous social interaction. However, we acknowledge that a fixed-order design may introduce the possibility of unforeseen confounds in the current study.
2. Readers may contact the authors for details about the behavior coding protocols.
3. Analyses were also conducted discarding responses in Blocks 3 and 6 (which presumably are more sensitive to task learning effects), as reported by Greenwald et al. (1998). Identical results obtained. Additional analyses using other trimming criteria (e.g., omitting incorrect trials, omitting trials with responses slower than 2 standard deviations from the mean) produced equivalent results.

References

Ajzen, I., & Fishbein, M. (1973). Attitudinal and normative variables as predictors of specific behaviors. *Journal of Personality and Social Psychology*, **27**, 41–57.

Ajzen, I., & Fishbein, M. (1980). *Understanding attitudes and predicting social behavior.* Englewood Cliffs, NJ: Prentice Hall.

Bargh, J. A., & Chartrand, T. L. (1999). The unbearable automaticity of being. *American Psychologist*, **54**, 462–479.

Cohen, J. (1988). *Statistical power analysis for the behavioral sciences* (2nd ed.). Hillsdale, NJ: Erlbaum.

Crosby, F., Bromley, S., & Saxe, L. (1980). Recent unobtrusive studies of black and white discrimination and prejudice: A literature review. *Psychological Bulletin*, **87**, 546–563.

DePaulo, B. M. (1992). Nonverbal behavior and self-presentation. *Psychological Bulletin*, **111**, 203–243.

DePaulo, B. M., & Friedman, H. S. (1998). Nonverbal communication. In D. T. Gilbert, S. T. Fiske, & G. Lindzey (Eds.), *Handbook of social psychology* (4th ed., Vol. 2, pp. 3–40). New York: McGraw-Hill.

Devine, P. G. (1989). Stereotypes and prejudice: Their automatic and controlled components. *Journal of Personality and Social Psychology*, **56**, 5–18.

Dovidio, J. F., Kawakami, K., Johnson, C., Johnson, B., & Howard, A. (1997). On the nature of prejudice: Automatic and controlled processes. *Journal of Experimental Social Psychology*, **33**, 510–540.

Duncan, S. (1969). Nonverbal communication. *Psychological Bulletin*, **72**, 118–137.

Dunton, B. C., & Fazio, R. H. (1997). An individual difference measure of motivation to control prejudiced reactions. *Personality and Social Psychology Bulletin*, **23**, 316–326.

Eckman, P., & Friesen, W. V. (1967). Head and body cues in the judgment of emotion: A reformulation. *Perceptual and Motor Skills*, **24**, 711–724.

Fazio, R. H. (1990). Multiple processes by which attitudes guide behavior: The MODE model as an integrative framework. In M. P. Zanna (Ed.), *Advances in experimental social psychology* (Vol. 23, pp. 75–109). New York: Academic Press.

Fazio, R. H. (1995). Attitudes as object–evaluation associations: Determinants, consequences, and correlates of attitude accessibility. In R. E. Petty & J. A. Krosnick (Eds.), *Attitude strength: Antecedents and consequences* (pp. 247–282). Mahwah, NJ: Erlbaum.

Fazio, R. H., Jackson, J. R., Dunton, B. C., & Williams, C. J. (1995). Variability in automatic activation as an unobtrusive measure of racial stereotypes: A bona fide pipeline? *Journal of Personality and Social Psychology*, **69**, 1013–1027.

Fazio, R. H., Powell, M. C., & Williams, C. J. (1989). The role of attitude accessibility in the attitude-to-behavior process? *Journal of Consumer Research*, **16**, 280–288.

Fazio, R. H., & Williams, C. J. (1986). Attitude accessibility as a moderator of the attitude–perception and attitude–behavior relations: An investigation of the 1984 presidential election. *Journal of Personality and Social Psychology*, **51**, 505–514.

Greenwald, A. G., & Banaji, M. R. (1995). Implicit social cognition: Attitudes, self-esteem, and stereotypes. *Psychological Review*, **102**, 4–27.

Greenwald, A. G., McGhee, D. E., & Schwartz, J. L. K. (1998). Measuring individual differences in implicit cognition: The Implicit Association Test. *Journal of Personality and Social Psychology*, **74**, 1464–1480.

Hendricks, M., & Bootzin, R. (1976). Race and sex as stimuli for negative affect and physical avoidance. *Journal of Social Psychology*, **98**, 111–120.

Kleinke, C. L. (1986). Gaze and eye contact: A research review. *Psychological Bulletin*, **100**, 78–100.

LaPiere, R. T. (1934). Attitudes vs. actions. *Social Forces*, **13**, 230–237.

Nisbett, R. E., & Wilson, T. D. (1977). Telling more than we can know: Verbal reports on mental processes. *Psychological Review*, **84**, 231–259.

Nosek, B. A., Banaji, M. R., & Greenwald, A. G. (2000). Harvesting implicit group attitudes and stereotypes from a demonstration website. Unpublished manuscript, Yale University.

Plant, E. A., & Devine, P. G. (1998). Internal and external motivation to respond without prejudice. *Journal of Personality and Social Psychology*, **75**, 811–832.

Ratcliff, R. (1993). Methods for dealing with reaction time outliers. *Psychological Bulletin*, **114**, 510–532.

Rudman, L. A., Greenwald, A. G., Mellott, D. S., & Schwartz, J. L. K. (1999). Measuring the automatic components of prejudice: Flexibility and generality of the Implicit Association Test. *Social Cognition*, **17**, 437–465.

Smith, E. R., Fazio, R. H., & Cejka, M. A. (1996). Accessible attitudes influence categorization of multiply categorizable objects. *Journal of Personality and Social Psychology*, **71**, 888–898.

Snyder, M., & Kendzierski, D. (1982). Acting on one's attitudes: Procedures for linking attitude and behavior. *Journal of Experimental Social Psychology*, **18**, 165–183.

Snyder, M., & Swann, W. B. (1976). When actions reflect attitudes: The politics of impression management. *Journal of Personality and Social Psychology*, **34**, 1034–1042.

Wegner, D. M., & Bargh, J. A. (1998). Control and automaticity in social life. In D. T. Gilbert, S. T. Fiske, & G. Lindzey (Eds.), *Handbook of social psychology* (4th ed., Vol. 1, pp. 446–496). New York: McGraw-Hill.

Wicker, A. W. (1969). Attitudes versus actions: The relationship of verbal and overt behavioral responses to attitude objects. *Journal of Social Issues*, **25**, 41–78.

Wilson, T. D., Hodges, S. D., & LaFleur, S. J. (1995). Effects of introspecting about reasons: Inferring attitudes from accessible thoughts. *Journal of Personality and Social Psychology*, **69**, 16–28.

Wittenbrink, B., Judd, C. M., & Park, B. (1997). Evidence for racial prejudice in the implicit level and its relationship with questionnaire measures. *Journal of Personality and Social Psychology*, **72**, 262–274.

Word, C. O., Zanna, M. P., & Cooper, J. (1974). The nonverbal mediation of self-fulfilling prophecies in interracial interaction. *Journal of Experimental Social Psychology*, **10**, 109–120.

Questions for Review and Discussion

1. What is an implicit attitude and how does the IAT measure implicit attitudes?
2. How did the researchers measure discriminatory behavior in their study?
3. What relationship was observed between scores on the IAT and explicit measures of prejudice in the study?

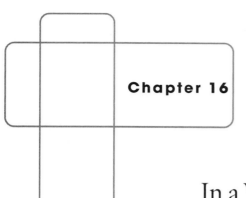

Chapter 16

In a Very Different Voice: Unmasking Moral Hypocrisy

C. Daniel Batson, Diane Kobrynowicz, Jessica L. Dinnerstein, Hannah C. Kampf, and Angela D. Wilson

Moral principles motivate moral action. This truism undergirds much preaching, teaching, parenting, and politicking. But is it true? Is the person who learns to value moral responsibility more likely to be responsible? Or, as astute observers of the human condition such as Jane Austen (1811/1969), Charles Dickens (1843–1844/1982), and Mark Twain (1884/ 1959) have noted, do valued morals often serve another master, providing convenient and high-sounding rationalizations for self-interest? Even though the term sounds harsh, we know no better name for this latter possibility than *moral hypocrisy:* Morality is extolled—even enacted—not with an eye to producing a good and right outcome but in order to appear moral yet still benefit oneself. *Webster's Desk Dictionary of the English Language* (1990) defines *moral* as "1. of or concerned with principles of right or wrong conduct. 2. Being in accordance with such principles" (p. 589); it defines *hypocrisy* as "a pretense of having desirable or publicly approved attitudes, beliefs, principles, etc., that one does not actually possess" (p. 444).

From *Journal of Personality and Social Psychology*, Vol. 72, No. 6, pp. 1335–1348. Copyright © 1997 by the American Psychological Association. Reproduced with permission.

Reasons to Neglect Moral Motivation

The questions in the preceding paragraph concern moral motivation, a topic that has received remarkably little attention from psychologists. Considerable attention has been given to moral behavior, that is, acting in accord with some moral principle or standard (see Bandura, 1991; Blasi, 1980; Hartshorne & May, 1928, Hartshorne, May, & Maller, 1929; Wright, 1971), and considerably more attention has been given to moral thought, that is, deciding what is morally right (see Bandura, 1991; Gilligan, 1982; Gilligan, Ward, & Taylor, 1988; Kohlberg, 1969, 1976, 1984; Kurtines & Gewirtz, 1991; Kurtines & Greif, 1974), but very little attention has been given to moral motivation, that is, the goal of acting morally (see Oliner & Oliner, 1988, chap. 8; Rushton, 1980; Staub, 1974).

The limited attention given to moral motivation can be explained in several ways. First, in the behaviorist environment, in which research on moral behavior came of age, moral principles were conceived of as secondary rewards and punishments—sources of pride and guilt—used to bring moral action within the purview of self-interest. In that environment, questions about the nature of moral motivation did not arise, because one knew from the outset that self-interest was the only form of motivation. Moral principles served self-interest in a forthright and honest way; there was no hint of hypocrisy.

Second, in the cognitivist environment, in which research on moral thought flourished, it was assumed that if a person analyzed a decision in terms of principled morality, then he or she would automatically be motivated to uphold the principle. Kohlberg (1976) emphasized early on this link of moral reasoning to moral action: "To act in a morally high way requires a high stage of moral reasoning. . . . Moral stage is a good predictor of action" (p. 32). Limited evidence for this link (see Blasi, 1980), as well as increased reliance on research procedures that focused on thinking about complex moral dilemmas—often hypothetical—in which the most moral act was debatable (e.g., Should Heinz steal the drug? Should I have an abortion?), soon led to a strategic retreat from the broad plain of moral motivation back inside the more secure fortress of moral thought. Behavioral measures and motivational issues disappeared from the research.

A third reason to neglect moral motivation is the impropriety of questioning the motives of one's betters. It seems decidedly in bad taste to ask of Mother Teresa why, really, she acted as she did (Hitchens, 1995). Yet might this taboo itself suggest a fear that there could be something to hide? If we think honestly about our own lapses into morality, we find ample reason to question our motives (Batson, Fultz, Schoenrade, & Paduano, 1987). Often, that which we convince others—and even ourselves—is done in the service of some noble principle is actually done to serve our own interest. This is a disquieting prospect, especially to those wishing to create a more moral society.

Looking at Moral Motivation

Still, belief in the motivating power of moral principles persists. Moral philosophers typically call for action motivated by the goal of upholding some universal and impartial moral principle, such as justice (Rawls, 1971) or care (Blum, 1980; Noddings, 1984). Philosophers have not, however, ignored the question of whether acting with an ultimate goal of upholding moral principle is really possible. When Kant (1785/1898) briefly shifted from his analysis of what ought to be to what is, he was ready to admit that even if one's action appears to be prompted by duty to principle, it may actually be prompted by self-love:

> We like to flatter ourselves by falsely taking credit for a more noble motive. . . . A cool observer, one that does not mistake the wish for the good, however lively, for its reality, may sometimes doubt whether true virtue is actually found anywhere in the world. . . . (sec. 2, para. 2)

Kant quickly let this issue drop. With some trepidation, we wish to pick it up again, considering why and how people might be motivated to appear moral yet still remain steadfastly focused on self-benefit.

Why Be a Moral Hypocrite?

There are many possible reasons for wanting to appear moral. Most obviously, one can garner the social and self-rewards of being seen and seeing oneself as upstanding, and one can avoid the social and self-punishments for failing to be so. Freud (1930/1961) suggested that society inculcates moral principles in the young in order to bridle their selfish impulses by making it in their best personal interest to act morally. But this bridle chafes; there is an unrelenting impulse to break free and be oneself (see also Campbell, 1975). One way out of this bind is to assume a moral masquerade, to make a show of morality, but only a show.

If moral principles are part of a masquerade, then the motivational potential that has attracted philosophers is in jeopardy. An antipathy may develop between the spirit of the principle and the inclination of the individual, just as antipathy is likely to develop in a child who is paid to get good grades (Lepper, Greene, & Nisbett, 1973). Adherence to principle may become selective and limited. If I can convince myself and others that I am serving principle while actually serving myself, then I should jump at the chance. And often I can.

How?

From the perspective of moral philosophy, the generality and abstractness of universal moral principles such as justice and care is a major virtue. They transcend the narrow partialities of self-interest, of kinship, friendship, and group interest; they apply to all people in all situations. From the perspective of moral psychology, especially the psychology of moral motivation, this generality and abstractness is an Achilles' heel. The more general and abstract a moral principle is, the more vulnerable it is to rationalization.

Most people are adept at moral rationalization, at justifying to themselves—if not to others—why a situation that benefits them or those they care about does not violate their principles: why, in Jonathan Kozol's (1991) apt phrase, the "savage inequalities" between the public school systems of rich and poor communities in the United States are just; why storing one's nuclear waste in someone else's backyard or using a disproportionate amount of the earth's natural resources is fair; why terrorist attacks by one's own side are regrettable but necessary evils, whereas terrorist attacks by the other side are atrocities. The abstractness of most moral principles makes such rationalization especially easy. Skill in dodging the thrust of principles one espouses may explain the disappointingly weak empirical relation between principled morality and moral action. Principles may be used more reactively than proactively, more to justify or condemn action than to motivate it.

Economist Robert Frank (1988), building on sociobiologist Robert Trivers's (1971) ideas about reciprocal altruism, presented a similar analysis of moral motivation, but with an interesting twist. Frank argued that people are motivated to present themselves as passionately committed to moral principles in order to gain the self-benefits that the ensuing trust provides. He also argued that the effort involved in shamming this commitment is so great that the more evolutionary stable strategy is genuine commitment. Our ancient ancestors may have taken up morality lightly as part of a masquerade, but over time, natural selection favored those whose appearance of morality was genuine, because only in them was hypocrisy likely to be undetected.

If Frank is right, then moral principles should motivate moral action. Trivers (1985, pp. 415–420; see also Alexander, 1987, pp. 114–125) suggested another possibility: If one can convince oneself that serving one's own interests does not violate one's principles, then one can honestly appear moral and so avoid detection without paying the price of actually upholding the principles.

In the moral masquerade, self-deception may be an asset, making it easier to deceive others.

These observations about moral hypocrisy suggest a two-step process. The first step is perceptual; it involves seeing a choice or decision as moral, as an opportunity to uphold or violate one's moral principles. The second step is motivational; it involves seeking to maximize personal gain by appearing moral while, if possible, not incurring the costs associated with a moral outcome.

Moral Integrity

Perhaps, however, the cynical claim that moral principles lack intrinsic motivating power is wrong. Perhaps moral responsibility can come to be valued in its own right and not simply as a means to self-serving ends (Gilligan, 1982; Gilligan et al., 1988; Kohlberg, 1976, 1984; Staub, 1989a). Even if principles are inculcated in childhood through appeals to reward and punishment, once they are internalized, upholding them may become an ultimate rather than an instrumental goal. One may be motivated to uphold not simply the appearance of morality but morality itself; one may be motivated to produce a moral outcome. We shall call intrinsic moral motivation of this kind, if it exists, *moral integrity* (McKinnon, 1991; Williams, 1976).

The Present Research

What is the nature of moral motivation—hypocrisy, integrity, both, or neither? To address this question empirically, we needed a research strategy that would enable us to determine the ultimate goal motivating some moral act. Following the same logic used over the past decade to determine the ultimate goal motivating helping behavior (Batson, 1991), we pursued a two-step strategy.

First, we had to elicit moral action. In so value-laden an area as morality, trusting self-reports or judgments about what one would do in a hypothetical situation seems unwise; we must infer motivation from behavior. Moral action by itself would, however, tell us only that there was some motivation; it would not reveal the nature of that motivation. Therefore, second, we had to vary the circumstances under which the moral act occurred, doing so in a way that would reveal whether the goal was to uphold one's moral principles (integrity) or to uphold the appearance of morality while serving self-interest (hypocrisy). One way to do this was suggested by the classic research by M. L. Snyder, Kleck, Strenta, and Mentzer (1979) on attributional ambiguity. They varied circumstances in a way that allowed individuals to justify a morally questionable outcome—avoiding a person with a disability—as an innocent and unintended consequence of preference for one movie over another. If we could introduce ambiguity so that benefiting oneself could appear to be the innocent and unintended consequence of moral action, then moral hypocrisy should unmask itself in a preference for moral action that, seemingly innocently, leads to a self-beneficial rather than moral outcome. Moral integrity—motivation to uphold moral principle as an ultimate goal—should be unaffected by the introduction of such ambiguity; the link between moral action and moral outcome should be as strong as when no ambiguity is present.

A Moral Dilemma in the Lab

To implement this strategy, we created a moral dilemma in the laboratory. Our dilemma was neither as profound nor as complex as those studied by Kohlberg, Gilligan, and their colleagues. Ours was a simple, straightforward zero-sum conflict between self-interest and the interest of another person. We purposely wanted a dilemma that was real, not hypothetical, so that we could observe actual behavior. We wanted a dilemma that was simple, not complex, so that individuals would have no problem understanding what was at stake and so that we could easily create variations to introduce ambiguity. We wanted a dilemma that pitted self-interest against the interest of another individual, not against the interest of a hallowed institution such as church or state, so that responses would not be affected by institutional affiliation or allegiance. We wanted a dilemma that was mundane and bland, not stereotypically moral and dramatic, so that we would get less scripted responses. We wanted a dilemma in which there would be broad consensus about the morally right course of action, not one in which opinions would conflict, so that we could know what action was moral.

Drawing on the maxims "Power is responsibility" and "Power corrupts," we gave research participants the chance to assign themselves and another participant (actually fictitious) to tasks. There were two tasks: a positive consequences task, in which each correct response earned a raffle ticket for a $30 prize, and a neutral consequences task, in which each correct response earned nothing and which was described as rather dull and boring. One person had to be assigned to each task. Participants were told that the other person would not know that they were allowed to assign the tasks. We assumed participants would think that taking advantage of their privileged position and assigning themselves the positive consequences task was less moral than either assigning the other person to the positive consequences task or using an evenhanded strategy, such as flipping a coin.

Individual Differences in Moral Responsibility

A standard assumption of those interested in inculcating moral principles is that by adolescence, some people are more moral than others, having internalized the principles to a higher degree. (Otherwise, why fret about inculcation?) A standard assumption among personality researchers studying morality is that this variation in morality is reflected in scores on individual-difference measures of prosocial orientation (Staub, 1974), the "altruistic personality" (Oliner & Oliner, 1988; Rushton, 1980), and moral reasoning (Gilligan, 1982; Gilligan et al., 1988; Kohlberg, 1976, 1984). Among the dozen or so measures of personal morality that researchers have used, we focused on four. Two measured the justice and the relationship–care perspectives of Kohlberg and Gilligan, respectively; two measured personal responsibility. Together, they measured four major constructs in the domain of moral responsibility. Each construct has been claimed to be an important source of moral motivation (see Berkowitz & Lutterman, 1968; Gilligan, 1982; Kohlberg, 1976; Schwartz & Howard, 1981; Staub, 1974).

Predictions

To the extent that one or more of these measures of moral responsibility taps a source of moral motivation, this measure should correlate positively with acting morally in our laboratory dilemma. If the action is only part of a masquerade of moral hypocrisy, however, then this hypocrisy should be unmasked by the introduction of ambiguity so that benefiting oneself can appear to be the innocent and unintended consequence of moral action; ambiguity should produce a pattern of moral action but not moral outcome. If upholding the moral principle is an ultimate goal, then introducing ambiguity should have no effect on the link between moral action and outcome; the link should remain strong, providing evidence of moral integrity.

We tested these predictions in three small, closely related, and simultaneously run studies. In the first, participants encountered the laboratory dilemma in as direct and simple a form as possible; no attention was called to the moral implications of their task assignment decision, nor was a morally right course of action suggested. Studies 2 and 3 were designed to provide more insight into the nature of moral motivation by introducing ambiguity that would allow a self-interested outcome to masquerade as an unintended consequence of moral action. Participants in all three studies completed the measures of moral responsibility at a questionnaire session held 1 to 14 days before their laboratory session.

Questionnaire Session: Measuring
Moral Responsibility

Method

Participants.   Eighty participants took part in one of several questionnaire sessions. Ostensibly, the questionnaires were part of a national survey of "the social attitudes and values of today's undergraduates." All participants were female general psychology students at the University of Kansas, who received partial credit toward a course requirement.[1]

Procedure.   When originally scheduled for the questionnaire session, participants were told that there would be two sessions and that they would receive research credit for each. After they arrived for the first session, participants learned that it had been necessary to cancel the second session. Ostensibly to fulfill the researchers' obligation for two sessions and the associated research credit, arrangements had been made to schedule participants for a second, unrelated study. This second study was actually one of our three. We scheduled participants in this way to reduce the likelihood that they would perceive a relation between the questionnaire session and subsequent laboratory experience.

Justice and relationship–care perspectives.   Included among the attitude and value scales completed at the questionnaire session were single-item measures of the justice and relationship–care perspectives. These measures were adapted from those developed by Ford and Lowery (1986). Participants were first asked to think about how they go about deciding what they should do in social conflict situations, such as when a friend who rarely attends class asks to borrow notes, when an accident-prone friend wants to borrow their car, or when friends want them to mediate an argument. They were then asked to rate on a 9-point scale the extent to which each of the following perspectives reflects their thinking when "trying to decide what you should do in a social conflict situation" (1 = *not at all*, 9 = *totally*). The *justice perspective*, labeled only as *Perspective A*, read:

> One way to approach thinking about a social conflict is to see yourself in a process of deciding what is most just. This includes standing back from the problem at hand to consider the most fair way to resolve the dilemma. It often means invoking certain principles which you personally believe should govern the way people behave. The problem, as you perceive it, involves competing sets of values. You seek what is most just by considering the rights of all involved.

This perspective was designed to capture the key elements of Kohlberg's (1976) postconventional morality.

The *relationship–care perspective*, labeled only as *Perspective C* (Perspective B concerned "deciding what is best for you personally"), read:

> One way to approach thinking about a social conflict is to see yourself involved in relationship with others. This means you have certain responsibilities to be concerned for others and to consider how what you do will help or hurt those involved. Conflicts are considered in the context of their effect on relationships between people, and whether those relationships will be maintained, restored, or damaged. You seek a way to respond that will minimize the hurt to all involved.

This perspective was designed to capture elements of Gilligan's (1982) description of mature morality: "Care becomes the self-chosen principle of a judgment that remains psychological in its concern with relationships and response but becomes universal in its condemnation of exploitation and hurt" (p. 74).

Social responsibility and ascription of responsibility. Also included were two measures of personal responsibility. These were Berkowitz and Lutterman's (1968) 8-item Social Responsibility Scale (sample item: "It is the duty of each person to do his or her job the very best that he or she can," where 1 = *strongly disagree,* 5 = *strongly agree*) and Schwartz's (1968) 28-item Ascription of Responsibility Scale (sample item: "If I hurt someone unintentionally, I would feel almost as guilty as I would if I had done the same thing intentionally," where 1 = *strongly disagree,* 4 = *strongly agree*).

Results

Means and standard deviations for each of these four moral responsibility measures, as well as intercorrelations among them, are presented in Table 1. As can be seen, means were well above the midpoint for each measure, indicating that on average, participants perceived (or at least presented) themselves as quite morally responsible. A principal-components analysis and a principal-axes factor analysis produced one-component and one-factor solutions (with the criterion of eigenvalue greater than 1.0); the single component accounted for 54% of the variance, and the single factor accounted for 39%. Although these analyses indicated that our measures shared considerable common variance, Table 1 reveals that the correlations among the measures were not overly high. Therefore, we decided that when analyzing results of our three studies, we should look at the relation to moral behavior of each moral responsibility measure in addition to creating an overall index.

	TABLE 1					

Means and Standard Deviations for, and Intercorrelations Among, the Moral
Responsibility Measures Administered in the Questionnaire Session

			Measure			
Measure	M	SD	1	2	3	4
1. Justice perspective	6.37	1.42	—	.45***	.24**	.43***
2. Relationship–care perspective	6.90	1.27		—	.31***	.40***
3. Social responsibility	4.22	0.41			—	.51***
4. Ascription of responsibility	2.89	0.26				—

Note. $N = 80$. The response scale range for the justice and relationship–care perspectives was 1–9, the response scale range for the Social Responsibility Scale was 1–5, and the response scale range for the Ascription of Responsibility Scale was 1–4. For each measure, higher values indicate stronger endorsement of this form of mortality.

**$p < .025$, one-tailed.   ***$p < .01$, one-tailed.

Study 1

The goal of Study 1 was to use our laboratory dilemma to test the relation of the moral responsibility measures to moral action and to do so in a "weak" psychological situation that provided no explicit cues to the moral nature of the task assignment decision or to the most moral course of action. M. Snyder and Ickes (1985) have suggested that in such situations individual difference measures are most likely to show their power to predict behavior. If moral principles motivate moral action, then in this situation, high scores on our moral responsibility measures should correlate positively with refusing to exploit the opportunity to assign the tasks, that is, with assigning the other participant to the positive consequences.

Method

Participants.   Of the 80 participants from the questionnaire sessions, 20 took part in Study 1. One additional participant was dropped from the sample and replaced because during debriefing she expressed doubts about the presence of another participant.

Procedure.   Participation was by individual appointment. Upon arrival, participants were greeted by a female experimenter and escorted to a research room on another floor of the building. The experimenter explained that there were 2 participants in the study and it was important that they not meet or even see one another, so each was being met at a different location. (As we mentioned, no other participant was actually present.) Once seated at a table in the research room, participants were left alone to read a typewritten introduction. The introduction explained that the study was part of ongoing research concerning "how a variety of task characteristics affect people's feelings and reactions after performing a task":

> We are currently examining the effects of task consequences on feelings and reactions. Task consequences can be either positive, negative, or neutral. In this particular study, we are focusing on the effects of *positive* task consequences—where correct responses are rewarded, and there are no consequences for incorrect responses. As a comparison, we are also considering *neutral* task consequences—where feedback is given about correct and incorrect responses but there are no consequences at all.

The introduction went on to explain that one of the two participants in the session would be assigned to do a positive consequences task and the other to do a neutral consequences task. "By having different types of tasks performed simultaneously by different people, we are able to control for the subtle effects on feelings and reactions of time of day, day of week, and so on." The introduction stated that the two participants would work on their tasks independently and would not meet. Finally, the introduction explained the consequences:

> To ensure that you care about the consequences of your performance, it is necessary to use real consequences. The consequences we are using in this study are the following: If you are assigned to the task with *positive consequences,* then for an incorrect response you will receive nothing. For each correct response, however, you will receive one raffle ticket; the prize in the raffle is a $30.00 gift certificate at the store of your choice. Only participants in this study are eligible for this raffle, so if you receive a number of tickets you have a good chance of winning a gift certificate.

> If you are assigned to the task with *neutral consequences,* you will simply perform a task and be given feedback about your performance. Your responses are not related to any consequences. (You should be aware that most participants assigned to the neutral consequences task find it rather dull and boring. If you are assigned to this task, we hope you will not find it too bad.)

Assigning the tasks.   After participants finished reading the introduction, the experimenter returned, answered any questions about the study, gave participants a folder containing a typewritten information sheet about the task assignment, and left them alone to read it. The sheet began:

> There is one aspect of the procedure of this study that we purposely did not explain earlier, but about which we can tell you now. In addition to studying the effect of task consequences—positive or neutral—on feelings and reactions, we are also interested in studying the effect of assigning people to the different tasks. To this end, in some sessions one of the two participants is asked to assign both participants to their tasks. The other participant is entirely unaware of this, simply being told that the tasks were assigned by chance.
>
> As you have probably guessed by now, you are the participant in this session who will assign the tasks. You must assign one of you—yourself or the other participant—to the positive consequences task and the other of you to the neutral consequences task.
>
> The decision is entirely up to you. You can assign yourself and the other participant however you choose. The other participant does not and will not know that you are assigning tasks; he or she will think that the task assignment was purely by chance. Because of this and because the two of you will never meet, your anonymity is assured.

The sheet reiterated that the participant assigned to the positive consequences task would receive a raffle ticket for each correct response and the participant assigned to the neutral consequences task would receive only information; it also included the reminder "People tend to find the neutral consequences task somewhat dull and boring."

Finally, the sheet instructed participants to indicate their decision on an enclosed task assignment form and return the form to the folder. On the form, one line said, "Participant assigned to *positive* consequences task _____"; the next line said, "Participant assigned to *neutral* consequences task _____." Instructions were as follows: "Please indicate your assignment of yourself and the other participant to the tasks by putting an *S* in one blank (for self) and an *O* in the other blank (for other participant). Thank you." The response on this form was the measure of moral action and outcome.

Feelings of pride and guilt about the decision.   Once participants filled out the form and indicated that they were ready to proceed, the experimenter returned, collected the folder, gave participants several questionnaires concerning the task assignment decision, and left them alone to complete these questionnaires while she ostensibly went to prepare the tasks. The first questionnaire concerned participants' feelings both during and after making the task assign-ment decision. For each of a number of emotion adjectives, participants were asked to indicate how strongly they felt that emotion on a scale of 1 (*not at all*) to 7 (*extremely*). Among the adjectives concerning feelings after making the task assignment decision were *proud* and *guilty*. Ratings of these feelings were used to assess self-rewards and self-punishments associated with the decision.

Perceptions of morality of the decision.   The next questionnaire focused on the decision. Among other questions it contained two concerned with perceptions of morality. The first question, which was open-ended, asked about the morally right way to assign the tasks: "In your opinion, what was the most *morally right* way to assign the task consequences?" Three blank lines were provided to write an answer. Later, in a different part of the questionnaire, par-ticipants were asked to rate the morality of their own decision on a 9-point scale: "Do you think the way you made the task assignment was morally right?" (where 1 = *not at all*, 9 = *yes, totally*). We used responses to the first question to check the assumption that participants would think that assigning the other participant to the positive consequences task was more moral than assigning themselves to it. We used the second to check participants' percep-tions of the morality of their own action.

Debriefing.   Once participants completed these questionnaires, the experi-menter returned and said she wished to discuss reactions to the study so far, before getting to the tasks. This discussion led to a full and careful debriefing in which the true purpose of the research and all deceptions were explained. Partici-pants did not actually perform a task. Because they had been presented with the prospect of earning raffle tickets, all participants were informed that they would receive 20 tickets in a raffle to be held following completion of data collection. After debriefing, participants were thanked for their time and excused. Once data collection was complete, the raffle was held and a $30 gift certificate awarded to the winner.

Results and Discussion

Moral action and its moral responsibility correlates.   Of the 20 participants in Study 1, 16 took advantage of the opportunity to assign themselves to the positive consequences task, giving the other participant the dull, boring neutral conse-quences task, whereas 4 assigned the other to the positive consequences task (.20). Coding the assignment of other to positive as 1 and self to positive as 0, we found that only one of the moral responsibility measures, ascription of responsibility, significantly predicted who would assign the other to the positive consequences task, $r(18) = .39$, $p < .05$.[2] Rated importance of a justice perspective in dealing with social conflicts had a marginal positive correlation, $r(18) = .29$, $p < .12$. Correlations with assignment for our measures of a relationship–care perspective and social responsibility were both weak, $rs(18) = .14$ and $.04$, respectively. Correlation for a combined index of moral responsibility (created by averaging standardized responses to the four measures) was not significant, $r(18) = .25$, $p < .15$. The size of these correlations may have been restricted somewhat by the rather low proportion of participants assigning the other to the positive consequences task, limiting variance on the assignment measure.

Perception of the morally right course of action.   The low proportion of participants assigning the other to the positive consequences task could not be explained by perceptions of what was morally right. When participants were asked in the open-ended question what was the most morally right way to assign the tasks, only 1 of the 16 who assigned themselves the positive consequences task said that assigning oneself to the positive consequences task was most morally right, whereas 12 said assigning the other participant to the positive consequences task was most moral, 2 judged using some even-handed method such as flipping a coin as most moral, and 1 said there was no morally right way to assign the tasks. Of the 4 participants who assigned the other to the positive consequences task, 3 said this was the most morally right way, and 1 said flipping a coin was most moral.

When asked later about the morality of the way they assigned the tasks, participants who assigned the other to the positive consequences task said that what they had done was more morally right ($M = 8.25$ on the 1–9 scale) than did participants who took the positive consequences task themselves ($M = 4.38$), $t(18) = 4.31$, $p < .0005$. These ratings suggested that those who gave the other participant the positive consequences task felt they had acted in a highly moral manner. Those who took the positive consequences task themselves felt they had acted less morally, but even they, on average, rated the morality of their action near the midpoint of the scale.

Among the 16 participants who took the positive consequences task themselves, those scoring higher on the measures of a relationship–care perspective and ascription of responsibility rated their action as less morally right, $rs(14) = -.51$ and $-.59$, $ps < .025$ and $.01$, respectively. The correlation with rating this action as morally right was also negative, but not reliable, for social responsibility, $r(14) = -.25$. It was positive, but not reliable, for a justice perspective, $r(14) = .25$. The correlation for the combined index was negative, $r(14) = -.46$, $p < .04$. The nonsignificant reversal for a justice perspective may have occurred because the zero-sum nature of the decision made it impossible to treat both participants equally in terms of distributive justice, so those who highly valued justice may have felt that they had not violated this principle.

Feeling proud or guilty after acting.   Consistent with the perceptions of the morality of their action, those who gave the positive consequences task to the other reported feeling more proud ($M = 3.25$ on the 1–7 scale) and less guilty ($M = 1.25$) than did those who took the positive consequences themselves ($Ms = 1.63$ and 3.25, respectively), $ts(18) = 2.72$ and 2.03, $ps < .02$ and $.03$, respectively. (Recall that feeling ratings were made before participants were asked about the morality of their decision.) These results suggest that those who assigned the other to positive consequences were able to self-reward more and self-punish less following their action. Whether obtaining these self-benefits was the goal of their action or was an unintended consequence we cannot say on the basis of the results of Study 1. If it was the goal, their moral motivation was instrumental, serving self-interest. If it was an unintended consequence, their ultimate goal may have been to uphold moral principle, showing integrity.

Summary.   Even though our sample for Study 1 was small, results were clear. When faced with the simple and straightforward dilemma of assigning self and other to positions of unequal attractiveness in the absence of clear moral cues or direction, only a small proportion of participants acted in the way that, in retrospect, they considered most moral. Moral motivation seemed rather weak. Under these circumstances, only one of the moral responsibility measures, ascription of responsibility, significantly predicted moral action. In retrospective judgments, endorsement of a relationship–care perspective and ascription of responsibility predicted rating the assignment of oneself to the positive consequences task as less morally right. Those who assigned the other participant to the positive consequences task reported more pride and less guilt, placing themselves in line for more self-benefits, than did those who assigned themselves to the positive consequences. We cannot say, however, whether obtaining self-benefits was the motive behind their action or simply an unintended consequence.

Study 2

Study 2 was designed to provide additional information concerning the scope and nature of moral motivation by introducing two new features into our laboratory dilemma. In Study 1, no explicit moral cues were provided, and there was no easy way to serve justice. In Study 2, we provided an explicit statement about the moral nature of the dilemma, saying that most people think the most fair way to assign the tasks is to give both participants an equal chance of being assigned the positive consequences task by, for example, flipping a coin. To facilitate use of this strategy, we provided a coin. We reasoned that this explicit moral cue would bring out more moral motivation and thus more moral action. Providing the coin also introduced ambiguity that could serve to unmask moral hypocrisy because it permitted moral action—flipping the coin—that could lead to a self-serving outcome—assignment of self to the positive consequences task. A sincere coin flip motivated by moral integrity should have led roughly 50% of those flipping to assign the other participant to the positive consequences task; significant deviation from 50% in the direction of assigning self the positive consequences task would suggest motivation to appear moral yet still serve self-interest, that is, moral hypocrisy.

Method

Participants.   A second 20 of the 80 participants from the questionnaire sessions took part in Study 2. One additional participant was dropped from the sample and replaced because during debriefing she expressed doubts about the presence of another participant.

Procedure.   The procedure for Study 2 was exactly the same as for Study 1, except for (a) the addition of a statement to the task assignment information sheet that said most participants think flipping a coin is most fair and (b) the presence of a coin to flip. After the information sheet explanation that the participant would be assigning "one of you—yourself or the other participant—to the positive consequences task and the other of you to the neutral consequences task," the following statement was added:

> Most participants feel that giving both people an equal chance—by, for example, flipping a coin—is the fairest way to assign themselves and the other participant to the tasks (we have provided a coin for you to flip if you wish). But the decision is entirely up to you.

The rest of the information sheet was identical to the one used in Study 1. When participants opened the folder that contained the information sheet, they found a clear plastic pouch taped to the inside of the folder. The pouch contained a coin (a quarter) for them to flip if they wished. All of the measures reported for Study 1 were taken in Study 2, in exactly the same order.

Results and Discussion

Moral action and its moral responsibility correlates.   Of the 20 participants in Study 2, 10 flipped the coin and 10 did not. Coding flipping as 1 and not flipping as 0, we found that two of the moral responsibility measures significantly predicted who would flip the coin, a relationship–care perspective, $r(17) = .41$, $p < .05$, and social responsibility, $r(18) = .47$, $p < .02$. (One participant failed to complete the relationship–care perspective measure.) Correlations with flipping for the other two moral responsibility measures, a justice perspective and ascription of responsibility, were also positive but were weaker and not reliably different from zero, $rs(18) = .24$ and $.14$, respectively. The correlation for the combined index was positive and significant, $r(17) = .40, p < .05$.

Recall that in Study 1 the relationship–care perspective and the Social Responsibility Scale had been relatively weak predictors of assigning the other to the positive consequences task. Moral motivation associated with these measures may have been more effectively activated in Study 2 by the explicit mention of an equal chance and by provision of the coin. The explicit moral cue may have weakened the predictive power of the Ascription of Responsibility Scale, which had been created to tap felt responsibility to act morally even when the situation does not demand it.

Perception of the morally right course of action.   When participants were asked in the open-ended question what was the most morally right way to assign the tasks, flipping the coin was the most frequent response for both those who flipped and those who did not. Of the 10 who flipped, 8 said flipping the coin was most morally right, whereas the other 2 said letting the experimenter assign the tasks was most morally right. Of the 10 who did not flip, 6 said flipping the coin was most morally right, 2 judged assigning the other the positive consequences as most moral, 1 judged assigning oneself the positive consequences as most moral, and 1 said there was no morally right way to assign the tasks.

When asked later about the morality of the way they assigned the tasks, participants who flipped the coin said that what they had done was more morally right ($M = 7.30$ on the 1–9 scale) than did participants who did not flip ($M = 4.00$), $t(18) = 3.59$, $p < .002$. These ratings suggest that those who flipped the coin felt they had acted quite morally. Those who did not flip felt they had acted less morally, but even they on average rated the morality of their action near the midpoint of the scale.

Feeling proud or guilty after acting.   Consistent with perceptions of the morality of their action, those who flipped the coin reported feeling more proud ($M = 2.90$ vs. 2.40 on the 1–7 scale) and less guilty ($M = 2.80$ vs. 3.40) than did those who did not flip. Neither of these differences, however, approached statistical reliability, both $ts < 1.0$.

Moral outcome: Assignment to tasks.   Did moral action lead to a moral outcome? Of the 10 participants who did not flip the coin, only 1 assigned the other participant to the positive consequences task. This proportion (.10) was very similar to the proportion in Study 1 (.20). More revealing, of the 10 participants who flipped the coin, only 1 assigned the other to the positive consequences task. This proportion (.10) differed significantly from the .50 that would occur by chance when flipping a coin, $z = 2.53$, $p < .01$. This result was in stark contrast to results reported by Batson, Klein, Highberger, and Shaw (1995, Study 1), whose participants were in the role of supervisor assigning two other participants to tasks. With self-interest not an issue in their study, assignment proportion by coin flip was quite close to .50. Apparently, either ours was a very charitable coin, or with self-interest an issue, flipping the coin introduced enough ambiguity into the decision process that participants could feel moral while still favoring themselves. ("It's heads. Let's see, that means . . . I get the positive task." "It's tails. Let's see, that means . . . the other participant gets the neutral task.") Apparently, some of those flipping the coin took advantage of this ambiguity to hide self-interest in the guise of morality. Aggregating responses across participants, we were able to unmask this moral hypocrisy.

Summary.   Once again, even though the sample for Study 2 was small, results were clear. Receiving an explicit cue to the morally right course of action led a substantial proportion of the participants (10 of 20) to perform the prescribed moral action. Two of our moral responsibility measures, a relationship–care perspective and social responsibility, predicted who would perform this act. Those who performed the moral act rated themselves as having acted more morally and as feeling more proud and less guilty, although the feeling effects were not statistically reliable. One reason that the differences in pride and guilt were weaker in Study 2 than in Study 1 may be that at least some participants in Study 2 were aware that their "moral" act was a sham. A high percentage (9 of 10) of those who did not flip the coin took the positive consequences task for themselves, even though only 1 said this was the morally right thing to do. An equally high percentage of those who flipped the coin took the positive consequences task for themselves, even though none of them said this was the morally right thing to do. Still, those who flipped the coin rated their action as highly moral and as more moral than did those who did not flip. This pattern indicated the presence of moral hypocrisy.

Study 3

If a hypocrisy interpretation of the results of Study 2 is correct—that the coin provided enough ambiguity to permit participants to mask self-interest in moral guise—then reducing ambiguity by making it more difficult to justify assigning oneself the positive consequences task should increase assignment of the other to that task. In contrast, increasing the ambiguity of a self-interested choice by providing a seemingly fair solution that participants know gives them the positive consequences should lead to ready acceptance of this solution and perception of acceptance as moral.

Pursuing this logic, in Study 3 we added yet another feature to our moral dilemma: an experimental manipulation. In addition to stating that most participants think an equal chance is most fair and providing a coin, we informed participants of another option: They could accept a task assignment made by the experimenter, arbitrarily based on odd and even participant numbers. All participants knew that their number was odd. Some were told that because of this, the experimenter's assignment gave them the positive consequences task; others were told that it gave them the neutral consequences task.

To the degree that participants were motivated to uphold moral principle as an ultimate goal (moral integrity), they should be no more likely to accept the experimenter's assignment in the assigned positive condition than in the assigned neutral condition. To the degree that they were seeking to mask self-interest in the guise of morality (moral hypocrisy), they should be more likely to accept the experimenter's assignment in the former condition than in the latter.

Method

Participants.   The last 40 of the 80 participants from the questionnaire sessions took part in Study 3. Using a randomized block procedure, we assigned half to each of two experimental conditions: We informed 20 that the experimenter's assignment gave them the positive consequences task (*assigned positive condition*) and 20 that it gave them the neutral consequences task (*assigned neutral condition*).

Procedure.   The procedure for Study 3 was exactly the same as for Study 2, except for (a) the addition of information about the experimenter's assignment and (b) the inclusion on the task assignment form of an option to accept the experimenter's assignment. As in Study 2, the information sheet explained the assignment options, stated that most participants felt flipping a coin was most fair, and noted that a coin had been provided; then it asked participants to turn to a second page. The second page provided a typewritten description, with the heading "Another Option: Accepting the Experimenter's Assignment," which contained blanks into which handwritten information had been added:

> You also have another option. Instead of assigning the tasks yourself, you can accept the assignment that has already been made by the experimenter. The experimenter's assignment is arbitrarily based on odd and even participant

numbers. Your participant number is _____, an _____ number. Therefore, if you accept the experimenter's assignment, *you* will do the _____ consequences task; the *other participant* will do the _____ consequences task. You can simply accept this arbitrary assignment by the experimenter, or you can assign yourself and the other participant to tasks, making the assignment decision however you choose. Once again, your anonymity is assured.

Manipulation of experimenter's assignment.   Handwritten inserts in the first two blanks informed all participants that their number was "023," an "odd" number. Inserts in the last two blanks differed by experimental condition. Participants in the assigned positive condition read that if they accepted the experimenter's arbitrary assignment, they would do the "positive" consequences task and the other participant would do the "neutral" consequences task; participants in the assigned neutral condition read that they would do the "neutral" consequences task and the other participant would do the "positive" consequences task. A number of copies of the two versions of this page had been prepared in advance and placed in task assignment information folders so that the experimenter could remain unaware of each participant's experimental condition.

Assigning the tasks.   Prior to allowing participants to insert an *S* and *O* for self and other, respectively, to indicate whom they had assigned to the positive and neutral consequences tasks (as in Studies 1 and 2), the task assignment form in Study 3 provided another option:

> If you prefer to accept the experimenter's arbitrary assignment, place a check mark here: _____
>
> (If you placed a check mark above, then please leave the rest of this form blank.)

With the exception of this additional task assignment option, all of the measures reported for Studies 1 and 2 were used in Study 3, in exactly the same order.

Results and Discussion

Perception of the morally right course of action.   When participants were asked in the open-ended question what was the most morally right way to assign the tasks, their responses in the two experimental conditions differed very little, $\chi^2(3, N = 40) = 1.35, p > .70$. Of the 20 in the assigned positive condition, 7 said accepting the experimenter's assignment was most morally right, 6 said flipping the coin was most moral, 6 said assigning the other participant to the positive consequences task was most moral, and 1 said there was no morally right way. Of the 20 in the assigned neutral condition, 8 judged accepting the experimenter's assignment as most moral, 8 said flipping the coin was most moral, 3 said assigning the other participant to the positive consequences task was most moral, and 1 said there was no morally right way.

Acceptance of the experimenter's assignment.   Although there was little difference between experimental conditions in perceptions of the most moral course of action, there was a clear difference in acceptance of the experimenter's task assignment. In the assigned positive condition, 17 of 20 (.85) accepted the experimenter's assignment; in the assigned neutral condition, 11 of 20 (.55) accepted the experimenter's assignment. This difference was statistically reliable, $z = 2.14$, $p < .02$ (determined using a normal approximation based on arcsin transformation, Langer & Abelson, 1972; Winer, 1971, pp. 399–400). When the experimenter's arbitrary assignment favored oneself, it was very likely to be accepted. When it favored the other participant, it was less likely to be accepted, although it was still accepted slightly over half the time. Participants in the assigned neutral condition were free to ignore the experimenter's arbitrary assignment and either flip the coin or assign the tasks as they chose; still, many accepted assignment by the experimenter to the neutral consequences task. This condition was the only one across all three studies that produced any substantial proportion (beyond .20) of assignment of the other to the positive consequences task.

Moral responsibility correlates of accepting the experimenter's assignment in each experimental condition.   Coding accepting the experimenter's assignment as 1 and not accepting as 0, we found that the high proportion of participants in the assigned positive condition who accepted the experimenter's assignment (.85) restricted variance and limited correlations. It is not surprising, then, that none of the moral responsibility measures were reliably correlated with accepting the experimenter's assignment in this condition; the highest correlations were for ascription of responsibility and for the combined index, both $rs(18) = .23$, $.15 < ps < .20$. Nor was accepting the experimenter's assignment correlated with thinking that the way one assigned the tasks was morally right, $r(18) = .15$, $p > .25$, or with feeling proud or guilty, $rs(18) = -.01$ and .01, respectively.

In the assigned neutral condition, one moral responsibility measure, social responsibility, reliably predicted acceptance of the experimenter's assignment, $r(18) = .39$, $p < .05$. The justice perspective showed a nonsignificant negative correlation, $r(17) = -.21$, $p < .20$ (one participant failed to complete the justice

CHAPTER SIXTEEN

perspective measure). Correlations for the relationship–care perspective and ascription of responsibility were .02 and .22, respectively. The correlation for the combined measure was .14.

Perception of morality of and feelings after one's own action. Independent of experimental condition, the 28 participants who accepted the experimenter's assignment felt that the way they made the task assignment was morally right (*Ms* = 7.06 and 7.91 on the 1–9 scale for the assigned positive and assigned neutral conditions, respectively), $t(26) = 1.14$, $p > .25$, for test of difference between conditions. They also felt relatively little guilt (*Ms* = 2.38 and 1.00 on the 1–7 scale; no statistical test of difference was performed because there was no variance in the assigned neutral condition) and a moderate amount of pride (*Ms* = 2.63 and 3.09, respectively), $t(25) = 0.70$, *ns* (one participant in the assigned positive condition failed to complete the feeling questionnaire). These results indicated that the 11 participants who accepted the experimenter's assignment of themselves to the neutral consequences clearly felt that they had done the morally right thing, but the 17 who accepted the experimenter's assignment of themselves to the positive consequences felt almost as strongly that they had, too.

Perceptions of morality of and feelings after deciding whether to accept the experimenter's assignment to the neutral task. When asked about the morality of the way they assigned the tasks, participants in the assigned neutral condition who accepted the experimenter's assignment rated the morality of their action higher ($M = 7.91$) than did participants who did not accept the experimenter's assignment ($M = 5.89$), $t(18) = 2.95$, $p < .005$, although even the latter group, on average, rated the morality of their action above the midpoint of the 1–9 scale. There was also a clear difference in reported feelings of guilt (*Ms* = 1.00 and 3.67 for those who did and did not accept the experimenter's assignment to the neutral task, respectively; no statistical test of difference was performed because of the lack of variance among those who accepted the experimenter's assignment). There was no reliable difference in reported feelings of pride (*Ms* = 3.09 and 2.56, respectively), $t(18) = 0.67$, *ns*.

Moral outcome: Assignment to tasks. Next, we considered moral outcome by looking at task assignment in each experimental condition. In the assigned positive condition, of the 3 participants who did not accept the experimenter's assignment, 1 assigned herself the positive consequences task, and the other 2 flipped the coin. Both who flipped gave themselves the positive consequences task. This meant that, one way or another, all 20 participants in the assigned positive condition ended up with the positive consequences task.

	Individual whom participant assigned to positive consequences task	
TABLE 2		
Summary of Assignment of Other and Self to the Positive Consequences Task Across Three Studies		
Study	Other	Self
1: No moral cues ($N = 20$)	4	16
2: Fairness cue, coin ($N = 20$)	2	18
3: Fairness cue, coin, experimenter's assignment		
Assigned positive condition ($n = 20$)	0	20
Assigned neutral condition ($n = 20$)	11	9
Total	17	63

In the assigned neutral condition, of the 9 participants who did not accept the experimenter's assignment, 3 assigned themselves the positive consequences task, and the other 6 flipped the coin. Once again, all 6 who flipped gave themselves the positive consequences task. This meant that all 9 of the 20 participants in the assigned neutral condition who did not accept the experimenter's assignment ended up with the positive consequences task.

Combining Results of the Three Studies

Task assignment decision, our outcome measure in each study, is summarized in Table 2. As can be seen, across all three studies only 17 of 80 participants (.21) assigned the other participant to the positive consequences task. The lone circumstance in which participants assigned the other to positive consequences with any regularity was the assigned neutral condition of Study 3; the pattern of decisions in this condition clearly differed from that in the other condition of Study 3 and in Studies 1 and 2, $\chi^2(3, N = 80) = 29.54, p < .0002$. Apparently, making the conflict between self-interest and moral action less ambiguous by informing participants that they had been fairly assigned to the neutral consequences task trapped at least some participants into acting in accord with their moral principles. We say "trapped" because in Study 2, acting morally by flipping the coin had no effect on the morality of the outcome, and in Study 3, participants were significantly more likely to accept the experimenter's

TABLE 3

Summary of Correlations of Moral Responsibility Measures with
Moral Action Across Three Studies

| Study | Moral responsibility measure | | | | |
	Justice perspective	Relationship–care perspective	Social Responsibility Scale	Ascription of Responsibility Scale	Combined index[a]
1: No moral cues ($N = 20$)					
Assigning other to positive (4 of 20)	.29	.14	.04	.39*	.24
2: Fairness cue, coin ($N = 20$)					
Flipping the coin (10 of 20)	.24	.41*	.47**	.14	.40*
Assigning other to positive (2 of 20)[b]	—	—	—	—	—
3: Fairness cue, coin, experimenter's assignment;[c] assigned neutral condition ($n = 20$)					
Accepted experimenter's assignment (11 of 20)[d]	−.21	.02	.39*	.22	.14

[a] Average of standardized responses to the four responsibility measures.
[b] Responses on moral action measure were too imbalanced for meaningful analysis.
[c] In the assigned positive consequences task condition, no one assigned the other to positive consequences.
[d] Only those who accepted the experimenter's assignment gave the other the positive consequences.

*$p < .05$, one-tailed.   **$p < .025$, one-tailed.

assignment when it gave them the positive consequences task than when it gave them the neutral consequences task. In addition, of the 18 participants across Studies 2 and 3 who satisfied the dictates of morality by flipping the coin, 17 ended up with the positive consequences task. The likelihood of this occurring in an unbiased coin toss is very small ($z = 3.77$, $p < .0001$).

Correlations with the moral responsibility measures indicated that who could be trapped into acting morally was best predicted by the Social Responsibility Scale. As summarized in Table 3, this scale predicted moral action in both Study 2 (flipping the coin) and Study 3 (accepting the experimenter's assignment to the neutral task). In Study 2, this moral action had no effect on the morality of the outcome; those high-social-responsibility individuals who flipped the coin were no more likely to assign the other the positive consequences task than were the low-social-responsibility individuals who did not flip. In the assigned neutral condition of Study 3, in which there was more direct moral pressure to take the neutral consequences task oneself and give the other the positive consequences task, the Social Responsibility Scale significantly predicted moral outcome as well as action. None of the other measures of moral responsibility did.

General Discussion

The goal of the present research was to begin exploration of the scope and nature of moral motivation by using a simple, real, zero-sum dilemma in the laboratory. In Study 1, in which morality was not mentioned, 16 of 20 participants assigned themselves to the positive consequences task, even though in retrospect only 1 of these said this was the most moral way to assign the tasks. Of the four measures of moral responsibility, only ascription of responsibility significantly predicted assigning the other participant to the positive consequences task.

In Studies 2 and 3, a moral strategy was proposed: either flipping a coin or accepting assignment by the experimenter based on odd and even participant numbers. Also in Studies 2 and 3, ambiguity was introduced, allowing participants to act in a way that appeared moral yet still served self-interest. In Study 2, 10 of 20 participants flipped the coin, but of these 10, only 1 assigned the other participant to the positive consequences task. Measures of both a relationship–care perspective and social responsibility were significantly positively correlated with flipping the coin. In Study 3, participants were significantly more likely to accept the experimenter's assignment when it gave them the positive consequences. Indeed, all 20 participants in the assigned positive condition ended up with the positive consequences task. In the assigned neutral condition, 11 of 20 participants accepted the experimenter's assignment; they were the only participants in this condition to end up with neutral consequences. Social responsibility was the only moral responsibility measure that significantly correlated with accepting the experimenter's assignment in the assigned neutral condition. Much as in Study 2, all 8 participants in Study 3 who flipped the coin assigned themselves the positive consequences task.

Our samples were small in each study, yet results were clear. Moral action increased when the moral dimension of the assignment decision was made salient, but whenever ambiguity allowed, this action was likely to produce a self-serving outcome. Across the three studies, results clearly suggested the presence of moral hypocrisy, not moral integrity.

A Research Strategy for Uncovering Moral Motivation

The simplicity of our dilemma made it relatively easy for us to unmask the nature of the moral motivation by introducing ambiguity into the link between moral action and moral outcome, permitting individuals to pursue self-interest without having to look selfish. The general strategy was, first, to make the morality of the situation salient and, second, to either provide or not provide an opportunity to appear moral without having to incur the personal cost of a moral outcome. If one's ultimate goal is to uphold moral principle (moral integrity), then having this opportunity should not affect one's behavior, because the appearance of morality without the outcome does not reach the goal. If one's ultimate goal is to gain the self-benefits of appearing moral while, if possible, not incurring any personal cost (moral hypocrisy), then having this opportunity should affect one's behavior. The opportunity to act morally yet still benefit oneself should be especially attractive; only when the action–outcome link is unambiguous and unbreakable should moral action lead to moral outcome.

In our research, we used two strategies to introduce ambiguity into the action–outcome link. In Study 2, we encouraged flipping a coin, but we did not specify the task assignment associated with heads or tails, and we left participants alone to make their decision. These features allowed participants to act fairly and nonexploitatively, by flipping the coin, yet still ensure an outcome favorable to themselves. We do not know which participants adjusted the outcome in their own favor, but it seems almost certain that some did. We do know (from observing through a carefully disguised one-way mirror) that several flipped the coin more than once. Perhaps some flips were designated "practice" after seeing the result.

In Study 3, the same opportunity to flip the coin was presented along with yet another way to act morally—to accept the experimenter's assignment based on odd and even participant numbers. We assessed the effect of ambiguity by comparing acceptance of the experimenter's assignment when it led to a self-beneficial outcome and when it did not. Participants were very ready to accept the experimenter's evenhanded solution when it benefited them; they were less ready to do so when it meant giving up the positive consequences task, although slightly over half accepted the experimenter's assignment to the neutral consequences task. Having been assigned this task by an evenhanded method, these participants, who scored relatively high on social responsibility, may have found it impossible to do otherwise and still perceive themselves as being morally responsible.

Individual Differences in Moral Motivation

Across our three studies, the measures of the justice and relationship–care perspectives were related only weakly to moral action and outcome. The lone statistically reliable relation was for the relationship–care perspective with moral action (flipping the coin), but not moral outcome, in Study 2.

Whether the lack of association we found is a valid indication of the motivational impotence of the widely celebrated principles of justice and care or is an indication of the weakness of our measures of these principles we cannot say. It certainly seems prudent to suspect the measures first. Based on measures used by Ford and Lowery (1986), our measures of justice and care, like theirs, have unknown validity beyond obvious face validity. Regrettably, uncertain validity is not a problem unique to our measures; we know of no easily administered objective measures of justice or care perspectives with established validity (now that Rest's, 1979, Defining Issues Test is out of date). Until we have more confidence in our—or someone else's—measures of justice and care morality, we can draw no clear conclusions about the motivational impotence of these hallowed principles. We can entertain doubts but nothing more.

Our two responsibility measures were related more clearly to moral action, although in different ways. Schwartz's (1968) Ascription of Responsibility Scale, which was designed to measure a transsituational sense of responsibility, predicted moral action (and outcome) only in Study 1, in which explicit moral cues were absent. Berkowitz and Lutterman's (1968) Social Responsibility Scale predicted moral action in Studies 2 and 3, in which explicit moral cues were present; it predicted moral outcome only in the assigned neutral condition of Study 3, in which the action–outcome link was unambiguous and unavoidable.

Overall, this pattern of associations suggests that the Ascription of Responsibility Scale was measuring an individual difference relevant to the first step in the two-step process of moral hypocrisy: perception of the situation as morally relevant. The Social Responsibility Scale was measuring an individual difference relevant to the second step: desire to appear moral while, if possible, avoiding the cost of a moral outcome.

Qualifiers on the Evidence for Moral Hypocrisy

Given that, on the one hand, participants tended to express great adherence to moral responsibility in their self-reports on the four measures in the questionnaire session and that, on the other hand, when possible they acted in a way that had the surface appearance of morality yet still served self-interest, the label *moral hypocrisy* seems accurate—even unavoidable. Yet hypocrisy is a heavily value-laden label, and it is important to emphasize that we are not singling out our research participants as uniquely deserving of it. We assume that moral hypocrisy of the kind we observed is far more general. Although our research participants were all undergraduate women at the University of Kansas, we can think of no reason to believe that this population is any more prone to moral hypocrisy than most. To the contrary, one reason we selected women as participants was because they tend to describe themselves—and to be described by others—as more morally responsible than men (Eagly & Crowley, 1986; Ford & Lowery, 1986; Maccoby & Jacklin, 1974).

Even as our sample of research participants was limited by certain characteristics, so too was the moral dilemma they faced. Compared with the dilemmas posed by Kohlberg (1976) and Gilligan (1982), ours was simple, pedestrian, even banal. Getting or giving raffle tickets rather than performing a dull, boring task is not the kind of decision that immediately leaps to mind when one thinks of moral dilemmas. One may not even think of it as moral, although virtually all of our participants did. No doubt, had we posed a choice between getting raffle tickets and saving someone's life, we would have seen a very different pattern of results; everyone would have immediately recognized the moral dimension of the decision and would have acted to achieve a moral outcome. But such a finding would tell us nothing about the nature of their motivation. In order to gain insight into the nature of moral motivation, it seems best to avoid stereotypical, dramatic dilemmas in favor of the banal. The actor needs some psychological space in which to move, some opportunity to rationalize self-interest without setting off social and self-evaluation alarms.

Of course, if banal decisions that pit one's own interests against the interests of another have only trivial consequences, then evidence of moral hypocrisy in this context may seem of little significance. It is, however, not the specific behavior that is significant but the psychological process—the tendency to respond to explicit identification of the morality of a decision with motivation to appear moral yet still, if possible, serve self-interest. There is no reason to think that because this process can be seen most clearly in a banal context, it occurs only there. Bandura, Barbaranelli, Caprara, and Pastorelli (1996) recently documented the role of moral rationalization—for example, of convincing oneself that no real harm was done or, if harm was done, that it served a higher purpose—in adolescent aggression and delinquency. And as Arendt (1964), Staub (1989b), and others have observed, truly atrocious evil can arise from a chain of benign, banal decisions, each extending one's moral myopia to include the next link.

Theoretical Implications of the Evidence for Moral Hypocrisy

We found no support for Frank's (1988) optimistic suggestion of an evolutionary stable strategy of moral integrity; our results were instead consistent with Trivers's (1985) more cynical suggestion of moral deception, possibly including self-deception. Of course, our results provide no evidence that the moral hypocrisy we observed was based on a genetic allele for reciprocal altruism, as Trivers assumed; it could have evolved socially or strategically as a direct product of self-interest.

Nor do our results provide clear evidence that self-deception was involved. Did participants consciously cheat on the coin flip; were they aware of greater willingness to accept an arbitrary assignment that served self-interest? We cannot be sure, but the way in which participants spoke of their actions during debriefing, as well as their ratings of the morality of their action, leads us to believe that at least some self-deception occurred. In philosophical terms, more was involved than *akrasia* (weakness of will), in which the desire to do right is overpowered by selfish desires (Aristotle, 1911); there were also signs of the subtle hypocrisy involving self-deceit discussed by Butler (1722/1896) and Hegel (1821/1952; see Kittay, 1992, for a summary of the philosophical literature on hypocrisy).

When self-interest and morality conflict, one must deceive oneself if one is to serve self-interest and still reap self-rewards for being moral. How might this happen? In their bystander intervention studies, Latané and Darley (1970, pp. 121–122) reported evidence of suspended and reconstructed thought—blocking and cycling—among individuals trying to decide what to do in an emergency. Similarly, some participants in our dilemma may not have clearly decided what heads and tails meant until they saw which side of the coin was up.

The underlying psychological process seems akin to deindividuation (Zimbardo, 1969; also see Diener, 1977). Our participants were left alone to make the task assignment decision (including flipping the coin), and they thought the other participant would never know they did the assigning. To the extent that self-deception was involved, however, our results take us beyond deindividuation: Rather than masking one's personal identity from others, one's true motivation is masked from oneself. Clearly, we need to understand more about the level and nature of moral self-deception.

Distinguishing Altruistic and Moral Motivation

Our results suggest that the goal of moral motivation is to appear moral while, if possible, still serving self-interest. Do these results cast doubt on recent claims (e.g., Batson, 1991) for the existence of empathy-induced altruism? Might benefiting the person for whom one feels empathy be an instrumental goal on the way to the ultimate goal of gaining the social and self-rewards for appearing altruistic? Research evidence suggests not. Using a strategy for disentangling instrumental and ultimate goals similar to the one we used, Batson et al. (1988) found clear and consistent evidence across five studies that the motivation to help evoked by empathy was directed toward benefiting the target of empathy as an ultimate goal, not as an instrumental means to benefit oneself.

It is becoming increasingly clear that empathy-induced altruism and moral motivation should not be equated or confused. The goal of the former is to benefit the person(s) for whom empathy is felt; the goal of the latter is to uphold a moral principle. The empathy–altruism research suggests that the former goal can be ultimate; the present research casts doubt on whether the latter goal can be. Highlighting the difference between these two distinct forms of prosocial motivation, Batson et al. (1995) found evidence that empathy-induced altruism—much like self-interested egoism—can conflict with and even overpower moral motivation, leading to an immoral outcome.

Conclusion

None of our moral responsibility measures were able to predict moral integrity. This may have been, however, because we found so little moral integrity to predict. Rather than accepting the straightforward, optimistic assumption of integrity that undergirds so much preaching, teaching, and politicking and so much moral psychology, a social psychological analysis of moral motivation may need to start with the more complex, cynical assumption of moral hypocrisy. To understand moral motivation, one may need to listen to those speaking in a very different voice, the voice of Austen, Dickens, and Twain.

Notes

1. Only women participated, for two reasons. First, the experimenters for each study were women, and to reduce impression-management concerns, we wished to keep gender of experimenter and participant the same. Second, we wanted to be sure that both justice and relationship–care perspectives were well represented among our participants. Previous research has indicated that women are as likely to endorse a justice perspective as men and are slightly more likely to endorse a relationship–care perspective (Dyck, Batson, Oden, & Weeks, 1989; Ford & Lowery, 1986).

2. Given the clear directional prediction for association of the moral responsibility measures with moral action, and in the interest of consistency, all statistical tests we report are one-tailed.

References

Alexander, R. D. (1987). *The biology of moral systems.* New York: Aldine de Gruyter.

Arendt, H. (1964). *Eichmann in Jerusalem: A report on the banality of evil.* New York: Penguin Books.

Aristotle. (1911). *The Nicomachian ethics* (D. P. Chase, Trans.). New York: E. P. Dutton.

Austen, J. (1969). *Sense and sensibility.* Baltimore: Penguin Books. (Original work published 1811)

Bandura, A. (1991). Social cognitive theory of moral thought and action. In W. M. Kurtines & W. M. Gewirtz (Eds.), *Handbook of moral behavior and development: Vol. 1. Theory* (pp. 45–103). Hillsdale, NJ: Erlbaum.

Bandura, A., Barbaranelli, C., Caprara, G. V., & Pastorelli, C. (1996). Mechanisms of moral disengagement in the exercise of moral agency. *Journal of Personality and Social Psychology, 71,* 364–374.

Batson, C. D. (1991). *The altruism question: Toward a social-psychological answer.* Hillsdale, NJ: Erlbaum.

Batson, C. D., Dyck, J. L., Brandt, J. R., Batson, J. G., Powell, A. L., McMaster, M. R., & Griffitt, C. (1988). Five studies testing two new egoistic alternatives to the empathy–altruism hypothesis. *Journal of Personality and Social Psychology, 55,* 52–77.

Batson, C. D., Fultz, J., Schoenrade, P. A., & Paduano, A. (1987). Critical self-reflection and self-perceived altruism: When self-reward fails. *Journal of Personality and Social Psychology, 53,* 594–602.

Batson, C. D., Klein, T. R., Highberger, L., & Shaw, L. L. (1995). Immorality from empathy-induced altruism: When compassion and justice conflict. *Journal of Personality and Social Psychology, 68,* 1042–1054.

Berkowitz, L., & Lutterman, K. (1968). The traditionally socially responsible personality. *Public Opinion Quarterly, 32,* 169–185.

Blasi, A. (1980). Bridging moral cognition and moral action: A critical review of the literature. *Psychological Bulletin, 88,* 1–45.

Blum, L. A. (1980). *Friendship, altruism, and morality.* London: Routledge & Kegan Paul.

Butler, J. (1896). Upon self-deceit. In W. E. Gladstone (Ed.), *The works of Joseph Butler, D. C. L.: Vol. 2. Sermons.* Oxford: Clarendon Press. (Original work published 1722)

Campbell, D. T. (1975). On the conflicts between biological and social evolution and between psychology and moral tradition. *American Psychologist, 30,* 1103–1126.

Dickens, C. (1982). *Martin Chuzzlewit.* New York: Oxford University Press. (Original work published 1843–1844)

Diener, E. (1977). Deindividuation: Causes and consequences. *Social Behavior and Personality, 5,* 143–156.

Dyck, J. L., Batson, C. D., Oden, A., & Weeks, J. L. (1989, April). *Another look at the altruism in the altruistic personality: Hers and his.* Paper presented at the meeting of the Midwestern Sociological Association, St. Louis, MO.

Eagly, A. H., & Crowley, M. (1986). Gender and helping behavior: A meta-analytic review of the social-psychological literature. *Psychological Bulletin, 100,* 283–308.

Ford, M. R., & Lowery, C. R. (1986). Gender differences in moral reasoning: A comparison of the use of justice and care orientations. *Journal of Personality and Social Psychology, 50,* 777–783.

Frank, R. H. (1988). *Passions within reason: The strategic role of the emotions.* New York: Norton.

Freud, S. (1961). *Civilization and its discontents* (J. Strachey, Trans.). New York: Norton. (Original work published 1930)

Gilligan, C. (1982). *In a different voice: Psychological theory and women's development.* Cambridge, MA: Harvard University Press.

Gilligan, C., Ward, J. V., & Taylor, J. M. (1988). *Mapping the moral domain: A contribution of women's thinking to psychological theory and education.* Cambridge, MA: Harvard University Press.

Hartshorne, H., & May, M. A. (1928). *Studies in the nature of character: Vol. 1. Studies in deceit.* New York: Macmillan.

Hartshorne, H., May, M. A., & Maller, J. B. (1929). *Studies in the nature of character: Vol. 2. Studies in self-control.* New York: Macmillan.

Hegel, G. W. F. (1952). *The philosophy of right* (T. M. Knox, Trans.). Oxford: Clarendon Press. (Original work published 1821)

Hitchens, C. (1995). *The missionary position: Mother Teresa in theory and practice.* New York: Verso.

Kant, I. (1898). *Kant's critique of practical reason and other works on the theory of ethics* (4th ed., T. K. Abbott, Trans.). New York: Longmans, Green. (Original work published 1785)

Kittay, E. F. (1992). Hypocrisy. In L. C. Becker & C. B. Becker (Eds.), *Encyclopedia of ethics* (pp. 582–587). New York: Garland.

Kohlberg, L. (1969). Stage and sequence: The cognitive-developmental approach to socialization. In D. A. Goslin (Ed.), *Handbook of socialization theory and research* (pp. 347–480). Chicago: Rand McNally.

Kohlberg, L. (1976). Moral stages and moralization: The cognitive-developmental approach. In T. Lickona (Ed.), *Moral development and behavior: Theory, research, and social issues* (pp. 31–53). New York: Holt, Rinehart, & Winston.

Kohlberg, L. (1984). *Essays on moral development: Vol. 2. The psychology of moral development.* San Francisco: Harper & Row.

Kozol, J. (1991). *Savage inequalities: Children in America's schools.* New York: Crown.

Kurtines, W. M., & Gewirtz. W. M. (Eds.), (1991). *Handbook of moral behavior and development.* Hillsdale, NJ: Erlbaum.

Kurtines, W. M., & Greif, E. B. (1974). The development of moral thought: Review and evaluation of Kohlberg's approach. *Psychological Bulletin, 81,* 453–470.

Langer, E. J., & Abelson, R. P. (1972). The semantics of asking a favor: How to succeed in getting help without really dying. *Journal of Personality and Social Psychology, 24,* 26–32.

Latané, B., & Darley, J. M. (1970). *The unresponsive bystander: Why doesn't he help?* New York: Appleton-Century-Crofts.

Lepper, M. R., Greene, D., & Nisbett, R. E. (1973). Undermining children's intrinsic interest with extrinsic reward: A test of the "overjustification" hypothesis. *Journal of Personality and Social Psychology, 28,* 129–137.

Maccoby, E. E., & Jacklin, C. N. (1974). *The psychology of sex differences.* Stanford, CA: Stanford University Press.

McKinnon, C. (1991). Hypocrisy, with a note on integrity. *American Philosophical Quarterly, 28,* 321–330.

Noddings, N. (1984). *Caring: A feminine approach to ethics and moral education.* Berkeley: University of California Press.

Oliner, S. P., & Oliner, P. M. (1988). *The altruistic personality: Rescuers of Jews in Nazi Europe.* New York: Free Press.

Rawls, J. (1971). *A theory of justice.* Cambridge, MA: Harvard University Press.

Rest, J. R. (1979). *Development in judging moral issues.* Minneapolis: University of Minnesota Press.

Rushton, J. P. (1980). *Altruism, socialization and society.* Englewood Cliffs, NJ: Prentice Hall.

Schwartz, S. H. (1968). Words, deeds, and the perception of consequences and responsibility in action situations. *Journal of Personality and Social Psychology, 10,* 232–242.

Schwartz, S. H., & Howard, J. (1981). A normative decision-making model of altruism. In J. P. Rushton & R. M. Sorrentino (Eds.), *Altruism and helping behavior* (pp. 189–211). Hillsdale, NJ: Erlbaum.

Snyder, M., & Ickes, W. (1985). Personality and social behavior. In G. Lindzey & E. Aronson (Eds.), *Handbook of social psychology (3rd ed.): Vol. 2. Special fields and applications* (pp. 883–948). New York: Random House.

Snyder, M. L., Kleck, R. E., Strenta, A., & Mentzer, S. J. (1979). Avoidance of the handicapped: An attributional ambiguity analysis. *Journal of Personality and Social Psychology, 37,* 2297–2306.

Staub, E. (1974). Helping a distressed person: Social, personality, and stimulus determinants. In L. Berkowitz (Ed.), *Advances in experimental social psychology* (Vol. 7, pp. 293–341). New York: Academic Press.

Staub, E. (1989a). Individual and societal (group) values in a motivational perspective and their role in benevolence and harmdoing. In N. Eisenberg, J. Reykowski, & E. Staub (Eds.), *Social and moral values: Individual and societal perspectives* (pp. 45–61). Hillsdale, NJ: Erlbaum.

Staub, E. (1989b). *The roots of evil: The origins of genocide and other group violence.* New York: Cambridge University Press.

Trivers, R. L. (1971). The evolution of reciprocal altruism. *Quarterly Review of Biology, 46,* 35–57.

Trivers, R. L. (1985). *Social evolution.* Menlo Park. CA: Benjamin/Cummings.

Twain, M. (1959). *Adventures of Huckleberry Finn.* New York: Penguin Books. (Original work published 1884)

Webster's desk dictionary of the English language. (1990). New York: Portland House.

Williams, B. (1976). Utilitarianism and moral self-indulgence. In H. D. Lewis (Ed.), *Contemporary British philosophy* (4th ser., pp. 306–321). London: Allen & Unwin.

Winer, B. J. (1971). *Statistical principles in experimental design* (2nd ed.). New York: McGraw-Hill.

Wright, D. (1971). *The psychology of moral behavior.* Baltimore: Penguin Books.

Zimbardo, P. G. (1969). The human choice: Individuation, reason, and order versus deindividuation, impulse, and chaos. In W. J. Arnold & D. Levine (Eds.), *Nebraska Symposium on Motivation: Vol. 17* (pp. 237–309). Lincoln: University of Nebraska Press.

Questions for Review and Discussion

1. How did Batson et al. define moral hypocrisy?
2. What task did most of those participants in Study 2 who flipped a coin assign to themselves and why?
3. How well did individual differences in moral motivation predict moral behavior in these studies?

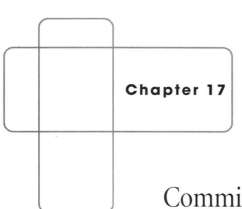

Chapter 17

Committing Altruism under the Cloak of Self-Interest: The Exchange Fiction

John G. Holmes, Dale T. Miller, and Melvin J. Lerner

Neoclassical economists do not mince words when articulating the role of self-interest in human affairs. Statements such as "the only assumption essential to a descriptive and predictive science of human behavior is egoism" (Mueller, 1986) and "the average human being is about 95 percent selfish in the narrow sense of the word" (Tullock, 1976) are as clear as they are bold. And it is not only rational choice theorists who view self-interest as the cardinal human motive. The layperson seems equally persuaded in this regard. For example, surveys routinely find that the vast majority of respondents consider most individuals to be motivated primarily by self-interest (e.g., Kohn, 1990; Wuthnow, 1991). Further, when laypersons are asked to predict the attitudes and behaviors of others they rely heavily on the assumption of self-interest (Miller & Ratner, 1996, 1998). Given this, it is hardly surprising that even efforts to promote social virtue emphasize self-interest. "Ethics pay," as the familiar corporate slogan puts it.

Despite the motivational power that self-interest is accorded by theorists and laypersons alike, a growing body of social science research points to the inadequacy of simple self-interest models of human behavior (for reviews, see Abelson, 1995; Etzioni, 1988; Green & Shapiro, 1994; Kohn, 1990; Lerner, 1980; Mansbridge, 1990; Sears & Funk, 1991; Sen, 1977; Tyler & Dawes, 1993). Although people certainly do care about their own material well-being, they

Reprinted from *Journal of Experimental Social Psychology*, Vol. 38, pp. 144–151, © 2002, with permission from Elsevier.

also care about the well-being of others (Batson, 1991) and about general principles of justice and fairness (Lerner, 1975, 1977, 1987; Lerner, Miller, & Holmes, 1976). This leaves us with a puzzle: Why does the assumption of self-interest have such wide currency in the face of so much evidence to the contrary? We consider one possibility in this article. We propose that even individuals experiencing strong feelings of compassion will be hesitant to act, or appear to act, on those feelings if doing so is inconsistent with their self-interest, a circumstance that reinforces and perpetuates a collective belief in the power of self-interest (Miller & Prentice, 1994; Miller & Ratner, 1996; Miller, 1999; Ratner & Miller, 2001).

The claim that individuals often conceal their more noble sentiments under the guise of self-interest is not new. Over 100 years ago, the French social philosopher Alexis deTocqueville observed that: "Americans . . . enjoy explaining almost every act of their lives on the principle of self-interest . . . I think that in this they often do themselves less than justice, for sometimes in the United States, as elsewhere, one sees people carried away by the . . . spontaneous impulses natural to man. But the Americans are hardly prepared to admit that they do give way to emotions of this sort" (1835/1969, p. 546).

Robert Wuthnow (1991) reached a similar conclusion in his recent examination of *Acts of Compassion.* According to Wuthnow, although people engage in many acts of genuine compassion, their vocabulary for talking about their motives in these cases is extremely impoverished. The language they seem most comfortable with in explaining their acts of compassion is one that emphasizes self-interest. For example, their accounts for giving to charity generally emphasize pragmatic or instrumental reasons: "It gave me something to do," "I liked the other volunteers," "It got me out of the house." People seem loathe to acknowledge that their behavior may have been motivated by genuine compassion or kindness. Indeed, the people Wuthnow interviewed seemed to go out of their way to stress that they were not "a bleeding heart, a goody two-shoes, or a do-gooder."

Why might people be inhibited from expressing the compassion they feel for others? Lerner's formulation of the justice motive (Lerner, 1975, 1980; Lerner, Miller, & Holmes, 1976; Miller, 1977) offers one possibility. According to Lerner, people confronted by the innocent suffering of another face a conflict. On the one hand, this experience is disturbing because it threatens the person's belief that the world is just and hence prompts the impulse to help eliminate the injustice. On the other hand, the impulse to help is itself threatening because acting upon it could undermine the person's ability to maintain just outcomes for him- or herself. Were the person to offer unconditional help to the person or group in need, he or she would confront difficult questions of the following kind: "If this person or group is worthy of my assistance, are the myriad other similar victims whose suffering I am exposed to on a regular basis not also worthy of my help?" and "If this type of person or group is worthy of help now are they not also worthy of help in the future?"

It will not be easy to answer these questions negatively and deny any further commitments, yet to answer them affirmatively renders the would-be helper vulnerable to becoming a victim him- or herself. For this reason, Lerner argues people may resist responding to appeals for unconditional help and instead rely on various psychological techniques (e.g., victim derogation) to convince themselves that help from them is unwarranted. Indeed, recent research by Hafer (2000), using a cognitive interference procedure, supports the proposed link between victim derogation and the experience of preconscious threat induced by the observation of innocent suffering. Alternatively, a possibility that we explore in the current research is that people may actually act upon their feelings of compassion but find ways of "conditionalizing" the action so as to minimize its implications for their ability to achieve deserved outcomes for themselves. Convincing oneself that one's action comports with one's self-interest is one important means of finding psychological cover for helping.

The Exchange Fiction

If people generate self-interested accounts for their prosocial acts so as not to appear motivated by compassion, either to themselves or to others, perhaps they also welcome those opportunities that provide them with self-interested accounts for acting compassionately. Tax deductions in exchange for charitable donations may provide a case in point. When people receive a tax deduction in exchange for their assistance, they do not have to feel like a do-gooder. They can construe their action as something to feel good about, but not as something that implies a responsibility to help all victim groups or even this victim group in the future. From the perspective of the present analysis, it is the symbolic or psychological value of a tax deduction, and not merely its material value that makes tax-deductible donations so attractive.

The wisdom of offering people psychological cover for their altruistic behavior also may, knowingly or unknowingly, underlie the practice of offering potential charity donors some product (e.g., light bulbs, address stickers, and magazine subscriptions) for their donations. The commonness of this practice suggests that the net profit elicited by product-for-donation exchanges might well exceed that elicited by strict charity appeals alone. If so, the explanation for the success of the strategy might reside in the fact that the offer of an exchange creates a *fiction* that permits people to act on their impulse to help without committing themselves to unwanted psychological burdens, such as an enduring, open-ended relationship with either the victim or similar victims. That is, the offer of an exchange permits people to still feel good about doing "their part" without committing themselves to a hard-to-live-up-to psychological contract. In effect, the exchange fiction provides the mask under which the altruist can express her compassion and concerns with justice without having to reveal, or even recognize, her motives—after all, she is merely engaging in an economic transaction. Two field studies were designed to test this hypothesis.

Study 1

Study 1 tested the main empirical prediction of the exchange fiction hypothesis—namely that the offer of a product in exchange for a charitable donation will increase contributions.[1] We approached participants with a request to assist a charity by making a financial contribution either through a direct donation or by purchasing decorative candles. In order to probe further the reasoning behind the exchange fiction hypothesis, we also manipulated the level of need characterizing the target group. We predicted that because compassion should increase with victim need, so should the disinhibiting effect of a "rational" economic explanation for helping. That is, when victim need is high, people should most wish to disguise their compassion, thereby rendering especially great the increment in financial yield produced by the offer of an exchange.

Method

Participants   Eighty-eight (44 male and 44 female) undergraduates were approached for donations. All participants were alone on campus when approached.

Design and procedure   Four experimenters, two male and two female, presented themselves to participants as representatives of one of three charitable organizations. The charities represented were real organizations, although their names were modified slightly. The content of the appeals was developed from literature provided by these groups. All donations were given directly to these charities at the conclusion of the study. Experimenters were instructed to approach an equal number of male and female participants and to vary the location and time of day of their solicitations. Experimenters memorized and rehearsed each appeal to the point where they could deliver it naturally and without reference to notes. They were blind to the hypotheses.

Need manipulation. The appeal with which experimenters approached participants portrayed one of three levels of victim need. The specific appeals were as follows.

> **Low Need:** Hello, I'm from the Kitchener-Waterloo Recreational Society. We are interested in helping our midget softball team buy equipment for their members who are seven to ten years old. They are being sponsored for some of the necessary equipment but we'd like them to be fully fitted out and feel they should have the best available equipment.

> **Moderate Need:** Hello, I'm from the Kitchener-Waterloo Perceptually Handicapped Society. We're starting a training program for handicapped children from seven to ten years old who have problems in performing various normal activities. We hope that this program will be able to help them deal with their problems. There are over two hundred children in the program and we need a lot of support to make it effective.

> **High Need:** Hello, I'm from the Kitchener-Waterloo Society for Emotionally Disturbed Children. We're starting a training and remedial program for handicapped and emotionally disturbed children from seven to ten years of age who have severe problems in coping with most normal activities. We hope that with this program we can avert the tragedy that will result if these children are left to cope alone with their problems. There are over two hundred children who could remain damaged for life if they don't get help, so we need a lot of support to make the program effective.

Exchange manipulation. A set of decorative candles was chosen as the product for the economic transaction. The candles varied from a small 2 × 3 in. cylinder at .75¢ to a large 12 × 3 in. model at $3.50. We chose candles as the product because a civic group on campus had used candles in their appeals for various charities. According to representatives from this group, the candles were perceived as a reasonable, high-quality product, although not one that people normally rushed to buy.

In the *exchange* condition the experimenter brought out the candles after he or she had introduced the need manipulation. The positive attributes of the candles were emphasized in a "soft-sell" pitch:

> We're selling and distributing four different types of candles, each offered at a good price. The candles range from this smaller one at seventy-five cents to this larger candle at three dollars and fifty cents. We feel these are interesting designs and would make an excellent gift for friends and relatives. They are of excellent quality and are long-lasting.

		TABLE 1		
The Average Contribution and Proportion of Persons Contributing in Study I				
	Level of deserving			
Condition	Low	Moderate	High	Marginal means
Donation	14.47	34.06	40.50	28.78
	0.16	0.44	0.44	0.33
Exchange	38.46	33.33	131.25	66.89
	0.23	0.17	0.69	0.35
Marginal means	24.22	33.75	79.39	
	0.19	0.32	0.54	

Note.   The first number in each cell is the amount of contribution in cents. The second number is the proportion of people who made a donation.

In the *donation* condition, the experimenter followed the need manipulation by simply stating that "any donation of seventy-five cents or more would be very helpful to the children." The requested minimum donation was .75¢ in order to equate for the minimum candle price in the exchange condition.

Results and Discussion

The amount of money contributed to the charity was analyzed in a 2 (Solicitation Form: exchange vs donation) $\times$ 3 (Need: low, medium, and high) analysis of variance (ANOVA) (see Table 1). (Because the proportion of participants helping by either making a donation or buying candles was highly correlated with amount contributed, $r = .76$, the results for the proportion measure will only be presented when they differ from those for amount.) The effects of sex of experimenter and sex of subject did not approach significance and are not discussed further.

The ANOVA revealed main effects on the amount contributed for both need of the victim group, $F(2, 82) = 4.35$, $p < .025$, and form of solicitation, $F(1, 82) = 5.30$, $p < .025$. We had hypothesized that the impact of an exchange offer on donation behavior would be most apparent when the need of the victim group was high. Consistent with this prediction, the ANOVA revealed a marginally significant interaction between victim need and solicitation form for the contribution measure, $F(2, 82) = 2.72, p < .075$, and for the proportion measure, $F(2, 82) = 2.33, p < .10$.

Simple effects analyses provided further support for the *a priori* experimental hypothesis. As expected, in the donation condition need of the victim group had no significant impact on contributions ($F < 1$). In the exchange condition, however, victim need strongly affected the amount of contributions, $F(2, 82) = 6.39, p < .005$. More specifically, the high-need condition induced greater helping responses than either of the other two need conditions, which did not differ from one another, $F(1, 82) = 12.72, p < .001$.

Finally, consistent with the exchange fiction analysis, the offer of an exchange in the high-need condition produced significantly larger contributions than did the strict donation appeal, $F(1, 82) = 7.67, p < .005$. As expected, the offer of an exchange had no effect in the low-need condition ($Fs < 1$), indicating that people had little interest in the candles for their own sake. The offer of an exchange also did not facilitate helping in the moderate-need condition.

The results of Study 1 generally supported the hypothesis that people are more likely to act upon compassionate impulses when doing so can be disguised as an economic transaction. The psychological cover provided by the transaction is perhaps all the more intriguing when viewed in the context of the results in the low-need condition, which indicated that participants had no interest in the candles themselves. Despite this, the presumably heightened sympathy aroused in the high-need condition only produced corresponding levels of help when the act of help could be explained as an exchange for such a candle. Together, these findings suggest that the reason that the offer of candles increased net donations is that this offer provided not an incentive, but an "excuse" for giving.

Study 2

Study 2 provided a second test of the hypothesis that people's willingness to express compassion for a victim will increase if it can take the form of an economic transaction. This study, like the previous study, manipulated victim need. However, it did not merely vary whether an exchange was offered as did Study 1, but actually varied how much of a bargain the exchange was purported to be. In all the exchange conditions the cost of the candles ($3) and the alleged "profit" to the charity from the exchange ($1) were held constant. The manipulation involved describing the $3 price of the candles as (1) a "Fair Price," allegedly similar to that found in most area stores; (2) a "Bargain Price," allegedly $1 less than in most area stores; or (3) an "Altruist's Price," allegedly

$1 more than in most area stores. Donation-only appeals within each level of need were included for baseline purposes.

The pricing conditions were designed to vary the extent to which psychological cover was provided by the transaction descriptions. The more attractive the "deal" offered, the easier it would be to interpret the transaction in instrumental terms and obscure any compassion experienced by the helper. Essentially, favorable terms of exchange provide "sufficient explanation" for the act. Closet altruists in the Bargain Price condition, for instance, could help without exposing themselves to threats from either a burdensome person attribution ("I am the sort of person who feels compelled to help such needy victims") or a burdensome entity attribution ("These victims legitimately need and are deserving of help"). Such attributions are potentially troublesome because they leave the actor open to future demands and internal conflicts.

Two specific hypotheses guided Study 2. First, it was hypothesized that greater helping rates would occur in the exchange conditions than in the strict donation conditions. Second, it was hypothesized that the impact of need on helping rates would depend on the extent to which the act of help could be economically justified. Specifically, need was expected to have least impact under the altruist price framing, intermediate impact under the fair price framing, and greatest impact under the bargain price framing.

Method

Participants   One hundred (50 male and 50 female) undergraduates were approached for donations. All participants were alone on campus when approached.

Procedure   The procedure for Study 2 closely paralleled that of Study 1. Two male and two female experimenters presented themselves to participants on the university campus as representatives of one of two charitable organizations. The experimenter introduced each appeal by describing the charity and the plight of the "victims" it represented. In one condition the victims were characterized in low-need terms and in the other in high-need terms. The wording of these appeals was virtually identical to that used in the corresponding conditions of Study 1. In all three exchange conditions, the experimenter next showed the participant the candle (a 3-in. cube with an abstract design in various colors) and explained: "We're selling and distributing these candles at three dollars each. We feel that it's an interesting design and would make an excellent gift for friends and relatives, or simply for yourself." Following this statement, the experimenter made one of three pitches:

Fair Price condition: Three dollars is the normal price for this type of candle in stores in the area. Even at this good price it allows us a one-dollar profit that goes to our organization for each candle sold. Would you be interested in buying one or more of these candles?

Bargain Price condition: The normal price for this type of candle in stores in the area is in the four-dollar range. Three dollars is therefore an extremely good price that gives you very good value in return for your money. In addition, we can still have a one-dollar profit that goes to our organization for each candle sold. Would you be interested in buying one or more of these candles?

Altruist's Price condition: The normal price for this type of candle in stores in the area is approximately two dollars but we're charging three dollars so that the one-dollar profit can go as a donation to our organization for each candle sold. Would you be interested in buying one or more of these candles?

Two different donation baseline groups were employed. In the first, the experimenter followed a description of the charity with the request: "Any donation of one dollar or more would be very helpful to the children." In the second, the experimenter followed a description of the charity with the request: "Any donation of three dollars or more would be very helpful to the children." The $1 donation condition was included because this was the amount of alleged profit in the exchange conditions; the $3 donation condition was included because this was the amount of the total request in the exchange conditions.

Results and Discussion

The amount of money contributed in each condition and the proportions of contributors are reported in Table 2. As in Study 1, the amount of money received and the proportion of individuals contributing were highly correlated, $r = .86$, and analyses are reported only for amount. The results were first analyzed in a 2 (Victim Need: high vs low) $\times$ 4 (Solicitation Form: bargain price, fair price, altruist's price, and donation) ANOVA. The $1.00 donation condition was included as the donation appeal in this analysis as it provided a much more conservative point of comparison for proportions in the exchange conditions than the $3.00 donation condition.

The analysis of participants' contributions revealed main effects for need of the victim group, $F(1, 98) = 14.62$, $p < .001$, and for the form of solicitation, $F(3, 98) = 4.00$, $p < .01$. Qualifying the main effects was a

	TABLE 2				
	The Average Contributions and Proportion of Persons Contributing in Study 2				
			Solicitation form		
	Donation type		Exchange framing		
Condition	$1	$3	Altruist's price	Fair price	Bargain price
Low need	31.3	25.0	27.3	27.3	30.0
	0.25	0.08	0.09	0.09	0.10
High need	41.2	50.0	120.0	150.0	184.6
	0.40	0.17	0.40	0.50	0.62

Note.   The first number in each condition is the amount of the contribution in cents. The bottom number is the proportion of people making a contribution.

Victim Need $\times$ Solicitation Form interaction, $F(3, 98) = 3.06$, $p < .05$. As predicted, the form of appeal affected the amount of contributions within the high-need case, $F(3, 98) = 4.88$, $p < .005$, but not within the low-need case ($F < 1$). In fact, while the offer of an exchange elicited higher contributions than a mere request for a donation in the high-need condition, $F(1, 98) = 7.92$, $p < .005$, there was no difference between these conditions in the low-need condition ($F < 1$). The absence of a difference between the donation condition and the exchange conditions in the low-need conditions is noteworthy because it suggests that the candle held no intrinsic or economic value for participants—indeed, only one person purchased a candle in each of the low-need conditions.

There was a strong linear trend for amount contributed across the four solicitation conditions under high-need, $F(1, 98) = 10.31$, $p < .005$ [though a weaker one for the proportion of contributions, $F(1, 98) = 2.63$, $p = .11$; for both measures combined, Multivariate $F(2, 97) = 18.01$, $p < .001$]. Comparisons were made among the three types of exchange appeals, using conservative Scheffe contrasts. Consistent with predictions, participants contributed more in the bargain price condition than in the altruist's price condition, $F(1, 98) = 2.19$, $p < .075$. The amount of contributions elicited by the fair price appeal fell in between the latter two conditions as expected, although it did not differ significantly from either.

Finally, the effects described above are stronger in every case for the proportions analysis when the $3 donation condition is included in the analysis because the proportion of contributors in the $3 condition was significantly lower than in the $1 condition. This result, consistent with our theoretical perspective, suggests that the $3 condition is the more appropriate control group. Indeed, we included the $1 donation condition because of concerns that the $3 request might elicit *greater* contributions by serving to define a higher standard for an "act of help." Apparently though, the $3 criterion represents a much more substantial request, a hurdle that contributors, including those in the exchange conditions, had to overcome in order to help.

The results from Study 2 were generally consistent with the hypothesized relation between the "economics" of the transaction and donation behavior. They also supported our speculation concerning the dynamics underlying this relation. The framing of the sales appeal had no impact on donation behavior in the low-need case, but the ordering of means in the high-need condition was consistent with our analysis of the relative disinhibiting power inherent in each of the experimental framings. The most psychological cover for acting upon compassionate impulses was presumably provided by the framing in the bargain price condition, the second most in the fair price condition, and the least in the altruist's price condition. This was exactly the pattern that donation rates followed.

General Discussion

The present results suggest that people often are inhibited from engaging in unambiguous acts of help. Specifically, the results demonstrate that people are more willing to act on their feelings of compassion when they are provided with a self-interested justification. But why are people uncomfortable with appearing too compassionate or concerned with justice? We suggest one possible reason is that an act of unambiguous help in a situation likely to recur exposes the actor to future demands and internal conflicts. Offering an unconditional act of help to one victim makes it difficult both psychologically and socially for the actor to deny future requests for help from that victim or from other deserving victims that, if obliged, would threaten the actor's personal entitlements (Lerner, 1977; Miller, 1977).

A second, related reason that people may be uncomfortable engaging in unconditional acts of help is that such acts frequently will violate collective representations of appropriate, reasonable conduct (Miller, 1999). Because our culture values individualism over collectivism, appearing too sociocentric can make one suspect (Ratner & Miller, 2001). To avoid this, people are often motivated to provide accounts for their behavior that exaggerate their basis in self-interest. For example, as we saw earlier, people tend to generate self-interested accounts for their compassionate actions (Wuthnow, 1991). A similar psychology possibly underlies the fact that despite the low correlation between voting behavior and self-interest, people's accounts for their voting behavior tend to prominently feature self-interest (Sears & Lau, 1983; Stein, 1990). Apparently, people feel uncomfortable voting for a candidate merely because they think it is the right thing to do. From the present results it also appears that they feel uncomfortable helping others merely because it is the right thing to do. In fact, one's image as a good and just person may not be compromised as much by pursuing self-interest as one's image as a reasonable person is compromised by unconditionally pursuing justice.

Alternative Explanations

One potential alternative account for the present results deserves mention. By this account, the offer of an economic exchange increases donations by creating psychological coercion, not psychological liberation. More specifically, this account suggests that the reason the offer of an economic exchange increases helping is because it renders it difficult for people to refuse to help and still see themselves as just and decent people (see Cialdini & Schroeder, 1976). In other words, the offer of an economic exchange may facilitate helping not because it provides psychological cover as the exchange fiction analysis suggests, but because it removes psychological cover and leaves people feeling "trapped."

This alternative cannot be ruled out decisively without additional process data. Nevertheless, we doubt its validity on two counts. First, it is not obvious that framing a donation in terms of an exchange would leave people feeling more as opposed to less obligated to help. Once a request is framed in terms of an exchange, people could reasonably see themselves as having more, not less, justification for rejecting the transaction by claiming not to like or need the product itself. Second, the overall pattern of results across the two field experiments is less consistent with the alternative account than ours. The key to the alternative explanation would seem to rest with the perceived attractiveness of the object of exchange—the candle. For the alternative account to be tenable this product would need to be perceived as sufficiently desirable that its proffer, in combination with the chance to help a needy group, constituted an offer too good to refuse. There is no evidence to suggest that this is the case. In neither study was there any indication that participants found the candle attractive on its own—this was true *even* when it was described as a "bargain" (in the low need condition in Study 2). Furthermore, while the price for the candle was described as a "good deal" in the Bargain condition of Study 2, in all other conditions it was described as at or above the "normal price" for candles of that type. It is difficult to see how this "soft-sell" pitch could have left participants feeling that they had no choice but to help. In summary, we feel the evidence suggests that the candles were sufficiently "attractive" to constitute a convenient excuse for people to do what they wanted to, but not so attractive as to constitute an "excuse-remover" that shamed people into doing what they did not want to do.

Conclusion

The major contribution of the present studies is the finding that helping behavior is facilitated when the framing of the helping act permits people to see themselves as altruistic but not unconditionally so. Although a commercial product (a candle) was employed as the disinhibiting instrument here, appealing to a person's noneconomic self-interest may also facilitate helping behavior. For example, recent psychological analyses of volunteerism have argued that emphasizing the link between volunteerism and self-interest (e.g., personal needs and goals) may be an effective means of increasing and sustaining the former (Perloff, 1987; Snyder, 1993; Snyder & Omoto, 1990). No doubt appeals to self-interest are effective, at least partially, because they provide an incentive to help. But the present results suggest that their effectiveness may also stem from the fact that they provide an excuse for helping. In effect, they provide people with the license to act on their sympathies. Lacking a self-interested account, people may feel they lack both the moral authorization and psychological cover to act. The claim that self-interest serves to disinhibit the impulse to help as well as to facilitate the incentive to help underscores a point made by Kurt Lewin (1951) many years ago. When confronted with people behaving in undesirable ways (e.g., not volunteering), it is generally more effective to remove obstacles that inhibit them from taking the desired action than to provide them with additional reasons for taking the desired action.

Note

1. A brief description of this experiment was presented in Lerner, Miller, and Holmes (1976).

References

Abelson, R. P. (1995). The secret existence of expressive behavior. *Critical Review,* **1–2,** 25–36.

Batson, C. D. (1991). *The altruism question: Toward a social psychological answer.* Hillsdale, NJ: Erlbaum.

Cialdini, R. B., & Schroeder, D. A. (1976). Increasing compliance by legitimizing paltry contributions: When even a penny helps. *Journal of Personality and Social Psychology,* **34,** 599–604.

deTocqueville, A. (1835/1969). *Democracy in America,* J. P. Mayer (Ed.), G. Lawrence (Trans.). Garden City, NY: Anchor Books.

Etzioni, A. (1988). *The moral dimension: Toward a new economics.* New York: The Free Press.

Green, D. P., & Shapiro, I. (1994). *Pathologies of rational choice theory.* New Haven, CT: Yale University Press.

Hafer, C. L. (2000). Do innocent victims threaten the belief in a just world? Evidence from a modified stroop task. *Journal of Personality and Social Psychology,* **79,** 165–173.

Kohn, A. (1990). *The brighter side of human nature.* New York: Basic Books.

Lerner, M. J. (1975). The justice motive in social behavior: Introduction. *Journal of Social Issues,* **31,** 1–19.

Lerner, M. J. (1977). The justice motive in social behavior: Some hypotheses as to its origins and forms. *Journal of Personality,* **45,** 1–52.

Lerner, M. J. (1980). *The belief in a just world.* New York: Plenum.

Lerner, M. J. (1987). Integrating societal and psychological rules of entitlement: The basic task of each social actor and fundamental problem for the social sciences. *Social Justice Research,* **1,** 107–125.

Lerner, M. J., Miller, D. T., & Holmes, J. G. (1976). Deserving and the emergence of forms of justice. In L. Berkowitz (Ed.), *Advances in experimental social psychology* (Vol. 9, pp. 134–160). New York: Academic Press.

Lewin, K. (1951). *Field theory in social science,* D. Cartwright, (Ed.). New York: Harper.

Long, G. T., & Lerner, M. J. (1974). Deserving, the "Personal Contract", and altruistic behavior by children. *Journal of Personality and Social Psychology,* **29,** 551–556.

Mansbridge, J. J. (Ed.) (1990). *Beyond self-interest.* Chicago: Univ. of Chicago Press.

Miller, D. T. (1977). Personal deserving versus justice for others: An exploration of the justice motive. *Journal of Experimental Social Psychology,* **13,** 1–13.

Miller, D. T. (1999). The norm of self-interest. *American Psychologist,* **54,** 1053–1060.

Miller, D. T., & Prentice, D. A. (1994). Collective errors and errors about the collective. *Personality and Social Psychology Bulletin,* **20,** 541–550.

Miller, D. T., & Ratner, R. K. (1996). The power of the myth of self-interest. In L. Montada & M. J. Lerner (Eds.), *Current societal issues in justice* (pp. 25–48). New York: Plenum.

Miller, D. T., & Ratner, R. K. (1998). The disparity between the actual and assumed power of self-interest. *Journal of Personality and Social Psychology,* **74,** 53–62.

Mueller, D. C. (1986). Rational egoism vs. adaptive egoism. *Public Choice*, **51**, 3–23.

Perloff, R. (1987). Self-interest and personal responsibility redux. *American Psychologist*, **42**, 3–11.

Ratner, R. K., & Miller, D. T. (2001). The norm of self-interest and its impact on social action. *Journal of Personality and Social Psychology*, **81**, 5–16.

Regan, D. T., & Fazio, R. (1977). On the consistency between attitudes and behavior: Look to the method of attitude formation. *Journal of Experimental Social Psychology*, **13**, 28–45.

Schwartz, B. (1986). *The battle for human nature*. New York: Norton.

Sears, D. O., & Funk, C. L. (1991). The role of self-interest in social and political attitudes. In M. P. Zanna (Ed.), *Advances in experimental social psychology* (Vol. 24, pp. 2–91). New York: Academic Press.

Sears, D. O., & Lau, R. R. (1983). Indicating apparently self-interested political preferences. *American Journal of Political Science*, **27**, 223–252.

Sen, A. K. (1977). Rational fools: A critique of the behavioral foundations of economic theory. *Philosophy and Public Affairs*, **6**, 317–344.

Snyder, M. (1993). Basic research and practical problems: The promise of a "functional" personality and social psychology. *Personality and Social Psychology Bulletin*, **19**, 251–264.

Snyder, M., & Omoto, A. M. (1990). Who helps and why? The psychology of AIDS volunteerism. In S. Spacapan & S. Oskamp (Eds.), *Helping and being helped: Naturalistic studies* (pp. 213–239). Newbury Park, CA: Sage.

Stein, R. M. (1990). Economic voting for governor and U.S. Senator: The electoral consequences of federalism. *Journal of Politics*, **52**, 29–53.

Tullock, G. (1976). *The vote motive*. London: Institute for Economic Affairs.

Tyler, T. R., & Dawes, R. M. (1993). Fairness in groups: Comparing the self-interest and social identity perspectives. In B. A. Mellers & J. Baron (Eds.), *Psychological perspectives on justice* (pp. 87–108). New York: Cambridge Univ. Press.

Wuthnow, R. (1991). *Acts of compassion*. Princeton, NJ: Princeton Univ. Press.

Questions for Review and Discussion

1. Define the exchange fiction.
2. Why did Holmes et al. predict (Study 1) that the offer of a candle in exchange for a donation would be especially effective when the deservingness of the victim group was especially high?
3. In addition to the exchange fiction, why else might the offer of a product such as a candle in exchange for a charitable donation produce higher contributions?

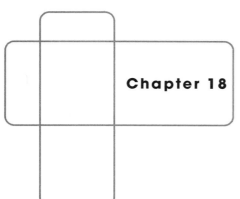

Chapter 18

Thinking Too Much:
Introspection Can Reduce
the Quality of Preferences
and Decisions

Timothy D. Wilson and Jonathan W. Schooler

When faced with a difficult decision, people sometimes spend a good deal of time thinking about the advantages and disadvantages of each alternative. At one point or another, most of us have even reached for a sheet of paper and made a list of pluses and minuses, hoping that the best course of action would become clear. Reflection of this kind is generally thought to be beneficial, organizing what might otherwise be a confusing jumble of thoughts and feelings. Benjamin Franklin, for example, relayed the following advice to the British scientist Joseph Priestley about how to make a difficult choice:

> My way is to divide half a sheet of paper by a line into two columns, writing over the one Pro, and over the other Con. Then, during three or four days consideration, I put down under the different heads short hints of the different motives, that at different times occur to me, for or against each measure . . . I find at length where the balance lies; and if, after a day or two of further consideration, nothing new that is of importance occurs on either side. I come to a determination accordingly . . . When each [reason]

From *Journal of Personality and Social Psychology*, Vol. 60, No. 2, pp. 181–192. Copyright © 1991 by the American Psychological Association. Reproduced with permission.

is thus considered, separately and comparatively, and the whole lies before me, I think I can judge better, and am less likely to make a rash step. (Quoted in Goodman, 1945, p. 746)

Franklin's advice has been captured, at least in spirit, by many years of research on decision analysis (e.g., Edwards, 1961; Keeney, 1977; Koriat, Lichtenstein, & Fischhoff, 1980; Raiffa, 1968; Slovic, 1982). Though the terms *decision theory* and *decision analysis* describe a myriad of theoretical formulations, an assumption made by most of these approaches is that decisions are best made deliberately, objectively, and with some reflection. For example, Raiffa (1968) states that

the spirit of decision analysis is divide and conquer: Decompose a complex problem into simpler problems, get your thinking straight in these simpler problems, paste these analyses together with a logical glue, and come out with a program for action for the complex problem. (p. 271)

Janis and Mann (1977) go so far as to predict that a "balance sheet" procedure similar to Benjamin Franklin's will become as commonplace among professional and personal decision makers as recording deposits and withdrawals in a bankbook.

Curiously, however, there has been almost no research on the effects of reflection and deliberation on the quality of decision making. One reason for this lack of research is the difficulty of assessing how good any particular decision is. For example, Janis and Mann (1977) arrived at the "somewhat demoralizing" conclusion that there is "no dependable way of objectively assessing the success of a decision" (p. 11). Whereas we agree with Janis and Mann that any one measure of the quality of a decision has its drawbacks, we argue that it is not impossible to evaluate people's decisions, particularly if converging measures are used. The purpose of the present studies was to examine the effects of two different kinds of introspection on decision making. We hypothesized that contrary to conventional wisdom, introspection is not always beneficial and might even be detrimental under some circumstances.

Our studies can be viewed as part of a growing literature on the drawbacks of introspection and rumination. Recent research from a variety of sources casts doubt on the view that introspection is always beneficial. Morrow and Nolan-Hoeksema (1990), for example, found that ruminating about a negative mood was less successful in improving this mood than was engaging in a distracting task. Schooler and Engstler-Schooler (1990) documented a deleterious effect of a different kind of reflection: Subjects who verbalized their memory for nonverbal stimuli (such as faces) were less likely than control subjects to recognize these faces on a subsequent recognition test. Most relevant to the present concerns, Wilson and his colleagues found that introspecting about the causes of one's attitudes can have disruptive effects, such as reducing attitude–behavior consistency and changing people's attitudes (Wilson, 1990; Wilson, Dunn, Kraft, & Lisle, 1989; see also Millar & Tesser, 1986a).

Effects of Analyzing Reasons

Forming preferences is akin to riding a bicycle; we can do it easily but cannot easily explain how. Just as automatic behaviors can be disrupted when people analyze and decompose them (Baumeister, 1984; Kimble & Perlmuter, 1970; Langer & Imber, 1979), so can preferences and decisions be disrupted when people reflect about the reasons for their feelings (Wilson, Dunn, Kraft, & Lisle, 1989). We suggest that this can occur as follows. First, people are often unaware of exactly why they feel the way they do about an attitude object. When they reflect about their reasons, they thus focus on explanations that are salient and plausible. The problem is that what seems like a plausible cause and what actually determines people's reactions are not always the same thing (Nisbett & Wilson, 1977). As a result, when asked why they feel the way they do, people focus on attributes that seem like plausible reasons for liking or disliking the stimulus, even if these attributes have no actual effect on their evaluations.

It might seem that people would focus only on attributes of the stimulus that are consistent with their initial attitude, to justify how they feel. That is, even if people do not know why they feel the way they do, and have to construct reasons, they might focus only on factors that could account for their present feelings. Undoubtedly such a justification process can occur. We suggest that under some circumstances, however, people will focus on reasons that imply a different attitude than they held before and will adopt the attitude implied by these reasons. These circumstances are hypothesized to be as follows. First, people often do not have a well-articulated, accessible attitude and thus do not start out with the bias to find only those reasons that are consistent with an initial reaction. They conduct a broader search for reasons, focusing on factors that are plausible and easy to verbalize even if they conflict with how they felt originally.

Even when people's initial attitude is inaccessible, analyzing reasons will not always change their attitude. A cause of people's attitude might be so powerful and obvious that it is difficult to miss when they analyze their reasons. For example, if we knew nothing about a stranger except that he was convicted of child abuse and then were asked why we felt the way we did about him, we would have little difficulty in pinpointing the actual cause of our feelings. Second, even if people miss an important cause of their feelings when they analyze reasons, they will not change their attitudes if the reasons that are salient and plausible are of the same valence as the actual cause. Thus, people might not realize that Attribute A was a major determinant of their reaction and instead might focus on Attribute B. If Attributes A and B imply the same feeling, however, no attitude change will occur.

In sum, we suggest that reflecting about reasons will change people's attitudes when their initial attitude is relatively inaccessible and the reasons that are salient and plausible happen to have a different valence than people's initial attitude. A considerable amount of evidence has been obtained that is consistent with these hypotheses. It is well documented, for example, that when people are asked to think about why they feel the way they do, they sometimes bring to mind reasons that are discrepant from their initial attitude and that they adopt the attitude implied by these reasons (e.g., Millar & Tesser, 1986a; Wilson, Dunn, Bybee, Hyman, & Rotondo, 1984; Wilson, Kraft, & Dunn, 1989). In addition, Wilson, Hodges, and Pollack (1990) found that thinking about reasons was most likely to change people's attitudes when their initial attitude was relatively inaccessible.

It has not been clear, however, whether there is any harm done by the attitude change that occurs when people analyze reasons. We suggest that thinking about reasons can alter people's preferences in such a way that they make less optimal choices. In many domains, people have developed an adaptive, functional means of how to weight different information about a stimulus. For example, when evaluating food items with which they are familiar, people have little difficulty deciding which ones they prefer the most. Asking people to think about why they feel that way might focus their attention on attributes that seem like plausible reasons for liking or disliking the items but that in fact have not been heavily weighted before. Similarly, people might dismiss attributes that seem like implausible reasons but that in fact had been weighted heavily before. As a result, they change their mind about how they feel. To the extent that their initial reaction was adaptive and functional, this change might be in a less optimal direction.

Effects of Evaluating Multiple Attributes of Stimuli

A related kind of introspection might also influence people's decisions in disadvantageous ways, but in a different manner. Sometimes, when evaluating a stimulus, people decompose it into many different attributes. For example, potential car buyers sometimes consider a wide array of information about cars—such as their price, safety, repair record, gas mileage, and resale value. There is evidence that evaluating a stimulus on several different dimensions causes people to moderate their evaluations. Linville (1982), for example, asked people to evaluate five different brands of chocolate chip cookies. She asked some subjects to consider six different attributes of the cookies before rating them, such as how sweet they were and the number of chocolate chips they contained. She asked others to consider only two of these attributes. As predicted, those who evaluated six attributes made more moderate evaluations than those who evaluated two attributes: The range and standard deviation of their ratings of the five cookies were significantly smaller.

This moderation effect is most likely to occur when the different attributes people consider are uncorrelated, so that some are positive and some are negative (Judd & Lusk, 1984; Millar & Tesser, 1986b). The more such attributes people consider, the more all the alternatives will seem to have some good and some bad qualities and thus will appear more similar to each other. To our knowledge, no one has examined the effects of considering multiple attributes of a set of alternatives on the quality of people's decisions. If this type of introspection makes the alternatives more difficult to distinguish from one another, people may be more likely to make a poor choice. And, as noted earlier, to the extent that people's initial preferences (before introspecting) are adaptive, any form of thought that changes people's preferences might lead to less optimal choices.

The present studies examined the effects of analyzing reasons (in Studies 1 and 2) and considering multiple attributes of the alternatives (in Study 2) on people's preferences and choices. We hypothesized that both types of introspection would lead to less optimal decisions, by means of the different mechanisms we have just reviewed. Our measure of the quality of people's preferences and choices was expert opinion. In Study 1, we compared subjects' preferences for different brands of a food item, strawberry jam, with the ratings of these brands by trained sensory experts. We assumed that left to their own devices, people's preferences would correspond reasonably well to the ratings of the experts. We predicted that analyzing the reasons for one's reactions to the jams would change people's preferences. Consistent with our hypothesis that analyzing reasons can produce attitudes that are nonoptimal, we predicted that the preferences of people in the reasons condition would not correspond very well with the experts' ratings of the jams. In Study 2, we examined college students' choices of which courses to take and compared these choices with various kinds of expert opinion about what the best choices were.

Study 1

Method

Subjects Subjects were 49 undergraduate psychology students (39 men, 10 women) at the University of Washington. They volunteered for a study entitled "Jam Taste Test" in return for course credit and were instructed not to eat anything for 3 hours before the study.

Materials and ratings of the experts We purchased five brands of strawberry jams or preserves that varied in their overall quality, as reported by *Consumer Reports* magazine ("Strawberry Jams", 1985). The *Consumer Reports* rankings were based on the ratings of seven consultants who were trained sensory panelists. These experts rated 16 sensory characteristics (e.g., sweetness, bitterness, aroma) of 45 jams; these ratings were averaged to compute the ranking of each jam (L. Mann, *Consumer Reports* magazine, personal communication, May 15, 1987). The jams we purchased were ranked 1st, 11th, 24th, 32nd, and 44th.

Procedure Subjects, seen individually, were told that the purpose of the study was to evaluate different kinds of jams under different conditions, as part of a consumer psychology experiment. Experimenter 1 explained that some subjects would taste the jams on crackers, whereas others would taste the jams on plastic spoons. All subjects were told that they had been randomly assigned to the condition in which they would taste the jams on spoons and that after tasting the jams, they would be asked to rate their liking for each one. After receiving these initial instructions and signing a consent form, subjects were randomly assigned to a control or a reasons analysis condition. Reasons analysis subjects received written instructions asking them to "analyze *why* you feel the way you do about each" jam, "in order to prepare yourself for your evaluations." They were told that they would be asked to list their reasons for liking or disliking the jams after they tasted them, the purpose of which was to organize their thoughts. They were also told that they would not be asked to hand in their list of reasons. Control subjects did not receive any additional instructions.

All subjects were then asked to sit at a table with five plates, each containing a plastic spoon with approximately 1/2 teaspoon (3.3 ml) of strawberry jam. The jams were labeled with a letter from A to E and were presented in one random order. Experimenter 1 left the room, during which time the subjects tasted each of the five jams.

Version 1.   The first five subjects in each condition followed a slightly different procedure than did those who followed. The initial subjects in the reasons analysis condition completed the reasons questionnaire while they tasted the five jams; that is, they tasted Jam 1, listed their reasons for liking or disliking Jam 1, tasted Jam 2, listed their reasons for liking or disliking Jam 2, and so on. The experimenter reiterated that the purpose of this questionnaire was to organize the subjects' thoughts and that they would not be asked to hand it in. When she returned, she picked up the reasons questionnaire, explained that it would not be needed anymore, and deposited it in a trash can. The initial subjects in the control condition tasted all five jams and then rated each one, without filling out any questionnaires.

Version 2.   To equalize the amount of time subjects spent on the tasting part of the study, subsequent subjects followed a slightly different procedure. All subjects tasted the jams without filling out any questionnaires and then were given a questionnaire to fill out when the experimenter returned. Subjects in the reasons condition received the reasons questionnaire. As in Version 1, they were told that they would not hand in this questionnaire, and the experimenter deposited it in the trash when she returned. Subjects in the control condition received a filler questionnaire instructing them to list reasons why they chose their major. The experimenter also left the room while control subjects completed this questionnaire. She collected the questionnaire when she returned.

The remainder of the experiment was identical for all subjects. Experimenter 1 introduced subjects to Experimenter 2, who was unaware of whether they had analyzed reasons. Experimenter 2 gave subjects a questionnaire on which to evaluate the jams, which consisted of a 9-point scale ranging from *disliked* (1) to *liked* (9) for each jam. Subjects were instructed to complete the questionnaire and to place it through a slot in a covered box, to maintain anonymity. Experimenter 2 left the room while subjects made their ratings. He fully debriefed subjects when he returned.

Results

We predicted that asking subjects to think about reasons would change their evaluations of the jams. Consistent with this prediction, a multivariate analysis on the mean ratings of the five jams found a significant effect of the reasons analysis manipulation, $F(5, 43) = 3.09$, $p = .02$. Individual t tests were significant on two of the jams, as seen in Table 1. We also predicted that analyzing reasons would produce preferences that were, in some sense, nonoptimal. To test

TABLE 1					
Study 1: Mean Liking Ratings for the Five Jams					
Condition	Jam 1	Jam 2	Jam 3	Jam 4	Jam 5
Control					
M	6.52	7.64	6.12	2.72	4.68
SD	2.22	1.66	2.05	2.26	2.66
Reasons					
M	4.54	6.25	5.42	2.88	4.92
SD	2.00	2.38	2.70	2.13	2.89
t	3.27	2.38	1.03	−.25	−.30
p	.002	.02	.31	.81	.77

Note.   The jams are listed in order of their rankings by the *Consumer Reports* experts; Jam 1 was the highest ranked jam, Jam 2 was the second highest, and so on. The liking ratings were made on 9-point scales that ranged from *disliked* (1) to *liked* (9).

this prediction, we computed the Spearman rank-order correlation between each subject's ratings of the five jams and the rank ordering of the jams by the *Consumer Reports* taste experts (for all analyses, these within-subject correlations were converted to z scores by means of Fisher's r-to-z transformation; the means reported here have been converted back to correlation coefficients). The mean correlation in the control condition was .55, reflecting a fair amount of agreement with the taste experts. As predicted, the mean correlation in the reasons condition was significantly lower ($M = .11$), $t(47) = 2.53$, $p = .02$.[1] The mean correlation in the control condition was significantly higher than zero, $t(24) = 4.27$, $p = .0003$, whereas the mean correlation in the reasons condition was not, $t(23) = .80$, $p = .43$.

We noted earlier that some kinds of introspection cause people to moderate their evaluations. We have not found this to be the case with analyzing reasons in previous studies (e.g., Wilson, Lisle, & Schooler, 1990). Nor does analyzing reasons reduce people's confidence in their attitudes (Wilson, Dunn, Kraft, & Lisle, 1989). Nonetheless, it is important to see if in the present study, asking people to explain their preferences led to moderation. If so, this reduced variability in people's ratings might account for the lower correlation between their ratings and the opinions of the *Consumer Reports* experts. Though the mean ratings of the jams displayed in Table 1 seem to support this interpretation (i.e., the range in ratings of the five jams was lower in the reasons condition), it is more appropriate to test this possibility on a within-subject basis.[2] We computed the range between each subject's highest and lowest rating of the jams, as well as the standard deviation of each subject's ratings. On average, these values were quite similar in both the reasons and control conditions, $ts(47) < .39$, $ps > .71$. Thus, there was no evidence that analyzing reasons caused people to evaluate the jams more similarly than did control subjects.

Instead, people seemed to have come up with reasons that conflicted with the experts' ratings and adopted the attitude implied by these reasons. Support for this interpretation comes from analyses of the reasons people wrote down in the reasons condition. Subjects' responses were first divided into individual reasons by a research assistant and then put into different categories of reasons for liking or disliking the jams. (Another research assistant coded a subset of the questionnaires and agreed with the first assistant's initial divisions into reasons 95% of the time and agreed with her placement of the reasons into individual categories 97% of the time.) Subjects gave an average of 2.93 reasons per jam. These reasons concerned some aspect of their taste (e.g., sweetness, tartness, fruitiness, 52%), texture (e.g., thickness, chunkiness, ease of spreading, 35%), appearance (e.g., color, how fresh they looked, 8%), smell (1%), naturalness or artificiality of the ingredients (1%), and miscellaneous (3%). Two research assistants also coded, on a 7-point scale, how much liking for each jam was expressed in subjects' reasons (reliability $r = .97$). Consistent with our hypothesis that the reasons people came up with would not match expert opinion, this index did not correlate significantly with the experts' ratings of the jams ($M = .25$), $t(23) = 1.74$, $p > .09$. Consistent with our hypothesis that people would base their attitude on the reasons they listed, this index correlated very highly with subjects' subsequent ratings of the jams (mean within-subject correlation $= .92$), $t(23) = 8.60$, $p < .0001$.

A closer look at how analyzing reasons changed people's attitudes is illuminating. In some of our previous studies, people who analyzed reasons changed their attitudes in the same direction, possibly because similar attributes of the stimuli became salient when people analyzed reasons, and people held similar causal theories about how these attributes affected their judgments (e.g., Wilson et al., 1984). In other studies, the attitude change was more idiosyncratic (e.g., Wilson, Kraft, & Dunn, 1989), which can occur for at least two reasons. First, for some stimuli, the attributes that become salient might differ from person to person. For example, when asked why they feel the way they do about a political candidate, people draw on different knowledge bases. The fact that is most salient to one person (e.g., that the candidate is antiabortion) may be completely unknown to another. Second, even if the same fact, such as the candidate's stance on abortion, is available to everyone, it may be evaluated quite differently by different people, leading to attitude change in different directions.

The fact that there were significant differences between conditions on ratings of two of the jams (see Table 1) indicates that at least some of the change in the present study was in a common direction: Subjects who analyzed reasons became more negative, on average, toward Jams 1 and 2. However, other changes may have occurred in idiosyncratic directions, so that some people who analyzed reasons became more positive, whereas others became more negative. To test this possibility, we correlated each subject's ratings of the five jams with the ratings of every other subject in his or her condition and then averaged these correlations, using Fisher's r-to-z-to-r transformation. The average correlation in the control condition was .55, indicating a fair amount of consensus about how likable the jams were. If subjects in the reasons condition changed their attitudes in a common direction, then their ratings should have correlated as highly, or possibly even higher, with other subjects in this condition. If these subjects changed their attitudes in idiosyncratic directions, then there should have been less consensus in the reasons condition. Supporting this latter possibility, the mean intercorrelation in the reasons condition was significantly lower than in the control condition ($M = .18$), $t(47) = 4.38, p < .0001$.[3]

Discussion

Left to their own devices, control subjects formed preferences for strawberry jams that corresponded well to the ratings of trained sensory experts. Subjects asked to think about why they liked or disliked the jams brought to mind reasons that did not correspond very well with the experts' ratings. They then seem to have based their preferences on these reasons (i.e., the correlation between the attitude implied by their reasons and their subsequent preferences was extremely high). As a result, their preferences did not correspond as well with expert opinion. No evidence was found for the possibility that analyzing reasons moderated subjects' judgments. Instead it changed people's minds about how they felt, presumably because certain aspects of the jams that were not central to their initial evaluations were weighted more heavily (e.g., their chunkiness or tartness).

It might be argued that there should have been a greater correspondence between the experts and subjects who analyzed reasons, because both sets of people made their ratings in an analytical frame of mind. The ratings made by the two groups, however, differed in important ways. First, the experts were provided in advance with a list of 16 criteria on which to evaluate the jams

(L. Mann, *Consumer Reports* magazine, personal communication, May 15, 1987). In contrast, our reasons subjects had to decide for themselves which criteria to use, increasing the probability that they would focus on a few attributes that were salient and plausible as causes of their preferences. Second, the experts were trained sensory panelists with a good deal of experience in tasting food items. Wilson, Kraft, and Dunn (1989) found that people who are knowledgeable about the attitude object are unaffected by analyzing their reasons. Thus, even if the experts evaluated the jams analytically, we would expect their ratings to differ from the subjects in our reasons condition, who were not experts.

It might also be argued that the different attitudes reported by subjects in the reasons condition were due to demand characteristics. Though we went to some length to convince these subjects that no one would see their reasons, they still might have believed we would compare their attitude responses with their reasons, and thus they might have purposely exaggerated the similarity of their attitudes to their reasons because of concerns about consistency. Note, however, that even if this interpretation were true, it would not explain why the reasons generated by subjects implied an attitude that was different from those held by control subjects and the *Consumer Reports* experts.

One way to rule out a demand characteristics explanation more definitively would be to allow people to choose one of the attitude objects for their own personal use. For example, suppose we had told subjects in Study 1 that they could choose one of the jams to take home and had set up the study in such a way that no one would know which brand subjects chose. If subjects in the reasons condition acted on their reported attitudes—that is, if they chose jams that they had rated highly—it would seem that they had genuinely changed their attitudes, rather than simply reporting a new attitude to please the experimenter. Though we did not follow such a procedure in Study 1, we did in two studies by Wilson et al. (1990). For example, in one study, subjects examined five art posters and chose one to take home. The results were inconsistent with a demand characteristics explanation: Subjects who analyzed reasons chose different posters, even though they believed that the experimenter would not know which one they chose.

The Wilson et al. (1990) studies addressed another possible concern with Study 1: the use of expert opinion as our criterion of decision quality. It might be argued that even though subjects in the reasons condition formed preferences that were at variance with the experts, there was no cost in doing so. As long as people like a particular kind of jam, what difference does it make that experts disagree with them? We suggest it can make a difference, because the attitude change caused by analyzing reasons is often temporary. Over time, people probably revert to the weighting schemes they habitually use. If they made a choice on the basis of a different weighting scheme, they might come to regret this choice. To test this prediction, Wilson et al. (1990) contacted subjects a few weeks after they had been in the study, and asked them how satisfied they were with the poster they had chosen. As predicted, subjects who analyzed reasons expressed significantly less satisfaction with their choice of poster. Thus, analyzing reasons has been shown to reduce the quality of preferences in two different ways: It can lower the correspondence between these preferences and expert opinion, and it can cause people to make decisions they later regret.

Study 2 attempted to extend these findings in a number of respects. First, it was a field experiment that examined a real-life decision of some importance to college students: their choice of which courses to take the following semester. Students were presented with detailed information about all of the sophomore-level psychology courses being offered the next semester, and we examined their ratings of each course and whether they actually registered for the different courses. As in Study 1, we included a measure of expert opinion of the desirability of the alternatives. The "experts" were students who had previously taken the courses. We predicted that subjects in the control conditions would be most likely to choose courses recommended by these experts; that is, they should be most likely to register for the courses that had received the highest course evaluations. Subjects who analyzed reasons, however, might change the criteria they used to make their decision and thus be less likely to sign up for the highly rated ones.

Second, as discussed in the Introduction, we examined the effects of another form of introspection, in addition to analyzing reasons. Some subjects were asked to consider how every attribute of every course (e.g., the topic matter, the time it met) influenced their preferences. We hypothesized that this form of introspection would moderate subjects' ratings of the courses, by making them more cognizant of the fact that every course had pluses and minuses (Linville, 1982). We also hypothesized that this form of introspection might confuse subjects about which information was the most important, causing them to assign more equal weights to the different information. This change in subjects' weighting scheme was also expected to change their decisions about which courses to take, possibly in a nonoptimal direction.

Third, we included a long-term measure of subjects' behavior: the courses they were enrolled in at the end of the following semester. Subjects had the opportunity to add and drop courses at the beginning of the semester; thus, even if our manipulations influenced their initial decision of which courses to take, they could revise these decisions later. Whether the manipulation would influence subjects' long-term behavior was an open question. On the one hand, we have argued that the attitude change caused by analyzing reasons is relatively temporary and will not influence long-term behavior. Consistent with this view, Wilson et al. (1984, Study 3) found that analyzing reasons did not influence dating couple's decision about whether to break up several months after the study was completed. On the other hand, if analyzing reasons changes subjects' decisions about the courses for which they register, they might experience a certain amount of inertia, so that they remain in these courses, even if they change their mind at a later point. Furthermore, Millar and Tesser (1986a, 1989) found that analyzing reasons highlights the cognitive component of attitudes and that these cognitively based attitudes will determine behaviors that are more cognitively based than affectively based. Given that the decision of whether to take a college course has a large cognitive component (e.g., whether it will advance one's career goals), the attitude change that results from analyzing reasons might cause long-term changes in behavior.[4]

Fourth, to test more directly the hypothesis that people who analyze reasons change the criteria they use to make decisions, we included some additional dependent measures assessing the criteria subjects used, and we compared these criteria with another kind of expert opinion: ratings by faculty members in psychology of the criteria students ought to use when choosing courses. We predicted that the criteria used by control subjects would correspond at least somewhat to the criteria faculty members said students ought to use but that there would be less of a correspondence in the reasons condition. This would be consistent with our hypothesis that analyzing reasons can cause people to alter the criteria they use in nonoptimal ways.

Study 2

Method

Subjects Two hundred and forty-three introductory psychology students at the University of Virginia volunteered for a study entitled "Choosing College Courses." The sign-up sheet indicated that participants would receive detailed information about all of the 200-level courses being offered by the psychology department the following semester (i.e., sophomore-level courses) and that only students who were considering taking one of these courses should volunteer for the study. Thirteen students were eliminated from the analyses for the following reasons: One participated in the study twice, 2 reported that they would not be enrolled in college the next semester, and 10 reported that they had already registered for classes, which was one of the major dependent variables. Other subjects failed to complete some of the individual questions and were eliminated from the analyses of these measures. Subjects received course credit for their participation.

Procedure   Subjects were run in large groups in the first 2 days of the pre-registration period, when students register for the classes they want to take the following semester. Subjects received written instructions indicating that the purpose of the study was both to provide people with more information than they would ordinarily receive about 200-level psychology courses and to "look at some issues in decision making of interest to psychologists, such as how people make decisions between alternatives." They were given a packet of materials and told to go through it page by page without looking ahead, though they could look back at any point. After filling out some demographic information, they received descriptions of the nine 200-level psychology classes.

Course descriptions.   Each course description included the name of the professor teaching the course, when and where it would meet, the required and recommended prerequisites for the course, the requirements for the psychology major satisfied by the course, whether a term paper was required, the format of the course (lecture or discussion), evaluations of the course by students who took the course the last time it was taught by the same professor, whether there was a required or optional discussion section, a description of the course contents, and a list of the books to be used. The course evaluations included a frequency distribution of the responses to two ratings, the overall teaching effectiveness of the instructor and the intellectual stimulation of the course, as well as the mean response to these two questions. Most, though not all, of this information was available for all nine courses. For example, one course was being taught by a new instructor—thus course evaluations were not available—and the format of one course was unknown. The course descriptions were presented in one of two counterbalanced orders.

Experimental conditions.   Subjects were randomly assigned to one of three experimental conditions within each group session. In the rate all information condition (hereafter referred to as rate all), subjects were asked to stop and think about each piece of information about every course and then to rate the extent to which it made them more or less likely to take the course. Underneath each item, subjects were reminded to "stop and think about this piece of information," after which they rated it on a 9-point scale ranging from *makes me much less likely to take it* (1) to *makes me much more likely to take it* (9). Subjects in the reasons condition were instructed to think about why they might want or not want to take a course as they read the course descriptions. They were told that they would be asked to write down their reasons and were asked to prepare themselves by "analyzing why you feel the way you do about each course." After reading the course descriptions (without making any ratings of the information), these subjects did in fact write down their reasons for each of the nine courses. They were told that the purpose of this was to organize their thoughts and that their responses would be completely anonymous. They were also reminded that they could refer back to the course descriptions if they wanted. Subjects in the control condition were instructed to read the information about the nine courses carefully, after which they received a filler questionnaire that asked their opinion of some university issues (e.g., what they thought about the advising and honor systems) and their leisure-time activities.[5]

Dependent measures   All subjects rated the likelihood that they would take each course on a scale ranging from *definitely will not take this course* (1) to *definitely will take this course* (9). If they had already taken a course, they were asked to indicate this and to not complete the rating scale. The courses were rated in the same order as they were presented in the course description packet. Subjects next rated each type of information they had received about the courses (e.g., the course evaluations, the course content), as well as two additional pieces of information (what they had heard about the courses from other students or professors and how interested they were in the topic), according to how much it influenced their decision about which courses to take. These ratings were made on scales ranging from *did not influence me at all* (1) to *influenced me a great deal* (9). The information about the courses was rated in one of two counterbalanced orders.

At this point, subjects handed in their packets and were given, unexpectedly, a recall questionnaire. They were asked to recall as much information about the courses as they could and to write it down in designated spaces for each course. Their responses were later coded by a research assistant who was unaware of the subjects' condition. She assigned subjects a 1 for each piece of information recalled correctly, a 0 for each piece not recalled, and a −1 for each piece recalled incorrectly. One of the authors also coded the recall questionnaires of 7 subjects; his codings agreed with the research assistant's 94% of the time.

After completing the recall measure, subjects were asked to sign a release form giving us permission to examine the registrar's records so that we could record the courses for which they actually registered. All subjects agreed to sign this form. They were then given a written explanation of the study that explained it in general terms; that is, that the study was concerned with the kinds of information people use when deciding what courses to take. Neither the hypotheses nor the different conditions of the study were discussed. At the end of the following semester, all subjects were sent a complete written description of the purpose of the study.

Expert opinion on the criteria for choosing courses   A questionnaire was distributed to the 34 faculty members in psychology in residence at the University of Virginia. They were given a description of the 10 pieces of information subjects had received about the psychology courses (e.g., "whether or not a term paper is required"), as well as the two other pieces of information that subjects had rated (what the student had heard about the courses from other students or professors and how interested the student was in the topic), in one of two counterbalanced orders. The faculty rated how much students should use each piece of information "to make sure they make the best decision they can" about which 200-level psychology course to take. These ratings were made on scales ranging from *should be given very little weight* (1) to *should be weighted very heavily* (9). A total of 18 (53%) of the faculty completed the questionnaire.

Results

Initial analyses revealed that neither the order in which the courses were presented, the order in which subjects rated how much the information about the courses influenced their likelihood of taking them, nor subjects' gender interacted significantly with the independent variables. There were a few significant main effects of gender and course order; for example, women recalled more information about the courses than did men, and the order in which the courses were presented had a significant effect on subjects' ratings of how likely they were to take some of the courses. Because the distributions of men and women and of people who received the courses in each order were nearly identical in each condition, however, we collapsed across gender and order in all subsequent analyses.

Recall for and ratings of influence of the course information   We predicted that the two introspection manipulations would alter the way subjects weighted the different information about the courses. To test this, we examined their recall for the information and their ratings of how much each type of information had influenced their decisions. We would certainly not argue that these measures were perfectly correlated with the weights subjects actually assigned to the different criteria. As one of us has noted elsewhere, subjects' causal reports are often inaccurate (Nisbett & Wilson, 1977). It is also well known that recall is often uncorrelated with people's weighting schemes (Hastie & Park, 1986). Few would argue, however, that such measures were orthogonal to the weights people used. Thus, relative differences in reported influence and recall between different conditions can be taken as rough indicators of what subjects in those conditions found important about the courses (Anderson & Pichert, 1978).

Recall. Interestingly, the total amount of information subjects recalled did not differ across the three conditions, $F(2, 226) < 1$. There were, however, differences in the kinds of information subjects recalled. Subjects' recall scores were averaged across the nine courses and analyzed in a 3 (introspection condition) × 10 (type of information, e.g., when the course met, whether a term paper was required) analysis of variance (ANOVA), with the last factor treated as a repeated measure. There was a very strong effect for type of information, $F(10, 217) = 59.53$, $p < .001$, reflecting the fact that subjects were more likely to recall some kinds of information about the courses than they were others. More interestingly, there was also a significant Condition × Type of Information interaction, $F(20, 434) = 2.53$, $p < .001$, indicating that the kinds of information subjects were most likely to remember differed by condition.

How well did subjects' recall correspond to the opinion of faculty as to how much people should weight each piece of information? We predicted that subjects in the control condition would do a reasonably good job of attending to the information that was important about the courses, whereas the introspection manipulations might disrupt this process. To test this prediction, we averaged subjects' recall for the three pieces of information faculty rated as most important (who was teaching the class, the course content, and the prerequisites for the class) and subjects' recall for the three pieces of information faculty rated as least important (when the class met, whether there was a required term paper, and whether the course had a discussion section). As seen in Table 2, control subjects recalled more of the "important" than "unimportant" information, $F(1, 226) = 10.09$, $p < .01$. As predicted, this was not the case in the two introspection conditions. Subjects in the reasons condition were no more likely to recall important than unimportant information, and subjects in the rate all condition actually recalled more of the unimportant information, $F(1, 226) = 3.46$, $p = .06$. These results were reflected by a significant Condition × Importance of Information interaction, $F(2, 226) = 8.28$, $p < .001$. This interaction was also significant when the control condition was compared with the reasons condition alone, $F(1, 226) = 5.25$, $p < .05$, and with the rate all condition alone, $F(1, 226) = 12.69$, $p < .001$.

Ratings of influence of the course information. Subjects rated how much each of the 10 pieces of information about the courses influenced how likely they were to take them, as well as the influence of 2 additional items: what they had heard about the course from others and how interested they were in the topic of the course. A 3 (condition) × 12 (information type) between/within ANOVA revealed a significant main effect for condition, $F(2, 223) = 8.46$, $p < .001$, reflecting the fact that subjects in the rate all condition ($M = 5.78$) thought

	Condition		
	TABLE 2		
Variable	Control	Reasons	Rate all
Recall			
Recall for 3 highest items	0.23	0.19	0.16
Recall for 3 lowest items	0.14	0.19	0.21
Ratings of influence			
Ratings of 3 highest items	6.41	6.47	6.26
Ratings of 3 lowest items	4.73	5.11	6.32

TABLE 2

Recall for and Reported Influence of the Course Information as a Function of the Importance Attributed to These Items by Faculty

Note. The higher the number, the more subjects recalled the information or thought the information influenced their decision of what courses to take.

that all of the information had influenced them more than did subjects in the control and reasons conditions ($Ms = 5.17$ and 5.26, respectively). The ANOVA also yielded a significant Condition $\times$ Information Type interaction, $F(22, 426) = 2.81$, $p < .001$, indicating that the manipulations influenced what kinds of information subjects thought influenced them.

As seen in Table 2, control subjects reported that the important information influenced them more than did the unimportant information, $F(1, 223) = 50.42$, $p < .001$. In contrast, subjects in the rate all condition reported that the two types of information had influenced them about equally, $F(1, 223) < 1$. Unexpectedly, subjects in the reasons condition responded similarly to control subjects. A 3 (condition) $\times$ 2 (importance of information) between/within ANOVA revealed a highly significant interaction, $F(2, 223) = 9.20$, $p < .001$. This interaction was also significant when considering the control and rate all conditions alone, $F(1, 223) = 30.91$, $p < .001$. It was not significant when the control condition was compared with the reasons condition, $F(1, 223) = 1.06$.[6]

We predicted that the rate all manipulation might confuse people about which attributes of the courses were most important, causing them to assign more equal weights to the different information. One piece of evidence for this prediction was that as just seen, subjects in the rate all condition rated all of the information, on average, as more influential than subjects in the other two conditions. Another was that the mean, within-subject range in subjects' ratings of the influence of the information was significantly smaller in the rate all condition ($M = 6.78$) than in the control and reasons conditions ($Ms = 7.35$

	Condition		
TABLE 3			
Ratings of Likelihood of Taking the Courses			
Evaluation of course	Control	Reasons	Rate all
Highly rated	4.77	4.55	4.45
Poorly rated	3.18	2.85	3.74

Note. The higher the number, the greater the reported likelihood that students would take the class.

and 7.47, respectively), $ts(224) > 3.31$, $ps < .001$. An identical pattern of results was found in an analysis of the within-subject standard deviations of the ratings of the course information.

Reported likelihood of taking each course   We expected that people instructed to reflect about their decision (i.e., those in the reasons and rate all conditions) would change their minds about which courses were the most desirable and that this change would be in a nonoptimal direction. To test this prediction, we computed the mean of subjects' reported likelihood of taking the five courses that had received the highest course evaluations by students who had taken the classes and the mean ratings of the three that had received the lowest ratings plus one for which no ratings were available (the results are nearly identical if this latter course is eliminated from the analyses). These means were analyzed with a 3 (condition) $\times$ 2 (course evaluation) between/within ANOVA.

The main effect for condition was not significant, $F(2, 199) = 1.88, p > .15$, indicating that subjects' condition did not influence their reported likelihood of taking psychology courses. The main effect for course evaluation was highly significant, $F(2, 199) = 195.61$, $p < .001$, reflecting the fact that subjects in all conditions preferred the highly rated courses to the poorly rated courses (see Table 3). Most relevant to our hypotheses, the Condition $\times$ Course Evaluation interaction was also significant, $F(2, 199) = 10.80$, $p < .001$. As predicted, subjects in the control condition showed more of a preference for highly rated courses than for poorly rated courses than subjects in the rate all condition (see Table 3). Considering these two conditions alone, the Condition $\times$ Course interaction was significant, $F(1, 199) = 14.25, p < .001$. Unexpectedly, there were no significant differences in the reports of subjects in the control versus reasons condition.

To see if subjects in the rate all condition moderated their ratings of the courses, we examined the range of each subjects' ratings of the nine courses. As predicted, the average range was significantly smaller in the rate all condition ($M = 5.19$) than in the control condition ($M = 6.01$), $t(224) = 3.18$, $p < .001$. The mean in the reasons condition was actually larger than in the control condition ($M = 6.53$), $t(224) = 1.95$, $p = .05$. An identical pattern of results was found in an analysis of the within-subject standard deviations of the ratings of the courses. Finally, we examined the intercorrelations between subjects' ratings within each condition, as we did in Study 1. The mean intercorrelations in the control and reasons conditions were very similar ($Ms = .24$ and $.23$, respectively). Both of these means were significantly higher than the mean in the rate all condition ($M = .16$), $ts(221) > 2.31$, $ps < .02$. The lower agreement in the rate all condition may be a result of the fact that there was less variation in these subjects' ratings—that is, the restricted variance in their ratings placed limits on the magnitude of the intercorrelations.

Course preregistration and enrollment   In the few days after our study, all the participants registered for the courses they wanted to take the next semester. We obtained the preregistration records for the nine psychology courses and assigned subjects a 1 if they had preregistered for a course, a 0 if they had not, and a missing value if they had already taken the course. We also analyzed the actual course enrollment data at the conclusion of the following semester, to see if any differences found in the preregistration data persisted, even after students had had the option to add and drop courses. These data were coded in an identical fashion to the preregistration data.

Preregistration for courses.   As predicted, the two introspection manipulations influenced the kind of courses for which subjects preregistered. As seen in Table 4, subjects in the introspection conditions (especially those who analyzed reasons) were less likely than control subjects to take the highly rated courses but about equally likely to take the poorly rated courses. The number of courses of each type that subjects registered for were analyzed in a 3 (condition) × 2 (course evaluation) between/within ANOVA, which yielded the predicted Condition × Course Evaluation interaction, $F(2, 206) = 6.40$, $p = .002$. This interaction was significant when the control and reasons conditions were considered alone, $F(1, 206) = 12.58$, $p < .001$, and when the control and rate all conditions were considered alone, $F(1, 206) = 4.12$, $p < .05$.

It can be seen by the low averages in Table 4 that the modal response in all conditions was not to take any of the nine psychology courses. Despite our request that people only participate in the study if they were considering taking a 200-level psychology course, many subjects opted not to take any. This created a bit of a statistical anomaly, in that the people who did not take any psychology

	Condition		
TABLE 4			
Courses Preregistered for and Actually Taken			
Variable	Control	Reasons	Rate all
Preregistration			
Highly rated courses	.41	.15	.21
Poorly rated courses	.04	.10	.01
Actual enrollment			
Highly rated courses	.37	.21	.24
Poorly rated courses	.03	.08	.03

Note. Subjects were assigned a 1 if they registered for or actually took a course and a 0 if they did not register or take a course.

classes lowered the variance and increased the sample size, thereby increasing the power of the significance tests. To avoid this problem, a 3 (condition) $\times$ 2 (course evaluation) chi-square analysis was performed after eliminating those students who did not register for any of the nine courses. This analysis was also significant, $\chi^2(2, N = 74) = 8.25, p = .02$, reinforcing the conclusion that the manipulations influenced the courses for which subjects registered.

Enrollment at the conclusion of the following semester. We did not make firm predictions about whether the effects of the introspection manipulations on people's choice of courses would persist over the long run. To see if they did, we analyzed the course enrollment data at the conclusion of the semester in the same manner as the preregistration data. The results were similar, though not as strong (see Table 4). The interaction effect in a 3 (condition) $\times$ 2 (course evaluation) ANOVA was significant, $F(2, 206) = 3.05, p = .05$. This interaction was significant when the control condition was compared only with the reasons condition, $F(1, 206) = 5.90, p < .05$, but not with the rate all condition, $F(1, 206) = 2.37, p = .13$. The chi-square on only those subjects enrolled in at least one course was not significant, $\chi^2(2, N = 74) = 2.84, p = .24$.

To test more definitively whether the effect of the manipulations had weakened over time, the preregistration and final enrollment data were entered into a 3 (condition) $\times$ 2 (course evaluation) $\times$ 2 (time of measurement: registration vs. final enrollment) ANOVA; the last two factors were treated as repeated measures. The Condition $\times$ Course Evaluation interaction was highly significant, $F(2, 206) = 5.31$, $p = .006$, reflecting the fact that at both times of measurement, subjects in the introspection conditions were less likely to take the highly rated courses but about equally likely to take the poorly rated courses. The Condition $\times$ Course Evaluation $\times$ Time of Measurement interaction was not significant, $F(2, 206) = 1.13$, $p = .32$, indicating that the attenuation of the Condition $\times$ Course interaction over time was not reliable.

Other analyses   Coding of reasons given in the reasons condition.   The reasons protocols were coded as described in Study 1, with similar levels of reliability. Subjects gave an average of 2.06 reasons for liking or disliking each course. The most frequently mentioned reasons were interest in the material (33%), the course evaluations (23%), the course content (13%), whether a term paper was required (7%), and when the course met (6%). The reasons were also coded according to how much liking for each course they conveyed (reliability $r = .98$). The average within-subject correlation between these ratings and subjects' ratings of how likely they were to take each course was .70, $t(63) = 10.93$, $p < .0001$.

Other factors potentially influencing course selection.   Some preference is given to upper-level students and majors when they enroll for psychology courses. This could not have accounted for the present results, however, because the number of such students was randomly distributed across conditions, $\chi^2(6, N = 229) = 4.49$, $p = .61$, for upper-level students; $\chi^2(2, N = 230) = 1.07$, $p = .58$, for majors.

Grades obtained in the psychology courses.   The grades received by those subjects who took one or more of the nine psychology courses were obtained from the final grade sheets. There were no significant differences between conditions in these grades. The means for the control, reasons, and rate all conditions, on a 5-point scale ranging from A (4) to F (0), were 2.82, 2.78, and 3.20, respectively.

Discussion

We predicted that subjects who introspected about their decision about which courses to take would change the way they evaluated the courses, causing them to make less optimal choices. The results in the rate all condition, in which subjects rated each piece of information about every course according to how it influenced their decision, were entirely consistent with this prediction. These subjects' recall and reports of how they had weighted the information differed significantly from control subjects' and were significantly less likely to correspond to the ratings of faculty members of how this information ought to be used. In addition, these subjects were less likely to register for and somewhat less likely to remain in courses that students who had taken the courses previously said were the best courses. Thus, regardless of whether the opinions of faculty members or students' peers (those who had previously taken the courses) were used as the criteria of an optimal choice, subjects in the rate all condition appeared to have made less optimal choices than control subjects. We predicted that the rate all manipulation would change subjects' choices by moderating their evaluations, so that the courses appeared more similar to each other. We found two pieces of evidence in support of this prediction. Both the range in their ratings of how likely they were to take the courses and the range in their ratings of how much they were influenced by the different information about the courses were significantly smaller than the ranges in the other two conditions.

Asking subjects to analyze the reasons for their evaluations of the courses also caused them to weight the course information in a less optimal way and to make less optimal choices. The effects of this manipulation, however, were not as strong as the effects of the rate all manipulation. On some measures, subjects who analyzed reasons responded similarly to control subjects, such as on their reports of how the different kinds of course information influenced their decisions. On those measures that were most objective and consequential, however, our predictions were confirmed. For example, subjects in the reasons condition were significantly less likely than control subjects to preregister for and enroll in courses that had received high course evaluations (see Table 4). In addition, the correspondence between their recall of the course information and faculty members' ratings of this information was significantly lower than it was for control subjects (see Table 2).

As predicted, analyzing reasons did not make the courses seem more similar to subjects. In fact, the range in their ratings of the courses was significantly larger than it was in the control condition. Nor did analyzing reasons lower the range in their ratings of how much they were influenced by the different kinds of information about the courses. Thus, subjects in the reasons condition seemed to have had little difficulty in forming an opinion about which courses they liked and how the course information influenced them; it is just that their opinions differed from control subjects' (at least as assessed by their recall of the course information and the courses for which they registered and in which they were enrolled). These results are consistent with our hypothesis that when people analyze their reasons, they often change their criteria by focusing on attributes that seem like plausible reasons for liking or disliking the attitude object, but that in fact have not been heavily weighted before. Similarly, they dismiss attributes that seem like implausible reasons, but that in fact have been weighted heavily before. As a result, people change their mind about how they feel.

Despite this support for our predictions, we should not overlook the inconsistent effects of the reasons manipulation in Study 2 (e.g., the failure of this manipulation to influence subjects' reported likelihood of taking the courses). We offer the following, speculative explanation for these inconsistent findings. Both Wilson, Dunn, Kraft, and Lisle (1989) and Millar and Tesser (1986a) suggested that analyzing reasons is most likely to change attitudes that have a large affective component, because people are less likely to know the actual causes of these attitudes and because analyzing reasons is likely to emphasize cognitions and obscure the affect (the Millar & Tesser (1986a) explanation). People's attitudes toward college courses may have less of an affective component than their attitudes toward food items (e.g., strawberry jams), explaining why the effects were less consistent in Study 2. In addition, analyzing reasons may have a greater effect when the different dimensions of the stimuli are ill-defined, because this increases the likelihood that people will overlook factors that initially influenced their judgments. Consistent with this view, the criteria used to evaluate the courses in Study 2 were much more explicit than were the criteria in Study 1. That is, in Study 2, we gave subjects a list of all the relevant attributes of the different courses, whereas in Study 1, subjects had to define the set of relevant attributes themselves (e.g., whether to consider the color or consistency of the jams). Clearly, further research is needed to verify these speculations.

Finally, we should mention a possible alternative explanation for the effects of the introspection manipulations. The manipulations may have caused people to attend less to the information about the courses, because they were concentrating on why they felt the way they did. According to this argument, any intervention that distracts people from the information about the alternatives would have similar deleterious effects to our introspection manipulations. The results of our recall measure, however, reduce the plausibility of this interpretation. If subjects in the introspection conditions were distracted, they should have recalled less information about the courses than did control subjects; in fact, there were no significant differences between conditions in the amount of information they recalled—only, as predicted, in the kinds of information they recalled (see Table 2).

General Discussion

Previous studies demonstrated that thinking about why we feel the way we do could change our attitudes (Wilson, 1990; Wilson, Dunn, Kraft, & Lisle, 1989). It has not been clear, however, whether the direction of this change is beneficial, detrimental, or neutral. The present studies demonstrated that analyzing reasons can lead to preferences and decisions that correspond less with expert opinion. This result, taken together with Wilson et al.'s (1990) finding that analyzing reasons reduces people's satisfaction with their choices, suggests that it may not always be a good idea to analyze the reasons for our preferences too carefully. In the present studies, analyzing reasons focused subjects' attention on characteristics of the stimuli that were, according to expert opinion, nonoptimal and caused them to use these characteristics to form preferences that were also nonoptimal. Nor may it be wise to analyze the effects of every attribute of every alternative. Evaluating multiple attributes led to nonoptimal preferences in Study 2 by moderating people's evaluations, so that the college courses seemed more equivalent than they did to subjects in the other conditions.

We do not mean to imply that the two kinds of introspection we examined will always lead to nonoptimal choices, and we certainly do not suggest that people studiously avoid all reflection before making decisions. Such a conclusion would be unwarranted for several reasons. First, we used stimuli in the present studies that were evaluated fairly optimally by control subjects, who were not instructed to reflect about the alternatives. That is, the evaluations and choices of control subjects in both studies corresponded fairly well with the experts' ratings. If people start out with feelings or preferences that are nonoptimal, the change that often results from introspection may be in a positive direction. Consistent with this possibility, Tesser, Leone, and Clary (1978) found that when people who experienced speech anxiety were asked to think about why they felt anxious, their anxiety was reduced.

Second, some people might be more likely to know why they feel the way they do about an attitude object and thus will be less likely to be misled by thinking about their reasons. Consistent with this hypothesis, Wilson, Kraft, and Dunn (1989) found that people who were knowledgeable about the attitude object and thus more likely to have attitudes that were based on objective, easily verbalizable attributes of it were relatively immune to the effects of thinking about reasons. Finally, in our studies, people were asked to reflect for a relatively brief amount of time. A more intensive, in-depth analysis, such as that advocated by Janis and Mann (1977), may have very different effects on the quality of people's decisions (see, for example, Mann, 1972).

We have just begun to explore the conditions under which people should and should not reflect about the reasons for their preferences, thus to make broad claims about the dangers of introspection would be inappropriate (or at least premature). Perhaps the best conclusion at this point is a variation of Socrates' oft-quoted statement that the "unexamined life is not worth living." We suggest that, at least at times, the unexamined choice *is* worth making.

Notes

1. Initial analyses revealed that the effects of analyzing reasons did not differ according to which version of the procedure was used. Subjects in both conditions who followed the initial procedure—in which the jams were rated right after tasting them, without an intervening questionnaire—had higher correlations between their ratings of the jams and the *Consumer Reports* experts' ratings of the jams, as indicated by a significant main effect of version ($p = .02$). The difference in correlations between the reasons and control conditions, however, was in the same direction in both versions, and the Reasons × Version interaction was nonsignificant ($p = .60$). Initial analyses also revealed that there were no significant effects of gender; thus subsequent analyses were collapsed across this variable.

2. For example, consider two hypothetical subjects in the reasons condition, one of whom gave ratings of 9, 7, 5, 3, and 1 to the five jams, the other of whom gave ratings of 1, 3, 5, 7, and 9. The mean of these two subjects' ratings would be 5 for every jam, making it appear as though they were not discriminating between the jams, when in fact they were making very strong discriminations.

3. Two points should be made about these mean intercorrelations: one statistical and one conceptual. First, the lowered consensus in the reasons condition might show that people's evaluations became more random—that is, by becoming unsure of how they felt, subjects' ratings contained more "error," and thus were not as correlated with each other. Though we cannot completely rule out this interpretation, the fact that analyzing reasons did not reduce the range in subjects' ratings and the fact that in previous studies, analyzing reasons has not made people less confident in their evaluations, reduces its plausibility (see Wilson, Dunn, Kraft, & Lisle, 1989). Second, note that to avoid the problem of lack of independence of the intercorrelations (e.g., there were 300 intercorrelations among the 25 subjects in the control condition), the *t* test was computed on the mean of each subject's intercorrelations with every other subject in his or her condition, so that there was one data point for each subject.

4. We should address some possible ethical objections to Study 2. It might be argued that it was unfair to ask subjects to reflect about their decision of which courses to take, given our hypothesis that it would change the courses for which they preregistered and possibly even change the courses they actually took the following semester. We struggled with this issue before conducting the study and discussed it with several colleagues. In the end, we decided that the potential knowledge gained—discovering some detrimental effects of introspection—out-weighed the possible harmful effects on the participants. It would have been unacceptable to give subjects misinformation about the courses—for example, telling them that a course was highly rated by students when in fact it was not. However, we gave all subjects accurate information

and then asked some of them to reflect more than they might ordinarily do when forming their preferences. According to the predominant theories of decision making (e.g., Janis & Mann, 1977), asking people to be more reflective about their choices should have beneficial effects. Probably thousands of decision analysts, counselors, and academic advisers urge people to make decisions in ways similar to subjects in our reasons and rate all conditions. Given that the effects of our manipulations were predicted to be relatively benign (altering the psychology courses for which subjects preregistered and possibly altering the courses they took the following semester), we felt it was worth testing the wisdom of such advice. We did not, of course, make this decision alone. The study was approved by a Human Subjects Committee.

5. The inclusion of the filler questionnaire in the control condition solved one problem but possibly created another. The problem it solved was controlling for the amount of time that elapsed between the examination of the course descriptions and the completion of the dependent variables in the reasons condition. It also, however, made the control and reasons conditions different in the amount of time spent thinking about unrelated matters between the examination of the courses and the dependent measures. That is, subjects in the reasons condition read the descriptions, spent several minutes thinking about why they felt the way they did about the courses, and then rated the courses. Control subjects spent several minutes thinking about unrelated matters after reading the course descriptions, which might have adversely affected their memory for the courses. To correct this problem, two versions of the control condition were run: one in which subjects completed the filler questionnaire between reading the descriptions and completing the dependent measures, to equalize the delay between these activities, and one in which subjects completed the dependent measures immediately after reading the descriptions so that they would not be distracted by thinking about unrelated matters before completing the dependent measures. As it happened, the presence or absence of the delay in the control group produced very few significant differences on the dependent measures. The only difference was that subjects who had no delay between the course descriptions and the dependent measures reported that they were significantly less likely to take two of the nine courses. Because there were no other differences on any other dependent measure (including the actual registration and enrollment figures and the recall data), the data from the two versions of the control condition were combined in all analyses reported later.

6. Subjects' ratings of the influence of and their recall for the course information were analyzed in several alternative ways. For example, we computed the within-subject correlations between subjects' recall and the faculty members' ratings of importance and then averaged these correlations across conditions. The results of these and other analyses were very similar to those reported in the text.

References

Anderson, R. C., & Pichert, J. W. (1978). Recall of previously unrecallable information following a shift in perspective. *Journal of Verbal Learning and Verbal Behavior, 17*, 1–12.

Baumeister, R. F. (1984). Choking under pressure: Self-consciousness and paradoxical effects of incentives on skillful performance. *Journal of Personality and Social Psychology, 46,* 610–620.

Edwards, W. (1961). Behavioral decision theory. *Annual Review of Psychology, 12,* 473–498.

Goodman, N. G. (Ed.). (1945). *A Benjamin Franklin reader,* New York: Crowell.

Hastie, R., & Park, B. (1986). The relationship between memory and judgment depends on whether the judgment task is memory-based or on-line. *Psychological Review, 93,* 258–268.

Janis, I. L., & Mann, L. (1977). *Decision making: A psychological analysis of conflict, choice, and commitment.* New York: Free Press.

Judd, C. M., & Lusk, C. M. (1984). Knowledge structures and evaluative judgments: Effects of structural variables on judgmental extremity. *Journal of Personality and Social Psychology, 46,* 1193–1207.

Keeney, R. L. (1977). The art of assessing multiattribute utility functions. *Organizational Behavior and Human Performance, 19,* 267–310.

Kimble, G. A., & Perlmuter, L. C. (1970). The problem of volition. *Psychological Review, 77,* 361–384.

Koriat, A., Lichtenstein, S., & Fischhoff, B. (1980). Reasons for confidence. *Journal of Experimental Psychology: Human Learning and Memory, 6,* 107–118.

Langer, E. J., & Imber, L. G. (1979). When practice makes imperfect: Debilitating effects of overlearning. *Journal of Personality and Social Psychology, 37,* 2014–2024.

Linville, P. W. (1982). The complexity–extremity effect and age-based stereotyping. *Journal of Personality and Social Psychology, 42,* 193–211.

Mann, L. (1972). Use of a "balance sheet" procedure to improve the quality of personal decision making: A field experiment with college applicants. *Journal of Vocational Behavior, 2,* 291–300.

Millar, M. G., & Tesser, A. (1986a). Effects of affective and cognitive focus on the attitude–behavior relationship. *Journal of Personality and Social Psychology, 51,* 270–276.

Millar, M. G., & Tesser, A. (1986b). Thought-induced attitude change: The effects of schema structure and commitment. *Journal of Personality and Social Psychology, 51,* 259–269.

Millar, M. G., & Tesser, A. (1989). The effects of affective–cognitive consistency and thought on the attitude–behavior relation. *Journal of Experimental Social Psychology, 25,* 189–202.

Morrow, J., & Nolan-Hoeksema, S. (1990). Effects of responses to depression on the remediation of depressive affect. *Journal of Personality and Social Psychology, 58,* 519–527.

Nisbett, R. E., & Wilson, T. D. (1977). Telling more than we can know: Verbal reports on mental processes. *Psychological Review, 84*, 231–259.

Raiffa, H. (1968). *Decision analysis.* Reading, MA: Addison-Wesley.

Schooler, J. W., & Engstler-Schooler, T. Y. (1990). Verbal overshadowing of visual memories: Some things are better left unsaid. *Cognitive Psychology, 22*, 36–71.

Slovic, P. (1982). Toward understanding and improving decisions. In W. C. Howell & E. A. Fleishman (Eds.), *Information processing and decision making* (pp. 157–183). Hillsdale, NJ: Erlbaum.

Strawberry jams and preserves. (1985, August). *Consumer Reports*, pp. 487–489.

Tesser, A., Leone, C., & Clary, G. (1978). Affect control: Process constraints versus catharsis. *Cognitive Therapy and Research, 2*, 265–274.

Wilson, T. D. (1990). Self-persuasion via self-reflection. In J. M. Olson & M. P. Zanna (Eds.), *Self-inference processes: The Ontario Symposium* (Vol. 6, pp. 43–67). Hillsdale, NJ: Erlbaum.

Wilson, T. D., Dunn, D. S., Bybee, J. A., Hyman, D. B., & Rotondo, J. A. (1984). Effects of analyzing reasons on attitude–behavior consistency. *Journal of Personality and Social Psychology, 47*, 5–16.

Wilson, T. D., Dunn, D. S., Kraft, D., & Lisle, D. J. (1989). Introspection, attitude change, and attitude–behavior consistency: The disruptive effects of explaining why we feel the way we do. In L. Berkowitz (Ed.), *Advances in experimental social psychology* (Vol. 19, pp. 123–205). San Diego, CA: Academic Press.

Wilson, T. D., Kraft, D., & Dunn, D. S. (1989). The disruptive effects of explaining attitudes: The moderating effect of knowledge about the attitude object. *Journal of Experimental Social Psychology, 25*, 379–400.

Wilson, T. D., Lisle, D. J., & Schooler, J. (1990). *Some undesirable effects of self-reflection.* Unpublished manuscript, University of Virginia, Department of Psychology, Charlottesville.

Wilson, T. D., Hodges, S. D., & Pollack, S. (1990). *Effects of explaining attitudes on survey responses: The moderating effects of attitude accessibility.* Unpublished manuscript, University of Virginia, Department of Psychology, Charlottesville.

Questions for Review and Discussion

1. What was Wilson and Schooler's reasoning behind their hypothesis that introspection will reduce the quality of decisions?
2. How did asking participants to analyze the way they felt about different brands of jam (Study 1) affect their ratings of the jam?
3. Why did Wilson and Schooler predict (Study 2) that asking students to think about their reasons for choosing a course would make them less likely to choose popular courses?

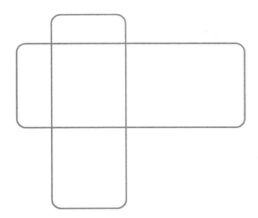

Name Index

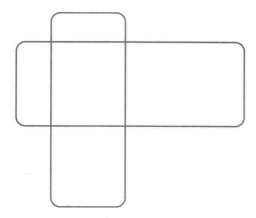

Subject Index

Abortion debate, pro-choice and pro-life views of partisanship in, 172–182

Acceptance by others, normative social influence and, 98

Accidental injury
self-presentational concerns and, 19, 20
self-presentational explanation of men vs. women in accidents, 31–32

Action concepts, 100

Actions, norms and, 18

Activation
automatic stereotype, 299
of normative behavior, 100–101
of stereotypes and personal beliefs, automatic and controlled processes and, 297–300

Activism
in Gender Role Journey Scale, 42
public confrontation of sexism and, 50, 55–56, 59n8

Acts of Compassion (Wuthnow), 382

Actual differences, in level of caring about community, 237 (fig.)

Actual norm vs. subjective norm, 138

Adjustment interpretation, of illusion of transparency, 273, 274

Adolescents, health-risk behaviors among, 33

Affect-Arousal Scale, in silence behavior in library experiments, 108, 109

Age, differences in littering and, 75–76

Alcohol use on campus

conclusions from studies on, 164
norms promoting, 141
peer influence and, 141
pluralist ignorance, misperception of social norm and, 137–164
self-presentational concerns and, 19, 20

Alienation, study on and feelings of, 153–158

Alone condition, and reaction to emergencies, 129

Alternatives
expert opinion on desirability of, 408, 409–420, 414 (table)
introspection about, 397–421

Altruism. *See also* Compliance studies; Helping behavior
conclusion about, 393
inhibitions against unrestricted acts of, 391–392
moral motivation vs. empathy-induced, 376
motivation for, 2
norms for, 2
psychology of, 1
reciprocal, 350
self-interest and, 381–393
underlying force toward, 2

Ambiguously hostile behaviors, examined in automatic stereotype priming effects for high-and low-prejudice subjects study, 303–312

Ambivalence, of aversive racists, 284